PHILI[P'S]

STR[EET ATLA]S

Cornwall

First published in 2003 by

Philip's, a division of
Octopus Publishing Group Ltd
2-4 Heron Quays, London E14 4JP

First edition 2003
Third impression 2005

ISBN-10   0-540-08329-1 (pocket)
ISBN-13   978-0-540-08329-9 (pocket)

© Philip's 2003

OS Ordnance Survey®

This product includes mapping data licensed
from Ordnance Survey® with the permission
of the Controller of Her Majesty's Stationery
Office. © Crown copyright 2003. All rights
reserved. Licence number 100011710.

Printed and bound in Spain
by Cayfosa-Quebecor

Contents

II	**Key to map pages**
IV	**Route planning**
VIII	**Administrative and Postcode boundaries**
1	**Key to map symbols**
2	**Street maps** at 1¼ inches to mile
104	**Street maps** at 2½ inches to 1 mile
148	**Street map of Plymouth city centre** at 5 inches to 1 mile
150	**Index** of towns and villages
152	**Index** of streets, hospitals, industrial estates, railway stations, schools, shopping centres, universities and places of interest

Digital Data

The exceptionally high-quality mapping found in this atlas is available as digital data in
TIFF format, which is easily convertible to other bitmapped (raster) image formats.

The index is also available in digital form as a standard database table. It contains all the
details found in the printed index together with the National Grid reference for the map
square in which each entry is named.

For further information and to discuss your requirements, please contact Philip's on
020 7644 6932 or james.mann@philips-maps.co.uk

Key to map pages

149	Map pages at 5 inches to 1 mile
128	Map pages at 2½ inches to 1 mile
100	Map pages at 1¼ inches to 1 mile

Scale

0	5	10	15	20	25 km
0		5		10	15 miles

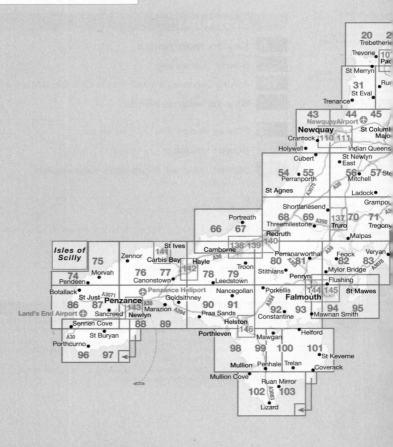

20 2
Trebetherie
Trevone 10
Pad
St Merryn
31 Rur
St Eval
Trenance

43 44 45
Newquay Airport
Newquay St Colum
Majo
Crantock 110 111
Holywell Indian Queens
Cubert St Newlyn
East
54 55 56 57 Ste
Perranporth Mitchell
St Agnes Ladock
Grampou
Shortlanesend
Portreath 68 69 137 70 71
66 67 Threemilestone Truro Tregony
Redruth Malpas
140
Isles of St Ives Camborne 138 139
Scilly 75 141 Perranarworthal Feock Veryan
74 Zennor Carbis Bay 80 81 82 83
Morvah 76 77 Hayle 142 Troon Stithians Penryn Mylor Bridge
Pendeen Canonstown 78 79 Flushing
Botallack Leedstown 144 145 St Mawes
St Just A3071 Penzance Heliport Nancegollan Porkellis Falmouth
86 87 Penzance Goldsithney 90 91 92 93 94 95
Land's End Airport Sancreed 143 Marazion A394 Constantine Mawnan Smith
Newlyn Praa Sands
Sennen Cove 88 89 Helston Helford
Porthleven 146
Porthcurno St Buryan Mawgan Helford
A30 98 99 100 101
96 97 Mullion Penhale Trelan St Keverne
Mullion Cove Coverack
Ruan Mirror
102 103
Lizard

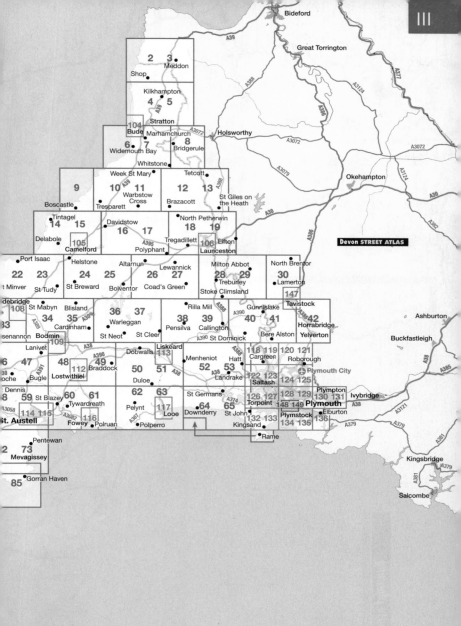

Bideford

Great Torrington

A39

A388

A3124

A377

2 **3** Meddon

Shop

A39

Kilkhampton

A3072

4 **5**

A3072

Stratton

A3072

Holsworthy

A3072

Okehampton

A3124

104

Bude Marhamchurch A3072

6 **7** **8**

Widemouth Bay Bridgerule

Whitstone

A3079

A386

A30

A382

Week St Mary Tetcott

9 **10** **11** **12** **13** St Giles on the Heath

Warbstow Cross Brazacott

Boscastle

Tresparrett

A30

Devon STREET ATLAS

Tintagel North Petherwin

14 **15** Davidstow **18** **19**

Delabole **16** **17** Tregadillett Lifton

105 Polyphant **106** Launceston

Camelford

Port Isaac Helstone Milton Abbot North Brentor

22 **23** **24** **25** Altarnun Lewannick **28** **29** **30**

St Minver St Tudy St Breward Bolventor Coad's Green Treburley Lamerton

26 **27** Stoke Climsland

147

edebridge Rilla Mill Tavistock

108 St Mabyn Blisland Gunnislake **42**

33 **34** **35** **36** **37** **38** **39** **40** **41** Horrabridge

senannon Cardinham Warleggan Pensilva Callington Bere Alston Yelverton

Bodmin St Neot St Cleer St Dominick

109 A38 Lanivet A390 Dobwalls Liskeard **118** **119** **120** **121**

113 Menheniot **52** **53** Roborough

Lanivet **48** **112** **49** **50** **51** Hatt Cargreen Plymouth City

6 **47** Braddock Landrake **122** **123**

30 **59** Lostwithiel Duloe St Germans **126** **127** Saltash **124** **125** Plympton

Dennis St Blazey **60** **61** **62** **63** **64** **65** Torpoint **128** **129** **130** **131** Ivybridge

8 **59** Tywardreath Pelynt **117** Downderry St John **148** **149** Plymouth

114 **115** **116** Looe Polperro Kingsand **132** **133** Plymstock Elburton A379

St. Austell Fowey Polruan **134** **135** **136**

Rame A379

Ashburton

Buckfastleigh

A38

A386

A3121

Kingsbridge

A381

A379

Salcombe

Pentewan

2 **73**

Mevagissey

85 Gorran Haven

Roche Bugle

Port Isaac

Lanivet

Route planning

Scale

0 1 2 3 4 5 6 7 8km
0 1 2 3 4 5 miles

ISLES OF SCILLY

VIII

Major administrative and Postcode boundaries

Scale
0 5 10 15 20 25 30 km
0 5 10 15 20 miles

County and unitary authority boundaries
District boundaries
Postcode boundaries
Area covered by this atlas

Devon

City of Plymouth
Plymouth

North Cornwall

Caradon

Cornwall

Restormel

Carrick

Kerrier

Penwith

Shop
EX39
EX21
EX22
EX23
Stratton
Bude
Week St Mary
PL16
Launceston
PL15
PL17
PL19
Tavistock
PL20
PL12
Callington
Saltash
PL11 Torpoint
Kingsand
PL7
PL5
PL6
PL9 PL8
PL1
PL2
PL3
PL4
PL10
St Cleer
PL14
Liskeard
Looe
PL13
Fowey
PL22
Lostwithiel
PL23
PL24
Bodmin
PL31
PL30
St Tudy
Camelford
Delabole
PL32
Tintagel
PL33
PL34
Boscastle
PL35
Port Isaac
PL29
PL27
Wadebridge
Padstow
PL28
St Columb Major
PL26
PL25
Sticker
St Austell
Mevagissey
Portloe
Tregony
Portscatho
St Newlyn East
TR8
TR9
Newquay
TR7
TR6
TR5
Perranporth
TR16
Portreath
Camborne
TR14
Redruth
TR15
TR1
Truro
TR3
TR2
TR4
Feock
Penryn
TR10
Falmouth
TR11
Helford
TR12
Lizard
Mullion
Porthleven
TR13
Helston
TR27
Hayle
St Ives
TR26
Penzance
TR20
TR18
Newlyn
TR19
Porthcurno
St Just
Land's End
Land's End

SS
SX
SS
SW
SX
SW

Symbol	Description
	Motorway with junction number
	Primary route – dual/single carriageway
	A road – dual/single carriageway
	B road – dual/single carriageway
	Minor road – dual/single carriageway
	Other minor road – dual/single carriageway
	Road under construction
	Tunnel, covered road
	Rural track, private road or narrow road in urban area
	Gate or obstruction to traffic (restrictions may not apply at all times or to all vehicles)
	Path, bridleway, byway open to all traffic, road used as a public path
	Pedestrianised area
DY7	Postcode boundaries
	County and unitary authority boundaries
	Railway, tunnel, railway under construction
	Tramway, tramway under construction
	Miniature railway
Walsall	Railway station
	Private railway station
South Shields	Metro station
	Tram stop, tram stop under construction
	Bus, coach station

Symbol	Description
◆	Ambulance station
◆	Coastguard station
◆	Fire station
◆	Police station
✚	Accident and Emergency entrance to hospital
H	Hospital
✝	Place of worship
𝒊	Information Centre (open all year)
P	Parking
P&R	Park and Ride
PO	Post Office
Ⅹ	Camping site
⛺	Caravan site
⚑	Golf course
⏃	Picnic site
Prim Sch	Important buildings, schools, colleges, universities and hospitals
River Medway	Water name
	River, weir, stream
	Canal, lock, tunnel
	Water
	Tidal water
	Woods
	Built up area
Church	Non-Roman antiquity
ROMAN FORT	Roman antiquity
87	Adjoining page indicators and overlap bands
228	The colour of the arrow and the band indicates the scale of the adjoining or overlapping page (see scales below)

Abbreviation	Full term	Abbreviation	Full term	Abbreviation	Full term
Acad	Academy	Inst	Institute	Recn Gd	Recreation Ground
Allot Gdns	Allotments	Ct	Law Court		
Cemy	Cemetery	L Ctr	Leisure Centre	Resr	Reservoir
C Ctr	Civic Centre	LC	Level Crossing	Ret Pk	Retail Park
CH	Club House	Liby	Library	Sch	School
Coll	College	Mkt	Market	Sh Ctr	Shopping Centre
Crem	Crematorium	Meml	Memorial	TH	Town Hall/House
Ent	Enterprise	Mon	Monument	Trad Est	Trading Estate
Ex H	Exhibition Hall	Mus	Museum	Univ	University
Ind Est	Industrial Estate	Obsy	Observatory	Wks	Works
IRB Sta	Inshore Rescue Boat Station	Pal	Royal Palace	YH	Youth Hostel
		PH	Public House		

The small numbers around the edges of the maps identify the 1 kilometre National grid lines

■ The dark grey border on the inside edge of some pages indicates that the mapping does not continue onto the adjacent page

The scale of the maps on the pages numbered in blue is 3.92 cm to 1 km • 2½ inches to 1 mile • 1: 25344

0	¼	½	¾	1 mile
0	250 m	500 m	750 m 1 kilometre	

The scale of the maps on the pages numbered in green is 1.96 cm to 1 km • 1¼ inches to 1 mile • 1: 50688

0	¼	½	¾	1 mile
0	250 m 500 m 750 m 1 kilometre			

The scale of the maps on the pages numbered in red is 7.84 cm to 1 km • 5 inches to 1 mile • 1: 12672

0	220 yards	440 yards	660 yards	½ mile
0	125 m	250 m	375 m ½ kilometre	

Manley Cliff
Elmscott
Edist

Docton

SANDHOLE CROSS

Sandhole Cliff

Mast

Hardisworthy

HARDISWORTHY CROSS

FIRE
D

Nabor Point

South Hole

Golden Park

Firebeacon

EX39

Wembsworthy

Embury Beacon

Cranham

Putshole Farm

Embury Beach

Henafor

Knaps Head

Linton

Linton LA

LINTON LA

KINGS CROSS

The Hermitage

Welcombe

LANE PARK LA

Tredown

UPCOTT CROSS

Welcombe Mouth

P

Mead

BELL LA

OLD SMITHY COTTS

Up

South West Coast Path

Mead CNR

Darraccott

Marsland Mouth

Berry Park

PO

Gull Rock

Marsland Cliff

Gooseham Mill

Marsland Water

Yeol Mouth

Cornakey Cliff

Marsland Manor

Gooseham

Hackmarsh

Cornakey Farm

Cory

Henna Cliff

Westcott Farm

Bryaton

Brownspit

Lopthorne

Hawker's Hut

Well

EX23

RULE CROSS

Vicarage Cliff

P

Morwenstow

WEST BECKON

St Mark's Prim Sch

Lucky Hole

Crosstown

PH

JAME'S CROSS

FURZE GDNS

PO

P

Higher Sharpnose Point

The Tidna

Shop

SARGENTS MOW

CROSSWATER

Ruxmoor

Tonacombe

WOODFORD CROSS

STANBURY CROSS

WOODVILLE RD

Darzle Farm

Middlefields

Milton

Scale: 1¼ inches to 1 mile
¼   ½ mile
250m 500m 750m 1 km

Devon STREET ATLAS A39 Bideford

A   B   C   D   E   F

Welsford

Stitworthy Farm

Seckington Farm

Trew Farm

Clifford

Tosberry Cross

Tosberry

Grove La

Painton Water

Green La

Tosberry Moor

Welsford Moor

EX39

Seckington Water

Clifford Water

Bursdon Moor

Bursdon Moor Cross

Summerville Cross

Summerwell Farm

Gorvin Farm

Gorvin Cross

Lutsford

Lutsford Cross

Bursdon

PH

Meddon Cross

CH

Huddisford

Lower Bideford Cross

River Torridge

Biteford

Runland Farm

Deptford

Meddon

Meddon Cross

Horton Bridge

Welcombe Cross

Shorestone Farm

Greadon

Horton Farm

Brimford Bridge

Brimford Cross

Holyrood House

Woolley

Dural

Dural Cross

Horton Cross

North Moor Cross

Northmoor

Newlands Farm

EX22

Loatmead

Loatmead Cross

Eastcott

Eastcott Cross

Hardsworthy

East Youlstone

Maddocks Cross

Redmonsford

Dinworthy

EX23

East Youlstone

East Youlstone Cross

River Waldon

Crimp

West Youlstone

River Tamar

Trentworthy Cross

Ryall Farm

Killarney Springs Leisure Park

Trentworthy Farm

West Down

Wrasford Moor

Blatchborough

Blatchborough Cross

A   26   B   27   C   28   D   29   E   30   F

5

8
21
7
20
6
19
5
18
4
17
3
16
2
15
1
14

Devon STREET ATLAS

Scale: 1¼ inches to 1 mile

| 0 | ¼ | ½ mile |
| 0 | 250m | 500m | 750m | 1 km |

EX23

A3072

STRATTON

BUDE

Stanbury

Woodford

Ham Farm

Stursdon

Hippa Rock

Stanbury Mouth

Lower Sharpnose Point

Hollamoor

Heathe

Woodlands Farm

Lee Barton

Edslee Farm

Lee Wood

Coombe Valley

Burridge Farm

Steeple Point

Duckpool

Coombe

Stowe Barton

Stowe Woods

Penstowe Park

Warren Gutter

South West Coast Path

Houndapitt Farm

Collery

Stanbury

Scadghill Farm

Stibb

Sandymouth Bay Holiday Pk

Sandy Mouth

Long Rock

Killock Farm

Barnacott

Collaton Farm

Halls

Dunsmouth Farm

Tiscott

Ivyleaf Farm

Hunthill Wood

WYE-LEAF Holiday Pk

River Nee

Menachurch Point

Northcott Mouth

Northcott

Crockwood Farm

Maer Cliff

104

Maer

Anthony Cl

Wooda Farm

Bush

St Petroc's Sch

Paize

Poughill

Colebrook Farm

Leigh

Wrangle Point

Crooklets Beach

Broomhill Manor

Stamford Hill

104

East Leigh Berrys

Bude Haven

Flexbury

Burn

104

Compass Point

Tower

Mus

BUDE

Diddies

Cross Lanes

A3072

Superstore

STRATTON RD

A3072

For full street detail of the highlighted area see page 104.

6

7

B1
1 POUNDFIELD HILL
2 POUNDFIELD CL
3 BAY TREE COTTS
4 WARD CL
5 BENTLEY DR
6 UNION HILL
7 BRIDGE ST
8 WOODLEY CL
9 ST MICHAEL'S RD

10 GLADWELL GDNS
11 ST PETERS RD
12 ST ANDREW'S RD
13 ST OLAF'S RD

E1
1 MAIDEN ST
2 COT HILL
3 MARKET ST
4 CHURCH SQ
5 CHURCH ST

6 GIBRALTER SQ
7 FORE ST
8 OLD POST OFFICE HILL
9 THE LEAT
10 HOWELL'S RD
11 SPICERS LA
12 SANCTUARY LA

19   20   21   22   23   24
A   B   C   D   E   F

13
7
12
6
11
5
10
4
09
3
08
2
07
1
06

8

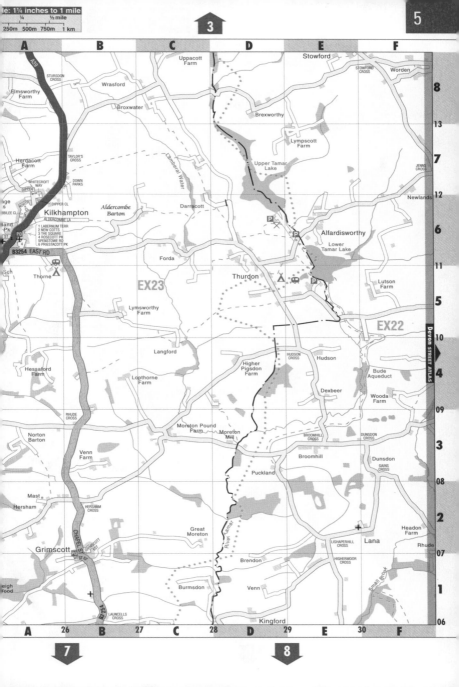

For full street detail of the
highlighted area see page 104.

4

Scale: 1¼ inches to 1 r

0   ¼   ½ mile
0   250m   500m   750m   1 k

A   **B**   **C**   **D**   **E**   **F**

Ebbingford
Manor

Efford
Beacon

8

Lynstone

05

Upton

7

Hotel   Phillip
             Farm

Phillip's
Point

104

04

Higher
Longbeak

6

Lower
Longbeak

03

Salthouse
Cottage

Bay View Inn
(PH)

5

BRAMBLE   1 ATLANTIC CL
CL   2 CRESCENT CL

MADEIRA DR

ASHTON WLK
BRANDON WLK

Widemouth
Sand

Widemouth
Bay

02

Black
Rock

4

WIDEMOUTH BAY
HOLIDAY VILLAGE

Wanson
Mouth

Widemouth
Farms

01

Foxhole
Point

South West Coast Path

WIDEMOUTH BAY
CVN PK

Wanson

3

Penhalt Cliff

Millock
Haven

EX23

PENHALT FARM
HOLIDAY PK

00

Millbrook

Trevisick

BANGORS EST

Cancleave
Strand

Bangors

2

Dizzard
Point

Millbrook
Common

VICARAGE LA

Poundstock

Cemy
Trekennard
Farm

Trebarfoote

99

Chipman
Strand

Long Cliff

Bynorth
Cliff

Trevoulter
Farm

Treskinnick
Cross

1

Dizzard

The
Den

Cleave
Strand

Tregole

98

15   **A**   **16**   **B**   **17**   **C**   **18**   **D**   **19**   **E**   **20**   **F**

10   11

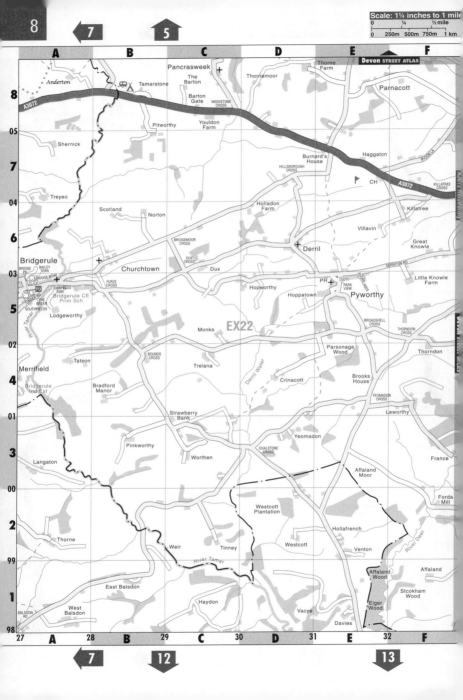

1¼ inches to 1 mile
¼   ½ mile
m 500m 750m 1 km

A   B   C   D   E   F

8

97

Cambeak   7

96

6

95

Voter
Run   PL23

High
Cliff   5

94

Rusey
Cliff

Buckator   4

Gull
Rock   93

Beeny
Sisters

Fire Beacon
Point

Seals
Hole

Beeny

South West Coast Path

Beeny
Cliff   3

Trebyla
Farm

B3263

92

Pentargon   Hillsborough   Tremorle

Meachard   Penally
Hill   VALENCY
ROW   Penally
House   Trewannett

Penally
Point   Mus   YH   Tresuck   PL35   2

Willapark   Harbour   PENALLY
P G1   Newmills   Trefalger

Visitor
Ctr   1 PENTARGON RD
2 EGLOS VIEW
3 TREFLOUR CL
4 LANSFORDS MDW
5 FORRABURY HILL
6 CLOVER LANE CL
7 WHITE SMOCK MDW
8 DOCTORS HILL
9 GUNPOOL LA
10 DUNN ST   River Valency   91

Forrabury   NEW RD   MARINE
TERR   Trebilfin

Short
Island   Mast   FORE
ST

rebeacon
Hill   Boscastle   Trewold   Trebilfin

Ladies
Window   Welltown
Manor   Home
Farm   1

nd   Paradise
House   MOUNT
PLEASANT

Trevalga   TINTAGEL RD   B3266

B3263   Paradise
Rd   B3266

90

A   08   B   09   C   10   D   11   E   12   F

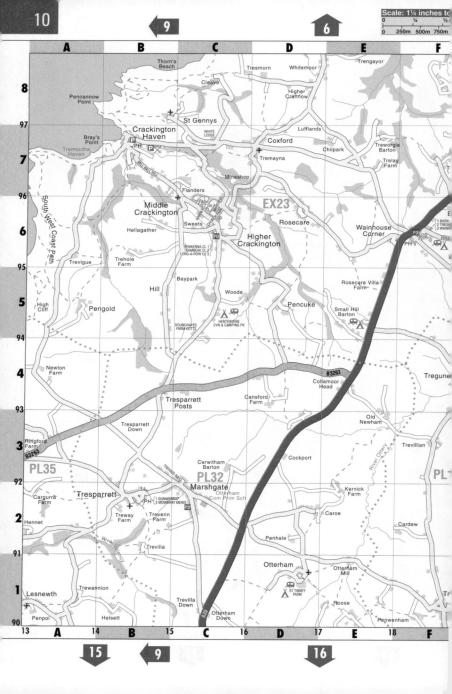

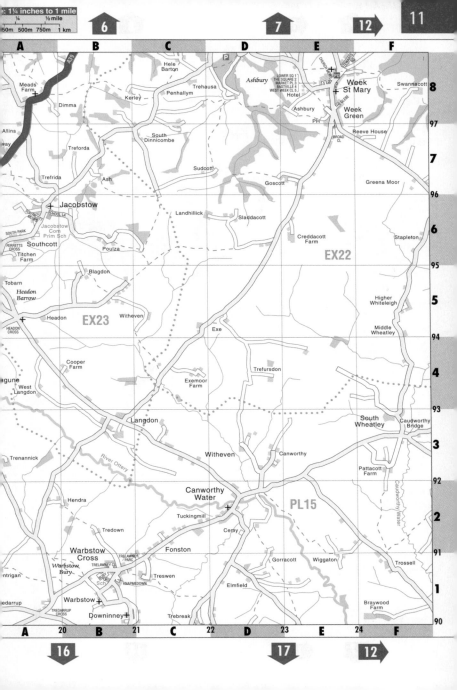

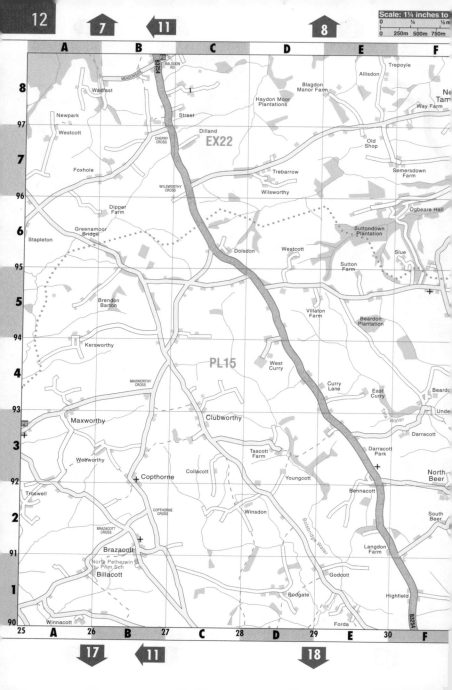

cale: 1¼ inches to 1 mile
¼ ½ mile
250m 500m 750m 1 km

8

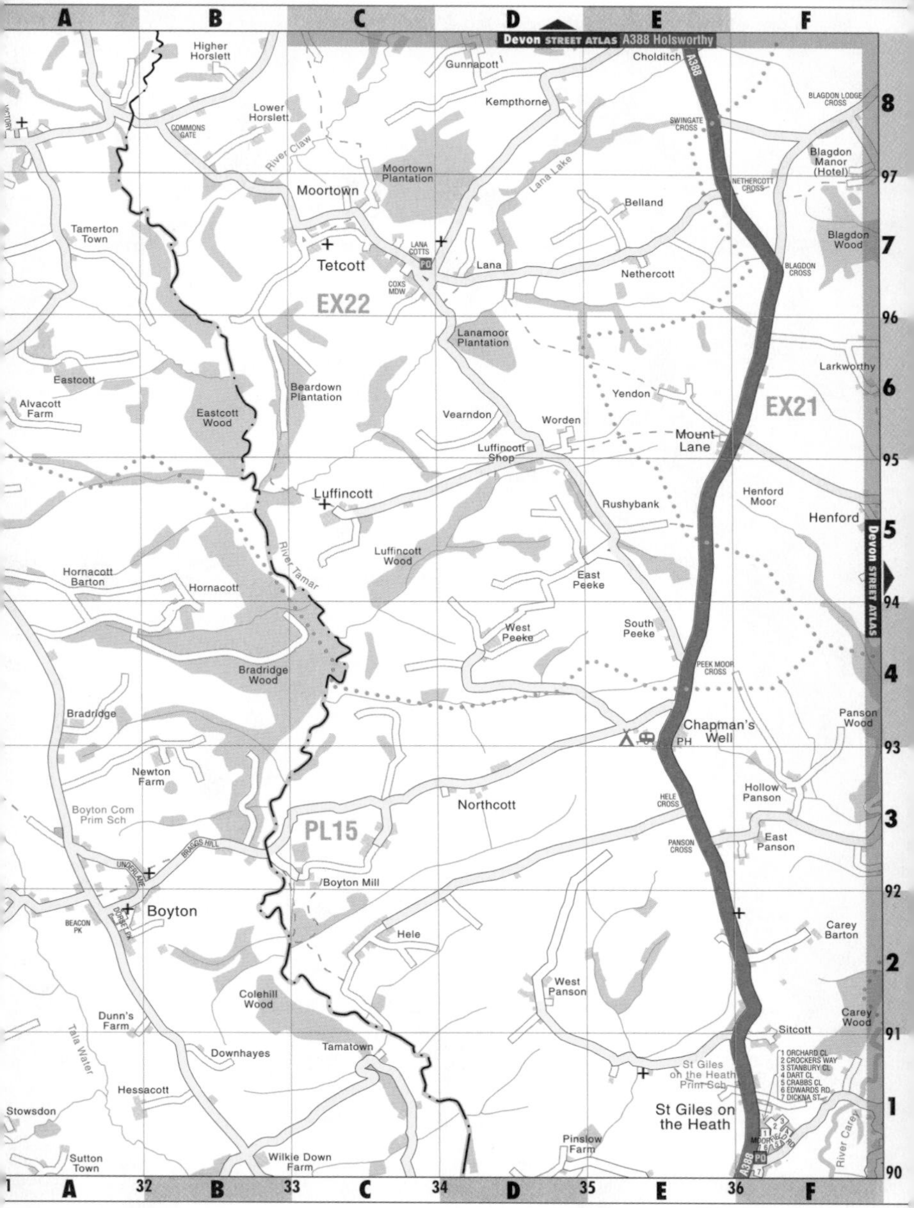

A
B
C
D
E
F
Devon STREET ATLAS A388 Holsworthy
Higher Horslett
Gunnacott
Cholditch
A388
Kempthorne
Lower Horslett
COMMONS GATE
River Claw
BLAGDON LODGE CROSS
SWINGATE CROSS
Blagdon Manor (Hotel)
Moortown Plantation
Lana Lake
Moortown
NETHERCOTT CROSS
Tamerton Town
Belland
LANA COTTS
PO
Tetcott
Lana
Blagdon Wood
BLAGDON CROSS
Nethercott
COXS MDW
EX22
Lanamoor Plantation
Larkworthy
Eastcott
Beardown Plantation
Yendon
Alvacott Farm
EX21
Eastcott Wood
Vearndon
Worden
Mount Lane
Luffincott Shop
Luffincott
Henford Moor
Henford
Rushybank
River Tamar
Luffincott Wood
Devon STREET ATLAS
Hornacott Barton
Hornacott
East Peeke
West Peeke
South Peeke
Bradridge Wood
PEEK MOOR CROSS
Bradridge
Panson Wood
Chapman's Well
PH
Newton Farm
Hollow Panson
HELE CROSS
Northcott
Boyton Com Prim Sch
PL15
PANSON CROSS
East Panson
BRAGGS HILL
UNDERLANE
Boyton Mill
Boyton
BEACON PK
DORSET PK
Hele
Carey Barton
West Panson
Colehill Wood
Dunn's Farm
Carey Wood
Tala Water
Sitcott
Downhayes
Tamatown
1 ORCHARD CL
2 CROCKERS WAY
3 STANBURY CL
4 DART CL
5 CRABBS CL
6 EDWARDS RD
7 DICKNA ST
St Giles on the Heath Prim Sch
Hessacott
St Giles on the Heath
Stowsdon
River Carey
Pinslow Farm
Sutton Town
Wilkie Down Farm
A388
PO
8
97
7
96
6
95
5
94
4
93
3
92
2
91
1
90
32
33
34
35
36

18

19

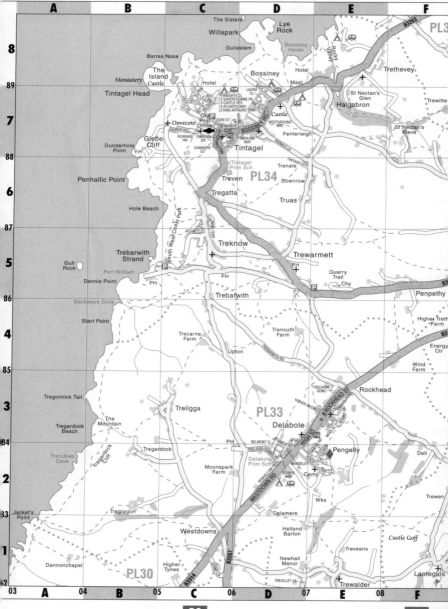

Scale: 1¼ inches to 1 mile
0   ¼   ½ mile
0   250m   500m   750m   1

| | A | B | C | D | E | F |

8

The Sisters

Willapark

Lye Rock

Gullastem

Bossiney Haven

Rocky Valley

PL3

B3263

Tretthevey

Barras Nose

Monastery

The Island Castle

Tintagel Head

89

Hotel

Bossiney

Mast

Hotel

St Nectan's Glen

Halgabron

Trewitte

Penhallic Point

Tintagel Head

KNIGHTS CL
GAVERCOMBE PK
CASTLE HTS
ATLANTIC WAY
KING ARTHURS TERR

Castle

St Nectan's Kieve

7

Dovecote

Old Post Office

FORE ST
Visitor Ctr

WESTGROUND WAY

Fenterleigh

CHURCH HILL

Glebe Cliff

VICARAGE HILL

TREVENA DR

MERLINS WAY

Tintagel

88

Dunderhole Point

YH

DANMORE CV

Tintagel Prim Sch

Trenale

Downrow

PL34

6

Penhallic Point

Treven

Tregatta

Truas

87

Hole Beach

South West Coast Path

ATLANT...

NEW TERR

Treknow

Trewarmett

5

Gull Rock

Trebarwith Strand

Port William

P

PH

PH

PH

Quarry Trail

Chy

Penpethy

86

Dennis Point

Backways Cove

P

Start Point

Higher Treth Farm

B3

4

Trecarne Farm

Trenouth Farm

Upton

TRELOWTH RD

Energy Ctr

B3

Wind Farm

85

Tregonnick Tail

The Mountain

Treligga

Trecarne Gdns

HIGHER MEDR...

STOCKHEAD ST

Rockhead

3

Tregardock Beach

Tregardock

Tregardock Cliff

PL33

Delabole

HIGH ST

Deli

84

Trerubies Cove

PH

BELMONT CL

TRELIGGA DOWNS RD

PH

PD

Pengelly

2

Jacket's Point

Tregragon

Moonspark Farm

Delabole Prim Sch

MANDELEY CL

EGAN'S WAY

Cemy

Wks

Trewen

83

Delamere

Westdowns

Helland Barton

Trewalder

Trewen

Castle Goff

1

Dannonchapel

Higher Tynes

B3314

B3267

BOSSO LA

Newhall Manor

TREVILLEY LA

Treveans

Trewalder

Lantegios

PL30

42

| | A | B | C | D | E | F |

03   04   05   06   07   08

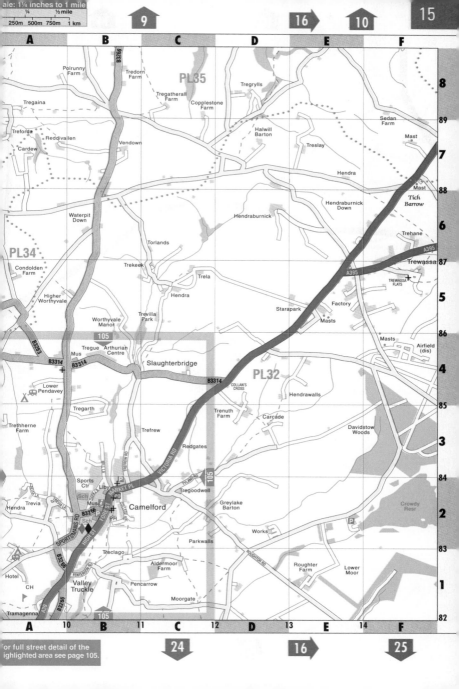

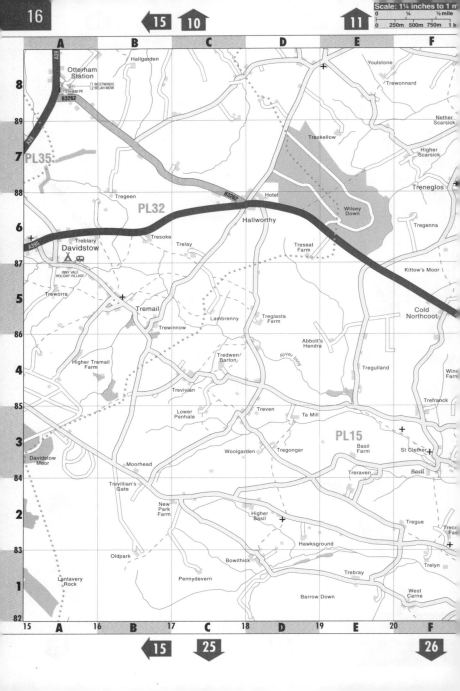

0   ¼   ½ mile
0   250m   500m   750m   1 k

15   10   11

A   B   C   D   E   F

8

Otterham Station
Hallgarden
1 WESTWINDS
2 BELAH MOW
OTTERHAM PK
B3262

Youlstone
Trewonnard

89

A39

Nether
Scarsick

7

PL35

Treskellow

Higher
Scarsick

88

B3262
Hotel

Tregeen

Treneglos

PL32

Wilsey
Down

Tregenna

6

Hallworthy

A395

Treblary
Davidstow
Tresoke
Trelay

Treseat
Farm

Kittow's Moor

87

INNY VALE
HOLIDAY VILLAGE

**Cold
Northcoot**

5

Treworra

Tremail

Lambrenny

Treglasta
Farm

86

Trewinnow

Abbott's
Hendra

4

Higher Tremail
Farm

Tredwen
Barton

River Inny

Tregulland

Wine
Farm

85

Trevivian

Treven
Ta Mill

Trefranck

3

Lower
Penhale

Woolgarden
Tregonger

PL15

Basil
Farm

St Clether

Basil

Davidstow
Moor

Moorhead

Treraven

84

Trevillian's
Gate

Higher
Basil

Tregue

Treco
Far

2

New
Park
Farm

Hawksground

83

Oldpark

Bowithick

Trelyn

1

Lanlavery
Rock

Pennydevern

Trebray

West
Carne

82

Barrow Down

15   A   16   B   17   C   18   D   19   E   20   F

15   25   26

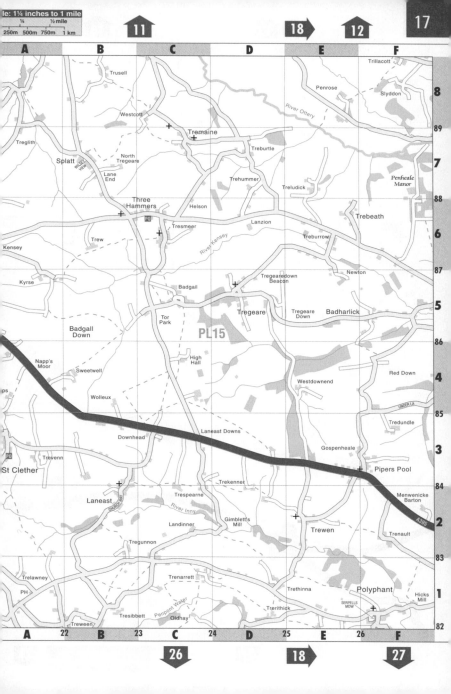

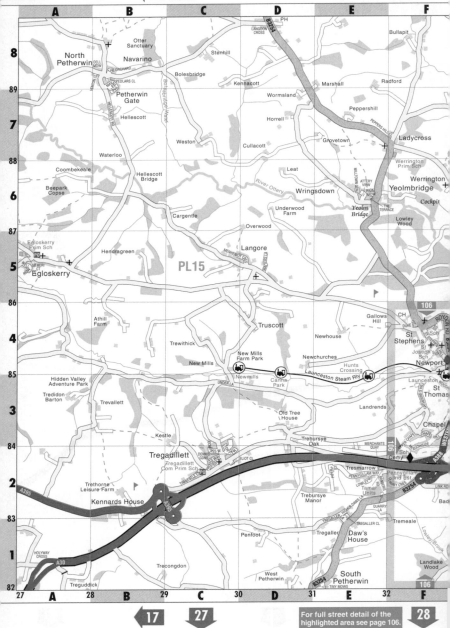

Scale: 1¼ inches to 1 mile
0   ¼   ½ mile
0   250m 500m 750m 1

A **B** **C** **D** **E** **F**

8

North
Petherwin
Otter
Sanctuary
Navarino
Stenhill
Bolesbridge
Kennacott
Marshall
Radford
Bullapit

89

Petherwin
Gate
Wormsland
Peppershill
Hellescott
Horrell
Grovetown
Ladycross

7

Waterloo
Weston
Cullacott
Werrington
Prim Sch
Werrington

88

Coombekeale
Hellescott
Bridge
Leat
Yeolmbridge
Cockpit

Beepark
Copse
Wringsdown
Yeolm
Bridge
Lowley
Wood

6

River Ottery
Cargentle
Underwood
Farm

87

Egloskerry
Prim Sch
Overwood
Langore

Hendragreen
Egloskerry
PL15

5

86

Athill
Farm
Truscott
Gallows
Hill
St
Stephens

4

Trewithick
Newhouse
Newport

New Mills
Farm Park
Newchurches
Hunts
Crossing

85

Hidden Valley
Adventure Park
New Mills
Newmills
Canna
Park
Launceston Steam Rly
St
Thomas

Tredidon
Barton
Trevallett
Landrends
Chapel

3

Kestle
Old Tree
House

84

Tregadillett
Trebursye
Oak
Merchants
Quay
Cemy

Tregadillett
Com Prim Sch

2

Trethorne
Leisure Farm
Tresmarrow
Tamar
Units
Pennygillam
Ind Est

Kennards House
Trebursye
Manor
Quarry
La
Tremeale

83

Tregaller
Daw's
House
Tregaller
Cl

1

Holyway
Cross
A30
Penfoot
Landlake
Wood

82

Treguddick
Trecongdon
West
Petherwin
South
Petherwin

27 **A** **28** **B** **29** **C** **30** **D** **31** **E** **32** **F**

17 27 28

For full street detail of the
highlighted area see page 106.

106

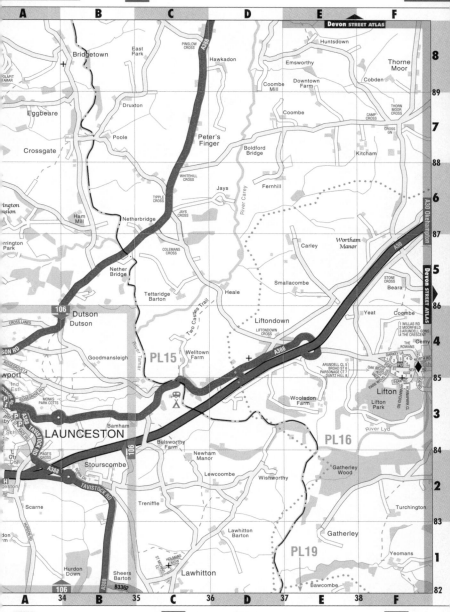

Gulland Rock

Gunver Head

Trevose Head

Cat's Cove

Merope Rocks

Stinking Cove

LB Sta

Polventon or Mother Ivey's Bay

Cataclews Point

Porthmissen Bridge

Round Hole

Trevone Bay

Porthmiss

The Bull

Dinas Head

Round Hole

St Cadoc's Point

Newtrian Bay

WEST RD
BEACH RD
SANDS
VIEW

Trevone

Trevose Farm

Harlyn Bay

IRB Sta

South West Coast Path

UPPER DOBBIN CL
DOBBIN CL
PARKENHEAD LA

Booby's Bay

St Cadoc Farm

Windmill

Harlyn

PH
BANK
HARLYN
BARTON
HARLYN
COTTS

Trenearne

South West Coast Path

St Constantine's Church

Constantine Bay

Harlyn House

Polmark

PL28

Trelowsa Farm

CH

Higher Harlyn

PEGUARRA CT

Treyarnon Point

P

Constantine Bay

PH

B3276

Treyarnon Bay

YH

CRESCENT RISE

Towan

PH

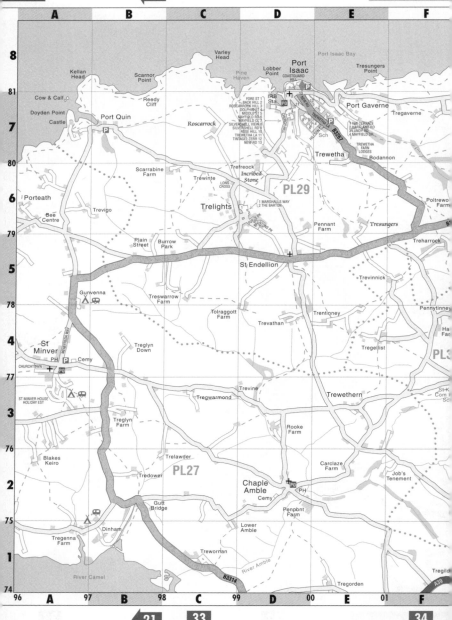

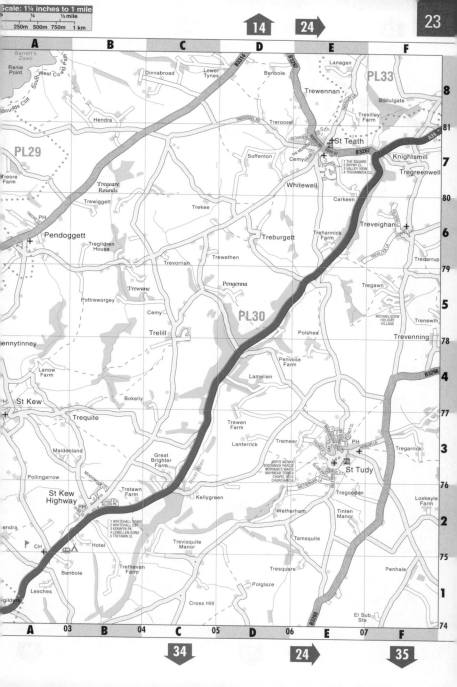

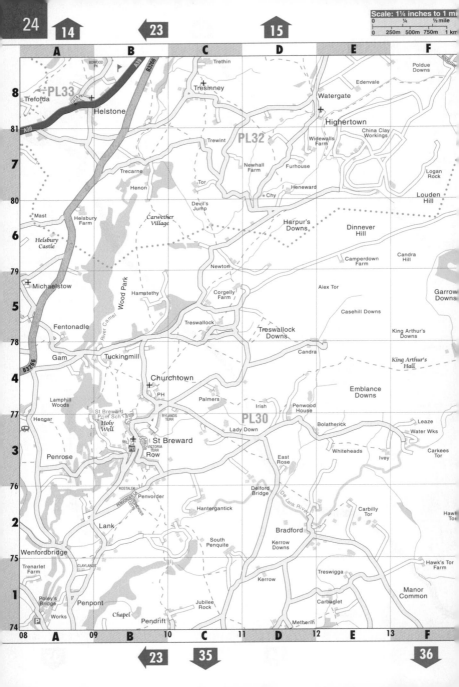

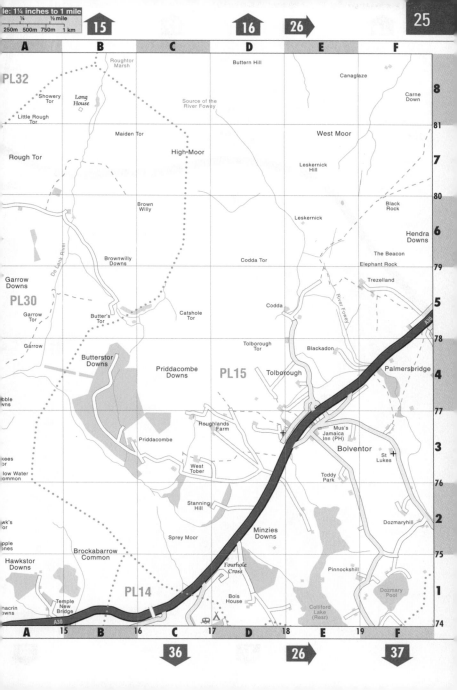

Scale: 1¼ inches to 1
0   ¼   ½ mile
0 250m 500m 750m 1

A **B** **C** **D** **E** **F**

Carne Down

Trekennick
Cross

Altarnun
Hotel
Tresmaine

Newhay

Bowden
Derra

8

South
Carne

Trevell

Hut
Circle

Tredaule

81

Trecorner

Darras

Wesley
Cottage

WESLEY
WAY

Trebant
Farm

Blackaton
Farm

Westmoorgate

Trewint

PH

7

Trewint Downs

Plusha

B3257

Tregirls

80

Midway

Hendra

Trenilk

Tregrenna

Knighton

Trevague

6

Poldhu

Upton
Barton

Tregune

Castle

Trekernell

79

Tolcarne
Tor

Cannaframe

Halvana

Fox
Tor

Tolcarne

5

Halvana
Plantation

A30

PL15

78

Stona

East Moor

4

North Bowda
Farm

77

Allabury

Tressellern

Bastreet
Downs

3

Works

Hawk's
Tor

Rushyford
Gate

76

King Arthur's
Bed

2

Trezibbett

Trewortha

75

Smallacoombe
Downs

Kilmar
Tor

PL14

Twelve Men's
Moor

1

Harrowbridge

River Fowey

Winsey Brook

PL14

Ninestones
Farm

Siblyback
Moor

Newel
Tor

74

20   21   22   23   24   25

A **B** **C** **D** **E** **F**

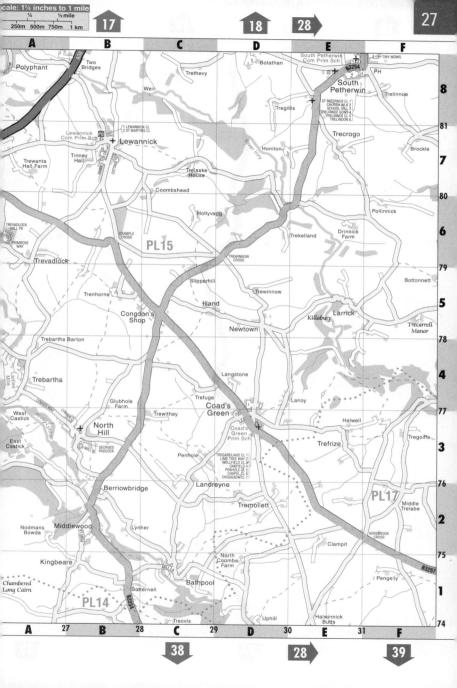

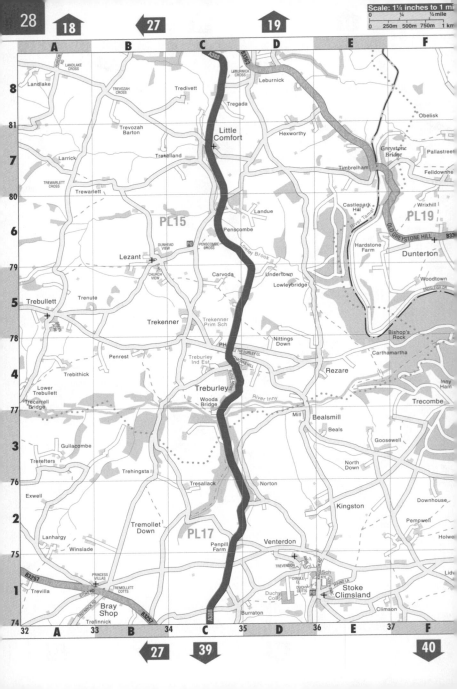

29

Scale: 1¼ inches to 1 mile

| 0 | ¼ | ½ mile |
| 0 | 250m | 500m | 750m | 1 |

Devon STREET ATLAS

PL16

8

Quither

Whitstone Farm

Rowden

North Brentor

West Blackdown

Westcott

PH

Cemy

STATION VIEW
STATION RD

81

Week

Monkstone

Metherell

7

P

Brent Tor

Quither Common

Blacknor Park

80

Holyeat

Brinsabach Farm

6

Mast

Heathfield

Higher Farm

River Burn

79

Higher Haye

The Four Winds

Wallabrook Farm

Burnford

5

Pittescombe

Cherrybrook House

Grendon Farm

Great Haye Farm

Heathfield Lodge

78

Hurlditch Court

PITLAND CNR

Pitland Farm

River Wallabrook

4

Chaddlehanger

PL19

Mana Butts

Wringwor Farm

CHESTNUT CL 1
CHESTNUT CERR 2

COURT BARTON MEWS

Kilworthy

77

B3362

GREEN HILL

THE PATHWAYS

Wilminston

A386

PH

Lamerton

CH

3

Rushford

Venn House

Hurdwick Farm

Grammerby Wood

76

ORCHARD COTTS

River Lumburn

Langford

147

Hazeldon

PH

2

Ottery Park Ind Est

OTTERY COTTS

147

TAVISTOCK

Weir Mount House Sch

Ottery

Kelly Coll

75

Ogbeare

147

B3357 MOUNT TAVY RD

1

Three Oaks

Millhill

Mus

Liby

CH

Sch

MILLHILL

Downhouse Farm

NEW LAUNCESTON RD

B3362

Sch

H
PO

P P

74

Artiscombe

Crease

| 44 | A | 45 | B | 46 | C | 47 | D | 48 | E | 49 | F |

29

41

For full street detail of the highlighted area see page 147.

42

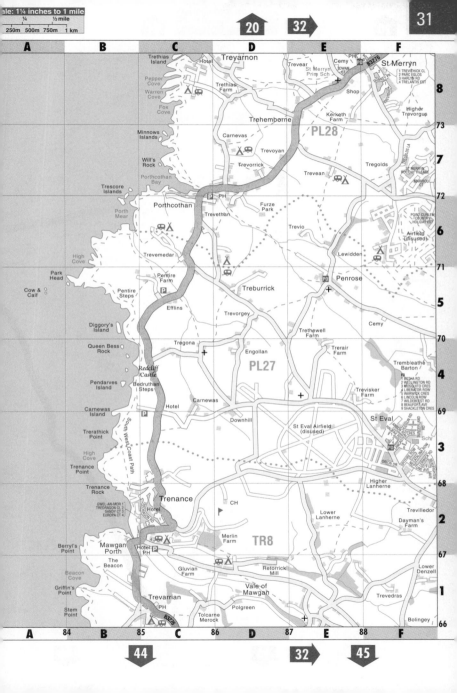

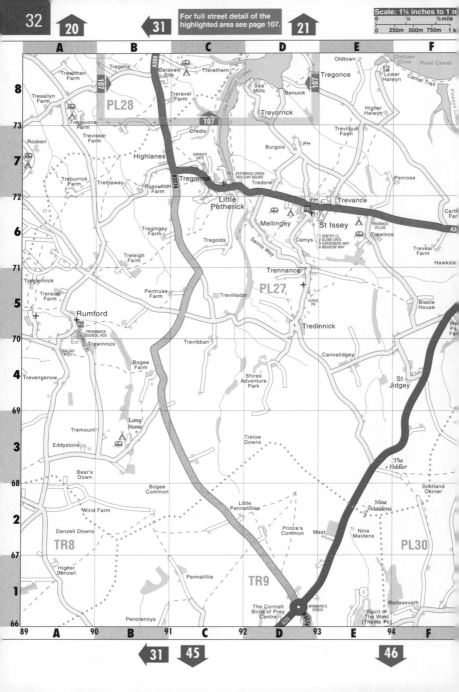

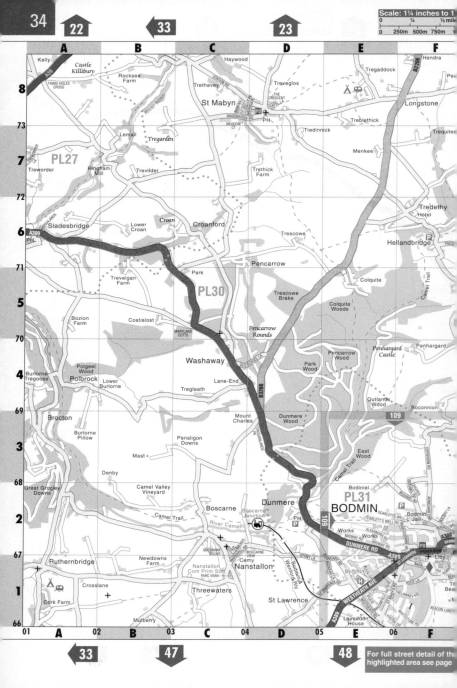

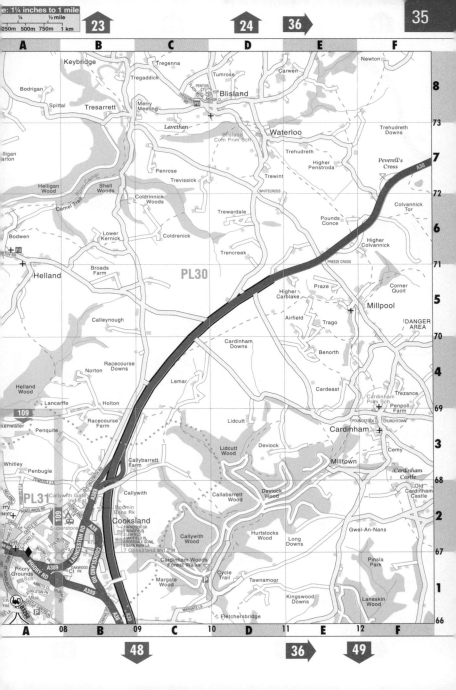

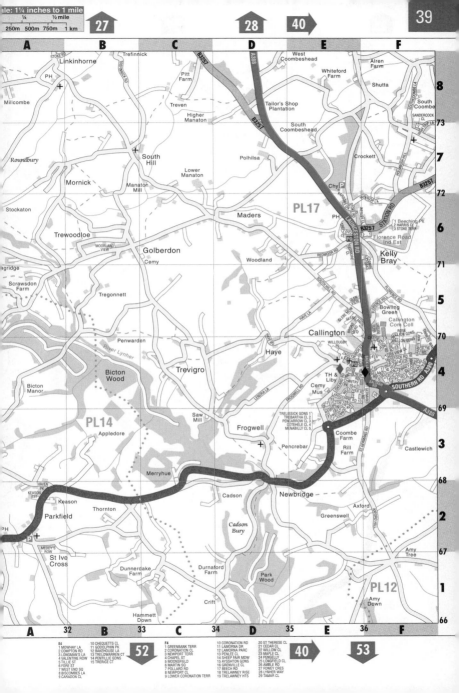

Scale: 1¼ inches to 1 mile

250m 500m 750m 1 km

A	B	C	D	E	F

8

65

7

64

6

63

Towan Head

110

Gazzle

P

5

62

Hotel

P

Fistral
Bay

Fistral
Beach

HEADLAND RD

NEWQUAY

South West Coast Path

CH

TR7

LB
Sta

Cemy

CRANTOCK S

P

P

4

The
Goose

Pentire
Point East

Pentire

ESPLANADE RD

PENTIRE RD

PO

Pentire
Point West

The
Chick

Kelsey
Head

Porth
Joke

Vugga
Cove

Ferry P
(summer only)

Crantock
Beach

P

Crantock

PENTIRE AVE

PENTIRE CRES

110

PENNARE DR

TREVEAN WAY

DRYNANCE DR

A392

A392

61

Hotel

West
Pentire

P

PH

WEST PENTIRE RD

Penpol

The
Gannel

South West Coast Path

3

Cave

South West Coast Path

Treago
Farm

ST CARANTOC
WAY

DUCTURY RD

GREENA

SELKET

GALWYN RD

Trevella

Treringey

60

Holywell
Bay

The
Kelseys

P

Trevowah

Trevella
Park

Carter's or
Gull Rocks

Holywell
Beach

Holywell

Cubert
Common

TR8

2

Penhale
Point

Dunes

Lewannick

Carines

110

P

59

Penhale
Camp

PH
CH
Fun
Park

BARB HILL

GOLDEN DR

TREGUTH CL

Treworgans

Treworthal

Trevornick

Tresean

Carevick

Cave

TREVAL
COTTS

Trevail

Cemy

CHYNOWEN
PARC

CHYNOWEN LA

PH

Cubert
Prim Sch

Trenissick

1

Hoblyn's
Cove

DANGER
AREA

Ligger
Point

58

A	76	B	77	C	78	D	79	E	80	F

55 ▼   44 ◀   For full street detail of the
highlighted area see page
110.

43
31

Scale: 1¼ inches to 1

| 0 | ¼ | ½ mile |

| 0 | 250m | 500m | 750m |

A B C D E F

8

Strasse
Cliff

South West Coast Path

Ce

65

Watergate
Bay

Hotel

Tregurrian

TREGURRIAN HILL

Newquay
Airport

7

Tregurrian or Watergate Beach

WATERGATE RD

Penvose
Farm

MARBEIN
COTTS

St
Mawgan
Airfield

64

Horse
Rock

Trebelsue
Farm

Twr

6

Zacry's
Island

Trevelgue

Higher
Trewince

Water
Tower

Flory
Island

Trevelgue
Head

1 THE WILLOWS
2 COASELINE CT
3 TREVELGUE CT

Whipsiderry

Tregustick
Farm

Trebarber

Caves

63

110

111

Penrose

Tregenna

CH

Treloy

Newquay
Bay

Lusty
Glaze

Porth

St Columb
Minor

5

Caves

PARKABBIT

Treviglas
Com Coll

HENVER RD

PRIORY RD

Cem'y

Rialton
Barton

Melancoose

Trebarber

62

Aquarium

Sh
Ctr

NARROWCLIFF

GLAMIS RD

Sports
Ctr

Tretherras
Sch

A3059

RIALTON RD

TR8

4

Liby

Newquay

MOUNT WISE

PITOR RD

TR7

Gusti
Veor

NEWQUAY

Trewollack
Farm

East
Penhill

Cola

Sch

Pk

Trenance

A3058 GANNEL RD

Trencreek

Gusti
Vean

QUINTRELL RD

Lowertown

61

A392

TREVEMPER RD

LC

Chapel

Bejowan

3

Treringey
Round

Trel Ind Est

Lane

LC

Quintrell
Downs

Quintrell
Downs

WEST RD

NORTH AVE

Lady
Nanc

111

EAST RD

Superstore

PH

Hendra

Manuels

Trethiggy
Farm

Coswart

60

Trevemper

A3075

Trevithick
Manor

Higher
Trevilley

River Gannel

Gwills

Trevilley Court
Farm

A3058

Kestle

Penhallow

Legonna

Kestle
Mill

PH

2

Rosecliston
Park

110

111

Trevean

Trevean

59

Sewage
Works

Polgreen

Trevarthian

A3058

Trewerry
Mill

Treg

1

Trerew
Farm

A3075

Tregair
Farm

Trerice

Tresillian
House

Dairyland
Farm World

58

81 A 82 B 83 C 84 D 85 E 86 F

43
56

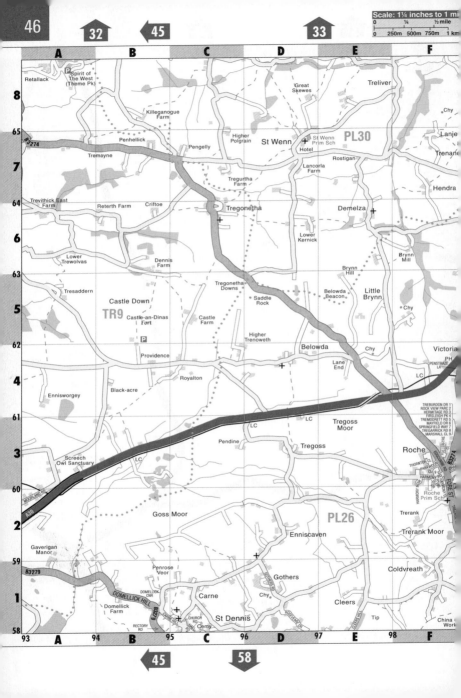

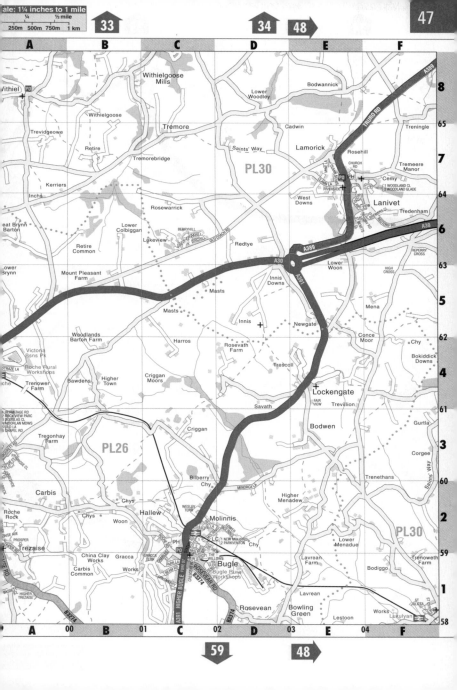

34
47
35

Scale: 1¼ inches to 1

0   ¼   ½ mile

0   250m 500m 750m   1

A   B   C   D   E   F

Laveddon
Mill

Kymsland

Little
Kirland

Kirland

Bodmin & Wenford Rlwy

Coll

Turfdown

SUNNY BANK

Fletchersb

Trekillick
Farm

Stephen
Gelly

Hawke's
Bridge

Halgavor
Farm

GREEN LA

Ind Est

CARMINOW
CROSS

Crem

Colesloggett
Halt

Lidcutt
Farm

109

L Ctr

BESPRYN RD

1 PAARDEBURG RD
2 LUCKNOW RD S
3 ISLAND LANES

CARMINOW
CROSS

PL31

Little
Cutmadoc
Farm

8

109

Tremabyn

Kirland
Bower

OM FORD

CH

THE
FAIRWAYS

Halgavor
Plantation

Bazley's
Plantation

Hart
Wood

7

Tregullon

Cemy

Cutmadoc

Treliggon

Tretoil

Treffry

Lanhydrock
House

Newton

Waterlake

6

St Ingunger
Farm

Foxpark

Great
Wood

Bof

Fenton
Pits

Mast

Trebyan

PL22

112

Trebell
Green

Lesquite
Farm

Tredinnickpits

Ford
Farm

Maudlin

Coombe
Farm

Works

Brownqueen
Wood

Brown
Queen

5

Bokiddick

Higher
Trevilmick

Creney
Farm

Sweetshouse

Woodlands
Farm

Slip
Wood

Helman

PL30

Boslymon

Leadenhill
Wood

Restormel
Castle

Restormel
Farm

4

Lowertown

Red Moor

Redmoor

B269

B3269

Barngate
Farm

Restormel

Restormel
Manor

Breney
Farm

Bowden
Farm

Chark

112

Hillhead

Penquite

TERRAS HILL

3

Roseney
Farm

Crift

Ruzza

Penhale

LOSTWITHIEL

Poldew
Wood
Poldew

Cemy

Crift
Downs

Streigh
Farm

Polgassick
Farm

Victoria

Penknight

Uplands

Sch

Rosehill

Lanwit

2

Luxulyan
Quarry

Tregantle

LANXON CRES
1 THOMAS BULLOCK CL

Crewell

PH

Pelyn

Cemy

112

Treganoon

Lanlivery

Puddle

PL22

Mast

1

Luxulyan

Middle
Greadow

Trethew

Sandyway
Wood

Castle

1 ST JULITTA
2 ST SULIEN

B3269

58

A   05   B   06   07   C   08   D   09   E   10   F

47
60

For full street detail of the
highlighted area see pages
109 and 112.

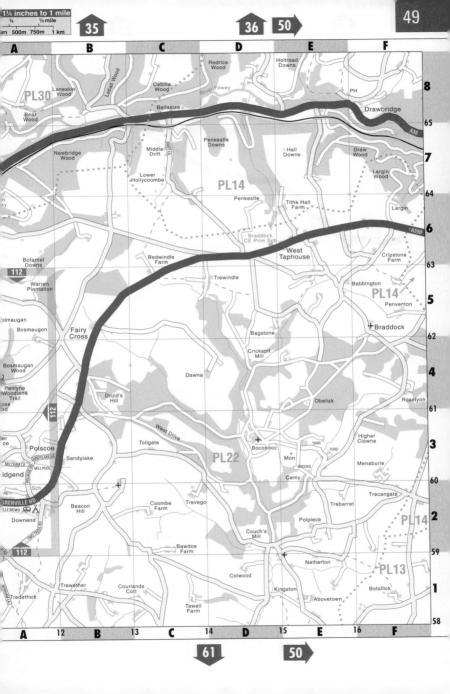

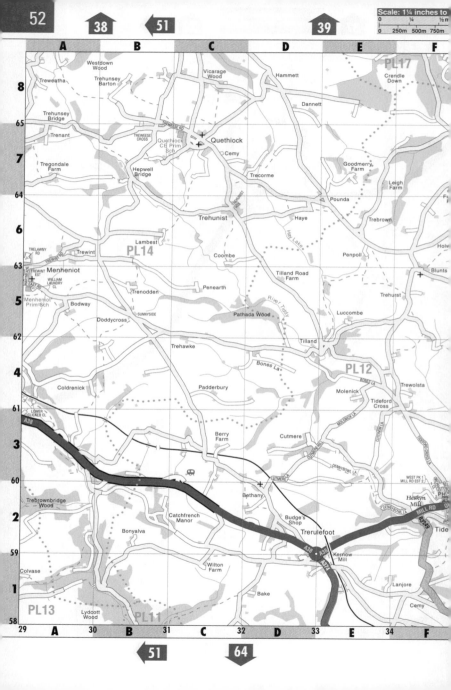

Scale: 1¼ inches to 1 mile
0 ¼ ½ mi
0 250m 500m 750m

Shag Rock

Cligga Head

Cligga Workshops 1
ST GEORGE'S TERR 2

Shafts (dis)

Hanover Cove

TR

Airfield

Anchor

Bawden Rocks

South West Coast Path

Trevellas

Green Island

Blowinst

Trevellas Porth

Cross Coombe

Trevaunance Cove

Chy

Newdowns Head

Blue Hill

Trevellas Coombe

Crams

Chy

PERRAN VIEW HOLIDAY PARK

Trevellas

New Downs

Shafts (dis)

St Agnes Head

PH

TREVAUNANCE CL

TR5

Carn Gowla

Higher Bal

Chy

Wheal Kitty

Peterville

Mithian Jun & Inf Sch

Barkla Shop

Hotel

Tubby's Head

Chy

St Agnes Beacon

St Agnes Prim Sch

Chy

TOWN HALL

B3285

St Agnes

Mithian

BEACON FARM

Lib

Mus

B3277

Goonown

68

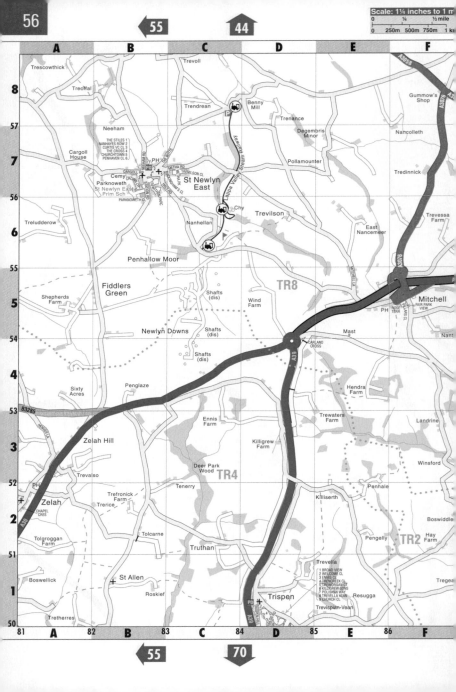

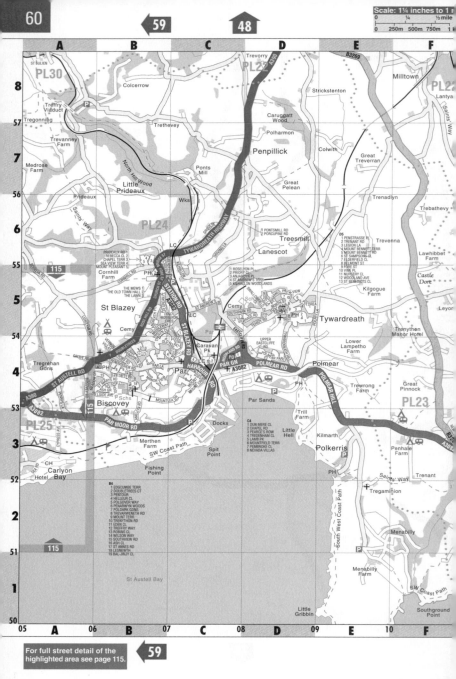

Scale: 1¼ inches to 1 mile

59
48
59

St Austell Bay

PL30
PL24
PL25
PL23

St Julien
Trevorry
Milltown
Lantya
Saints' Way

Colcerrow
Strickstenton
Treffry Viaduct
Caruggatt Wood
Polharmon
Tregonning
Trethevey
Penpillick
Colwith
Great Treverran

Trevanney Farm
Ponts Mill
Great Pelean
Trenadlyn
Trebathevy

Medrose Farm
North Hill Wood
Wks
Castle Dore
Leyor

Prideaux
Little Prideaux
Saints' Way
1 PONTSMILL RD
2 PORCUPINE RD
Treesmill
Trevenna
Lawhibbet Farm

Cornhill Farm
Lanescot
Kilgogue Farm

St Blazey
Cemy
Tywardreath
Tremython Manor Hotel

Tregrehan Gdns
Caravan Pk
Par
Lower Lampetho Farm
Polmear
Trewrong Farm
Great Pinnock

Biscovey
POLMEAR RD
A3082
PL23

A390
A3082
Par Sands
POLMEAR HILL

PAR MOOR RD
Merthen Farm
Docks
Spit Point
Trill Farm
Little Hell
Kilmarth
Polkerris
Penhale Farm
Trenant

Carlyon Bay Hotel
SW Coast Path
Fishing Point
South West Coast Path
Tregaminion

St Austell Bay
Menabilly
Menabilly Farm
SW Coast Path

Little Gribbin
Southground Point

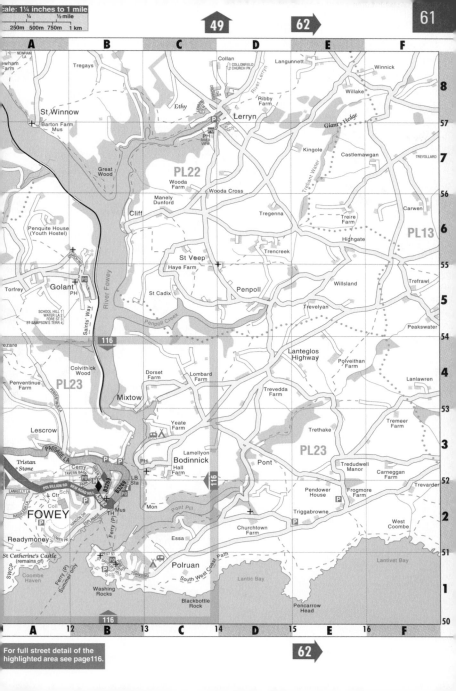

Scale: 1¼ inches to 1 mi

0   ¼   ½ mile
0 250m 500m 750m 1 km

A   B   C   D   E   F

8

47

7

46

6

45

5

44

Godrevy
Island

Navax Point

Godrevy Point

The
Knavocks

Fishing
Cove

Hell's
Mouth

Deadman's
Cove

North Cliffs

Reskaje
Down

South West Coast Path

Higher
Pencobben

Hudder Down

43

B3

St Ives Bay

Godrevy
Towans

BUTNEY
CNR

Carlean
Farm

Coombe

Cvn P

Magow
Rocks

42

78

Ashill Farm

79

Gwealavellan

Menadarva

TR14

Strap Rocks

Red River

THE
OLD BARNS

2

Gwithian Towans

CHURCHTOWN RD

Nanterrow
Farm

TR27

Kehelland

Peter's Point

Gwithian

PH

Nancemellin

Kehell
Village

PENTIONA
LA

CHAPEL
CL

Met

41

ST IVES RD

PROSPER HILL

MANERROW LA

GWITHIAN RD

B3301

GODREVY PK
(CVN PK)

GWITHIAN SANDS
CHALET PK

Trevarnon
Round

Chyo

Cornhill
Farm

A30

SANDBANK
HOLIDAY FLATS

40

57   A   58   B   59   C   60   D   61   E   62   F

78   78   79

Scale: 1¼ inches to 1 mile

¼   ½ mile
250m 500m 750m 1 km

E4
1 CORONATION RD
2 VENTONRAZE TERR
3 ROBARTES TERR
4 HARMONY TERR
5 ALEXANDRA CL
6 TREFORTHLAN CL

7 TREFORTHLAN
8 ILLOGAN PK
9 SUNNYSIDE PARC
10 KESTRAL WAY
11 BOSVEAN GDNS
12 POLDARK RD
13 PENCARROW RD

14 PENWARTHA VEAN
15 PENWARTHA RD
16 LAMANVA CL
17 LAMANVA RD
18 TREVELTHAN RD
19 VALLEY VIEW
20 VALLEY GDNS

21 FORTH DALL
22 LOWER MERRITTS HILL
23 BEACON VIEW PK

68

Tobban Horse
TR4
Chy
Factory Farm
Gullyn Rock
Sheep Rock
Nancekuke Common
Diamond
South West Coast Path
Airfield (dis)

HARBOUR TERR 1
KINGSLEY TERR 2
CAYFORTH FLATS 3
FORTH-AN-NANCE 4
THE SQUARE 5
HARBOUR CT 6
GLENFEADON TERR 7
SUNNYVALE CL 8
BAIRES HILL 9
GREENFIELD TERR 10

Cambrose
Horse Rock
Portreath
Gull Rock
Landmark
Pier
LIGHTHOUSE HILL
PH
TR16
Ralph's Cupboard
PENBERTHY RD
NEW PORTREATH RD
Cvn Pk
LAMORNA
Portreath Com Prim Sch
Samphire Island
PH
Bridge
Carvannel Downs
Basset's Cove
OLD BOYS SCHOOL 1
TANGYE EL 2
Nance
Tin Works
Crane Castle
Tehidy Barton
Sch
CHURCH TOW
Illogan
Sparnon Gate
...eage Downs
PH
Tehidy Ctry Pk
CH
THE STABLES
PRIMROSE GDNS 1
WOODBINE LA 2
COLBORNE AVE
WARWICK AVE 4
THE MEADOW 5
ALEXANDRA RD
Paynter's Lane End
BASSET RD
PH
Oak Wood
Old Merrose Farm
PH
Magor Farm
138
Home Farm
139
West Tolgus
Tolgus Mount
South Tehidy
Halgoss
Park Bottom
A30
A3300
TR14
MOUNT WHISTLE RD
CLIFTON RD
WEST TOLGUS
Chys
Roscroggan
Tolvaddon Downs
TR15
79
Chy
Sch
Mus
Illogan Highway
80
Tolskithy
BARNCOOSE TERR
A3047
Reskadinnick
Roskear Croft
Mast
Col
Mus
FORE ST
AGAR RD
Camborne Redruth Com
H
Carn Brae Village
Shafts (dis)
Trng Ctr
Chys
TREVENSON ST
Pool
Mus
A3047
Race Farm
Rosewarne
ROLLER WORKS RD
PENDARVES ST
EAST HILL
Mine (dis)
L Ctr
Carn Brae
Carn Brae Castle
TA Ctr
Tuckingmill
Tregajorran
Mon
CAMBORNE
DOLCOATH RD
DOLCOATH AVE
Coll (Annexe)
Brae
Tramways Ctr
Penhallick
...swithian
TRESWITHIAN RD
PENDARVES RD
THELDWARREN ST
Cemy
Sch
Coll (Annexe)
LC
Carn Arthen
Bosleake
TR16
A3047

For full street detail of the highlighted area see pages 138 and 139.

79

80

80

A   B   C   D   E   F

64   65   66   67   68

8 47 7 46 6 45 5 44 4 43 3 42 2 41 1 40

Scale: 1¼ inches to 1

| 0 | ¼ | ½ mile |
| 0 | 250m | 500m 750m 1 |

8

Chapel Porth
Goonvrea
BEACON DR
ALBANY RD
CHIVERTON
GREENACRES
KERENSA
GDNS
A.MILE CL

Goonbell

Mithian
Downs

Shaft
(dis)
Chy
Hurlingbarrow
Ind Est
TR5
White

49

Mingoose
Silverwell
Farm

South West Coast Path

1 EASTCLIFF AVE NO 1
2 EASTCLIFF AVENUE NO 2
3 EASTCLIFF AVE NO 2
4 LOWER EASTCLIFF
5 GOYNE'S FIELD
6 SEASPRAY LEISURE FLATS
7 KINGSLEY COVE
8 OCEAN CT
9 SANDY COVE TRAVEL LODGE
TOWAN RD

Towan
Cross

Silver

7

Porth
Towan
PH
Banns
PH

Gover
Farm

1 HENLEY CRES
2 HENLEY DR
3 HENLEY CL
4 SHORT CROSS MDWS
5 ALEXANDRA TERR
6 PEN HALLOW CL
7 TRENITHICK MDW
8 SCORIA CL
9 HIGH FIELD RD
10 MAITHALLEN RD
11 CHURCH RD
12 CHARLOTTE CL
13 ELLEN CL

48

Porthtowan
PO
PH
Trevissick
Farm
Chy
Mount
Hawke
ROPE WLK
PH
GLENDA
CRES
Penhallow
Farm
TR4
Works
PH

6

Chy
1 BEACHSIDE CT
2 BEACHVIEW FLATS
3 TYWARNHALE WAY
4 SOUTH VIEW PARC
Chys
MOUNT HAWKE
CHALET PK

PH
B3277
CHIVERTON
CROSS

47

ROSE HILL
TOURING PK

Wheal Bassett
Farm
Cemy
Gooseswartha
Farm
Two Burrows

5

Manor
Parsley
Menagissey

Blackwater

1 HIGHVIEW CRES
2 HIGHVIEW
3 SOUTH VIEW TERR
4 SYMONDS CL
5 CORONATION TERR
6 PASS NORE CL

The
Burr

46

Laity
Moor

Mawla

Skinners
Bottom

Blackwater
Com Prim
Sch
PH

CHAPEL HILL

4

Forge

Stencoose

Wheal
Plenty
Chy
Boscawen
Farm
STATION RD
Carnhot

45

Sinns
Barton

GLOBE VALE
CVN

GREEN LA
Chy
Wheal
Busy
BROOKSIDE 1
BUCKINGHAM NIP 2
SERGEANTS HILL 3
WHEAL BUSY LA

Parc
Erissey
Wheal
Rose

Chacewater

Parc Erissey
Ind Est
TR16
Chys
8 CHURCH ST

Salem

3

B3300

North
Downs

WHITE
LA

PH
1 SCORIA CL
2 ADAMS ROW
3 RADNOR RD
Chys
WHEAL BUSY LA
HIGH ST

Cox
Hill

44

Radnor
140
A3047
B3298
PO
Motel
Scorrier
Killifreth
Farm
POLICE

Creegbraw

North
Country
Treleigh
LC
Scorrier
House
Tregullow
1 TELEGRAPH HILL
2 HIGHVIEW
3 MILLS
4 SCORRIER ST
5 CAREW ST
7 BOSAWNE CL

2

140
A3047
Highway
Treskerby
WHEAL GORLAND RD 1
CHYROSE RD 2
FORTH-AN-PRAZE 3
BALODATH 4
TRENANT 5
CHAPEL ST 6
VOGUE TERR 7
TELEGRAPH ST 9
MARKET SQ 10
FORE ST 11
WEST END 12
CAREW RD 13

Todpool

REDRUTH HIGHWAY
Mount
Ambrose
140
Tolgullow

Chy

Go
Gum

43

A38
A393
TR15
SANDY LA
Chy
Vogue
PH
St Day
Chy
POLICE
HIGHER GOONGUMPAS LA
LOWER GOONGUMPAS LA

1

REDRUTH
Trefula
ST DAY DR
VICARAGE HILL
BARRE
CHAPEL
TERR
Crothandy
WHEAL
B3298

PO
Sch
Cemy
Ninnis
Chy
CHURCH HILL
Sch
Chys

42

A3047
B3300
Redruth
A393

For full street detail of the
highlighted area see page 140.

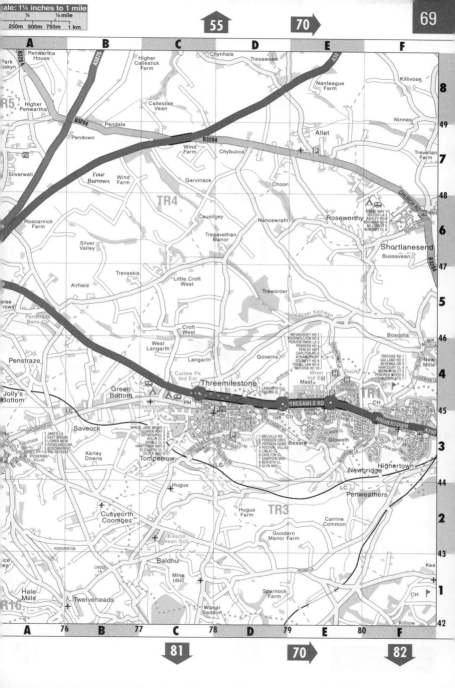

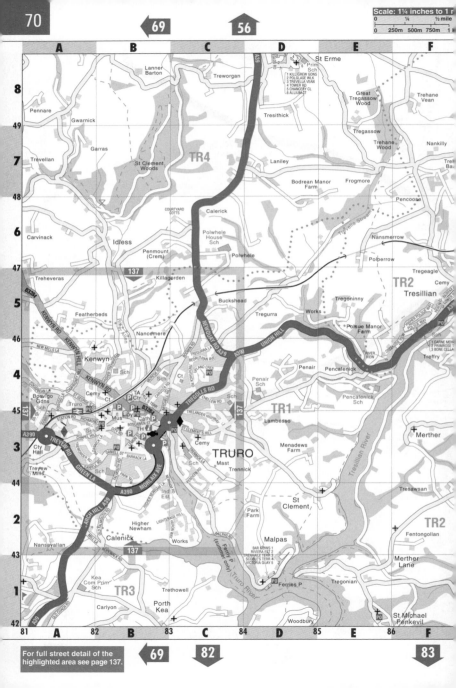

69 56

Scale: 1¼ inches to 1 mile

| 0 | ¼ | ½ mile |
| 0 | 250m | 500m | 750m | 1 km |

8

Lanner Barton
Treworgan
St Erme Prim

1 KILLIGREW GDNS
2 POLGLASE WLK
3 TREVELLA VEAN
4 TOWER RD
5 CHANCERY CL
6 ALLUAN CT

Pennare
Gwarnick
Tresithick
Great Tregassow Wood
Trehane Vean

49

Garras
TR4
Tregassow
Trehane Wood
Nankilly

7

Trevellan
St Clement Woods
Laniley
Frogmore
Treh Ba

48

Carvinack
Calerick
Bodrean Manor Farm
Pencoose

6

Idless
Polwhele House Sch
Polwhele
Travellis Stream
Nansmerrow

Penmount (Crem)
Polperrow
Tregeagle

47

Treheveras
COURTYARD COTTS
Killagorden
Buckshead
TR2
Tresillian
Cemy

5

Featherbeds
Nancemere
Tregurra
Tregoninny
Works
1 CARNE MDW
2 PRIMROSE
3 BONE CELLA
Treffry

Kenwyn Rd
River Allen
Polsue Manor Farm
RIVER VIEW
B3284

46

New Mills La
Kenwyn
Penair Sch
Pencalenick

4

Bosvigo Gdns Sch
Truro
TA P Ctr
Tregolls Rd
Penair
Pencalenick Sch

Cemy
Mus
Cath
Trelander Highway
TR1
Lambesso
Merther

45

Cty Hall
Treyew Mills
Station Rd
TH
St Clement's Hill
Cemy
TRURO
Mast
Trennick
Menadews Farm
Merther

3

Treyew Rd
Green La
Morlaix Ave
Ind Est
St Clement
Tresawsan

44

Arch Hill A39
Higher Newham
Lightdrage Hill
Park Farm
Malpas
TR2
Fentongollan

2

Nansavallan
Calenick
Works
BAR MDWS
RIVIERA EST
TRENHALE TERR
SCOBLES TERR
VICTORIA QUAY
Merther Lane

43

Kea Com Prim Sch
Trethowell
Ferry P (summer only)
Truro River
Ferries P
Tregonian
St Michael Penkevil

1

Carlyon
TR3
Porth Kea
Woodbury

42

| A | 81 | B | 82 | C | 83 | D | 84 | E | 85 | F | 86 |

69 82 83

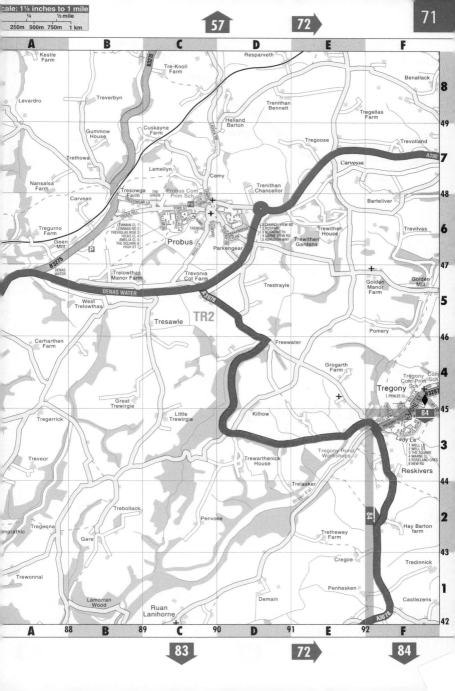

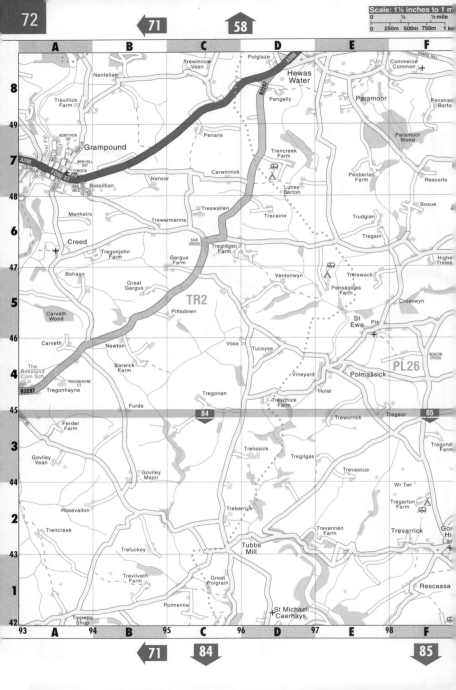

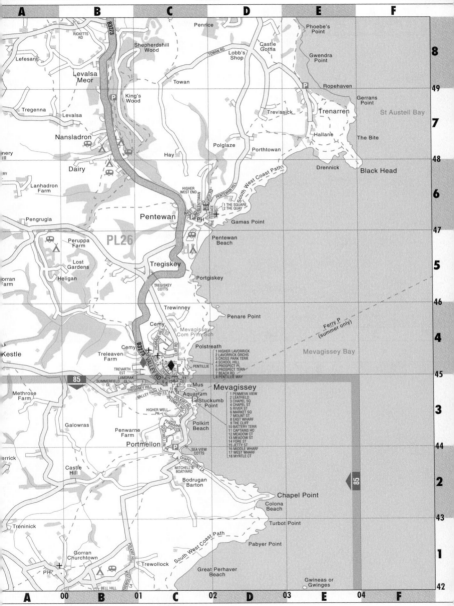

e: 1¼ inches to 1 mile

¼ ½ mile

250m 500m 750m 1 km

A	**B**	**C**	**D**	**E**	**F**

Penrice

RICKETTS RD

Shepherdshill Wood

Castle Gotha

Phoebe's Point

8

Lefesant

Levalsa Meor

King's Wood

Towan

Lobb's Shop

TOWAN RD

Gwendra Point

Ropehaven

49

Tregenna

Levalsa

Nansladron

Trevissick

Trenarren

Gerrans Point

St Austell Bay

7

Dairy

Hay

Polglaze

Porthtowan

Hallane

The Bite

48

Lanhadron Farm

Drennick

Black Head

6

Pengrugla

PL26

HIGHER WEST END

Pentewan

1 THE SQUARE
2 THE QUAY

South West Coast Path

47

Peruppa Farm

Gamas Point

Lost Gardens

Heligan

Tregiskey

Pentewan Beach

5

TREGISKEY COTTS

Portgiskey

46

Trewinney

Penare Point

Ferry P
(summer only)

Cemy

Mevagissey
Com Prim Sch

4

Cemy

Treleaven Farm

Polstreath

Mevagissey Bay

1 HIGHER LAVORRICK
2 LAVORRICK ORCHS
3 CROSS PARK TERR
4 SCHOOL HILL
5 PROSPECT PL
6 PROSPECT TERR
7 BEACH RD
8 PENTILLIE WAY

45

TREVARTH EST

SUMMERFIELD CL

LAMORAK

PENTILLIE

85

VALLEY RD

Mus

Mevagissey

1 PENMEVA VIEW
2 LEATHFIELD
3 CHAPEL SQ
4 CHAPEL ST
5 RIVER ST
6 MARKET SQ
7 MOUNT ST
8 EAST WHARF
9 THE CLIFF
10 BATTERY TERR
11 CAPTAINS HO
12 MEADOW CT
13 MEADOW ST
14 FORE ST
15 JETTY ST
16 MIDDLE WHARF
17 WEST WHARF
18 MYRTLE CT

3

Methrose Farm

Galowras

Aquarium

Stuckumb Point

HIGHER WELL

Penwarne Farm

Portmellon

Polkirt Beach

44

SEA VIEW COTTS

CHAPEL POINT LA

Chapel Point

85

2

Treninick

Castle Hill

MITCHELL'S BOATYARD

Bodrugan Barton

Colona Beach

Turbot Point

43

Gorran Churchtown

PH

Trewollock

South West Coast Path

Pabyer Point

1

BELL HILL

Great Perhaver Beach

Gwineas or Gwinges

42

A	**B**	**C**	**D**	**E**	**F**

00 01 02 03 04

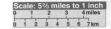

Scale: 5⅔ miles to 1 inch
0 1 2 3 4 miles
0 1 2 3 4 5 6 7 km

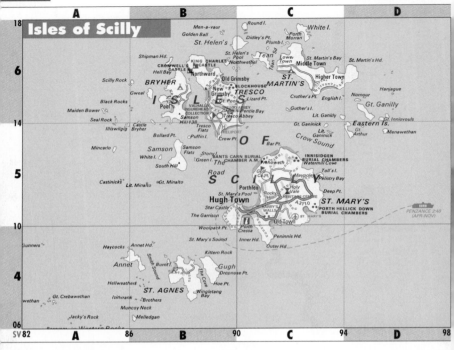

Isles of Scilly

Men-a-vaur
Golden Ball
Round I.
White I.
Didley's Pt.
Porth
Morran
Plumb I.
St. Helen's
St. Helen's
Pool
Northwethel
Lower
Town
Middle Town
St. Martin's Bay
St. Martin's Hd.
Shipman Hd.
St. Martin's Hd.
CROMWELL'S
CASTLE
KING CHARLES
CASTLE
McCARTIE
ST.
MARTIN'S
Higher Town
Hell Bay
Northward
Old Grimsby
Scilly Rock
BRYHER
BLOCKHOUSE
Hanjague
Gweal
New
Grimsby
Gt. Pool
TRESCO
Lizard Pt.
Cruther's Pt.
English I.
Nornour
Black Rocks
Pool
ISLES
Gt. Pentle Bay
Tresco Abbey
Guther's I.
Gt. Ganilly
Maiden Bower
VALHALLA
NQUREHA A D
COLLECTION
ABBEY
Lit. Ganilly
Gt. Innisvouls
Seal Rock
Samson
Hill 138
Tresco
Flats
HELIPORT
Gt. Ganinick
Eastern Is.
Illiswilgig
Castle
Bryher
Puffin I.
Gt. Ganinick
Lit.
Ganinick
Gt.
Arthur
Menawethan
Mincarlo
Bollard Pt.
Crow Pt.
Bar Pt.
OF
Crow Sound
Samson
Samson
Flats
Stony
Green I.
NANTS CARN BURIAL
CHAMBER A.M.
Toreboweth
INNISIDGEN
BURIAL CHAMBERS
White I.
The
Road
SCILLY
Watermill Cove
Castinicks
Lit. Minalto
Gt. Minalto
South Hill
Porthloo
Maypole
Pelistry Bay
Deep Pt.
St. Mary's Pool
Hugh Town
Rocky
Hill
Holy
Vale
HERITAGE CENTRE
ST. MARY'S
PENZANCE 2:40
(APR-NOV)
Star Castle
ST.
MARY'S
WALLS
A3710
PORTH HELLICK DOWN
BURIAL CHAMBERS
The Garrison
Old Town
ST.
MARY'S
Woolpack Pt.
Porth
Cressa
Peninnis Hd.
Inner Hd.
Gunners
St. Mary's Sound
Outer Hd.
Haycocks
Annet Hd.
Kittern Rock
Annet
Smith Sound
Burnt I.
Gugh
Dropnose Pt.
Hellweathers
The Cove
Hoe Pt.
wethan
Gt. Crebawethan
ST. AGNES
Wingletang
Bay
Isinvrank
Brothers
Jacky's Rock
Muncoy Neck
Melledgan
Bowers Western Rocks
SV 82   A   86   B   90   C   94   D   98

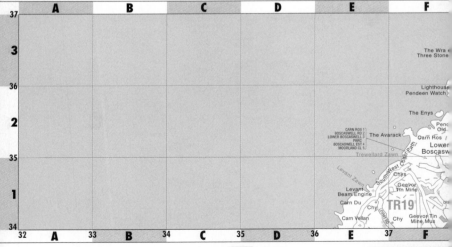

The Wra
Three Stone
Lighthouse
Pendeen Watch
The Enys
CARN ROS 1
BOSCASWELL RD 2
LOWER BOSCASWELL 3
PARC
BOSCADWELL EST 4
MOORLAND CL 5
The Avarack
Penc
Old
Carn Ros
Lower
Boscasw
Trewellard Zawn
Levant Zawn
Chys
Levant
Beam Engine
Geevor
Tin Mine
Carn Du
TR19
Carn Vellan
Geevor Tin
Mine, Mus
Chy

Scale: 1¼ inches to 1
0 ¼ ½ mile
0 250m 500m 750m 1

32   A   33   B   34   C   35   D   36   E   37   F

A B C D E F

8

41

7

40

6

39

Ebal Rocks

Porthglaze Cove

Gurnard's Head

5

38

Robin's Rocks

TR26

Treen

Porthmeor Point

PH

B3306

Porthmeor Cove

4

Great Zawn

37

Halldrine Cove

Bosigran Farm

Porthmeor

Porthmoina Cove

Bosigran Castle

The Mozens

Brandys

Bosporthennis

3

Greeb Point

Whirl Pool

Rosemergy

P

Carn Galver

Hannibal's Carn

Portheras Cove

South West Coast Path

Chair Carn

Long Carn

36

Little Galver

Carn Clough

Lower Chypraze

White Downs

TR20

2

Pendeen House

Morvah

Trevean

Watch Croft

Nine Maidens

Portheras Farm

TR19

Trevowhan

35

ETERS ROW
PARK-AN-PYTH
RRASE

4 BOSCASWELL TERR
5 CALARTHA TERR
6 CRESCENT PL
7 TR. SQUARE
8 ST. JOHN'S TERR
9 GWEL-MOR

LOWER HILL

Keigwin

The Carn

Bosullow Common

Pendeen

PORTHERRAS
CROSES

Higher Bojewyan

Tor Noon

Chun

Carn Downs

1

CARN
VIEW
TERR

10 PORTHERRAS VILLAS
11 PORTHERRAS TERR
12 BOJEWYAN STENNACK

B3318

Little Bosullow

Lanyon Farm

Bosiliack

Higher Boscaswell

A 39 B 40 C 41 D 42 E 43 F

34

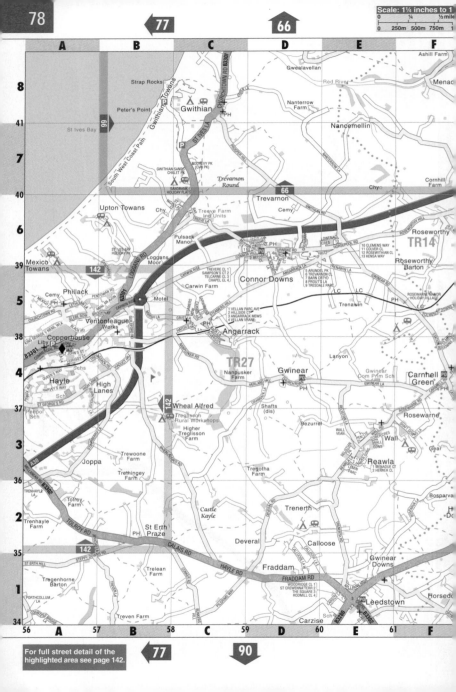

77

66

A   B   C   D   E   F

8

41

7

40

6

39

5

38

4

37

3

36

2

35

1

34

Ashill Farm

Menac

Gwealavellan

Red River

Strap Rocks

Peter's Point

Gwithian

Nanterrow Farm

Nancemellin

St Ives Bay

66

South West Coast Path

Gwithian Towans

St Ives La

Churchtown Rd B3301

GWITHIAN SANDS CHALET PK

Bodrevy Pk (CVN PK)

SANDBANK HOLIDAY FLATS

Trevarnon Round

Cornhill Farm

Chyo

66

Trevarnon

Cemy

Roseworthy

TR14

Upton Towans

Chy

Loggans Rd B3301

Treeve Farm Ind Units

Treeve La

Pulsack Manor

Owenac Cres

Horsepool Rd

Roseworthy Hill

Roseworthy Barton

Mexico Towans

142

St Ives Bay Holiday Pk

Loggans Moor

Phillack

Cemy

Pentowan Rd

Brockway

Klebe Rove

Carwin Rise

Carwin Farm

Trevere Cl 1
Telcarne Cl 3
Chapel Cl 4

Sampson's Ct 2

Turnpike Rd

Connor Downs

Trenawin La

Gwithian La

PH

Rosewarne Manor Holiday Village

10 Clemens Way
11 Colver Cl
12 Rosewithian Cl
13 Kenga Way

5 Arundel Pk
6 Trevarnon Cl
7 Barn Crtyd
8 Prout's La
9 Tresdale Parc

Trenawin

LC   LC

LC

Cot Wood Downs

Ventonleague Works

Copperhouse
Liby

Hayle

B3301

Schs

High Lanes

Queen's Way

Harvey's Way

142

Wheal Alfred

Treglisson Rural Workshops

Higher Treglisson Farm

1 Vellan Parc Ave
2 Hillside Ct
3 Angarrack Mews
4 Vellan Vrane

Griebe La

Hatches La

PH

Angarrack

Penhanover Rd

TR27

Nanpusker Farm

Gwinear

PH

Church Rd

Merland Way

Gwinear La

Lanyon

Gwinear Com Prm Sch

Carnhell Green

Bezurrel

Shafts (dis)

Wall Vean

Penty

Wall

Rosewarne

A30

Millennium Way

B3302

Joppa

Trewoone Farm

Trethingey Farm

Trelean Farm

Treweal Speed Rd

Gear

Reawla

1 Menadue Ct
2 Herver Cl

Gwinear Downs

Tregotha Farm

Trenerth

Bosparva

Trenhayle La

Tolroy Farm

Tolroy Rd

St Erth Praze

PH

Calais Rd

Castle Kayle

Deveral

Calloose

Trenhayle Farm

142

Steepy Downs Rd

St Erth Hill

Hayle Rd

Fraddam

Gwinear Downs

Tregenhorne Barton

Porthcollum La

Courtis Rd

Trelean Farm

Fraddam Rd

Woodridge Cl 1
St Crewenna Terr 2
The Square 3
Rodmill Cl 4

B3280

Sch

Leedstown

Horsed

Treven Farm

Carzise

For full street detail of the highlighted area see page 142.

56   A   57   B   58   C   59   D   60   E   61   F

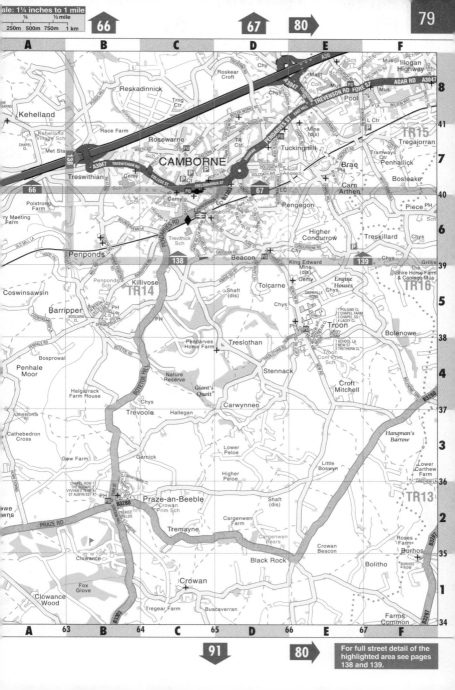

A   B   C   D   E   F

Illogan
Highway
8

Kehelland

Reskadinnick

Roskear
Croft

Chy

Mus

Sch
Mast
Coll
Mus

AGAR RD   A3047

TREVENSON RD   FORE ST

Pool

Trng
Ctr

Mine
(dis)

L Ctr

P

41

TR15

Tregajorran

Kehelland
Village Sch

Met Sta

Race Farm

Rosewarne

A3047   TRESWITHIAN RD

CAMBORNE

Mine
(dis)

Tuckingmill

Brae
PH

Penhallick

Bosleake

138

7

CHAPEL
CL

Treswithian

Cemy

Sch

P
Ct

P

TRELOWARREN ST

Carn
Arthen

66

Camborne

67   LC

40

Polstrong
Farm

Trevithick
Sch

Pengegon

Higher
Condurrow

Piece   PH

Sch

ry Meeting
Farm

OLD MILL LA

Penponds

CADOGAN RD

Beacon

138

King Edward
Mine
(dis)

Cemy

139

Treskillard

Chys

Chys

The
Shire Horse Farm
& Carriage Mus

39

Coswinsawsin

Penponds
Sch

Killivose

TR14

Shaft
(dis)

Tolcarne

Chys

Engine
Houses
Chys

TR16

Grillis

5

Barripper

PH

PH

Pendarves
Home Farm

Treslothan

Troon

1 POLGINE CL
2 CHAPEL FARM
3 CHAPEL SQ
4 LACEY CL

1 SCHOOL LA
2 NEW ST
3 TRETHERIN CL

Bolenowe

38

Bosprowal

Penhale
Moor

Halgarrack
Farm House

Nature
Reserve

Giant's
Quoit

Stennack

Croft
Mitchell

4

Cathebedron
Cross

Trevoole

Chys

Hallegan

Carwynnen

Hangman's
Barrow

37

3

Gew Farm

Garnick

Lower
Peloe

Higher
Peloe

Little
Boswyn

Lower
Carthew
Farm

TR13

36

Chapel Row 1
The Square 2
Vyvyan's Terr 3
St Aubyn Est 4

PH

B3280

Praze-an-Beeble

Crowan
Prim Sch

Tremayne

Cargenwen
Farm

Cargenwen
Resrs

Shaft
(dis)

Roses
Farm

Burhos

2

Clowance

PRAZE RD

Crowan
Beacon

Black Rock

Bolitho

Burhos
Row

35

Fox
Glove

Crowan

Buscaverran

Farms
Common

1

Clowance
Wood

Tregear Farm

34

A   63   B   64   C   65   D   66   E   67

91   80

For full street detail of the
highlighted area see pages
138 and 139.

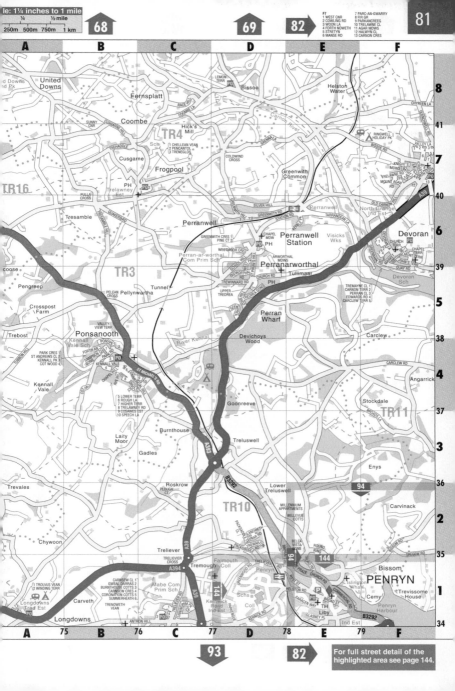

For full street detail of the highlighted area see page 144.

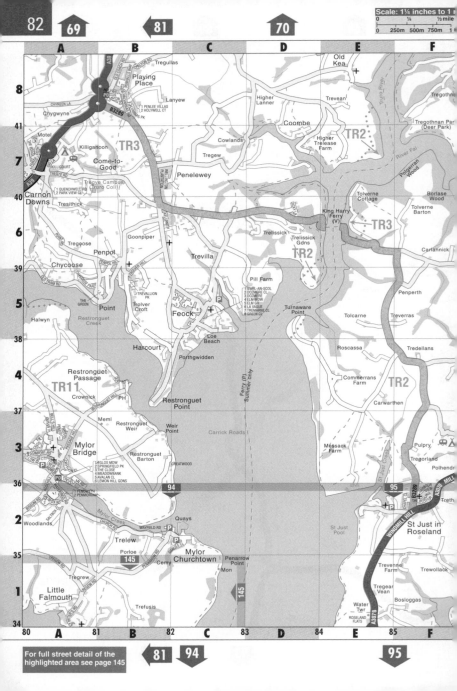

Mevagissey

1 PENHEVA VIEW
2 LEATFIELD
3 CHAPEL SQ
4 CHAPEL ST
5 RIVER ST
6 MARKET SQ
7 MOUNT ST
8 EAST WHARF
9 THE CLIFF
10 BATTERY TERR
11 CAPTAINS HO
12 MEADOW CT
13 MEADOW ST
14 FORE ST
15 JETTY ST
16 MIDDLE WHARF
17 WEST WHARF
18 MYRTLE CT

Mevagissey Bay

SUMMERFIELD   LAMORAK
CL   CL
TREGONEY HILL
VALLEY PARK LA
HIGHER WELL
PK

Stuckumb
Point

Polkirt
Beach

Methrose
Farm

Tregondean
Farm

Galowras

Penwarne
Farm

Portmellon

SEA VIEW
COTTS

Tregerrick

Castle
Hill

CHAPEL
MITCHELL'S
BOATYARD

Chapel Point

Bodrugan
Barton

Colona
Beach

Gorran
High
Lanes

Treninick

Turbot Point

PL26

Rescassa

Gorran
Churchtown

PH

Trewollock

South West Coast Path

Pabyer Point

Great Perhaver
Beach

Gwineas or
Gwinges

72   **73**

Treveor

Gorran
Sch

Gorran
Haven

1 QUILVER CL
2 RATTLE ST
3 CHURCH ST
4 ALEXANDER CT

Tregavarras
ROW
Tregavarras

Trevesson
Farm

DERBY'S LA 1
WILLS MOOR 2
COOKS LEVEL 3
TREWOLLOCK CL 4
PORTHEAST CL 5
LIGHTHOUSE LA 6

Tréveague
Farm

Lamledra

Pen-a-maen or
Maenease Point

Boswinger

YH

Cadythew
Rock

Hemmick
Beach

Penare

Bow or
Vault Beach

Gell Point

Penveor Point

High Point

Dodman Horse

Lizard Pool

Dodman Point

Scale: 1¼ inches to 1 mil

Scale: 1¼ inches to 1 mile

	A	B	C	D	E	F

8

Trythall Farm
Crankan
Noongallas
Trezelah
Badger's Cross
Tregadjack
Treass Man

Boswarthen

33

Bosoljack
Gear Farm

TR20

Kenegie Manor
Tregar

Madron Well Cross

Kennels
Trevaylor
Bone
Tremearne
Rosemorran Farm
Tolver

7

Trengwainton House

32

1 PARC-ABNAC
2 ALDREATH CL
3 TREGODICK CL
4 VINGOE'S LA
5 HILLSIDE PARC

1 TRENEGLOS TERR
2 TREVARRACK ROW
3 BARNFIELD GDNS
4 VLLANNOGGAN MEWS
5 MILLFIELD
6 BRAMWELL LA
7 FOXESFIELD
8 FRESHBROOK CL
9 GWEL LEWERN
10 MOUNT'S BAY HOL FLTS

Madron
Poltair
Trythogga
Gulval
Trevarrack
Heliport
Longrock

6

TR18

CHY-AN-MOR 1
Penwith Bsns Ctr 2
Longrock Bsns Pk 3
Longrock Ind Est 4

Mount's Bay Golf
Heamoor
Boscathnoe Resrv
Heamoor Jun & Inf Sch
West Cornwall
Cemy Coll Sch Inf Sch Prim Sch

Chyandour
Cressars
Western Cressar
Long F
Ryem

EASTERN GN

31

CUXHAVEN WAY 5
PONDU WAY 6
BAY VILLAS 7
GLADSTONE TERR 8
CASTLE VIEW 9
TRESCOE RD 10
DARLINGTON RD 11

Tremethick Cross
Rosehill
Penzance

PENZANCE

5

Tremethick Farm
Lesingey Round
Castle Horneck
YH
School of St Clare
Gall & Mus
Piers
Trinity House National Lighthouse Ctr

Tregavarah
Trewidden
Trereife
Libys

30

Buryas Bridge
Ind Est
Wherry Town
St Mary's CE Prim Sch
The Gear

4

Tolcarne Prim Sch

Edward Bolitho Ho (Hospl & Day Ctr)

29

The Pilchard Wks
Newlyn Art Gall

NEWLYN

Tredavoe
Newlyn Sch
LB Sta
Pier
Tidal Obsy

3

Chyenhal
Hotel

Gwavas Lake

Tresvennack

28

Tresvennack Pillar

97

Chywoone Grove
Trewarveneth Farm Cotts
Roskilly Cotts
Skilly

2

TR19

Karris
Paul
Roskilly
Meml
Penlee Point

1 ST POL-DE-LEON VIEW
2 TRUNGLE TERR
3 TRUNGLEMOOR COTTS
4 TRUNGLE PARC
5 BOSLANEW HILL

27

Rosevale Farm Penaluna
Cemy
PH
Trevithal

1

Redhouse
Lower Sheffield
Sheffield
Mousehole
St Clements Isle

Four Lanes End
Halwyn Farm

26

44	A	45	B	46	C	47	D	48	E	49	F

C1
1 LYNWOOD COTTS
2 PREVENNA RD
3 GWELENYS RD
4 PARKRYN RD
5 FOXES LA
6 MARCWHEAL
7 DUMBARTON TERR
8 SOUTHVIEW TERR
9 DUCK ST

10 COMMERCIAL RD
11 QUAY ST
12 NORTH CLIFF
13 FORE ST
14 NORTH ST
15 MILL POOL
16 BROOK ST
17 SOUTH CLIFF
18 GRENFELL ST
19 MILL LA

20 CHAPEL ST
21 THE WHARF
22 PORTLAND PL
23 GURNICK ST
24 RAGINNIS HILL
25 ST CLEMENTS TERR
26 SALTPONDS

For full street detail of the highlighted area see page 143

A   B   C   D   E   F

NANCEDDEN FARM

Vellanoweth

TRETHORNE CT
BOWJEY
PH
THE SQUARE
Ludgvan
CHY-AN-GWEAL EST

Crowlas
Crowlas Ind Est

CHURCH HILL
B3309
CARVOSSO EST
THEDENDER

GITCHELL LA

Trevorrow Farm

THE LONG BARN
Rosevidney Barton

Trewinnard Manor
Trevessa Farm

TR27

Porthcollum

Carbows Farm

8

33

MOUNT VIEW COTTS
Varfell

Giant's Grave

A30   A394

Tregilliowe Farm

Truthwall

Trevarthian Farm

TR20

Treveneague

Frythens Farm

PENBERTHY CROSS

Ennys

7

32

Gwallon

TREGURTHA FARM COTTS

Chy

Kestal

Chynoweth

St Hilary
Prim Sch

6

GREEN LA

TR17

Marazion

Pipin-an-Gwarry

Chy

Tregurtha Downs

Chy

St Hilary

Trevabyn

B3280

1 DARLINGTON RD
2 TRESCO RD
3 THE BUILDINGS

Sch
Mus
HIGHER FORE ST
CLIFF LA
COMORAN

Goldsithney
1 WOLCOCKE CL
2 MILLET CL

ALBYNS LA

WEST END

FORE ST

Higher Downs

31

Little Hogus

Chapel Rock

Ferry P
(summer only)

HARBOUR VIEW

ELIZABETH TERR

Priory

St Michael's Mount

CAUSEWAY

PH

Top Tieb
5 THE SQUARE
6 MARKET PL

CS
1 GWEL-AN-MOR
2 TURNPIKE HILL
3 SHOP MILL
4 OLD SMITHY CL
5 MOUNT VIEW TERR
6 HENFOR MEWS
7 ST LEVAN RD
8 ST LEVAN CL
9 TREWORVENNETH DR
10 FORNEGLOS DR
11 CHURCHWAY
12 HENFOR CL
13 HENFOR TERR

Little London

Camy

Trenow Cove

The Frenchman

Perranuthnoe

THE ELMS

PH

Perran Crossroads

Perran Downs

Wt Twr

JOHN'S CNR

ZELGOGY CROSS

Perran Downs

5

30

CHIVERTON CROSS

CHIVERTON WAY

PH

Rosudgeon

4

Basnore Point

The Greeb

Maen-du-Point

Perran Sands

Trebarvah

Trevean Farm

Rosudgeon Common

29

Trevean Cove

CS
1 NORTH ORCHARD CT
2 QUEEN'S WAY
3 RETALLACK GDNS
4 PRIMROSE LA
5 TREVELYAN WAY
6 ORCHARD WAY
7 MANOR FARM CL
8 MEADOW VIEW
9 PRIMROSE CL
10 TREVELYAN CL

Stackhouse Cove

Acton Castle (Hotel)

COASTGUARD COTTS

3

28

Prussia Cove

Bessy's Cove

Piskies Cove

Cudden Point

2

27

1

26

A   51   B   52   C   53   D   54   E   55   F

For full street detail of the
highlighted area see page 146.
98 92 99

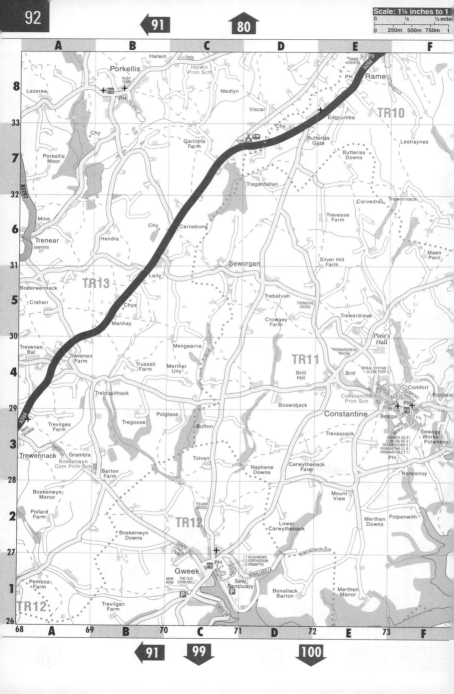

Scale: 1¼ inches to 1 mile

0   ¼   ½ mile
0   250m   500m   750m   1 km

A   **B**   **C**   **D**   **E**   **F**

Works

Hantertavis
ANTRON HILL

Trenoweth

ESTON CL 1
SPARGO CT 2

Antron Farm
College Resr

Mabe Burnthouse

Antron Way

Superstore Resr

Hillhead Farm

Ind Est

DRACAENA AVE

8

Halvosso

TR10

TRENOWETH TERR

Tregonhaye

PENRYN

Lower Kergillack

Budock
H

Sch

Falmouth

H

33

Lower Spargo

Water Sports Park

Argal Manor

Higher Kergillack

Lower Kergillack

Nangitha Farm

Bsns Pk

Mongleath

Penmere

7

Potter's

Trevone Farm

Higher Spargo

Argal Resr

Higher Argal

Sparnon

SCHOOL LA

Schs

Swanvale

32

Job's Water

Helland Mill

Lamanva

ELM GROVE COTTS

Higher Argal

ARGAL VIEW

Treverva

Helland House

Tresooth

Tresooth Bungalow

Trewen Farm

Higher Crill Farm

Budock Water

Roscarrack House

FALMOUTH

Boslowick

6

Meaallack Chease Farm

Trewoon Farm

144

CH

31

Tresahor Vean

Bosvathick

Bosawsack

Bosvarren House

Penwarne Manor

Penjerrick

Hotel

Tregedna

Trelevra Farm

Pennance Farm

5

Higher Treglidgwith Farm

Lower Treglidgwith

Trecombe Farm

TR11

Penwarne Barton

Rosemerryn Farm

Penrose

30

Treviades

HIGH CROSS

Treworval Farm

Drift Farm

Lower Tregarne

Bareppa

Carlidnack

MAENPORTH EST

Maenporth

High Cliff

4

29

Trenarth

Bosanath Mill

Boskensoe Farm

GOLDMARTIN CL 1
CARLIDNACK CL 2
TREVENA GDNS 3
GOODMARTIN SQ 4
GREENFIELDS CL 5
FIELD PL 6
ST MICHAELS CT 7
ROSEANNON 8

Mawnan Smith

Meudon Hotel

The Hutches

Bream Cove

3

TREWINCE

INOW TERR

Lower Penpoll

Higher Penpoll

DURGAN CROSSROADS

Sch

94

28

Porth Navas

Higher Calamansack

Hotel

CH

Trebah Gardens

Glendurgan Gardens

Durgan

Bosveal

Mawnan

Rosemullion

Trerose

Rosemullion Head

2

Lower Calamansack

Helford Passage

COASTGUARD COTTS

Polgwidden Cove

Porthallack

Toll Point

Parson's Beach

Mawnan Shear

August Rock

27

Groyne Point

Ferry (P)

Helford River

South West Coast Path

The Gew

1

ORCHARD LA

Helford

Treath

TR12

26

A 75 **B** 76 **C** 77 **D** 78 **E** 79 **F**

For full street detail of the highlighted area see page 144.

Scale: 1¼ inches to 1 mile
¼   ½ mile
250m 500m 750m 1 km

82   83

Trethewell
Lanhay
Tregassa
Pednvadan
Porthcurnick Beach

St Just
Pool

St Just in Roseland

Gerrans

Portscatho

Pencabe

1 ADMIRALTY TERR
2 SPRINGFIELD
3 PARC MERYS
4 HARBOUR CT FLATS
5 SUNNYSIDE
6 RIVER ST
7 THE SQUARE
8 VICTORIA TERR
9 CLIFTON TERR
10 TREVENTON CL
11 THE SQUARE

Trevennel Farm
Trewollack

Hotel
Gerrans Sch

Tregear Vean
Bosloggas

Tregassick
Treloan

Water Twr
ROSELAND FLATS

TR2

82   Percuil   83

St Mawes

Trewince

TREWINCE MANOR

1 PORTH VIEW
2 PERCUIL VIEW
3 PEN BREA CL

Quay

Froe

Hosteague

Greeb Point

UPPER CASTLE RD
POLVARTH RD
TREDENHAM RD

Porth Farm

Towan Beach

Ferry P
(summer only)

St Mawes Harbour

Castle Point

Bohortha

St Anthony

Killigerran Head

Carricknath Point

MANOR CT
ST AUSTELL ROW
THE SQUARE
KINGS RD
COMMERCIAL RD
GIBRALTAR TERR
CHURCH HILL
PEN-EGLOE
THE ROPE WLK
CHAPEL TERR
SEA VIEW CRES
SEA VIEW RD
NEWTON PK
HANCOCK LA
PLACE VIEW RD
KENNERLEY TERR
BROOKLYN TERR
BEECH HALL FLATS
BOHELLA RD

Place House

Porthbeor Beach

Porthmellin Head

Place Barton

MILITARY RD

St Anthony Head

Zone Point

85   86   87   88   89

86

87

Crows-an-wra

8

Tregiffian

Trevedra Farm

B3306

Treave

27

Escalls

Carn Barges

Carn Towan

THE GREENS

Rissick

Bosca

Trevorian Farm

Whitesand Bay

7

The Tribbens
Cowloe
Jetty

Sennen Cove

ATLANTIC

SEAVIEW TERR

Rospannel

Bar
Ha

LB Sta

COVE HILL

TREMBRASE

Pedn-mên-du

MARIA'S LA

Trevear Farm

Bosanketh Farm

26

Irish Lady

86

87

Gamper

Mayon Cliff

Mayon

Maen Castle

Sennen Prim Sch

Trevear Farm

Dr Syntax's Head

TOWER DE

Cemy

Mast

Penrose

Bosfranken Farm

Alsia Farm

6

The Peal

HALLAN VEAN

Sennen

Brew

TR19

Johnson's Head

Hotel

PH

Crean

25

Carn Kez

P

Theme Park

A30

B3315

Skewjack Farm

Trengothal Farm

Trebehor

Bottoms

Tresidder

Carn Greeb

Trevescan

St Levan Com Prim Sch

Sparnon

Armed Knight

Trevilley

5

Enys Dodnan

Trebehor

24

Pordenack Point

Zawn Reeth

Bosistow Farm

Polgigga

Trethewey

ST BURYAN HILL

Carn Boel

Raftra Farm

Trendrennen Farm

TREEN HILL

4

Mill Bay or Nanjizal

Carn Lês Boel

Treen

PH

23

Inner Pendower Cove

Arden-Sawah

Museum of Submarine Telegraphy

ZODIAC HOUSE

Zawn Kellys

Carn Barra

Roskestal

Röspletha

P

Porthcurno

Mên

Treryn Dinas

3

Folly Cove
Black Carn

St Levan

P

Porth Curno

Logan Rock

22

Porth Loe

Porthgwarra

Minack Theatre

Horrace

P

Carn Scathe

Vessacks

Pedn-mên-an-mere

2

Gwennap Head

Polostoc Zawn

Hella Point

21

1

20

34 A 35 B 36 C 37 D 38 E 39 F

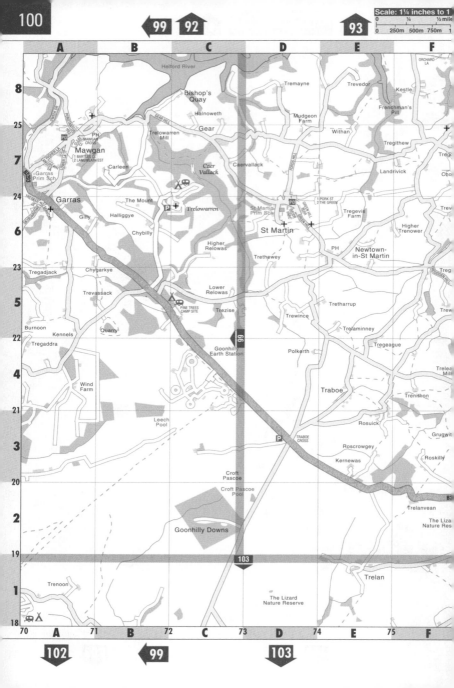

A   B   C   D   E   F

8
25
7
24
6
23
5
22
4
21
3
20
2
19
1
18

Bosaham Ho
Tendera
St Anthony-in-Meneage
Condurrow
Little Dennis
Dennis Head
Trudgwell
Gillan Harbour
vosé
1 MINSTER TERR
2 MINSTER MDW
VICARAGE LA
Flushing
Nare Point
Manaccan
Hotel
Gillan
Mên-aver Beach
Polnare Cove
Sch
PH
THE SQUARE
Tregithey
Lestowder
Nare Head
Carne
Tregasso
Lannarth Farm
Trewarnevas
Penare House
Nare Cove
Higher Bowden
Trewothaok
zabel
Roskruge Barton
Treglossick
Roskorwell
worgie
Roskruge Beacon Tumulus
Halwyn
SCHOOL HILL
Porthallow
Tregarne
PH
Porthkerris Point
idnick rm
Tregowris
TREGOWRIS COURT COTTS
Porthkerris Water Sports Ctr
Lesneague
TR12
Tregarminion
Porthellow Vineyard
Pencra Head
Trembraze
Treleague Farm
Trenowveth
Trenance
Nambol
1 MONASTERY CL
2 THE SQUARE
3 SCHOOL HILL
4 TREGELLAST CL
5 TREGELLAST PARC
Porthoustock
Trevallack
CORONATION COTTS
Quarry
Giant's Quoits
Manacle Point
Shark's Fin
Trelease Bean
Laddenvean
St Keverne
Sch
Rosenithon
Lanarth
B3293
Trythance
Godrevy Cove
Trevean
St Keverne Rural Workshops
Tregellast Barton
Quarry
Trevithian
Treskewes
Roskilly's Open Farm
Dean Point
Crousa Common
Chywoone
Trevean
Jetty
B3294
Three Brothers of Grugith
Main Dale
Trevalsoe
Trebarveth
Polcries
Kestlemerris Farm
Boscarnon Farm
Lowland Point
Great Wrea
Cow-y-Jack
Kilter
South West Coastal Path
Pedn-myin
103
ousa wns
North Corner
Polcoverack Farm
Hotel
POLCOVERACK LA
Coverack
103
Penhallick
GATEWNYACK
Sch
H
B3294
Dolor Point
ttle eaver

77   B   78   C   79   D   80   E   81   F

C4
1 TRESKEWES EST
2 TREVALLACK VIEW
3 TREVALLACK PARC
4 LAMHEVERNE PARC
5 DOCTORS HILL
6 POLVENTON PARC
7 PENMENNER EST
8 COMMERCIAL RD
9 TREGONNING PARC

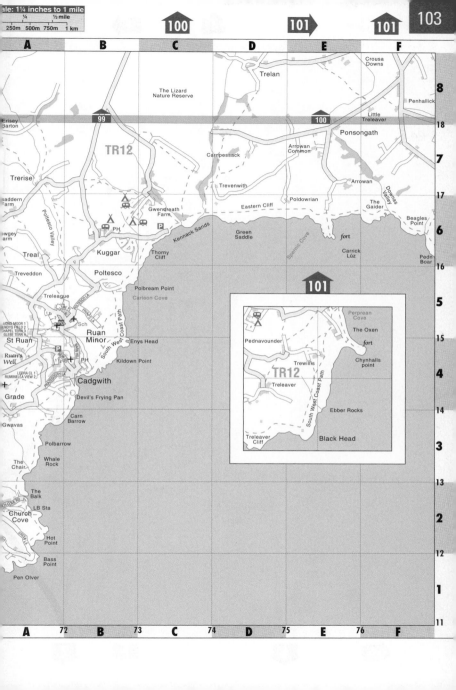

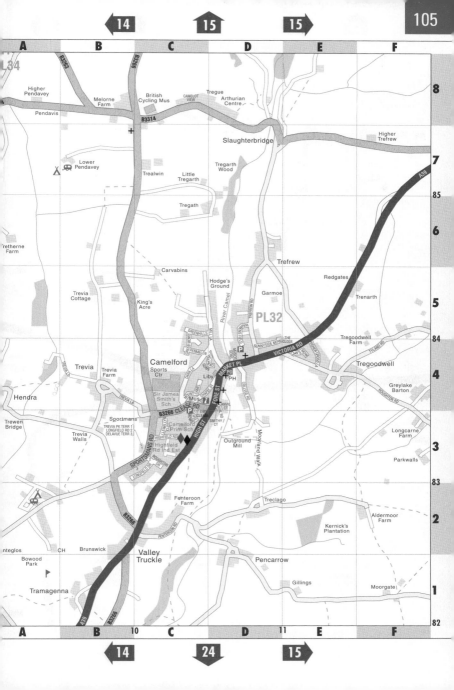

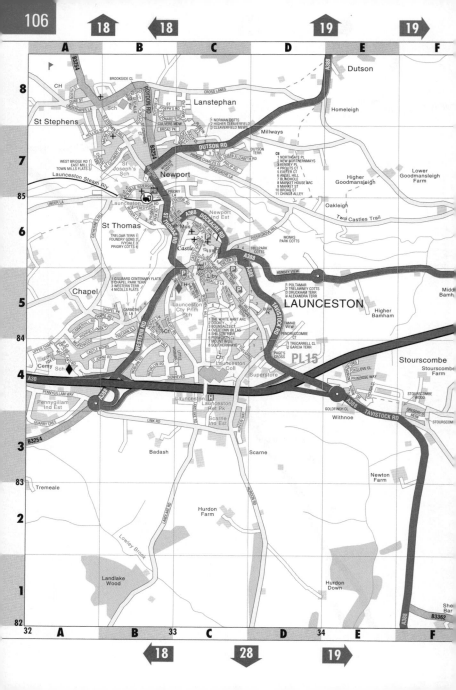

Map Legend

Ferry P locations:
1 NORTH QUAY PAR
2 WATERS EDGE
3 THE OLD BOAT-YARD

Street index:
1 OLD SCHOOL CT
2 ST EDMUNDS LA
3 COACHYARD MEWS
4 COMMERCIAL TERR
5 AVERY'S ROW
6 STRAND ST
7 BROAD ST
8 CHAPEL CT
9 GROVE PL
10 LANADWELL ST
11 MARKET PL
12 MARKET STRAND
13 MILL SQ
14 MIDDLE ST
15 BARRY'S LA
16 RUTHY'S LA
17 CROSS ST

Place labels:

Crugmeer

Tregirls Farm

St George's Well

Gun Point

South West Coast Path

PL27

Meml

Ferry P (Low Water)

Ferry P (High Water)

IRB Sta

River Camel

Trethillick

Prideaux Place

Cerny

Treator

PL28

Trecarus Ind Est

PADSTOW WORKSHOP UNITS

Padstow Jun & Inf Sch

ST PETROCS MDW

CHURCH ST

DUKE ST

VENTONLUNA LA

ST SAVIOUR'S LA

HIGH ST

CHURCH LA

LIBY & MUS

SOUTH QUAY

STATION RD

Padstow Harbour Ind Est

Town Bar

PADSTOW

Dinas

SARAH'S LA

SARAH'S CT

SARAH'S MDW

ANNETHY LOWEN

MOYLE RD

Dennis Hill

Obelisk

Camel Trail

Trerethern

Saints Way

Little Petherick Creek

Caravan Site

Tregella

Treravel Farm

Sea Mills

Benuick

PL27

Tregonce

Trevorrick

A389

B3276

B3215

A389

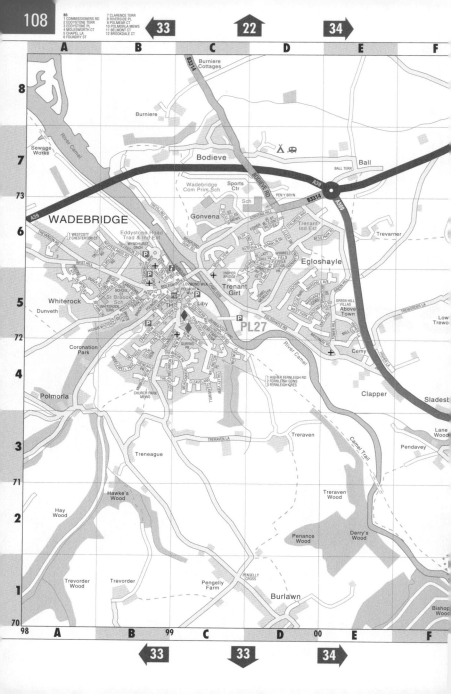

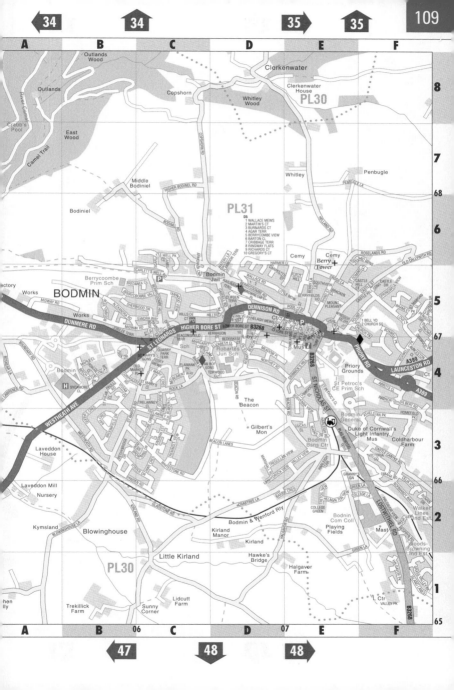

43 43 44

	A		B		C		D		E		F

8

Towan
Head

Lunvoy

Spy
Cove

Gazzle

Newquay
Bay

Hedgo
Cove

Old
Dane

Crigg

Beacon
Cove

Hotel

Pigeon
Cove

Tolcarne
Beach

7

Cross

Fly
Cove

Great Western
Beach

Fistral
Bay

Fistral
Beach

Tithy
Cove

Slip
Cove

Piers

Tolcarne
Point

62

CH

Aquarium

NEWQUAY

1 BROAD ST
2 CHAPEL HILL
3 KING ST
4 CENTRAL SQ
5 CHELTENHAM PL

6 PENHAVEN CT
7 CHYMEDOUR
8 JENKINS CT
9 SILVERDALE CT

1 STATION APP
2 ALBANY RD
3 TOLCARNE MEWS
4 PERGOLLA CT
5 MORRAB CT

LB
Sta

6

TR7

Trethellan

Cemy

Cemy

BANK

Trenance

Sch

H

5

Pentire

ESPLANADE RD

SURF VIEW

FISTRAL
CT

BAY
APARTMENTS

WATERS
EDGE

PENTIRE
CT

PD

PENTIRE RD

A392

ST CUTHBERT'S RD 10
KIMBERLEY CT 11
ST MARY'S CT 12

Trenance

MOUNT
WISE

WINDSOR

LINDEN AVE

RIVERSIDE
CRES

RIVERSIDE AVE

ALANTA
FLATS

HEADLEIGH RD

61

TREVEAR RD

QUARRY
TREGUNNEL
CVN PK

HOLT
CRES

THE
WHEWELL QUARRY

Stables

ST ANTHONY RD

TREDOUR

4

Penpol

The
Gannel

GANNEL RD

GANNEL RD

GALLEON
CT

PH

Little
Trevithich

3

Crantock

WINSTOWE
TERR

Trevella

Treringey

Treringey
Round

CHAPEL CL

HALWYN RD

TR8

60

Trevowah

Trevemper

2

Trevella
Park

Penhallow

1

Carines

Roseclistoll
Park

Works

59

79 **A** **B** 80 **C** **D** 81 **E** **F**

43 43 44

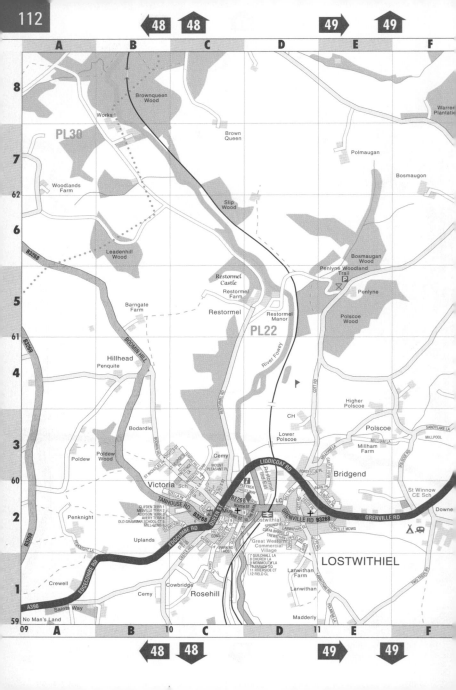

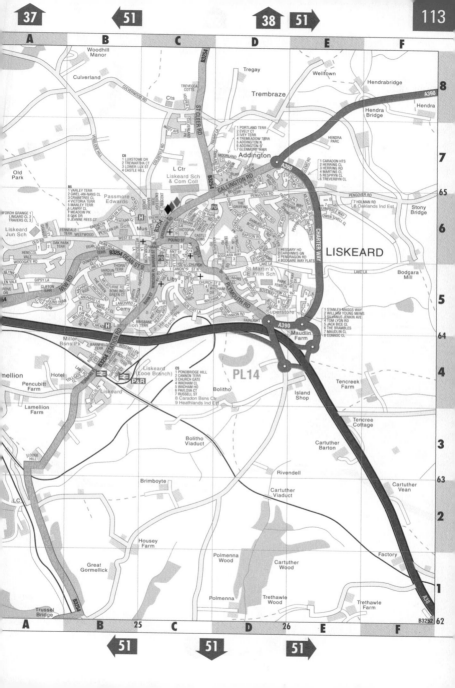

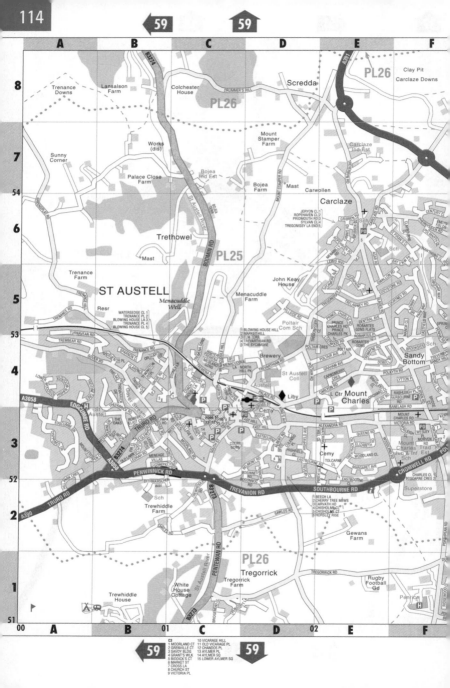

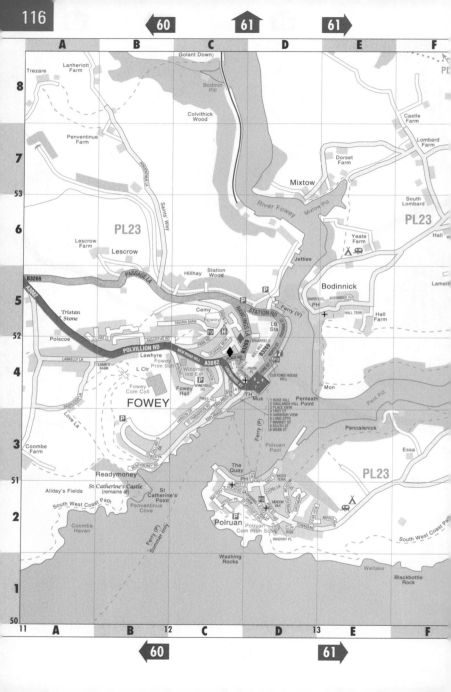

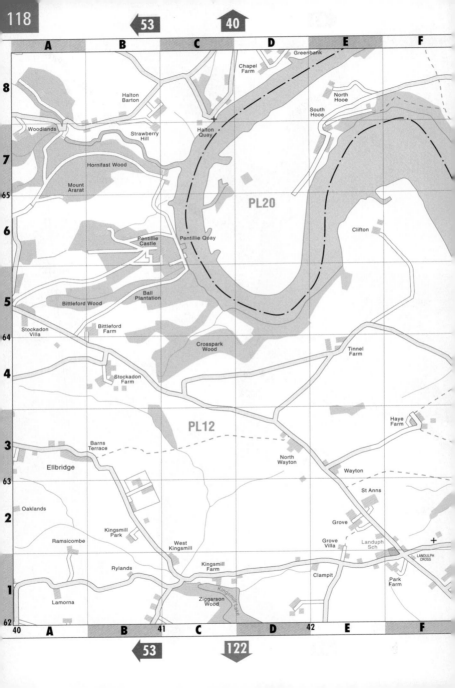

53   40

A   B   C   D   E   F

8

7

65

6

5

64

4

3

63

2

1

62

40   A   B   41   C   D   42   E   F

53   122

Woodlands

Halton
Barton

Strawberry
Hill

Hornifast Wood

Mount
Ararat

Chapel
Farm

Greenbank

Halton
Quay

North
Hooe

South
Hooe

PL20

Clifton

Pentillie
Castle

Pentillie Quay

Ball
Plantation

Bittleford Wood

Stockadon
Villa

Bittleford
Farm

Crosspark
Wood

Tinnel
Farm

Stockadon
Farm

PL12

Haye
Farm

Barns
Terrace

North
Wayton

Wayton

Ellbridge

St Anns

Oaklands

Grove

Kingsmill
Park

Ramsicombe

West
Kingsmill

Grove
Villa

Landuph
Sch

LANDULPH
CROSS

Rylands

Kingsmill
Farm

Clampit

Park
Farm

Lamorna

Ziggarson
Wood

Kingsmill Lake

A B C D E F

8

Wottons
Farm

Well
Farm

Higher
Birch

Down
Farm

Hewton

Cotts

Hole's
Hole

Down
Wood

HOLE
CROSS

7

Leeches

65

Quay

Weir
Quay

Shangri-La

Hole
Farm

6

Cleave
Farm

Clamoak

Clamoak
Poll Wood

Tuckham
Bridge

Ley
Farm

5

Clamoak
Quay

Ormonde
House

Fairway

64

River Tamar

Liphil
Quay

New Park
Farm

Parsonage
Farm

Shutecombe

4

PL20

Greystone

Bere
Ferrers

STATION RD

THE CHALK PK

FORE ST

SILVER ST

PO

PH

Bere
Ferrers

Bere
Barton

+

3

63

Thorn
Point

Cargreen

COOMBE LA

COOMBE DR

HOOPERS WAY

PH

CLOAKE
PL

FORE ST

Hall

Quays

New Barn
Farm

2

CHERHILL LA

THE GLENS

Penyoke

Pennard's
Point

River Tavy

1

PL12

62

A B C 44 C D 45 E F

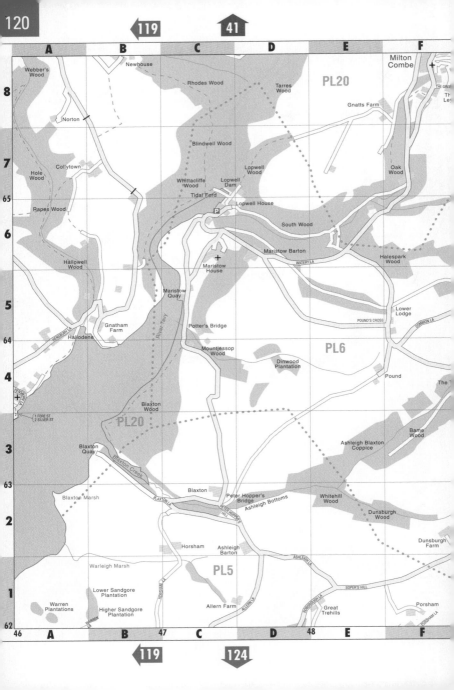

53
118

	A	B	C	D	E	F

8

Cross Park Farm
Rumbullion Farm
Sladeland
Marraborough
Collogett Hill
Collogett Quay
Marsh Farm
Holy Well
The Mars
PL12

7

Botusfleming
PH
Clark's Lake
Moditonham House
Moditonham Quay
South Down
Kingsmill La
Smallacombe

61
A388
The Marsh
Burrhills Farm
Burrhills Quay

6

Woodside Racing Stables
Atuba
East Town Farm
Carkeel
Hole Wood
Skinham Creek
Chine Fleet Country Clu

Broadmoor Wood
Carkeel Farm
River Ct
Tamar View Ind Est
Quarryfield Coppice

5

DIRTY LA
Saltash Service Area
AVERY WAY
PL12

Pill Farm
BEAUMONT TERR

60

Peninsular Pk
Gwel Avon Bsns Pk
Saltash
Castlend Est
Saltash Bsns Pk
Moorlands Trad Est
Mill Park
Saltmill Cre

4

A38 LISKEARD RD
WHITY CROSS
B3271
Saltash Parkway Ind Est
BURRATON RD
CALLINGTON RD
Burraton
Rogers Dr
ASHTON WAY
NEW RD
GOLDFINCH CRES
B3271
P

3

Latchbrook
LISKEARD RD
BARROW DOWN
PH
PLOUGH GN
FEARNSIDE
ST GEORGES RD
HILLSIDE RD
LONGMEADOW RD
WESTB

59

Wadgeworthy Farm
Latchbrook Leat
FOXGLOVE WAY
THE HEDGEROWS
South Pill
Saltash Leisure Ctr
Brunel Terr
Saltash Prim Sch
WINDMILL
Lib
TOP OF THE TOWN CT
GREENWICH PL
P

2

TOWER CL
CASTLE CL
YELLOW TOR CL
POLLARD CL
Burraton Coombe
ST ANDREWS
MANOR PK
St Stephens
Saltash Coll
Wearde
St Barnaba
Bishop Cornish CE Prim Sch

1

Longlands
LONGLANDS LA
MEADOWSWEET
NANCARROWS
CARINOUSTIE DR
BIRKDALE CL
SALTASH
ST STEPHEN'S HILL
Forder
GERALDINE TERR
COURTLANDS
CHURCHILL WLK
Saltash Com Sch
House on the Hill

58

Trehan
Little Trehan Farm
Cross
TAVRE VIEW
RIVERSIDE COTT

40	A	B	41	C	D	42	E	F

53
126

A   B   C   D   E   F

8

7

61

6

5

60

4

59

3

2

1

58

A   B   50   C   D   51   E   F

Arnold's Hill Coppice
Belliver Ind Est
Bickleigh Down
9 CROFT PK
10 COPPICE WOOD DR
11 BLACKTHORN CL
12 BIRCH CL
Pick Pie Plantation
1 ROCKWOOD RD
2 CHURCH PARK CT
3 CHURCHLANDS RD
Rock Wood

Widewell
Widewell Prim Sch
Factory
Woolwell
Darklake

West Wood
Darklake Wood

Glenholt
1 KINGFISHER CL
2 MAPLE CL
3 NELSON TERR
4 QUEENS CL
5 PRINCES RD
6 BAYTREE CL
7 BIRCH CT
8 WILLOW WLK
Common Wood
Common Wood Cottage

Plymouth City Airport
Notre Dame RC Sch

PLYMBRIDGE RD

Devon STREET ATLAS

Colwill Wood
Estover Ind Est
L Ctr
The Plymouth Nuffield
Coll of St Mark & St John
Derriford Rd
Works
Derriford
PL6
Tamar Science Pk
Prim Sch
Estover
Wentwood Cl
Earls Wood Cl
Plymouth Int Bsns Pk
TA Ctr
Seaton Bsns Pk
Fursdon
L Ctr
Mainstone
Swimming Pool

Mainstone Wood

PLYMOUTH
1 CROWN GDNS
2 BICKLEIGH CL
3 GEORGE DOWNING HO
4 SANDON WLK
5 ESTCOTT WLK
6 BRODKING CL
7 ALDERSLEY WLK
8 CRAFTON PL
9 BRIDGWATER CL
FRESHFORD WLK
FRESHFORD CL
CHILDREY CL
CHILDREY WLK
DUNLEY WLK
COCKINGTON WLK
Estover Com Coll
Estover Prim Sch

Bircham Farm
Poole Farm
Runnymede

Fort Austin Ave
Bowden Battery
Forder Valley Rd
Lanigham Inf & Jun Schs
Mast

F5
1 NEPEAN ST
2 ADELAIDE ST
3 BRUNEL TERR
4 EPWORTH TERR
5 SUSSEX TERR
6 RAILWAY COTTS
7 YORK TERR
8 ST MAWES TERR

8

PL5

Barne
Barton

Bull
Point

Kinterbury
House

Kinterbury
Point

Weston Mill

Weston
Mill

Cemy
Crem

1 DELAWARE GDNS
2 CAROLINA GDNS
3 COOMBE VIEW
4 MAUSHELL CL
5 OVERDALE RD

Camels
Head

7

57

Jetty

Cove Head

Looking
Glass

Cangapool

River Tamar Hamoaze

PL5

Dockyard

HMS Drake

Keyham Barton
RC Prim Sch

Keyham
Drake
Prim Sch

PL2

Keyham

WOLSELEY RD

6

Jetty
Yonderberry
Point

PL11

Torpoint
Com Sch

Thanckes
Lake

Torpoint
Inf Sch

Gravesend
Point

College Road
Prim Sch

Dockyard
Halt

ST VINCENT

Devonport

KEMYELL PL
ATHERTON PL
ALCESTER CL

5

56

4

TORPOINT

ANTONY RD   A374

1 HARBOUR ST
2 ELLIOT SQ
3 ST JAMES SQ
4 BELLEVUE SQ
5 ARTHUR TERR
6 HOOPER ST
7 WESLEY CT

Ferry
V

Moon
Cove

POTTERY RD
A374

TAMAR WHARF

FERRY RD

Parkside
Com Tech Coll

Liby

Devonport

B3396

ALBERT RD

3

55

Carew
Wharf

Marina

Jetty

RIVERSIDE PL
CHAPMANS OPE
MORICE SQ
WASHBOURNE CL
GRANBY
Quay
Landing Stage

Riverside
Bens Pk

Morice
Town

St Joseph's
RC Prim Sch

PARK AVE

DURRANT
CL PORTEOUS
CL KNOWLAND

PLYMOUTH

CHAPEL ST

BARRACK

CUMBERLAND RD

1 PRINCES ST
2 LOFOTEN CL
3 VIASSO CL
4 DEEPE CL
5 ST NAZAIRE APP
6 ST THERESE'S CT

Coll

The
Brickfields
(Recn Gd)

PL1

A374
DEVONPORT HILL

1 CUMBERLAND ST
2 MONUMENT ST
3 RAGLAN GDNS
4 RAGLAN CT
5 MOUNT
6 THEATRE OPE
7 ST GEORGE SQ
8 SUTTON CT

2

Mount Wise
Prim Sch

Mount Wise

ST MICHAEL'S

Mon

Admiralty
House

1

54

F3
1 CLARENDON HO
2 GARFIELD TERR
3 TRAFALGAR PL
4 THE MEWS
5 NELSON GDNS
6 BEYROUT PL
7 ST MICHAEL'S CT
8 ST MICHAEL'S TERR
9 PORTLAND CT

10 MOLYNEAUX PL
F4
1 ST GEORGES CT
2 HORNBY ST
3 PHILLIMORE ST
4 FREMANTLE GDNS
5 FAIRFAX TERR
6 HARGOOD TERR
7 HARRISON ST
8 KEPPEL TERR

9 HEALY CT
10 BRUNSWICK PL

A5
1 MELVILLE PL
2 Wolseley Bsns Pk
3 AUCKLAND RD
4 HALEY BARTON
5 GREATLANDS PL

6 WADHAM TERR
7 CRANTOCK TERR

E6
1 BRENT KNOLL RD
2 LUDLOW RD
3 SWANDALE RD
4 TYTHING WLK
5 GLENHURST RD
6 VENN CL

F4
1 GROSVENOR COTTS
2 HILLSBOROUGH
3 PEARSON AVE
4 PENLEE PL
5 PENROSE VILLAS
6 CROZIER RD

7 MARINA TERR
8 KENSINGTON PL

F6
1 RESERVOIR LA
2 PEARN COTTS
3 BRANDRETH RD
4 GLENEAGLE AVE

5 GLENEAGLE VILLAS
6 HENDERS CNR
7 ROSEVEAN RD
8 ROSEVEAN CT
9 FOSBROOKE CT

127 124

A3
1 UNDERHILL VILLAS
2 OSBORNE VILLAS
3 EDGCUMBE CT
4 NELSON GDNS
5 COLLINGWOOD VILLAS
6 PAVILAND GRANGE
7 FITZROY TERR

A4
1 WESLEY PL
2 MASTERMAN RD
3 DUCKWORTH ST
4 DUNEDAS ST
5 Stoke Damerel
Bsns Ctr
6 BROMLEY PL
7 SOMERSET COTTS

8 SOMERSET PLACE LA
9 PARK PLACE LA
10 BELMONT CT

E4
1 WARLEIGH RD
2 CONNAUGHT LA
3 CHESTER PL
4 ALEXANDRA PL
5 ROCHESTER RD

127 134

For full street detail of the highlighted area see pages 148 and 149.

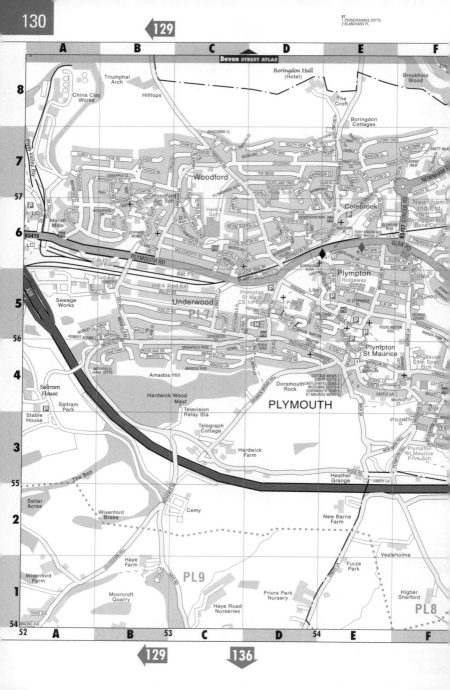

B5
1 CALEDONIA CL
2 ELDER CL
3 MAGNOLIA CL
4 TURBILL GDNS
5 PAYNTER WLK

C5
1 EIGHT ACRE CL
2 LAWN CL
3 ORCHARD CL
4 GREAT PARK CL
5 LONG TERRACE CL
6 CYPRESS CL

7 CAMPION CL
8 RODDICK WAY
9 BRANSON CT

Sparkwell Farm

Newnham Park

Furzeacre Wood

Furzeacre Bridge

Windwhistle

Sparkwell CE Prim Sch

Holly Wood

Lowdamoor

Hemerdon

Beechwood

Old Newnham Farm

Hemerdon Farm

Miners' Arms (PH)

Lodge

Hemerdon House

Beechwood

Old Newnham

Sherwell

Lodge

Newnham Ind Est

WEST PARK HILL

Sparkwell Bridge

Moor Bridge

LANGAGE CROSS

Chaddlewood

Langage Science Pk

Langage Way

Higher Langage

Lower Langage

Combe Farm

GLEN RD

Langage Ind Est

Applethorn Slade

SANDY RD

Langage Pk

PL7

MEADOW CL

CORNWOOD RD

WOLVERWOOD CL

Ley Farm

Yealmpstone Farm Prim Sch

B3416

WOLVERWOOD LA

The Lyneham Inn (PH)

Voss

A38

A38 Exeter, M5

Devon STREET ATLAS

Wiverton House

Tuxton Farm

Battisford

Butlas Farm

Wiverton Acre

Tuxton Wood

PL8

Blackpool

East Sherford

8

7

57

6

5

56

4

55

3

2

1

54

A   B   56   C   D   57   E   F

A B C D E F

8 Ford
Vanderbands
St John
Vanderbands Farm
PH
St John's Lake
San Isla

7 St John's Down
Mendennick
Penhale
PL11
Penhale Lake

Mendennick Hill

53 B3247
Works
Insworke

6 Sewage Wks
Trefusis Terr
Pottery Est
Millbrook CE Sch
1 Heanton Terr
Clinton Terr

5 New Barn
Millbrook Resr
Blindwell
Richards Terr
The Parade 2
St Andrew St
West St
PH
Mill View
Ande

Higher Hounster Farm

52 Withnoe Barton
Withnoe
Tregonhawke Farm
Dadbrook
Millbrook
Cemy

4 Tregonhawke
Whitsand Bay Holiday Pk
Mon
Treninnow Grove
Solla

3 Treninnow
Treninnow Plantation
Fourlanesend Com Prim Sch

51 Military Rd
The Hats

2 Whitsand Bay
South West Coast Path
PL10
Wiggle
Wringford Farm
Wring Dow

1 Wiggle Cliff
P
Hotel
Forder

50 Knatterbury

40 A B 41 C D 42 E F

8

St John's Lake

River Tamar
Hamoaze

Sango
Point

Inswork
Point

Mutton
Cove

Marina

Ferry
P

PL1

PH

Obelisk   Devil's
Point

St JULIAN'S
COTTS

Cremyll

Blockhouse

The Narrows

Wilderness
Point

PL10

ELM PK

WOODCOCK
CL

Southdown

SILVER
TERR

SOUTHVIEW

SOUTHDOWN RD

SOUTHDOWN
TERR

Quay

Palmer
Point

Quay

Empacombe
Cottage

Empacombe

Windmill
(disused)

Home Farm

Barrow Park

Mount
Edgcumbe

Barn Pool   53

7

6

Mount Edgcumbe
Country Park

The Raven's
Cliffs

MILL RD

Foss

oss
oint

LOWER ANDERTON
RD

Millbrook
Lake

Lower
Anderton

Clarrick
Woods

Pigshill
Wood

St Julian's
Well

Deer Park

Grotton
Plantation

5

52

Westpark

MAKER LA

PL10

Maker
Farm

Hooe Lake
Valley

Fort
Picklecombe

4

Maker
Heights

South West Coast Path

Hooe Lake
Point

Picklecombe
Point

3

51

combe
Farm

PORSPODER
PL

Blackendown   Mindew
Brakes

NEW RD

THE CLIFF TERR

Cavehole
Point

Cawsand Bay

2

Kingsand

Martin's
Cove

1 GREEN LA
2 THE GREEN
3 HEAVITREE RD
4 LITTLE LA
5 MARKET ST

Ferry P
(Summer Only)

THE FORT

ARMADA RD

ST ANDREW'S R

ST ANDREW'S R

SQUARE

Cawsand

Conger
Point

1

50

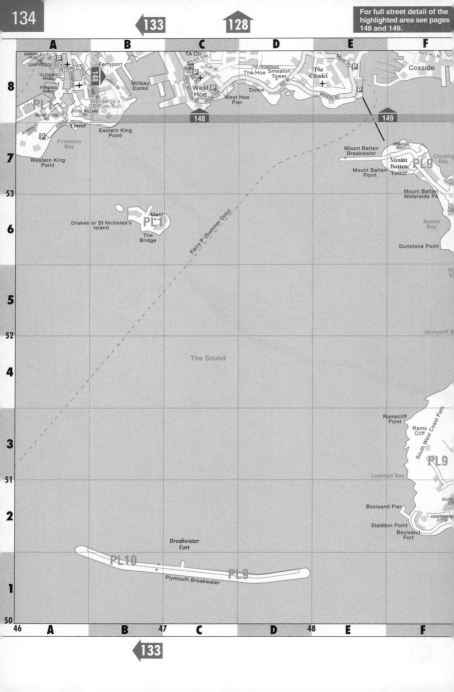

For full street detail of the highlighted area see pages 148 and 149.

A   B   C   D   E   F

8

Coxside

TA Ctr
WALKER TERR
CLIFF RD
THE PROMENADE
The Hoe
Smeaton Tower
The Citadel

Ferryport

Millbay Docks

West Hoe

St George's CE Com Sch
MOUNT ROAD
ROYAL WILLIAM RD
Dome
West Hoe Pier

TELEGRAPH WHARF
FREEMANS WHARF
ADMIRAL'S HARD
THE QUARTERDECK

MADEIRA RD
LAMBHAY HILL RD

148

149

PL1
Tower
Eastern King Point

7

ADMIRALS COTT
Firestone Bay

Western King Point

Mount Batten Breakwater

SPINNAKER QUAY
Mount Batten Tower
PL9
Clovelly Bay

Mount Batten Point

Mount Batten Waterside Pk

53

Batten Bay

6

Drakes or St Nicholas's Island

Mast
PL1
The Bridge

Ferry P (Summer Only)

Dunstone Point

5

52

Jennycliff B

The Sound

4

Ramscliff Point

Rams Cliff

South West Coast Path

3

PL9

51

Leekbed Bay

2

Bovisand Pier

BOVI
B
COASTGUARD COTTS

Staddon Point

Bovisand Fort

Breakwater Fort

1

PL10

PL9

Plymouth Breakwater

50

46   A   B   47   C   D   48   E   F

A B C D E F

8

PLYMOUTH

Moorcroft Quarry

A379

Widegate Nursery

Elburton Vineries

West Sherfor

ELBURTON RD

Dunstone Prim Sch

MOORLAND VIEW

Thornville Nurseries

STANBOROUGH CROSS

7

Dunstone Woods

Sch

53

Elburton

ELBURTON RD

Chittleburn Wood

Sterts Farm

6

Coombe Dean Sch

Jew's Wood

Dodovens Farm

CHITTLEBURN HILL A379

5

Coombe Wood

Halwell

Halwell Wood

Wopplewell

Combe

Fordbrook Farm

Brixton Lodge Gdns

52

Coombe Farm

PL9

Torr Hill Farm

Vicarage

COURT VIE

4

Higher Spriddlestone

Spriddlestone

PL8

Coflete

Leyford Parks

Cemy

Spriddlestone Barton

RIDGE CROSS

Higher Leyford

3

Knapps Wood

Spriddlestone House

51

Andron Wood

2

Hollacombe Hill

Hollacombe Wood Nature Res

Train Brake

Train Wood

HOLLACOMBE BRAKE

TRAINE BRAKE

Wembury Wood

Coflete Creek

Western Park Wood

South Barton

STEER POINT COTTS

Brick Works

1

Spirewell

Trescan

50

52 A B 53 C D 54 E F

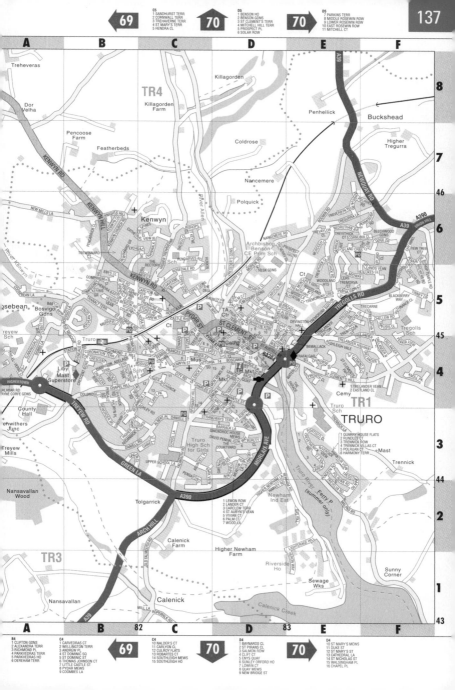

137

C6	D5	D5
1 SANDHURST TERR	1 BENSON HO	7 PARKINS TERR
2 CORNWALL TERR	2 BENSON GDNS	8 MIDDLE ROSEWIN ROW
3 TREHAVERNE TERR	3 ST CLEMENT'S TERR	9 LOWER ROSEWIN ROW
4 ST MARY'S TERR	4 MITCHELL HILL TERR	10 EAST ROSEWIN ROW
5 HENDRA CL	5 PROSPECT PL	11 MITCHELL CT
	6 SOLAR ROW	

← **69** ↑ **70** → **70**

← **69** ↑ **70** → **70**

B4	C4	D4	D4
1 CLIFTON GDNS	1 CARVEDRAS CT	1 BAYNARDS CL	10 ST MARY'S MEWS
2 ALEXANDRA TERR	2 WELLINGTON TERR	2 ST PIRANS CL	11 DUKE ST
3 RICHMOND PL	3 ANDREW PL	3 SALMON ROW	12 ST MARY'S ST
4 PARKVEDRAS TERR	4 ST DOMINIC SQ	4 CLIFT CT	13 CATHEDRAL LA
5 PARKVEDRAS HO	5 ST DOMINIC ST	5 ENYS QUAY	14 ST NICHOLAS ST
6 DEREHAM TERR	6 THOMAS JOHNSON CT	6 SUNLEY ORFORD HO	15 WALSINGHAM PL
	7 LITTLE CASTLE ST	7 LOWER CT	16 CHAPEL PL
	8 PYDAR MEWS	8 QUAY MEWS	
	9 COOMBES LA	9 NEW BRIDGE ST	
	10 NALDER'S CT		
	11 CARLYON CL		
	12 CULROY FLATS		
	13 ROBARTES CT		
	14 SOUTHLEIGH MEWS		
	15 SOUTHLEIGH HO		

C4 – 1 LEMON ROW / 2 LANDER CT / 3 CARCLEW TERR / 4 ST AUBYN'S VEAN / 5 VIVIAN CT / 6 PALM CT / 7 WOOD LA

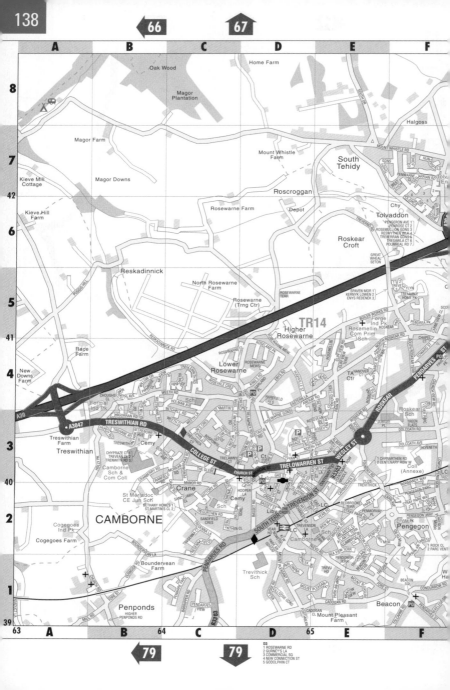

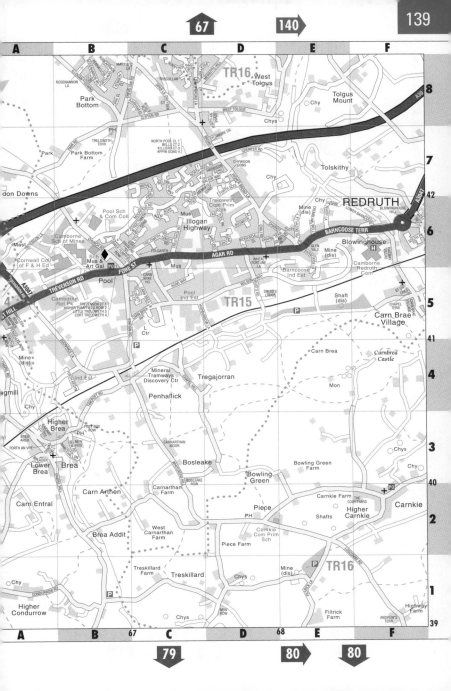

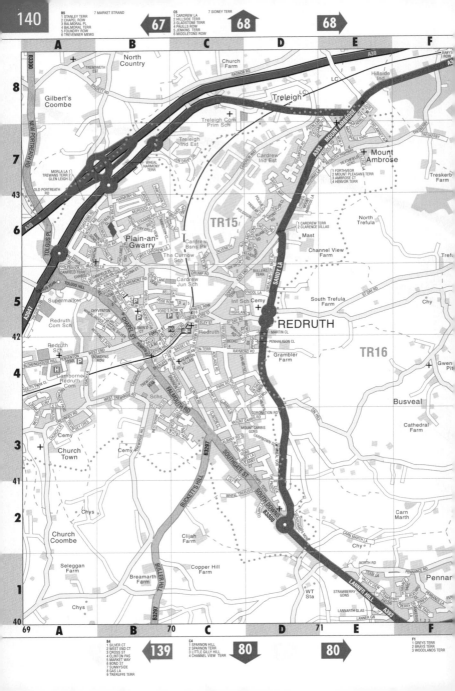

A B C D E F

8 7 41 6 5 40 4 3 39 2 1 38

B6
1 ST NICHOLAS CT
2 HALL LOFT FLATS
3 THE ROPE WLK
4 ISLAND RD
5 PENAMEYNE CT
6 PORTHMEOR RD
7 BACK ROAD E
8 ISLAND SQ
9 FISH ST
10 BETHESDA PL
11 VICTORIA PL
12 VICTORIA PL
13 BARNSLOFT
14 PIZZA
15 NORTH PL
16 ST PETERS ST
17 BACK LA
18 CHURCH PL
19 CHY-AN-CHY
20 BAILEYS LA
21 PORTHMEOR SQ

22 BUNKERS HILL
23 ROSE LA
24 LOVE LA
25 THE DIGEY
26 VIRGIN ST
27 MEADOW FLATS
28 GODREVY TERR
29 BRANDON TERR
30 ACADEMY TERR
31 MARKET STRAND
32 LIFEBOAT HILL
33 MARKET SQ
34 SPINKSLOT
35 BOWLING GN TERR
36 CARRACK DHU TERR
37 CARRACK DHU
38 BELLAIR TERR
39 MOUNT PLEASANT
40 RICHMOND PL
41 TREWYN FLATS
42 BACK ST
43 ATLANTIC TERR
44 CLODGY VIEW

1 PORTHGWIDDEN STUDIOS
2 CARNCROWS RD
3 CARNCROWS ST
4 TEETOTAL ST
5 ST EIA ST
6 BACK RD EAST
7 SEA VIEW PL

ARTHEW CT 1
HEW TERR 2
AYR TERR 3
AYR TERR 4
VIEW TERR 5
RYAN TERR 6
OUNT TERR 7
ANEL VIEW 8
ENOR TERR 9
LMONT PL 10
rrick

1 PENBEAGLE WAY
2 GWEL AN WHEAL
3 GWEL AN WHEAL CRES
4 PENWITH CL
5 PORTHIA CRES

Mean Derrens
The Island or St Ives Head
Crowner Rocks
Lookout Sta
Bamalüz Point
Mus
Porthmeor Beach
Tate Gallery
Cemy
Harbour
Pier
Smeaton's Pier
ST IVES
Pier LB Sta
Mus
PO
Pedn Olva
Park Ave
St Ives
Porthminster Beach
Schs
L Ctr
Bahavella
Edward Hain Mem
Albany Terr
Penbeagle
Corva
St Ives Sch
Hotel
CH
Trelyon
TR26
Steeple Woods
Hendra
Chy-an-Gweal
Knill's Mon
Superstore
Carbis Bay
Barrepta Cove or Carbis Bay
Carrack Gladden
GWEL MARTEN FLATS
Carbis Bay
Vorvas Vean
Lower Vorvas
Higher Vorvas
Withen
Trewartha
Carbis Water
South West Coast Path
Longstone
Gonwin Farm
Motel
Cemy
Schs

1 MOONRAKERS
2 GODREVY CT
3 CARBIS BEACH APARTMENTS
4 RIVIERA APARTMENTS
5 GWELAMMOR CL

1 HENDRAS CT
2 HEADLAND CT
3 KARENZA CT
4 PEDN-AN-...
5 KAMPARA CL
6 PORDENACK CL

HIGHER BOSKERRIS 1
BOSKERRIS MEWS 2
TREGENNA FLATS 3
TREWARTHA EST 4
SHEILA'S CT 5

A B C D E F
52 53

10 BOSTENNACK PL
11 BOSTENNACK TERR
12 PEARCE'S LA
13 HIGHER STENNACK COTTS
14 STENNACK GDNS
15 SANDOWS LA
16 ROSEWALL COTTS
17 ROSEWALL TERR

B5
1 ST ANDREW'S ST
2 REDFERN CT
3 STREET-AN-POL
4 TREGENNA PL
5 GABRIEL ST
6 BEDFORD PL
7 WESLEY PL
8 WINDSOR HILL
9 DRILLFIELD LA

B5
10 ALMA TERR
11 TRENWITH TERR
12 NORTH TERR
13 UMFULLA PL
14 TRENWITH PL
15 DOVE ST
16 TREGENNA HILL
17 STREET-AN-GARROW
18 SKIDDEN HILL

B5
19 FERN LEE TERR
20 SEA VIEW TERR
21 ALBERT PL
22 RADNOVER TERR
23 PORTHMINSTER TERR
24 PETES PL

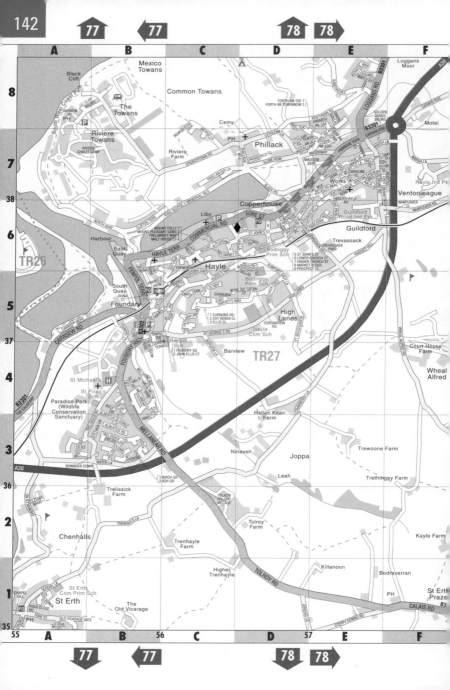

C7
1 ROSCADGHILL PARC
2 HEABROOK PARC
3 NICHOLAS PARC
4 MYTHYON CT
5 HEA COTTS
6 HAIG PL

7 POLTAIR TERR
8 BROOKWARD TERR
9 HOLLY TERR
10 CARMEN SQ
11 WESLEY ST
12 SILVERTON PL
13 JAMAICA TERR

14 JAMAICA PL
15 PLEASANT PL
16 NEVADA PL
17 MELBOURNE TERR
D5
1 GREENBANK
2 HAWKINS CT

3 TREVEAN GDNS
4 ALVERTON TERR
5 STANFORD CL
6 WEETHES COTTS
7 ALVERNE BLDGS
8 CARMINOWE CRES
9 LANDERYON GDNS

PENZANCE

TR20

Madron

St Maddern's CE Prim Sch

Heamoor

Mount's Bay Sch

Trythogga

Treneere

Higher Tranhack

Penwith Coll

The Humphry Davy Sch

Chyandour

North Lodge

Rosehill

West Cornwall

Lesingey Round

Castle Horneck

The Bolitho Sch

Harbour Pier

PENZANCE

TR18

Gall & Mus

Dock Pier

Trinity House National Lighthouse Ctr

Wherry Town

Trereife

The Gear

Alverton

St Mary's CE Prim Sch

Tolcarne

Stable Hobba Ind Est

Edward Bolitho Ho (Hospl & Day Ctr)

Newlyn Art Gall

The Pilchard Wks

NEWLYN

Newlyn Pier

Tredavoe

Gwavas Lake

Gurnick Est

LB Sta

Tidal Obsy Pier

Newlyn Sch

Hotel

E5
1 TRENDEAL GDNS
2 CAMELOT CT
3 TAROVEOR TERR
4 OLD BREWERY YD
5 ALMA PL
6 THE ARCADE
7 ST JOHNS CT
8 WHARFSIDE
9 WHARFSIDE VILLAGE
10 MANNINGTON CT
11 ST MICHAEL'S COTTS
12 PRINCESS CT
13 ST PIRANS CT
14 CHERRY GDNS
15 HARBOUR CT
16 CUSTOM HOUSE LA
17 KITTS CT
18 ST MICHAELS CT
19 ABBEY CT
20 VOUNDER/OUR LA
21 REGENT SQ
22 CHIRGWIN CT
23 CHANCERY LA
24 QUEEN'S SQ
25 MARKET PL
26 THE GREENMARKET
27 UNION SQ
28 PARADE PASS
29 SIMPSONS CT
30 SIMPSONS CT
31 VICTORIA PL
32 BURTON ROW
33 SOUTH PAR
34 MORRAB TERR
35 MORRAB TERR

E6
1 BARWIS TERR
2 PENARE GDNS
3 THE MEWS
4 ST HENRY ST
5 ST JOHN'S TERR
6 ST FRANCIS ST
7 ST WARREN ST
8 ST PHILP ST
9 ST DOMINIC ST
10 SWAINS ST
11 PENLEE CT
12 PENWITH ST
13 TREWARTHA TERR
14 CROSS ST
15 LESKINNICK PL
16 VICTORIA CT
17 VICTORIA SQ
18 VICTORIA MEWS
19 ALBERT TERR
20 ALBERT BLDGS
21 BELLE VUE TERR
22 MORDROS TERR
23 ROSE TERR
24 EMPRESS AVE
25 GARLONA
26 PROSPECT PL
27 FOLKSON CT
28 BULLOCK MARKET TERR
29 WINDSOR PL
30 CLARENCE PL
31 CLARENCE TERR

C1
1 TREVENETH PL
2 TREWINCE TERR
3 HIGHER GWAVAS RD
4 GWAVAS BGLWS
5 BOWJEY TERR
6 SEA VIEW TERR
7 LYN TERR
8 MEADOW VILLAS
9 BOWJEY CT
10 NAVY INN CT
11 HARBOUR LIGHTS
12 EBENEZER PL
13 EDEN GDNS
14 CHURCH ST
15 FRANWILL TERR
16 PARC VILLAS
17 PARK RD
18 PARC TERR
19 JUBILEE BGLWS

C2
1 NORTH CNR
2 MALT HOUSE GDNS
3 THE MALT HOUSE
4 ANTOINE CL
5 WESLEY PL
6 STRICKLAND COTTS
7 GWAVAS QUAY
8 FARMERS MEOW
9 CHAPEL ST

10 ORCHARD PL
11 ORCHARD HO
12 THE TERR
13 THE BRIDGE HO
14 CLIFTON HILL
15 VICTORIA TERR
16 PENWERRIS
17 BARLANDHU
18 ORCHARD CREST
19 LANE REDDIN TERR

20 HILLSIDE TERR
21 ANTOINE TERR
22 MOUNT VIEW TERR
23 ELMS CLOSE TERR
24 BAY VIEW TERR
25 GLOUCESTER PL

← 88   ↑ 88   → 88
← 88   → 88

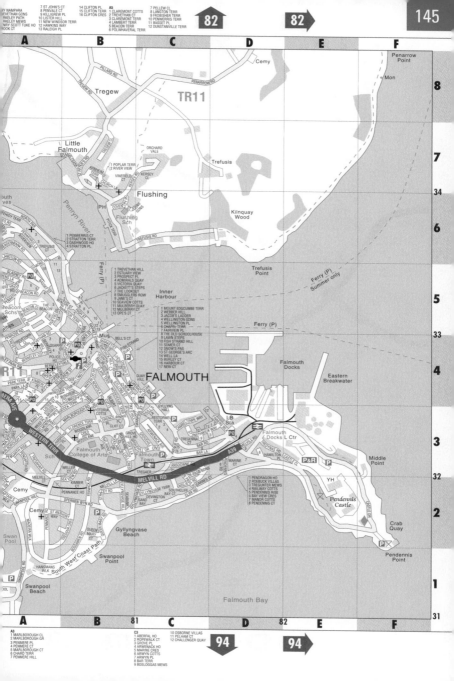

...Y NAMPARA
...REVETHAN GDNS
...RKELEY PATH
...RKELEY MEWS
...RY SCOTT TUKE HO
...OOK CT

7 ST JOHN'S CT
8 PENVALE CT
9 KILLIGREW PL
10 LISTER HILL
11 NEW WINDSOR TERR
12 HAWKINS WAY
13 RALEIGH PL

14 CLIFTON PL
15 CLIFTON TERR
16 CLIFTON CRES

A5
1 CLAREMONT COTTS
2 TREVETHAN CT
3 CLAREMONT TERR
4 LAMBERT TERR
5 BEACON TERR
6 POLWHAVERAL TERR

7 PELLEW CL
8 LANGTON TERR
9 FROBISHER TERR
10 PENWERRIS TERR
11 BASSET PL
12 DUNSTANVILLE TERR

Tregew

TR11

Penarrow Point

Mon

Little Falmouth

ORCHARD VALE

Trefusis

1 POPLAR TERR
2 RIVER VIEW

KERSEY CL

VINEFIELD CT

Flushing

Flushing Sch

Kilnquay Wood

Penryn River

PH

1 PENWERRIS CT
2 STRATTON TERR
3 DASHWOOD HO
4 STRATTON PL

Trefusis Point

Ferry (P)

Ferry (P) Summer only

1 TREVETHAN HILL
2 ESTUARY VIEW
3 PROSPECT PL
4 ADMIRALS QUAY
5 VICTORIA QUAY
6 JACKET'S STEPS
7 THE LOOKOUT
8 SMUGGLERS ROW
9 JANE'S CT
10 SEAVIEW COTTS
11 MULBERRY QUAY
12 MULBERRY CT
13 OPE'S CT

Inner Harbour

1 MOUNT EDGCUMBE TERR
2 WEBBER HILL
3 JACOB'S LADDER
4 WELLINGTON GDNS
5 WELLINGTON PL
6 CHAPEL TERR
7 FAIRVIEW PL
8 THE OLD SCHOOLHOUSE
9 LAWN STEPS
10 FISH STRAND HILL
11 SOMER CT
12 SNOW'S PAS
13 ST GEORGE'S ARC
14 WELL LA
15 BURLEY CT
16 HARBER CT
17 NEW CT

Ferry (P)

FALMOUTH

Falmouth Docks

Eastern Breakwater

Mus

BELL'S CT

GYLLYNG HALL

LB Sta

Falmouth Docks L Ctr

Middle Point

Falmouth College of Arts

Falmouth Town

A39

MARINE CT

P&R

YH

1 PENDRAGON HO
2 ROEBUCK VILLAS
3 TREGURTER MEWS
4 RAILWAY COTTS
5 PENDENNIS RISE
6 BAY VIEW CRES
7 MANOR COTTS
8 PENDENNIS CT

WESTERN TERR

MELVILL RD

Cemy

Swan Pool

Gyllyngvase Beach

Pendennis Castle

Crab Quay

Swanpool Point

South West Coast Path

HANGMANS WLK

Swanpool Beach

Pendennis Point

Falmouth Bay

A3
1 MARLBOROUGH CL
2 MARLBOROUGH GR
3 PENMERE PL
4 PENMERE CT
5 MARLBOROUGH CT
6 CHARD TERR
7 PENMERE HILL

C3
1 ABERFAL HO
2 ROPEWALK CT
3 GROVE PL
4 ARWENACK HO
5 MARINE CRES
6 ARWYN COTTS
7 ARWYN PL
8 BAR TERR
9 BOSLOGGAS MEWS

10 OSBORNE VILLAS
11 PELHAM CT
12 CHALLENGER QUAY

82 · 81 · 94 · 82 · 94

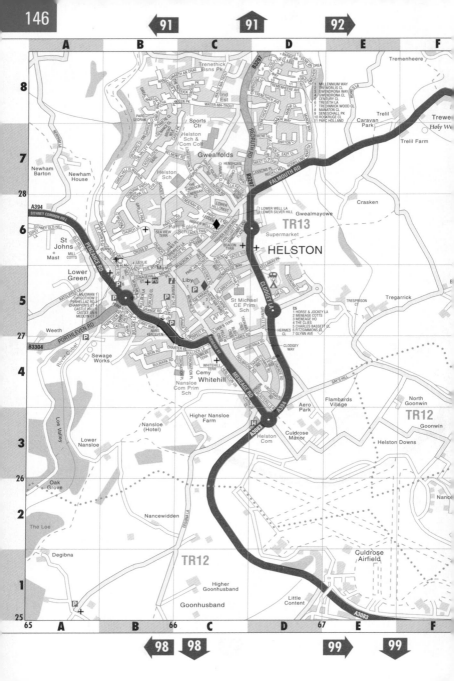

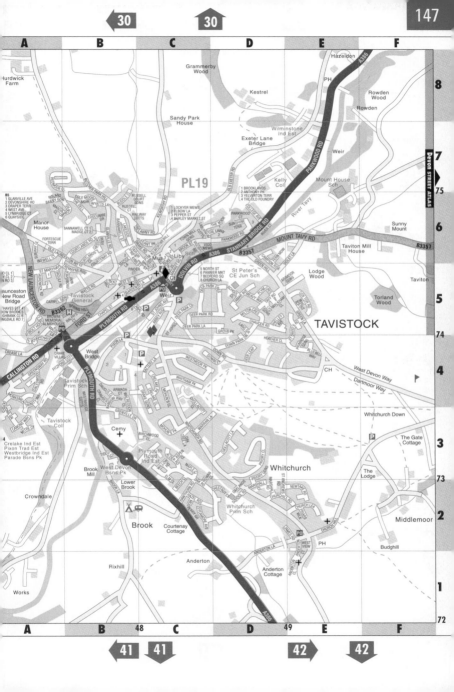

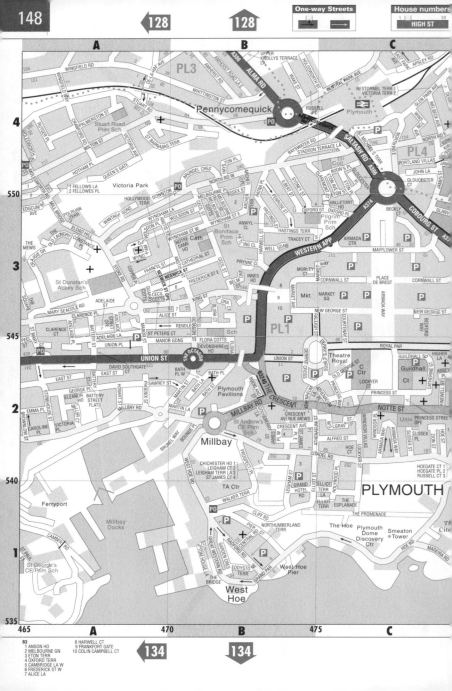

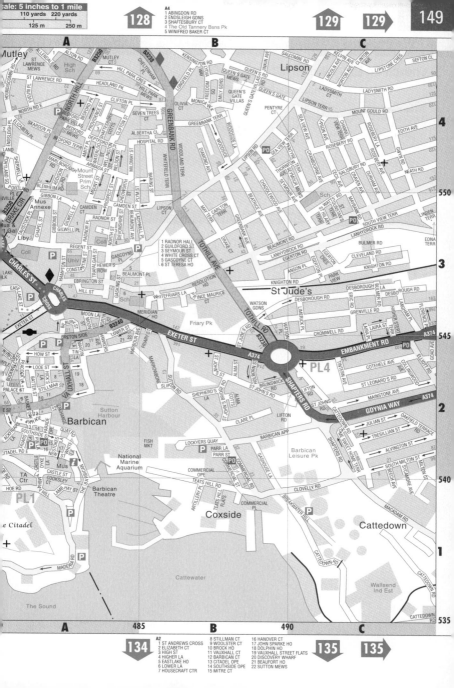

Church Rd **6** Beckenham BR2..........**53** C6

Place name	**Location number**	**Locality, town or village**	**Postcode district**	**Page and grid square**
May be abbreviated on the map	Present when a number indicates the place's position in a crowded area of mapping	Shown when more than one place has the same name	District for the indexed place	Page number and grid reference for the standard mapping

Public and commercial buildings are highlighted in magenta. Places of interest are highlighted in blue with a star★

Abbreviations used in the index

Acad	**Academy**	Comm	**Common**	Gd	**Ground**	L	**Leisure**	Prom	**Promenade**
App	**Approach**	Cott	**Cottage**	Gdn	**Garden**	La	**Lane**	Rd	**Road**
Arc	**Arcade**	Cres	**Crescent**	Gn	**Green**	Liby	**Library**	Recn	**Recreation**
Ave	**Avenue**	Cswy	**Causeway**	Gr	**Grove**	Mdw	**Meadow**	Ret	**Retail**
Bglw	**Bungalow**	Ct	**Court**	H	**Hall**	Meml	**Memorial**	Sh	**Shopping**
Bldg	**Building**	Ctr	**Centre**	Ho	**House**	Mkt	**Market**	Sq	**Square**
Bsns, Bus	**Business**	Ctry	**Country**	Hospl	**Hospital**	Mus	**Museum**	St	**Street**
Bvd	**Boulevard**	Cty	**County**	HQ	**Headquarters**	Orch	**Orchard**	Sta	**Station**
Cath	**Cathedral**	Dr	**Drive**	Hts	**Heights**	Pal	**Palace**	Terr	**Terrace**
Cir	**Circus**	Dro	**Drove**	Ind	**Industrial**	Par	**Parade**	TH	**Town Hall**
Cl	**Close**	Ed	**Education**	Inst	**Institute**	Pas	**Passage**	Univ	**University**
Cnr	**Corner**	Emb	**Embankment**	Int	**International**	Pk	**Park**	Wk, Wlk	**Walk**
Coll	**College**	Est	**Estate**	Intc	**Interchange**	Pl	**Place**	Wr	**Water**
Com	**Community**	Ex	**Exhibition**	Junc	**Junction**	Prec	**Precinct**	Yd	**Yard**

Index of localities, towns and villages

A

Altarnun 26 C8
Angarrack 78 C5
Antony 65 5
Ashton 90 E3

B

Barripper 79 A5
Bere Alston 41 B1
Bere Ferrers 119 E3
Blackwater 68 D5
Blisland 35 D8
Bodmin 109 B5
Bolventor 25 E3
Boscastle 9 C1
Boyton 13 B2
Bray Shop 28 B1
Breage 90 F3
Bridgerule 8 A6
Buckland Monachorum ...42 A3
Bude 104 E6
Budock Water 144 C2
Bugle 47 D1
Burras 80 A1

C

Callington 39 E5
Calstock 41 A3
Camborne 138 B2
Camelford 105 C4
Carbis Bay 141 D3
Cardinham 35 E3
Cargreen 119 A2
Carharrack 80 F8
Carnhell Green 78 F4
Carnkie 80 D1
Carnon Downs 82 A7
Cawsand 133 B1
Chacewater 68 F3
Coad's Green 27 D4
Common Moor 37 F4
Connor Downs 78 D5
Constantine 92 E3
Constantine Bay 20 D1
Coombe 58 B2
Coppathorne 7 A3
Coverack 101 C1
Crackington Haven ...10 B7
Crafthole 65 B5
Crantock 43 D3
Crapstone 42 B2
Cross Lanes 99 C4
Crowlas 89 C8
Crumplehorn 62 D2
Cubert 55 D8
Cury 99 B4

D

Delabole 14 D3
Devoran 81 F6
Dobwalls 50 E8
Dousland 42 F3
Down Thomas 135 C1
Downderry 64 C5
Downgate 39 A7
Duloe 51 A1
Dunterton 28 F6

E

East Portholland 84 E5
East Taphouse 50 B6
Edistone 2 F8
Egloskerry 18 A5

F

Falmouth 145 C4
Feock 82 C5
Flushing 145 C6

Four Lanes 80 A5
Fowey 116 B4
Foxhole 58 D5
Fraddam 78 D1
Fraddon 45 E1
Frogpool 81 C7

G

Gloweth 69 E3
Godolphin Cross 90 E6
Golant 61 A5
Goldsithney 89 D5
Goonbell 68 D8
Goonhavern 55 E4
Gorran Haven 85 D5
Grampound 72 B7
Grampound Road 57 E1
Grenofen 42 A6
Grimscott 5 A2
Gulval 88 E6
Gunnislake 40 F5
Gunwalloe 98 E5
Gweek 92 C1
Gwennap 80 F7
Gwinear 78 D4
Gwithian 66 B2

H

Harlyn 20 D2
Harrowbarrow 40 D5
Hatt 53 E4
Hayle 142 C6
Heamoor 143 B7
Helford 93 B1
Helston 146 D6
Helstone 24 B8
Herodsfoot 50 E3
Hessenford 64 C8
High Street 58 D4
Higher Town 74 C6
Holywell 43 B2
Horrabridge 42 C5
Horsebridge 29 C1
Hugh Town 74 C5

I

Illogan 67 E4
Indian Queens 45 E1

J

Jacobstow 11 B6

K

Kelly Bray 39 F6
Kilkhampton 5 A6

L

Ladock 57 C1
Lamerton 30 B3
Landrake 53 B3
Lane 111 B3
Langore 18 D5
Lanivet 47 F6
Lanjeth 58 E3
Lanlivery 48 C1
Lanner 80 D6
Lanreath 62 B7
Launceston 106 D5
Leedstown 78 E1
Lelant 77 E4
Lerryn 61 D8
Lewannick 27 B7
Lifton 19 F3
Linkinhorne 39 B8
Liskeard 113 E6
Little Petherick 32 C6
Lizard 102 F2
Longrock 88 F6

Looe 117 D3
Lostwithiel 112 E1
Luckett 40 B8
Luxulyan 48 A1
Lynstone 104 D3

M

Mabe Burnthouse 93 C8
Madron 143 A8
Maenporth 93 F4
Manaccan 101 A8
Marazion 89 B6
Marhamchurch 7 B6
Marshgate 10 C2
Mawgan 99 D7
Mawnan Smith 93 E3
Maxworthy 12 A3
Meavy 42 F2
Menheniot 52 A5
Merrymeet 38 C1
Metherell 40 D4
Mevagissey 73 D3
Middle Town 74 C6
Millbrook 132 E5
Milton Abbot 29 D6
Milton Combe 120 F8
Minions 38 D6
Mitchell 56 F5
Morwenstow 2 C2
Mount Hawke 68 C6
Mousehole 88 D1
Mullion 99 A1
Mylor Bridge 82 A3

N

Nancegollan 91 C7
Nancledra 76 F2
Nanpean 58 D7
Narkurs 64 C6
New Grimsby 74 B6
New Polzeath 21 E6
Newlyn 143 D2
Newquay 110 E7
North Brentor 30 E8
North Hill 27 B3
North Petherwin 18 A8
Northward 74 B6

O

Old Grimsby 74 B6
Old Town 74 C5

P

Padstow 107 C4
Par 60 C4
Paul 88 C2
Pelynt 62 D5
Pendeen 75 A1
Pendoggett 23 A6
Penponds 138 B1
Penryn 144 B7
Pensilva 38 E5
Pentewan 73 C6
Penwithick 59 D7
Penzance 143 F5
Perranarworthal 81 D6
Perranporth 55 A5
Perranuthnoe 89 D4
Perranwell Station ...81 E6
Petherwin Gate 18 B7
Phillack 142 D7
Pillaton 53 B6
Playing Place 82 B8
Plymouth 148 C1
Polbathic 64 F8
Polgooth 59 A1
Polmassick 72 E4
Polruan 116 C2
Polyphant 17 F1
Polzeath 21 E5
Ponsanooth 81 B5

Pool 74 B6
Porkellis 92 B8
Port Isaac 22 D8
Porth Navas 93 B2
Porthleven 98 B8
Porthlo 74 C5
Porthtowan 68 A6
Portloe 84 B3
Portmellon 73 C3
Portreath 67 C6
Portscatho 83 C2
Portwrinkle 65 B4
Poughill 4 D2
Poundstock 6 E2
Praa Sands 90 C3
Praze-an-Beeble 79 C2
Probus 71 C6
Pyworthy 8 E5

Q

Quethiock 52 C7
Quintrell Downs 44 E3

R

Rame 64 B2
Reawla 78 E3
Redruth 140 D5
Relubbus 90 A7
Rilla Mill 38 E8
Roborough 121 D1
Roche 46 F3
Rock 21 D2
Rosudgeon 89 F4
Ruan Minor 103 B6
Rumford 32 A5

S

St Agnes 54 D1
St Austell 114 B5
St Blazey Gate 115 F6
St Breock 33 C6
St Breward 24 B3
St Buryan 97 B6
St Cleer 37 F2
St Clether 17 A3
St Columb Major ...45 E6
St Columb Minor ...111 E7
St Columb Road 45 D2
St Day 68 E1
St Dennis 46 C1
St Dominick 40 D3
St Erme 70 E8
St Erth 142 A1
St Erth Praze 142 F5
St Eval 31 F3
St Germans 65 A8
St Giles-on-the-Heath ...13 E1
St Hilary 89 E6
St Issey 32 E6
St Ive 38 F2
St Ives 141 C6
St John 132 C8
St Just 86 E6
St Just in Roseland ...82 F2
St Keverne 101 C4
St Kew Highway 23 A2
St Martin 100 B6
St Mawes 95 B6
St Mawgan 45 A8
St Mellion 53 E8
St Merryn 31 F8
St Minver 22 A4
St Neot 36 C2
St Newlyn East 56 C7
St Stephen 58 B4
St Teath 23 E7
St Tudy 23 E3
St Wenn 46 D7
Saltash 122 B1
Seaton 64 B5
Sennen 96 B6
Sennen Cove 96 B7
Sheviock 65 B6
Shop 2 D1

Shortlanesend 69 F6
South Petherwin 27 E8
South Tehidy 138 E7
Staddiscombe 135 F3
Stenalees 59 B8
Sticker 58 F1
Stithians 80 F3
Stoke Climsland ...28 E3
Stowford 5 E8
Stratton 4 E1
Summercourt 57 C7

T

Tavistock 147 E5
Tetcott 13 C7
Threemilestone 69 D4
Tideford 52 F2
Tintagel 14 D7
Torpoint 127 C3
Townshend 90 D7
Trebetherick 21 D4
Trebullett 28 A5
Treburley 28 C4
Tregadillett 18 C2
Tregony 71 F4
Tregurrian 44 E8
Trehan 65 F8
Treknow 14 C5
Trelights 22 C6
Tremar 38 A2
Trematon 53 E2
Trenance 31 C2
Trencreek 111 C4
Trenear 92 A6
Tresillian 70 F5
Treverva 59 F6
Trevone 20 F2
Trewellard 86 F8
Trewennack 146 F8
Trewoon 59 A3
Treworlas 83 D5
Troon 79 E5
Truro 137 E3

U

Upton Cross 38 D6

V

Venterdon 28 D2
Veryan 83 F6

W

Wadebridge 108 A6
Wainhouse Corner ...10 E6
Walkhampton 42 D4
Warbstow Cross 11 B2
Week St Mary 11 F8
Welcombe 2 D5
Whipsiderry 44 C6
Whitchurch 147 D3
White Cross 45 C2
Whitemoor 58 E8
Whitstone 7 F1
Widegates 63 F8
Widemouth Bay ...6 F5
Woodford 4 D8

Y

Yelverton 42 D3
Yeolmbridge 18 F6

Z

Zelah 56 A2
Zennor 76 B5

A

Abbey Cl PL20 ....42 B2
Abbey Ct
  ⑯ Combe Martin TR13 ....143 E5
  Plymouth PL1 ....149 A2
Abbey Hill TR26 ....77 E3
Abbey Mdw TR26 ....77 E4
Abbey Mews PL31 ....109 C4
Abbey Pl Plymouth PL1 ....148 C2
  Tavistock PL19 ....147 C5
Abbey Rise PL19 ....147 C5
Abbey St TR18 ....143 E5
Abbots Cl PL2 ....128 E6
Abbotsbury Way PL2 ....127 F8
Abbotscourt La PL11 ....126 A2
Abbotsfield Cl PL19 ....41 D8
Abbotsfield Cres PL19 ....41 D8
Abbotts Rd PL3 ....128 E6
Aberdeen Ave PL5 ....124 D2
Aberdeen Cl PL24 ....60 B6
Aberfal Ho ❶ TR11 ....145 C3
Abingdon Rd PL4 ....149 A4
Abney Cres PL6 ....125 B6
Abscott La PL9 ....135 C5
Acacia Rd TR11 ....144 F4
Academy Terr ㉚ TR26 ....143 B6
Acklington Pl PL5 ....123 E4
Acland Cl EX23 ....104 E7
Acorn Dr PL25 ....115 A3
Acre Pl PL1 ....127 F3
Adams Cl Plymouth PL5 ....123 F1
  Torpoint PL11 ....126 F3
Adams Cres PL11 ....126 E3
Addington N PL14 ....113 D6
Addington S PL14 ....113 D6
Addison Rd PL4 ....149 A4
Addison Terr PL22 ....112 C2
Adela Rd PL11 ....127 A3
Adelaide La PL1 ....148 A2
Adelaide Pl PL1 ....148 A3
Adelaide Rd PL24 ....140 C4
Adelaide St
  Camborne TR14 ....138 E3
  Penzance TR18 ....143 E4
  Plymouth PL1 ....148 A3
  ❷ Plymouth, Ford PL2 ....127 F5
Adelaide Street Ope
  PL1 ....148 A3
Adelaide Terr TR17 ....137 B4
Adit La Newlyn TR18 ....143 C1
  Saltash PL12 ....122 E3
Adits The PL18 ....41 A3
Admiral's Hard PL1 ....134 A8
Admirals Quay TR11 ....145 B5
Admiralty Cotts PL1 ....134 A1
Admiralty Rd
  Plymouth, Millbay PL1 ....134 A8
  Plymouth, St Budeaux PL5 ...123 C2
Admiralty St
  Plymouth, Keyham PL2 ....127 E6
  Plymouth, Millbay PL1 ....134 A8
Admiralty Terr TR2 ....83 B2
Agar Cres TR15 ....139 D6
Agar Ct TR1 ....137 D5
Agar Mdws ⑪ TR3 ....81 F7
Agar Rd Camborne TR15 ....139 D6
  Newquay TR7 ....110 C5
  St Austell PL25 ....114 E6
  Truro TR1 ....137 E5
Agar Terr ❹ PL31 ....109 D5
Agar Way PL3 ....139 C5
Agaton Rd PL5 ....123 E3
Agnes Cl EX23 ....104 F4
Ainslie Terr PL2 ....127 E7
Aire Gdns PL3 ....129 B5
Alamein Cl PL12 ....122 E2
Alamein Rd PL12 ....122 D2
Alan Harvey Cl ⑪ TR26 ....77 A6
Alan Rd PL28 ....107 D4
Alansmere Ct TR2 ....57 A1
Alanta Flats PL7 ....110 B5
Albany Cl TR5 ....68 D8
Albany Ct TR15 ....140 D3
Albany La TR11 ....140 C4
Albany Rd TR11 ....140 C4
Albany Rd S TR11 ....140 C3
Albany St PL1 ....127 E2
Albany Terr TR26 ....141 B4
Albemarle Villas PL1 ....127 F3
Albert Bldgs ⑱ TR18 ....143 E6
Albert Cotts TR11 ....145 B4
Albert Pl ❷ Camborne TR14 ...138 E3
  ㉑ St Ives PL26 ....141 B5
  Truro TR1 ....137 C3
Albert Rd Plymouth PL2 ....127 F5
  Saltash PL12 ....123 A2
  St Austell PL25 ....114 D3
  St Ives PL26 ....141 B5
Albert St Camborne TR14 ....138 E3
  Penzance TR18 ....143 F6
Albert Terr
  Gunnislake PL18 ....40 F5
  ⑯ Penzance TR18 ....143 E6
Albertha Cl PL4 ....149 B4
Albertus Dr TR27 ....142 B3
Albertus Gdns TR27 ....142 B3
Albertus Rd TR27 ....142 B3

Albion Ct PL11 ....127 B3
Albion Dr PL2 ....128 B7
Albion Rd Helston TR13 ....146 B4
  Torpoint PL11 ....126 B3
Albion Row TR15 ....140 B5
Alcester Cl PL2 ....127 E4
Alcester St PL2 ....127 E4
Alden Wlk PL6 ....129 B7
Alder Rd PL19 ....147 C3
Aldercombe La EX23 ....5 A6
Aldermay Rd PL6 ....124 F7
Aldersley Wlk PL6 ....125 A1
Aldreath Cl TR20 ....88 B7
Aldreath Rd TR20 ....88 B7
Alexander Ct PL26 ....85 D5
Alexandra Cl
  ⑤ Illogan TR16 ....67 E4
  Plymouth PL19 ....136 B8
  St Ives TR26 ....77 A7
Alexandra Ct TR17 ....111 C8
Alexandra Dr PL20 ....41 C1
Alexandra Gdns TR18 ....143 D4
Alexandra Pl
  Penzance TR18 ....143 D4
  ❷ Plymouth PL4 ....128 E4
  St Ives TR26 ....77 A7
Alexandra Rd
  Mount Hawke TR4 ....68 C6
  Penzance TR18 ....143 D3
  Plymouth PL2 ....127 F5
  St Ives TR26 ....141 A5
  Tremar PL14 ....38 A4
  ❷ Truro TR1 ....137 B4
Alexandra Sq PL12 ....123 A2
Alexandra Terr
  Mount Hawke TR4 ....68 C6
  Penzance TR18 ....143 D3
  Plymouth PL2 ....127 F5
  St Ives TR26 ....141 A5
  Tremar PL14 ....38 A4
  ❷ Truro TR1 ....137 B4
Alford Cl EX23 ....104 F5
Alfred Pl PL2 ....127 F5
Alfred Rd PL2 ....127 F5
Alfred St PL1 ....148 C3
Alger Wlk PL6 ....124 E6
Alice La PL4 ....148 B3
Alice St PL1 ....148 B3
All Saints Pk PL18 ....40 E5
Alldritt Cl TR7 ....111 D7
Allen Pk PL30 ....23 B2
Allen Vale PL14 ....113 A5
Allenby Rd PL2 ....128 A6
Allern La PL5 ....120 C1
Allerton Wlk PL6 ....129 B7
Alley Hill PL20 ....42 A1
Alleyne Gdns PL3 ....128 E8
Allium Ct TR4 ....70 D8
Alma Cl TR5 ....68 D8
Alma Cotts PL4 ....149 B2
Alma Pl Heamoor TR18 ....143 C7
  Newquay TR7 ....110 D6
  ⑤ Penzance TR18 ....143 E5
  Redruth TR15 ....140 B5
Alma Rd Plymouth PL3 ....128 C4
  Truro TR1 ....137 C4
Alma St PL4 ....149 B2
Alma Terr Carharrack TR16 .....80 F8
  Penzance TR18 ....143 E5
  ⑤ St Ives TR26 ....141 B5
Almeria Ct PL7 ....130 D4
Almond Dr PL7 ....131 B6
Almshouse Hill PL15 ....146 B5
Alton Pl PL4 ....128 E4
Alton Rd PL4 ....149 A4
Alverne Bldgs ❼ TR18 ....143 D5
Alverton Com Prim Sch
  TR18 ....143 C4
Alverton Ct TR1 ....137 C5
Alverton Rd TR18 ....143 C4
Alverton St TR18 ....143 C5
Alverton Terr
  ❹ Penzance TR18 ....143 D5
  Truro TR1 ....137 C5
Alvington St PL4 ....149 C2
Alwin Pk PL6 ....125 A5
Alwyn Cl TR7 ....111 C6
Amacre Dr PL9 ....135 B6
Amados Cl PL7 ....130 B4
Amados Dr PL7 ....130 C4
Amados Rise PL7 ....130 C4
Aman An Avon TR27 ....142 F7
Amanda Way PL14 ....38 E4
Amble Rd ㉖ PL17 ....79 F4
Ambrose Ct PL15 ....140 E7
Amelia Ct PL7 ....71 C6
Amherst Rd PL3 ....148 B4
Amherst Road La E PL3 ....148 A4
Amity Pl PL4 ....149 A4
An Bof Gdns PL31 ....110 C6
An Vounder Goth TR13 ....146 B4
Anderton Cl PL19 ....147 E1
Anderton Ct TR9 ....45 D6
Anderton La PL19 ....147 D2
Anderton Rise PL10 ....132 F4
Andrew Pl ⑬ TR11 ....145 C3
Andrew's Terr TR16 ....139 F1
Andrewartha Rd TR10 ....144 B8
Andrews Way PL12 ....53 E5
Andurn Cl PL9 ....136 B6
Aneraj Rd TR14 ....138 D4
Angarrack La TR27 ....78 C5
Angarrack Mews TR27 ....78 C5

Angarvan Mdw TR8 ....55 D8
Angel Hill ❻ PL15 ....106 C6
Angwin Ave ❹ TR5 ....54 C1
Anjardyn Pl PL4 ....60 C5
Ankervis La TR16 ....140 F1
Ann's Pl PL3 ....128 A4
Annear Rd TR10 ....144 A6
Anson Ho ❶ PL1 ....148 B3
Anson Pl
  Plymouth, Devonport PL2 .....127 F4
  Plymouth, St Jude's PL4 ......149 C3
Anson Rd PL27 ....31 F3
Anson Way TR13 ....146 D4
Anstis St Plymouth PL1 ....148 A3
Anthony Cl EX23 ....4 C3
Anthony Lowen PL28 ....107 D4
Anthony Pk PL19 ....147 D6
Anthony Rd TR7 ....110 D6
Antoine Cl ❹ TR18 ....143 C2
Antoine Terr ❺ TR18 ....143 C2
Antony CE Jun & Inf Sch
  PL11 ....65 E5
Antony Gdns PL2 ....128 E8
Antony Ho* PL11 ....126 D5
Antony Rd PL11 ....127 B3
Antony Woodland Gdn*
  PL11 ....126 D6
Antron Hill TR10 ....81 B1
Antron La PL10 ....93 C8
Antron Way TR10 ....93 C8
Anvil Cl PL32 ....105 D4
Anwyl Cl PL1 ....148 B3
Anzac Ave PL5 ....124 B4
Appin Gdns TR15 ....139 C7
Appleby Wlk PL5 ....124 D4
Appletree La PL25 ....115 D3
Apsley Rd PL4 ....128 D4
Arch Barrow PL6 ....124 E5
Arcade The ❽ TR18 ....143 E5
Arcadia TR1 ....137 D3
Arcadia Rd PL9 ....136 D6
Arch Hill TR1 ....137 C2
Arch La TR27 ....77 D1
Archbishop Benson CE Prim
  Sch TR1 ....137 D6
Archer Pl PL1 ....148 B4
Archer Terr PL1 ....148 B4
Archway Ave PL4 ....129 B3
Arden Cl PL22 ....128 C8
Arena Cres PL25 ....115 B4
Argal View TR13 ....93 B6
Arimoor Gdns PL19 ....147 E5
Ark Royal Cl PL5 ....127 D8
Arkwright Gdns PL5 ....123 F2
Arley Cl PL6 ....124 E6
Arlington Rd PL4 ....128 F4
Armada Ct PL19 ....147 B4
Armada Ctr PL1 ....148 C3
Armada Rd PL10 ....133 A1
Armada St PL4 ....149 A4
Armada Way
  Plymouth PL1 ....148 C2
  ⑤ Plymouth PL19 ....136 E4
Armchair Cnr PL31 ....109 C5
Armistead Terr ❼ TR11 ....145 C3
Armoury Cl TR13 ....146 B5
Arnison Cl PL9 ....135 F5
Arnold's Point PL4 ....129 C3
Arnside Cl PL6 ....125 D3
Arralas Barns TR2 ....57 B4
Arscott Gdns PL9 ....135 D5
Arscott La PL9 ....135 D5
Art Gallery Terr TR1 ....143 C3
Arthur Terr PL11 ....127 B2
Arthurian Centre The*
  PL32 ....105 D8
Artillery Pl PL4 ....149 B1
Arun Cl PL3 ....129 C5
Arundel Cres PL1 ....148 B4
Arundel Cl PL27 ....78 D6
Arundel Pk TR7 ....78 B6
Arundel Terr Bude EX23 ....104 D4
  Plymouth PL1 ....127 F4
Arundel Way
  Connor Downs TR27 ....78 D6
  Newquay TR7 ....111 B7
Arundell Cl PL16 ....119 E4
Arundell Gdns
  Falmouth TR11 ....144 E6
  Lifton PL16 ....119 F4
Arundell Pl TR17 ....137 C3
Arundell La PL26 ....58 C8
Arwenack Ave TR11 ....144 E5
Arwenack Ho ⑫ TR11 ....145 C4
Arwenack St TR11 ....145 C4
Arworthal Mdws TR3 ....81 D6
Arwyn Cotts ❻ TR11 ....145 C3
Arwyn Pl TR11 ....145 C3
Ascension Pl Par PL24 ....60 B4
  ⑭ Yelverton PL20 ....42 C3
Ash Dr TR27 ....142 B3
Ash Gr Hayle TR27 ....142 B3
  Par PL24 ....60 B4
Ash La TR27 ....142 B4
Ashburgh Parc PL12 ....122 B3
Ashburnham Rd PL5 ....124 A3
Ashbury Ct PL14 ....113 D7
Ashcombe Cl PL7 ....131 C7
Ashdown Cl
  Plymouth PL6 ....125 E3
  Sticker PL26 ....58 E1
Ashdown Wlk PL6 ....125 E3
Ashery Dr PL9 ....135 C6
Ashfield Gdns TR11 ....144 E6

Ashfield Rd TR11 ....144 F6
Ashfield Villas TR11 ....144 F6
Ashford Cl PL3 ....129 A4
Ashford Cres PL3 ....129 A4
Ashford Hill PL4 ....129 A4
Ashford Rd PL4 ....129 A4
Ashleigh Cl PL5 ....124 C7
Ashleigh La PL5 ....120 D1
Ashleigh Way
  Plymouth PL7 ....131 C4
  Probus TR2 ....71 D6
Ashley Cl ❾ PL26 ....59 D7
Ashley Rd
  Shortlanesend TR4 ....69 F6
  Truro TR1 ....137 C4
Ashmead TR2 ....57 E1
Ashridge Gdns PL5 ....124 B2
Ashton Cl PL6 ....125 C6
Ashton Ctr TR1 ....111 D6
Ashton Way PL12 ....122 D3
Ashton Wlk EX23 ....6 F5
Ashtree Cl PL6 ....125 D7
Ashtree Gr PL9 ....136 C8
Ashwood Cl PL7 ....131 C6
Ashwood Park Rd PL7 ....131 C6
Aspen Cl PL9 ....147 C3
Aspen Gdns PL7 ....131 B5
Astor Dr PL4 ....129 C3
Astwood Devopments
  PL13 ....63 F8
Athelstan Pk PL31 ....109 F3
Athenaeum La PL1 ....148 B2
Athenaeum Pl PL1 ....148 C2
Athenaeum St PL1 ....148 B2
Atherton Pl PL1 ....127 E4
Atlantic Bay ❶ TR6 ....55 A5
Atlantic Cl
  Camborne TR14 ....138 E2
  Treknow PL34 ....14 C5
  Widemouth Bay EX23 ....6 F5
Atlantic Coast Cvn Pk
  TR6 ....55 B6
Atlantic Cres TR19 ....96 C7
Atlantic Mews PL27 ....31 D6
Atlantic Rd Delabole PL33 .....14 D2
  Newquay TR7 ....110 C6
  Tintagel PL34 ....14 C7
Atlantic Terr
  Camborne TR14 ....138 E2
  New Polzeath PL27 ....21 D6
  ㉖ St Ives TR26 ....141 B6
Atlantic Way
  Porthtowan TR4 ....68 A6
  Tintagel PL34 ....14 C7
Attery View PL15 ....106 B6
Auckland Rd ❸ PL2 ....128 A5
Audierne TR10 ....144 C7
Austin Ave PL2 ....128 A6
Austin Cres PL6 ....125 C1
Austin Farm Prim Sch
  PL6 ....129 C7
Automobilia Motor Mus*
  PL26 ....58 A4
Avent Wlk PL7 ....130 F7
Avenue Rd TR11 ....145 C3
Avenue The St Hilary TR20 .....89 F6
  Truro TR1 ....137 D5
Avery Terr PL22 ....112 C2
Avery Way PL12 ....122 C5
Avon Cl Plymouth PL3 ....129 C6
  St Austell PL25 ....115 A5
Avondale Rd TR1 ....137 B4
Avrack Cl TR19 ....87 F3
Axe Cl PL3 ....129 D6
Axford Hill PL7 ....37 F2
Axtown La PL20 ....42 C2
Aycliffe Gdns PL7 ....131 A1
Aylesbury Cres PL5 ....124 B5
Aylmer Pl ⑱ PL25 ....114 C3
Aylmer Sq ⑭ PL25 ....114 C3
Aylwin Cl PL7 ....130 C6
Ayr Cliff Gdns TR11 ....141 A5
Ayr La TR26 ....141 B6
Ayr Terr TR26 ....141 A6
Ayreville Rd PL2 ....128 B7
Ayshston Gdns ⑱ PL7 ....39 F4

B

Babbacombe Cl PL6 ....129 E8
Baber Cl PL12 ....40 C2
Baber La PL12 ....40 D2
Babis Farm Cl PL12 ....122 F1
Babis Farm Ct PL12 ....122 F1
Babis Farm Mews PL12 ....122 F2
Babis Farm Row PL12 ....122 F1
Babis Farm Way PL12 ....122 F1
Babis La PL12 ....122 F1
Baby Beach La PL27 ....26 B8
Back Hill Port Isaac PL27 ....22 D7
  Saltash PL12 ....122 D2
Back La Angarrack TR27 ....78 C5
  Callington PL17 ....39 F4
  Marazion TR17 ....89 B6
  Plymouth PL7 ....130 E4
  St Erth TR27 ....77 D2
  ⑰ St Ives TR26 ....141 B6
  Tintagel PL34 ....14 C7
  Tregony TR2 ....71 F4
  Veryan TR2 ....83 F6
Back La W TR26 ....141 B6
Back Lane TR15 ....139 E6
Barncoose Ind Est TR15 ......139 E5
Barncoose La TR15 ....139 E5
Barncoose Terr TR15 ....139 E6
Barndale Cres PL6 ....125 B6
Barne Barton Prim Sch
  PL5 ....127 D8
Barne Cl PL5 ....123 D1
Barne La PL5 ....123 D1
Barne Rd PL5 ....123 D1
Barncoul Cl ❹ PL14 ....38 D4
Barnfield Dr PL7 ....131 C5
Barnfield Gdns TR18 ....143 D4
Barnfield Rd
  ❸ Indian Queens TR9 ....45 E1
  Liskeard PL14 ....113 B4
Barningham Gdns PL6 ....125 A6
Barnoon Hill TR26 ....141 B6
Barnpark Rd PL35 ....9 C1
Barnsloft ⑯ TR26 ....141 B6
Barnstaple Ct PL6 ....129 E8
Barnwarren Cl PL9 ....135 E5
Barnwood Ch PL7 ....135 E5
Barons Rd PL20 ....42 E3
Barossa Rd PL11 ....127 B3
Barr's Ct PL23 ....116 D5
Barrack La TR1 ....137 A3
Barrack Pl PL1 ....128 A1

Back St ❹❷ TR26 ....141 B6
Badgers Wlk PL12 ....122 D4
Bag La Polbathic PL12 ....64 F8
  St Germans PL12 ....65 A8
Bagbury Rd EX23 ....104 E3
Bahavella Dr TR26 ....141 B4
Bailey Terr EX22 ....8 A5
Baileys La ㉚ TR26 ....141 B6
Bainbridge Ave PL3 ....128 F7
Bainbridge Ct PL7 ....130 E7
Baines Hill TR16 ....67 C6
Bakehouse La ⑫ PL17 ....39 E4
Bakers Cl PL7 ....131 C5
Bakers Pl PL1 ....127 F1
Bakers Row TR13 ....90 F3
Bal Rd TR13 ....91 E4
Bal-Jinjy Cl ⑩ PL24 ....60 B4
Balcoath TR16 ....68 D1
Baldhu Row TR20 ....76 F2
Balfield Rd ⑱ TR13 ....98 C8
Balfour Terr PL2 ....127 E4
Balkin Way TR15 ....139 D7
Ball Terr PL27 ....108 E7
Ballard Est TR16 ....80 B5
Balmoral Ave PL2 ....127 F5
Balmoral Pl ❸ TR11 ....140 B5
Balmoral Terr ❹ TR15 ....140 B5
Balnoon Flats TR26 ....77 A4
Balson Pl PL9 ....135 E5
Bampfylde Way PL6 ....124 D6
Bampfylde Way
  Goldsithney TR20 ....89 F5
  Plymouth PL6 ....124 E6
Bampton Rd PL6 ....125 E1
Band House La PL26 ....59 C7
Bangors Est EX23 ....6 F2
Bangors Rd PL15 ....18 E2
Bank Cotts ⑤ TR10 ....144 C7
Bank Sq TR19 ....86 F6
Bank St Newquay TR7 ....110 D6
  St Columb Major TR9 ....45 E6
Bannawell St PL19 ....147 B6
Banns Rd TR4 ....68 C6
Baptist Hill TR27 ....142 C6
Baptist St PL17 ....41 A3
Bar La Connor Downs TR27 .....78 C6
  Falmouth TR11 ....145 C3
Bar Mdws TR11 ....70 D2
Bar Rd Falmouth TR11 ....145 C3
  Mawnan Smith TR11 ....93 C2
Barbara Hepworth Mus*
  TR26 ....141 B6
Barbican App PL4 ....149 B2
Barbican Cl
  Helston TR13 ....146 D8
  Looe PL13 ....117 D4
Barbican Ct Looe PL13 ....117 D5
  ⑫ Plymouth PL7 ....149 A2
Barbican Hill PL13 ....117 D4
Barbican La TR18 ....143 F4
Barbican Leisure Pk
  PL4 ....149 C2
Barbican Rd Looe PL13 ....117 E6
  Plymouth PL7 ....130 E4
Barbican The PL1 ....149 A2
Barbican Theatre PL1 ....149 A1
Barbury Cres PL6 ....125 B8
Barcote Wlk PL6 ....129 C8
Bardsey Cl PL6 ....125 A7
Baring St PL4 ....149 B4
Barker's Hill PL12 ....122 C1
Barkhouse La PL25 ....115 B2
Barlandew Cl PL14 ....38 C2
Barley Market St PL19 ....147 C6
Barlowena TR14 ....138 D1
Barn Cl Plymouth PL7 ....131 C5
  Wainhouse Corner EX23 ....10 F6
Barn Crtyd TR27 ....78 D6
Barn Hill Polbathic PL12 ....64 F8
  Ruan Minor PL12 ....103 B4
  Tideford PL12 ....52 F1
Barn La Bodmin PL31 ....109 C4
  ⑱ St Columb Major TR9 ....45 E6
Barn Meadow Pk PL13 ....117 B2
Barn Park La PL31 ....35 B2
Barn Park Rd PL3 ....128 D6
Barn Park Rd PL12 ....112 C2
  Saltash PL12 ....122 C1
Barns St PL14 ....113 C5

arrack St PL1 .....127 E2
arrack's La TR16 .....68 E1
arras Cross PL14 .....113 C6
arras Pl PL14 .....113 C6
arras Rd PL14 .....113 C6
arrepta Cl TR26 .....141 D1
arrie Cres PL31 .....109 E2
arripper Rd
Camborne TR14 .....138 B3
Penponds TR14 .....79 C5
arrow Down PL12 .....122 B3
arry's La PL28 .....107 D5
artholomew Rd PL2 .....128 B5
arties Cl TR12 .....99 D7
arties Row TR14 .....139 A5
arton Ave PL2 .....127 E5
arton Cl
  Bodmin PL31 .....109 D5
  Heamoor TR18 .....143 D7
Plymouth PL7 .....131 C5
andrake PL12 .....53 C3
Plymouth PL7 .....131 C5
arton La TR9 .....58 A7
arton Mdw Pelynt PL13 .....62 D6
Truro TR1 .....137 A5
arton Mdws PL12 .....53 B7
arton Mews
andrake PL12 .....53 C3
Millbrook PL10 .....132 F6
arton Rd Plymouth PL9 .....135 B6
St Dennis PL26 .....58 A7
arton The PL29 .....22 C6
arview La TR27 .....142 C4
arwis Hill TR13 .....143 E6
arwis Terr TR18 .....143 E6
assinghall Cl PL9 .....135 E5
asket Ope PL4 .....149 A2
asset Rd TR14 .....138 D2
asset St Camborne TR14 .....138 D2
  Falmouth TR11 .....145 A5
  Redruth TR15 .....140 C4
assett Cl PL26 .....47 A1
assett Pl TR11 .....145 A5
assett Rd Illogan TR16 .....67 E4
  Redruth TR15 .....140 B8
astville EX22 .....11 E8
ath La PL1 .....148 B2
ath Pl PL1 .....148 B2
ath Pl W PL1 .....148 B2
ath St PL1 .....148 B2
atter St PL4 .....149 A2
attershall Cl PL9 .....135 F5
attery Hill TR16 .....142 C6
attery La Polruan PL23 .....116 C2
  Tavistock PL19 .....147 C4
attery Mill La TR27 .....77 E1
attery Pk PL23 .....116 C2
attery Rd TR13 .....143 F4
attery St PL1 .....148 A2
attery Street Flats
PL1 .....148 A2
attery The TR7 .....73 C3
attery The TR7 .....110 D7
awden Rd PL31 .....109 B3
ay Apartments TR7 .....110 A6
ay Ct TR11 .....145 C2
ay Rd PL18 .....20 F2
ay St PL13 .....117 D3
ay The PL13 .....117 D3
ay Tree Cotts EX23 .....4 D1
ay View Cres TR11 .....145 D3
ay View Pk PL25 .....114 F6
ay View Rd PL13 .....117 D4
ay View Terr
Hayle TR27 .....142 C6
  Newlyn TR18 .....143 C2
  Penzance TR18 .....143 D4
  Porthleven TR13 .....98 B8
ay Villas TR20 .....88 F6
aydon Cl PL6 .....125 C1
aydon PL13 .....117 D5
ayly's Rd PL9 .....135 B7
aynards Cl PL3 .....137 D4
aynes Ct PL14 .....38 A3
aytree Ave PL1 .....148 B4
aytree Cl PL6 .....125 D6
aytree Gdns PL2 .....128 A7
aytree Hill PL14 .....113 C5
ayview Dr PL13 .....117 E4
ayview Rd TR7 .....110 D7
ayview Wlk TR27 .....142 A8
each Hill PL11 .....64 C4
each Rd
Carbis Bay TR26 .....141 D2
Crantock TR8 .....42 A3
Mevagissey PL26 .....73 C4
  Newquay TR7 .....110 D6
Newquay, Porth TR7 .....111 B8
Perranporth TR6 .....55 A5
Porthtowan TR4 .....68 A6
St Austell PL25 .....115 D3
St Ives TR26 .....141 A6
Trevone PL28 .....20 F2
each View Cl TR7 .....111 C7
eachfield Ave TR7 .....110 D6
eachfield Cl TR18 .....143 D4
eachside Cl TR4 .....68 A6
eachside L Pk TR7 .....78 A6
eachview Flats TR4 .....68 A6
eacon Bsns Pk Pl2 .....128 C7
eacon Cl Falmouth TR11 .....145 A5
  St Austell PL25 .....115 A5
eacon Com Jun Sch
TR11 .....145 A5
eacon Cross PL26 .....72 F4
eacon Down Ave PL2 .....128 B7
eacon Dr TR5 .....54 B1

Beacon Est TR20 .....87 D4
Beacon Farm TR5 .....54 C1
Beacon Fields TR14 .....138 E2
Beacon Hill PL31 .....109 D4
Beacon Hill Mews PL31 .....109 D4
Beacon Ho PL3 .....129 D4
Beacon Inf Sch TR11 .....145 A5
Beacon Lanes PL31 .....109 D3
Beacon Parc TR13 .....146 C6
Beacon Park Rd PL2 .....128 B7
Pelynt PL13 .....62 D5
Beacon Rd Bodmin PL31 .....109 E3
  Falmouth TR11 .....145 A5
Foxhole PL26 .....58 D5
Marazion TR17 .....89 B5
Newquay TR7 .....110 D7
Porthleven TR13 .....98 B8
St Agnes TR5 .....54 C1
Summercourt TR8 .....57 B7
Beacon Sq TR11 .....138 E1
Beacon St TR11 .....145 B5
Beacon Terr
Camborne TR14 .....138 E1
  Falmouth TR11 .....145 A5
Helston TR13 .....58 D5
Lizard TR12 .....102 F2
Beacon View Pk TR16 .....67 E4
Beaconfield Rd PL2 .....128 B7
Beaconfield Pl TR5 .....54 C1
Beaconsfield Pl TR31 .....109 C5
Beaconside Foxhole PL26 .....58 D5
Summercourt TR8 .....57 B7
Bealswood Cl PL18 .....41 A6
Bealswood Rd PL18 .....41 A6
Beam Rd PL26 .....47 C1
Beare Cl PL9 .....135 F5
Bears Terr TR16 .....80 E7
Bearsdown Cl PL6 .....129 C8
Bearsdown Rd PL6 .....129 C8
Beatrice Ave
Plymouth Keyham PL2 .....127 E5
Plymouth St Jude's PL4 .....149 B3
Saltash PL12 .....122 C2
Beatrice Gdns PL12 .....122 C1
Beatrice Rd PL11 .....48 D8
Beatrice Terr TR27 .....142 D7
Beatrice Rd PL5 .....127 B8
Beatty Cl PL1 .....125 A4
Beauchamp Cres PL2 .....128 C7
Beauchamp Rd PL2 .....128 C7
Beauchamps Mdw TR15 .....140 D2
Beaudyn Wlk PL6 .....129 C7
Beaufighter Ave PL27 .....31 F3
Beaufort Ave PL27 .....31 F3
Beaufort Ho PL4 .....149 A2
Beauly Cl PL7 .....131 A5
Beaumaris Gdns PL3 .....128 F8
Beaumaris Rd PL3 .....128 F7
Beaumont Ave PL4 .....149 A3
Beaumont Pl PL4 .....149 A3
Beaumont Rd PL4 .....149 A3
Beaumont St PL11 .....128 A5
Beaumont Terr PL12 .....122 F4
Beck Adams PL12 .....53 C3
Beckett Cl TR15 .....140 C4
Beckford Cl PL7 .....131 A5
Beckham Pl PL4 .....129 A6
Beckly Ct PL1 .....148 C3
Bede Gdns PL5 .....124 C1
Bede Haven Cl EX23 .....104 E4
Bedford Ct PL31 .....109 D4
Bedford Mews PL4 .....149 A4
Bedford Park Villas PL4 .....149 A4
Bedford Pk
  Bere Alston PL20 .....41 B3
Plymouth PL4 .....149 A4
Bedford Pl
  Bere Alston PL20 .....41 B3
  St Ives TR26 .....141 B5
Bedford Rd
Horrabridge PL20 .....42 C4
Plymouth PL9 .....135 C7
  St Ives TR26 .....141 B5
Bedford Sq PL19 .....147 C5
Bedford St
Bere Alston PL20 .....41 B3
Plymouth PL2 .....127 F5
Bedford Terr PL4 .....149 A4
Bedford Villas PL4 .....41 B3
Bedford Way PL1 .....148 C3
Bedowan Mdws TR7 .....111 A6
Bedruthan Ave TR7 .....137 E6
Bee Cr PL27 .....22 A6
Beech Ave Liskeard PL14 .....113 B5
Plymouth PL4 .....149 C2
Beech Cl Falmouth TR11 .....144 F5
Tavistock PL19 .....147 C2
Torpoint PL11 .....127 A3
Beech Ct PL6 .....125 D5
Beech Dr Bodmin PL31 .....109 B4
  St Columb Major TR9 .....45 D6
Beech Hall Flats PL8 .....95 A6
Beech La PL25 .....114 D3
Beech Rd
  Callington PL17 .....39 F4
  Falmouth TR11 .....144 F5
St Austell PL25 .....114 D3
Beech Terr PL13 .....117 C4
Beechcroft Rd
Plymouth Lower Compton
PL3 .....129 A6
Plymouth, Deacon Park
PL2 .....128 B7

Beeches The PL14 .....38 E4
Beechfield Ave PL20 .....42 D3
Beechfield Gr PL3 .....128 E6
Beeching Pk PL17 .....39 F6
Beechwood Ave PL4 .....128 D4
Beechwood Cross PL7 .....131 F7
Beechwood Gdns TR1 .....137 E6
Beechwood Rise PL6 .....125 E1
Beechwood Terr PL4 .....128 D4
Beechwood Way PL7 .....131 D5
Beehive Workshops
TR10 .....144 A7
Beeston Wlk PL6 .....129 C7
Behenna Dr TR1 .....145 E3
Bekelege Dr TR14 .....138 F1
Belah Mdw PL32 .....16 A8
Belair Rd PL2 .....128 C7
Belair Villas PL2 .....128 C7
Belerion Rd TR16 .....67 C5
Belgrave La PL4 .....128 F4
Belgrave Rd PL4 .....128 F4
Belgrave Terr PL14 .....113 D6
Belgravia St TR18 .....143 E5
Bell Cl PL4 .....130 F6
Bell Hill PL26 .....85 C5
Bell La Bodmin PL31 .....109 E5
Lanner TR16 .....80 D6
Bell Veor TR16 .....80 E6
Bell View TR13 .....146 B6
Bella Vista Gdns TR10 .....81 E2
Bellair Rd TR20 .....143 A8
Bellair Terr TR11 .....141 B6
Bellamy Cl PL6 .....125 A1
Bellatt PL27 .....108 D6
Belle Acre Cl PL3 .....128 F6
Belle La Bude EX23 .....104 D6
Newlyn TR18 .....143 C1
Belle Vue Ave
Bude EX23 .....104 D6
Plymouth PL9 .....135 B5
Belle Vue La EX23 .....104 D6
Belle Vue Rd
Plymouth PL9 .....135 C5
Saltash PL12 .....122 F2
Belle Vue Rise PL9 .....135 B5
Belle Vue Terr
Gunnislake PL18 .....41 A6
  Penzance TR18 .....143 E6
Bellever Parc TR14 .....138 F4
Bellevue Hill PL16 .....27 C7
Bellevue Cotts TR10 .....81 E2
Bellevue Sq PL11 .....127 B2
Bellingham Cres PL7 .....131 C4
Belliver Ind Est PL6 .....121 B1
Belliver Way PL6 .....121 B1
Bells Ct TR15 .....139 C7
Belmont Cl PL19 .....147 C3
Belmont Ct
  Plymouth PL3 .....128 A4
  Wadebridge PL27 .....108 B5
Belmont Mews PL14 .....38 D4
Belmont Pk PL14 .....38 D4
Belmont Pl Newquay TR7 .....110 D7
Plymouth PL3 .....128 A4
  St Ives TR26 .....141 A6
Belmont Rd
Falmouth TR11 .....145 A3
Helston TR13 .....146 B7
St Austell PL25 .....114 C3
Belmont St Par PL24 .....60 D5
Plymouth PL1 .....148 B3
Belmont Terr Devoran TR3 .....81 F6
  St Ives TR26 .....141 A6
Belstone Cl PL5 .....124 B4
Belstone La TR20 .....89 F5
Belvedere Rd PL4 .....129 B2
Belyars Ct TR26 .....141 B4
Belyars La TR26 .....141 A4
Bemallack Ct TR11 .....137 E4
Benbow St PL2 .....127 F4
Bencoolen Rd EX23 .....104 D5
Beneathway PL14 .....50 E7
Benhole La PL12 .....121 D5
Bennett La PL12 .....122 C1
Bennett St PL2 .....127 F4
Bennetts Cotts TR10 .....144 C7
Benson Gdns TR1 .....137 D5
Benson Ho TR1 .....137 D5
Benson Rd TR1 .....137 D5
Bentley Dr EX23 .....4 D1
Beramic Cl PL27 .....78 D6
Bere Alston Prim Sch
PL20 .....41 B2
Bere Alston Sta PL20 .....41 B2
Bere Ferrers Sta PL20 .....119 E3
Berepper Cross TR12 .....98 E5
Beresford St PL2 .....127 A4
Berkeley Cl EX23 .....4 D1
Berkeley Cotts TR11 .....145 A4
Berkeley Path TR11 .....145 A4
Berkeley Vale TR11 .....145 A4
Berkshire Dr PL2 .....127 F5
Bernice Cl PL4 .....129 B4
Bernice Terr PL4 .....129 B4
Berries Ave EX23 .....104 F4
Berries Mount EX23 .....104 F4
Berrow Park Rd PL3 .....128 E6
Berry Head Gdns PL6 .....124 E1
Berry La PL31 .....109 E5
Berry Park Cl PL9 .....135 E6
Berry Park Rd PL9 .....135 E6
Berry Rd TR7 .....110 E6

Berrycombe View
PL31 .....109 D5
Berrycoombe Hill PL31 .....109 C5
Berrycoombe Prim Sch
PL31 .....109 A4
Berrycoombe Rd PL31 .....109 C5
Berrycombe Vale PL31 .....109 C5
Berryfields Ho PL31 .....109 A5
Berryhill PL31 .....47 C6
Berryman Cres TR11 .....144 F3
Berthon Rd PL5 .....127 C8
Berveth Cl TR13 .....69 D3
Berwick Ave PL5 .....124 E3
Bess Park Rd PL27 .....108 B6
Bethan Dr PL27 .....108 B5
Bethany Homes PL14 .....138 C2
Bethany Pl TR19 .....86 F6
Bethel Rd PL25 .....114 C3
Bethesda Gdns TR26 .....141 B6
Betjeman Wlk PL7 .....124 C3
Beverley Cres TR27 .....142 E7
Beverley Rd PL3 .....129 C4
Beverston Way PL6 .....125 B8
Beweys Pk PL12 .....122 C2
Beyrout Pl PL1 .....127 F3
Bickern Rd PL11 .....127 B3
Bickford Cres TR13 .....91 B1
Bickford Rd PL15 .....106 B8
Bickham Park Rd PL3 .....128 D7
Bickham Rd PL5 .....123 D2
Bickland Hill TR11 .....144 D4
Bickland Water Rd
TR11 .....144 D2
Bickleigh Cl PL6 .....125 D7
Bickleigh Down CE Prim Sch
PL6 .....125 D7
Bickleigh Down Rd PL6 .....121 D1
Bicton Cl PL5 .....125 D1
Biddick Dr PL2 .....127 F6
Biddick's Ct PL25 .....115 B5
Bideford Wlk PL6 .....129 E8
Big Gn PL13 .....62 D1
Bigbury Wlk PL6 .....129 E8
Biggin Hill PL5 .....123 F4
Bilbury St PL4 .....149 A3
Billacombe Rd PL9 .....129 E1
Billacombe Villas PL9 .....135 F8
Billing Cl PL6 .....124 D6
Billings Dr TR7 .....111 B5
Billington Cl PL4 .....129 B7
Binhamy Cl EX23 .....104 F4
Binhamy Rd EX23 .....7 B8
Binkham Hill PL20 .....42 D3
Birch Cl PL6 .....125 D7
Birch Gr TR27 .....142 B3
Birch Pond Rd PL9 .....135 D7
Bircham View PL6 .....125 C1
Birches The PL6 .....125 D6
Birchfield Ave PL2 .....128 C6
Birchill PL30 .....47 C6
Birchwood Dr PL19 .....147 A7
Birchwood Gdns PL7 .....131 A7
Birkbeck Cl PL7 .....131 E7
Birkdale Cl PL12 .....122 C2
Biscombe Gdns PL12 .....122 C2
Biscombes La PL17 .....39 E4
Biscovey Jun & Inf Schs
PL24 .....115 F5
Biscovey Rd PL24 .....60 B4
Biscovey Rd PL25 .....115 B5
Bishop Bronescombe CE Sch
PL25 .....115 B5
Bishop Cornish CE Prim Sch
PL12 .....122 F1
Bishop Temple Rd TR1 .....137 F6
Bishop's CE Prim Sch The
TR7 .....110 F4
Bishop's Hill Rd PL27 .....21 D5
Bishop's Rd TR26 .....141 B5
Bishops Cl TR1 .....137 C6
Bissoe Rd TR3 .....81 F7
Bissom TR10 .....144 C8
Bitterne Dr PL5 .....124 B3
Black Rd TR27 .....142 D7
Blackall Gdns PL6 .....124 D6
Blackberry La PL15 .....135 E8
Blackberry Way TR1 .....137 F5
Blackbrook Cl PL20 .....42 E4
Blackberry Ct TR14 .....68 E5
Blackfriars La PL1 .....149 A2
Blackmore Cres PL6 .....124 D6
Blacksmith La PL27 .....78 D6
Blackstone Cl PL9 .....136 B6
Blackthorn Cl
Plymouth, Honicknowle
PL5 .....124 B3
Plymouth, Woolwell PL6 .....125 D8
Blackwater Com Prim Sch
TR4 .....68 C5
Bladder La PL5 .....124 E2
Blagdon Cross EX21 .....13 F8
Blagdon Lodge Cross
EX21 .....13 F8
Blairgowrie Rd PL5 .....123 C2
Blake Gdns PL5 .....113 D7
Blakes Pk PL14 .....113 D7
Blanchard Pl PL7 .....130 E7
Blanchdown Dr PL18 .....40 F7
Blanchminster Rd EX23 .....104 E5
Blandford Rd PL3 .....129 C6
Blatchborough Cross
EX22 .....3 D2
Blaxton La PL5 .....120 E1
Blenheim Rd PL4 .....149 A4

Bligh Cres TR13 .....146 C5
Blight's Row TR15 .....140 B5
Blind La PL11 .....64 D6
Blindhole PL15 .....106 C6
Blindwell Hill PL10 .....132 E5
Blisland Com Prim Sch
PL30 .....35 D7
Bloom Fields TR18 .....143 C5
Bloomball Cl PL3 .....129 B6
Blowing House Cl PL25 .....114 B4
Blowing House Hill
Crowlas TR20 .....89 B8
Hayle TR20 .....77 A1
St Austell PL25 .....114 C4
Blowing House La PL25 .....114 B4
Blowinghouse Hill TR15 .....140 A4
Blowinghouse La PL30 .....109 B2
Blue Haze Cl PL6 .....125 D5
Bluebell Cl PL12 .....122 D4
Bluebell Way PL19 .....147 E4
Blunts La PL6 .....125 C3
Boaden Cl PL12 .....53 E5
Boakanza St TR26 .....141 C2
Boase St TR18 .....143 C1
Bochym Hill TR12 .....99 C3
Boconnic La TR20 .....42 D3
Boconnoc Ave PL27 .....39 F3
Boconnoc Rd PL25 .....114 D2
Bodelva Rd PL24 .....115 E8
Bodgara Way PL15 .....113 D6
Bodgare Way Flats
PL14 .....113 D6
Bodieve Rd PL27 .....108 D7
Bodinar Rd PL31 .....81 D2
Bodinel Rd PL31 .....109 C6
Bodinnick Rd PL31 .....109 C6
Bodiniel View PL31 .....109 B5
Bodinnar Cl TR20 .....87 E6
Bodinnar La TR20 .....87 E6
Bodinnick Hts PL23 .....116 E5
Bodinnick Parc PL30 .....23 E3
Bodinnick Rd PL30 .....23 C3
Bodmin & Wenford Rly
PL30,PL31 .....109 D2
Bodmin Bsns Ctr PL31 .....109 E3
Bodmin Bsns Pk PL31 .....35 B2
Bodmin Com Coll PL31 .....109 E3
Bodmin General Sta
PL31 .....109 E3
Bodmin Hill PL22 .....112 B4
Bodmin Hospl PL31 .....109 B4
Bodmin Jail PL31 .....109 D5
Bodmin Parkway Sta
PL30 .....49 A7
Bodmin Rd Plymouth PL5 .....124 D3
St Austell PL25 .....114 C6
Truro TR1 .....137 E6
Bodmin Town Mus
PL31 .....109 E4
Bodrigan Rd PL13 .....117 D5
Bodriggy Cres TR27 .....142 C5
Bodriggy St TR27 .....142 D6
Bodriggy Prim Sch
Hayle TR27 .....142 D5
Hayle TR27 .....142 D6
Bodriggy St TR27 .....142 D6
Bodriggy Villas TR27 .....142 D6
Body's Cr PL18 .....40 F6
Bohella Rd TR2 .....95 A6
Bohelland Rd TR10 .....144 D8
Bohelland Rise TR10 .....144 D8
Bohill TR10 .....144 D7
Bohill Ct TR10 .....144 D7
Boiler Works Rd TR14 .....138 E5
Bojea Ind Est PL25 .....114 C7
Bojea Terr PL25 .....114 C6
Bojewyan Stennack TR19 .....75 B1
Bokenna Cross PL14 .....37 C1
Boldventure Ave PL25 .....115 B5
Boldventure Cl PL25 .....115 B5
Bolenna La TR6 .....55 A4
Bolenowe Terr TR14 .....79 E4
Bolingey Chapel Flats
TR6 .....55 B4
Bolingey Rd TR6 .....55 B4
Bolitho Rd TR18 .....143 C4
Bolitho Sch The TR18 .....143 C5
Bolowthas Cnr TR7 .....111 A7
Bolowthas Way TR7 .....111 C7
Bolster Cl TR5 .....54 C1
Bolt House Ct PL9 .....147 A5
Boltern Rd TR17 .....89 C5
Bolventor La PL13 .....63 E8
Bon Cot Rd TR18 .....143 C2
Bonallack La TR12 .....92 D1
Bonathon Cl TR11 .....82 A3
Bonville Rd PL6 .....124 E6
Bonython Cl TR11 .....72 A7
Bonython Rd TR7 .....111 B7
Bonython Terr PL14 .....111 B3
Boon's Pl PL1 .....148 C4
Borgwitha TR16 .....80 B5
Borington Ave PL5 .....127 D8
Borington Cl PL7 .....130 D7
Borrington Hill PL7 .....130 E7

Boringdon Mill Bsns Ctr PL7 .130 F6
Boringdon Prim Sch PL7 .130 D7
Boringdon Rd
Plymouth, Plympton PL7 .130 D6
Plymouth, Turnchapel PL9 .135 A7
Boringdon Terr
Plymouth, Plympton PL7 .130 D6
Plymouth, Turnchapel PL9 .135 A7
Boringdon Villas PL7 .130 D6
Borlase CI TR13 .146 B5
Borough Cross EX22 .7 F5
Borough Ct PL11 .126 D4
Borough Pk PL11 .126 E4
Borrowdale CI PL6 .124 D5
Bosawna CI TR16 .68 E1
Boscarn CI TR14 .79 B5
Boscarn Rd TR15 .140 D6
Boscarne Cres PL25 .114 F3
Boscarne Junction Sta* PL30 .34 D2
Boscarne View PL30 .34 D2
Boscarnek TR27 .142 A1
Boscastle Com Prim Sch PL35 .9 C1
Boscastle Gdns PL2 .128 C8
Boscastle Visitor Ctr* PL35 .9 D2
Boscaswell Downs TR19 .75 A1
Boscaswell Est TR19 .74 F1
Boscaswell Rd TR19 .75 A1
Boscathnoe La TR18 .143 B7
Boscathnoe Way TR18 .143 B7
Boscawen Gdns 11 TR6 .55 A4
Boscawen Pk PL26 .58 B8
Boscawen PI PL22 .127 E4
Boscawen Rd
Chacewater TR4 .69 A3
Falmouth TR11 .145 B2
Helston TR13 .146 D4
Perranporth TR6 .55 A4
St Dennis PL26 .58 C8
Boscawen St TR1 .137 D4
Boscean CI TR14 .79 E4
Boscoppa CI TR15 .140 D7
Boscoppa Rd
St Austell PL25 .115 A5
St Austell PL25 .115 B5
Boscundle Ave TR11 .144 F1
Boscundle CI PL25 .115 D5
Boscundle Row PL12 .123 A2
Bosence Rd TR27 .90 C7
Bosillion La TR2 .72 A7
Bosinney Rd PL25 .114 D3
Bosinver La PL26 .59 A1
Boskear La PL31 .109 A4
Boskennal Barton TR19 .97 B6
Boskennal La TR19 .97 B6
Boskennal Dr TR27 .142 B4
Boskenwyn Com Prim Sch TR13 .92 A3
Boskernick CI TR18 .143 B1
Boskerris Cres TR26 .141 D2
Boskerris Mews TR26 .141 D1
Boskerris Rd TR26 .141 D2
Boslandew Hill TR19 .88 C2
Bosleake Row TR15 .139 C3
Bosloggas Mews 9 TR11 .145 C3
Boslowick CI TR11 .144 F3
Boslowick Ct TR11 .144 E2
Boslowick Rd TR11 .144 E2
Bosmeor CI TR11 .144 E2
Bosmeor Pk TR11 .139 D6
Bosmeor Rd TR11 .144 E3
Bosnoweth Helston TR13 .146 D5
Probus TR2 .71 D6
Bosolllow Vean TR20 .87 D8
Bosorne CI TR19 .86 E6
Bosorne Rd TR19 .86 E6
Bosorne St TR19 .86 E6
Bosorne Terr TR19 .86 E6
Bosparva La
Leedstown TR27 .78 F2
Praze-an-Beeble TR14 .79 A3
Bospolvans Rd 2 TR9 .45 D6
Bospowis TR14 .138 C3
Bossiney Rd PL34 .14 D7
Bostennack PI PL26 .141 A5
Bostennack Terr 11 TR26 .141 A5
Bosuen Rd PL7 .111 A7
Bosvean Gdns
11 Illogan TR16 .67 E4
Truro TR1 .137 B5
Bosvean Rd TR14 .69 F6
Bosvenna View PL31 .109 E4
Bosvenna Way TR18 .143 B7
Bosvenning PI TR20 .87 E6
Bosvigo Gdns* TR1 .137 A5
Bosvigo La TR1 .137 B5
Bosvigo Rd TR1 .137 C4
Bosvigo Sch TR1 .137 C4
Boswedden PI TR19 .86 E6
Boswedden Rd TR19 .86 E6
Boswell CI PL6 .124 E2
Boswerry TR23 .143 C5
Boswithian Rd TR14 .138 F6
Bosworgey CI 3 TR9 .45 D6
Bosworthy Rd TR27 .90 B8
Botallack La TR19 .86 E7

Botetoe Hill TR14 .79 C4
Botetoe Rd TR14 .79 B4
Botha Rd 11 PL7 .31 F3
Bothwicks Rd TR7 .110 E6
Boughhayes Est PL19 .147 A5
Boulden CI PL7 .131 C5
Boulter CI PL6 .121 C1
Bound The PL10 .133 A1
Boundary Rd
Bodmin PL31 .109 A4
Dousland PL20 .42 E3
Bounder Treath PL12 .101 C3
Bounders La TR6 .55 B4
Boundervean La TR14 .138 B2
Bounds Cross EX22 .8 B4
Bounds PI PL1 .148 B2
Bounsall's La PL15 .106 C5
Bounsalls Ct PL15 .106 C5
Bourne CI PL12 .129 D6
Boveway Dr PL14 .113 E5
Boveway La PL14 .113 D5
Boville La PL9 .136 C7
Bovisand Ct PL9 .134 F2
Bovisand La
Down Thomas PL9 .135 B2
Staddiscombe PL9 .135 D3
Bovisand Pk PL9 .135 A3
Bovisand Rd PL9 .135 E3
Bow La PL6/3 .4 E6
Bowden Park Rd PL6 .125 A1
Bowdens Row TR15 .140 A4
Bowers Park Dr PL6 .125 E7
Bowers Rd PL2 .128 B5
Bowglas CI TR20 .89 A8
Bowhays Wlk 2 PL6 .129 C7
Bowjey Ct 11 TR18 .143 C1
Bowjey Hill TR18 .143 C1
Bowjey Terr 5 TR18 .143 C1
Bowles Rd PL11 .145 A6
Bowling Gn
Menheniot PL14 .51 F5
34 St Ives TR26 .141 B6
Bowling Gn Terr 35
Bowling Gn The TR2 .82 F2
Bowling Green Ct
Hayle TR27 .142 D5
Liskeard PL14 .113 B5
Bowling Green Rd TR13 .92 F3
Bowmder Dower TR27 .142 B3
Bowmder Vean PL25 .115 A5
Bowood Pk PL32 .24 B8
Box's Shop EX23 .7 A4
Boxhill Ct PL5 .124 B3
Boxhill Gdns PL12 .128 C8
Boxwell Pk PL31 .109 F4
Boyd Ave PL28 .107 C5
Boyton Com Prim Sch PL15 .13 A3
Bracken CI Bodmin PL31 .109 F5
Plymouth PL6 .125 D8
Bracken Terr TR7 .110 E5
Brackenside PL13 .62 D1
Brackwell PI PL27 .108 B5
Braddock CE Prim Sch PL22 .49 D6
Braddock CI PL26 .58 C6
Braddons Hill PL7 .130 B7
Bradfield CI PL6 .125 E1
Bradford CI PL6 .125 D8
Bradford Quay Rd PL27 .108 C6
Bradley Rd Newquay TR7 .111 C7
Plymouth PL4 .128 F4
Braemar CI PL4 .131 C4
Braeside Pk PL14 .50 E8
Braggs Hill PL15 .101 D8
Brake La PL10 .132 B5
Brake Rd PL5 .124 E2
Brake The PL14 .37 F4
Bramble CI Newquay TR7 .111 A4
Widemouth Bay EX23 .6 F5
Bramble Hill EX23 .104 E5
Bramble Wlk 11 PL6 .129 C7
Bramblebank TR11 .145 B7
Brambles The PL14 .111 C7
Bramfield PI PL6 .129 D7
Bramley CI PL25 .114 E4
Bramley Pk PL31 .109 F5
Brancker Rd PL2 .128 C6
Brandon Rd PL2 .129 C4
Brandon Terr 2B TR26 .141 B6
Brandon Wlk PL25 .6 F5
Brandreth Rd 4 PL3 .128 F6
Brandy La TR20 .89 A8
Branksome Dr PL27 .108 E5
Brannel Sch PL26 .58 B3
Branscombe Gdns PL5 .124 A3
Branson Ct 8 PL7 .131 C5
Branson Pk PL19 .42 A6
Branwell La TR18 .88 E6
Braunton Wlk PL6 .129 E8
Bray CI PL9 .147 A5
Bray's PI PL25 .114 F4
Brayford CI PL5 .124 B3
Brays Terr 2 TR16 .140 F1
Brazacott Cross PL15 .12 B2
Brea Arch TR14 .69 A5
Brea Rd PL27 .21 D2
Bread St PL18 .143 E5
Breage CE Prim Sch TR13 .90 F3
Break My Neck La TR20 .88 E8
Breakwater Hill PL4 .149 C1
Breakwater Ind Est PL9 .135 C8
Breakwater Rd
Bude EX23 .104 D5

Breakwater Rd continued
Plymouth PL9 .135 C8
Brean Down CI PL3 .128 E6
Brean Down Rd PL3 .128 E7
Breaside TR14 .139 A3
Brecon CI Plymouth PL3 .129 A7
2 St Agnes TR5 .54 C1
Bree Shute La PL31 .109 E5
Brent Knoll Rd 3 PL3 .128 E6
Brent Tor* PL19 .30 D7
Brentford Ave PL5 .124 B5
Brenton Rd PL11 .64 B5
Brentons Pk PL29 .22 D6
Brentor Rd
Mary Tavy PL19 .30 F6
Plymouth PL4 .129 B2
Brentwartha PL13 .62 E2
Breoke Hts PL27 .108 A5
Brest Rd PL6 .125 A3
Brest Way PL6 .125 A3
Breton Side PL4 .149 A2
Brett Wlk PL7 .130 F7
Brewers CI PL30 .47 F6
Brewers Hill PL26 .58 C8
Brewers Rd TR1 .137 F5
Brewery Hill TR2 .146 B6
Brewery La TR13 .146 B6
Briansway PL22 .122 D2
Briar Rd Bude EX23 .104 E4
Plymouth PL3 .128 F7
Briar Tor PL20 .42 D3
Briardale Rd PL2 .127 F6
Briarfield PL23 .116 D4
Briarleigh CI PL6 .125 F2
Briars Row PL12 .122 D4
Briars Ryns PL12 .33 D7
Briarwood PL14 .113 D5
Brickworks Hill TR16 .68 D1
Bridals La PL13 .62 E2
Bridge TR9 .45 E7
Bridge CI PL7 .111 A4
Bridge Ct PL25 .114 F4
Bridge Hill Illogan TR16 .67 E5
St Columb Major TR9 .45 E6
Bridge Ho The 16 TR18 .143 C2
Bridge La PL12 .53 A3
Bridge Pk EX22 .8 A5
Bridge Rd Goonhavern TR4 .55 D6
Illogan TR16 .67 E4
Mousehole TR19 .88 C1
Tideford PL12 .52 F2
Bridge St Par PL24 .60 B6
2 Stratton EX23 .4 D1
Bridge The PL1 .148 B1
Bridge View PL27 .108 C6
Bridgemead CI PL26 .114 C1
Bridgemoor Cross EX22 .8 C6
Bridgerule CE Prim Sch EX22 .8 A5
Bridgerule Ind Est EX22 .7 F4
Bridges The PL12 .122 E1
Bridie CI PL7 .131 B7
Bridle Way
Quintrell Downs TR8 .44 E3
Saltash PL12 .122 D2
Bridwell CI PL5 .127 E8
Bridwell La N PL5 .127 E8
Bridwell Rd PL5 .127 E8
Brillwater Rd TR11 .92 E4
Brimford Cross EX39 .3 D4
Brimhill CI PL7 .131 B3
Brisbane Terr PL11 .113 C5
Brismar Wlk 2 PL6 .129 C7
Briston Orch PL12 .53 E7
Britannia PI PL4 .149 A3
British Cycling Mus* PL32 .105 C8
British Rd TR5 .54 D1
Briton's Hill TR18 .143 F6
Brixham Wlk PL6 .129 E8
Brixton Lodge Gdns PL8 .136 F5
Brixton Terr TR13 .146 C6
Broad CI EX22 .11 E7
Broad La Illogan TR15 .139 D7
Trematon PL12 .53 E2
Broad Mead PL17 .39 E5
Broad Park Rd
Bere Alston PL20 .41 B2
Plymouth PL3 .128 D6
Broad Pk
Launceston PL15 .106 B7
Tavistock PL19 .147 B6
Broad St
10 Launceston PL15 .106 C6
Lifton PL16 .19 F4
Newquay TR7 .110 D6
Padstow PL28 .107 D5
Penryn TR10 .144 D7
7 St Columb Major TR9 .45 E6
Truro TR1 .137 C5
Broad View TR4 .56 D1
Broad Wlk Helston TR13 .146 B7
Saltash PL12 .122 E1
Broadclose Hill EX23 .104 E5
Broadland Gdns PL9 .136 A8
Broadland La PL9 .135 F8
Broadlands CI PL7 .131 A3
Broadley CI PL6 .121 B2
Broadley Ind Pk PL6 .121 B2
Broadley Park Rd PL6 .121 B2
Broads La TR11 .81 F3
Broads Yd PL11 .64 C5
Broadshaft Cross EX22 .8 A4
Broadway The PL9 .135 C7

Brock Ho 10 PL4 .149 A2
Brockley Rd PL3 .129 C4
Brockstone Rd PL25 .115 A5
Brockton Gdns PL4 .125 B6
Brokenhill Cres TR2 .57 E1
Bromhead CI PL6 .129 A8
Bromley 6 PL2 .128 A4
Bromscombe Dr TR10 .144 D7
Bronte PI PL5 .124 D1
Brook CI Helston TR13 .146 B7
Plymouth PL7 .131 A3
Brook Ct 6 TR11 .145 A4
Brook Dr EX23 .104 E7
Brook La PL19 .147 B2
Brook PI Falmouth TR11 .145 A4
Penryn TR10 .144 C7
Brook Rd Falmouth TR11 .144 F3
Wadebridge PL27 .108 B5
Brook St Falmouth TR11 .145 A4
10 Mousehole TR19 .88 C1
Tavistock PL19 .147 C6
Brookdale CI PL27 .108 B5
Brookdown Terr PL12 .122 E3
Brookdown Villas PL12 .122 E3
Brooke CI PL12 .123 A2
Brookfield CI Lanjeth PL26 .58 E3
Plymouth PL7 .131 B5
Brooking Way PL12 .122 C3
Brookingfield CI PL7 .130 C5
Brooklands La PL6 .124 E3
Brooklands CI PL6 .124 E3
Brooklyn Flats 11 TR2 .95 A6
Brooklyn Terr 11 TR2 .95 A6
Brooks PL22 .49 E3
Brooks La PL10 .132 F5
Brookside St Austell PL25 .114 F4
Chacewater TR4 .69 A3
Brookside CI PL15 .106 B8
Brookward Terr 8 TR18 .143 C7
Brookway TR27 .142 E7
Brookwood Rd PL9 .136 D7
Broom Hill PL12 .122 D2
Broome CI PL25 .114 C3
Broomfield Dr
Bodmin PL31 .109 B3
Plymouth PL9 .135 C5
Broomfield Rd PL27 .108 D5
Broomhill Cross EX22 .5 E3
Broughton CI PL3 .128 F7
Brown's Hill TR10 .144 C8
Browne Meml Almshouses PL19 .147 A5
Browning Dr PL31 .109 C3
Browning Rd PL2 .128 A5
Brownlow PI PL31 .109 D5
Brownlow St PL1 .148 A2
Browns Hill PL23 .116 C4
Broxton Dr PL9 .129 E1
Brunel Ave PL2 .127 F5
Brunel Prim Sch PL12 .122 E2
Brunel Terr 8 PL2 .127 F5
Brunel Way PL1 .148 A2
Brunswick PI 10 PL2 .127 F4
Brunswick Rd PL4 .149 B2
Brush End TR26 .77 E4
Brynmoor CI PL3 .129 A7
Brynmoor Pk PL3 .129 A6
Brynmoor Wlk PL3 .129 A6
Bryny CI PL30 .23 E7
Buckett's Hill TR15 .140 C2
Buckeys La TR2 .95 B6
Buckfast CI PL2 .128 A8
Buckingham Nip TR4 .68 F3
Buckingham PI PL5 .123 E2
Buckingham Terr TR16 .68 A1
Buckingham's CI TR8 .56 B7
Buckland Abbey* PL20 .41 F1
Buckland CI PL7 .130 D7
Buckland St PL1 .148 B2
Buckland Terr PL20 .42 C2
Bucklawren Rd PL13 .63 C7
Buckler Village (Mobile Homes Pk) PL25 .115 B4
Bucklers La PL25 .115 B4
Buckwell St PL1/4 .149 A2
Buctor Pk PL19 .41 D8
Buddle CI Plymouth PL9 .136 A5
Tavistock PL19 .147 B6
Bude Ind Est EX23 .104 E4
Bude Inf Sch EX23 .104 E5
Bude Jun Sch EX23 .104 E5
Bude-stratton Mus* EX23 .104 D5
Budehaven Cvn Site EX23 .104 E5
Budemeadows Cvn Site EX23 .7 A4
Budge Mdws PL15 .106 C6
Budleigh Ct PL9 .135 E5
Budnic Est TR6 .55 B5
Budnic Hill TR6 .55 B5
Budock Hospl TR11 .144 D5
Budock CI PR TR11 .145 B4
Budock Vean La TR11 .93 B2
Budshead Gn PL5 .124 C3
Budshead Rd PL5 .124 C4
Budshead Way PL5 .124 E2
Buena Vista CI PL6 .125 D6
Buena Vista Dr PL6 .125 D6
Buena Vista Gdns PL6 .125 C6
Buena Vista Way PL6 .125 C6

Bugle Prim Sch PL26 .47
Bugle Rural Workshops PL26 .47
Bugle Sta The TR20 .89
Buildings The TR20 .89
Bull Hill PL23 .116
Bull Point Prim Sch
PL26 .122
Bullan's La TR26 .141
Bullans Terr 5 TR26 .141
Bulleid CI PL2 .127
Bulleid Way EX23 .104
Bulleid Way EX23 .104
Buller CI Plymouth PL7 .130
Torpoint PL11 .127
Buller Hill TR16 .80
Buller Pk Liskeard PL14 .113
Saltash PL12 .122
Buller Rd PL11 .127
Buller St PL13 .117
Bullers Terr TR15 .140
Bullock La Helston TR13 .146
Helston, Whitehill TR13 .146
Bullock Market Terr 28
TR18 .143
Bulmer Rd PL4 .149
Bulteel Gdns PL6 .124
Bulwark Rd TR13 .146
Bungalows The PL7 .117
Bunkers Hill
8 St Ives TR26 .141
Townshend TR27 .90
Bunyan CI PL5 .124
Burden CI PL3 .109
Burgess CI EX23 .4
Burfos Row TR13 .79
Burhos Row EX22 .79
Burias Row TR18 .143
Burleigh La PL3 .128
Burleigh Manor PL3 .128
Burleigh Park Rd PL3 .128
Burley Ct TR1 .137
Burley St TR11 .145
Burn Layne PL19 .30
Burn View EX23 .104
Burnard CI PL6 .124
Burnards CI 8 PL31 .109
Burnett CI PL12 .122
Burnett Rd PL6 .128
Burnham Park Rd PL3 .128
Burnistone CI PL7 .131
Burns Ave PL5 .124
Burns View PL11 .65
Burnthouse PL14 .37
Burnthouse Cotts TR10 .81
Burnthouse La TR27 .142
Burraton Com Prim Sch
PL12 .122
Burraton Rd PL12 .122
Burrator Rd PL20 .42
Burrington Ind Est PL5 .124
Burrington Rd PL5 .124
Burrington Way PL5 .124
Burrow Hill PL9 .135
Burrows The TR20 .141
Burslam Door Cross EX39 .3
Burthallan La TR26 .77
Burton CI PL6 .125
Burwell CI PL6 .125
Bury CI PL15 .11
Bush Hill PL14 .36
Bush Pk Launceston PL15 .106
Plymouth PL6 .125
Butcher Park Hill PL19 .147
Bute Rd PL4 .129
Butney Cnr TR14 .66
Butt Park Rd PL5 .124
Butterdown PL12 .122
Buttlegate PL11 .64
Butts La PL35 .9
Butts Pk PL22 .112
Butts The PL13 .56
Buttsbear Cross EX22 .7
Byard CI PL5 .123
Byland Rd PL3 .129
Byron Ave PL5 .124

C

Cabot CI PL12 .122
Cades Parc TR13 .146
Cadoc CI PL28 .107
Cadogan CI TR14 .138
Cadogan Rd TR14 .138
Cadover CI PL6 .125
Caernarron Gdns PL2 .128
Cai Hill TR16 .140
Calais Rd PL2 .142
Calartha Rd TR19 .75
Calartha Terr TR19 .75
Calder CI PL3 .129
Caldicot Gdns PL6 .125
Caldwells Rd PL14 .113
Caledonia CI 11 PL7 .131
Calenick St TR1 .137
California Gdns PL3 .129
Callestock Cider Farm* TR4 .55
Callington Com Coll PL17 .39
Callington Mus* PL17 .39
Callington Prim Sch PL17 .39
Callington Rd
Harrowbarrow PL17 .40
Liskeard PL14 .113
Saltash PL12 .122
Tavistock PL19 .147

loose Farm Cvn Pk
27 78 D2
loose La E TR27 78 D1
loose La W TR27 78 D1
lywith Gate Ind Est
31 35 B2
shot Cl TR7 111 E7
stock Com Prim Sch
18 41 A3
stock Rd PL18 41 A6
stock Sta PL17 41 A3
vez Cl PL10 132 F6
naret Dr TR26 141 B4
nbeak PL35 9 C1
nbeak Cl EX23 10 C6
nbeltown Way TR11 145 C3
nber Rd PL1 148 A1
mborne Cl PL5 124 A5
mborne Geological Mus &
rt Gal TR15 139 B6
mborne Redruth Com
ospl
edruth TR15 140 A4
edruth, Blowinghouse
R15 139 F6
mborne Ret Pk TR15 139 B5
mborne Sch & Com Coll
R14 138 B3
mborne Sch of Mines
R15 139 B6
mborne Sta TR14 138 D2
mbridge La W 5 PL1 148 B3
mbridge Pl TR11 145 A3
mbridge Rd PL2 127 F5
mden Ct PL4 149 A3
mden St PL4 149 A3
mel Cl PL28 107 D4
mel Ct PL30 109 C6
mel Valley Vineyard*
L30 34 B2
melford Prim Sch
L32 105 C3
melot Ct 2 TR18 143 E5
melot View PL32 105 C8
melside PL27 108 C5
meron Cl EX23 104 D7
meron Way PL6 125 B1
milla Terr PL2 128 D7
mp Cross PL15 19 F7
mp Hall Rd TR8 43 B1
mpbell Rd PL9 135 F7
mperdown St PL2 127 F4
mperknowle Cl PL10 132 F6
mpfield Hill TR1 137 D5
mpion Cl
Plymouth PL7 131 C5
altash PL12 122 D4
mpion Rise PL19 147 D6
mpion View PL6 125 E8
mullas Way TR7 110 A5
nal Rd PL19 147 B5
ndish Dr PL9 136 D7
nefields Ave PL7 131 B3
nfield Pl TR15 140 A5
nfield Terr TR15 140 A5
nhaye Cl PL7 131 A3
nn Gdns PL6 124 D6
nn Wood View PL6 125 E7
nna Pk* PL15 18 D3
nnamanning Rd 3
L26 59 D7
nnis Rd PL25 114 E6
nnon Hill PL14 113 C5
nnon St PL1 127 D2
nnon Terr 2 PL14 113 C5
nnons Pl TR13 146 D7
nons Way PL19 147 A3
nterbury Dr PL5 124 B4
ntillion Cl PL27 21 E3
nton PL26 85 D5
nyke Rd PL31 48 D8
pe Cl TR19 86 E6
pe Cornwall Rd TR19 86 E6
pe Cornwall Sch TR19 86 E6
pe Cornwall St TR19 86 E6
pe Terr TR19 86 E6
pe Trelew TR19 86 E6
ptain's Wlk TR11 145 A2
ptains Gdns PL5 124 E1
ptains Ho PL26 73 C3
radon Bsns Ctr 8
L14 113 C5
radon Cl
9 Callington PL17 39 E4
1 Pensilva PL14 38 E4
Plymouth PL6 125 A5
radon Ct 2 PL20 42 C4
radon Dr PL14 113 B6
radon Hts
iskeard PL14 113 D7
remar PL14 38 B4
radon Terr PL12 122 E3
radon View PL14 37 F3
rbeile Rd PL11 127 A2
rbeile Sch PL11 127 A3
rbes La PL22 112 C2
rbis Bay Holiday Pk
TR26 77 C4
rbis Bay Sta TR26 141 D2
rbis Beach Apartments
TR26 141 D2
rbis Ct TR15 140 A5
rboth La PL15 106 B5
rclaze Com Inf Sch
PL25 114 E6
rclaze Com Jun Sch
PL25 114 E6
rclaze Ind Est PL25 114 E7
Carclaze Rd PL25 114 E6
Carclew Ave TR7 110 E6
Carclew Rd TR11 81 F4
Carclew St TR1 137 D3
Carclew Terr Devoran TR3 81 F6
Truro TR1 137 D3
Cardell Rd PL31 109 D5
Cardell Way TR7 111 A5
Cardiff Cl PL7 131 B4
Cardigan Rd PL6 125 C1
Cardinal Ave PL5 127 D8
Cardinham Prim Sch
PL30 35 F3
Cardinham Woods Forest
Walks* PL30 35 C1
Cardinnis Gn PL14 113 D6
Cardinnis Rd TR18 143 B5
Cardrew Bsns Pk TR15 140 C6
Cardrew Cl TR15 140 B6
Cardrew Ind Est TR15 140 D7
Cardrew Jun Sch TR15 140 C5
Cardrew La 1 TR15 140 C5
Cardrew Terr TR15 140 D6
Cardrew Way TR15 140 D7
Cardwen Est PL13 62 C6
Careswell Ave PL2 127 F8
Carew Ave PL5 124 B3
Carew Cl Crafthole PL11 65 B5
St Day TR16 68 E1
Carew Gdns
Plymouth PL5 124 B3
Saltash PL12 122 D3
Carew Gr PL5 124 B3
Carew Rd St Day TR16 68 D1
Truro TR1 137 C5
Carew Terr PL11 127 B2
Carew Wharf PL11 127 C2
Carew-Pole Cl TR1 137 E3
Carey Ct PL12 122 E3
Carey Pk Helston TR13 146 B7
Polperro PL13 62 E2
Truro TR1 137 C4
Cargoll Rd TR8 56 B7
Cargwyn PL26 59 D6
Carisbrooke Rd PL6 125 C1
Carkeek's Cl PL26 58 B3
Carland Cross TR8 56 D4
Carlidnack Cl TR11 93 D3
Carlidnack La TR11 93 D4
Carlidnack Rd TR11 93 E4
Carlisle Rd PL5 124 D3
Carloggas Cl TR8 45 A8
Carloggas Farm TR8 45 A8
Carloggas Gr 6 TR9 45 D6
Carloggas Way 10 TR9 45 D6
Carlton Cl PL3 129 B5
Carlton Terr
Plymouth, Lipson PL4 149 B3
Plymouth, Weston Mill PL5 127 E8
Carlton Vills PL12 53 E4
Carlyon Cl
Threemilestone TR3 69 D3
Torpoint PL11 126 F4
11 Truro TR1 137 C4
Carlyon Ho TR1 69 E4
Carlyon Rd
Playing Place TR3 82 B8
St Austell PL25 114 E4
Truro TR1 137 C5
Carmarthen Rd PL4 129 B2
Carmel Gdns PL19 147 A5
Carmen Sq 10 TR18 143 C7
Carminow Cross PL30 48 D8
Carminow Rd PL31 48 D8
Carminow Road Ind Est
PL31 48 D8
Carminow Way TR7 111 A7
Carminowe Cres 8
TR18 143 D5
Carmython Ct TR7 111 B7
Carn Ave TR14 138 F2
Carn Bosavern TR19 86 F6
Carn Bosavern Cl TR19 86 F6
Carn Brae Ho TR15 139 C5
Carn Brae Village TR15 139 F5
Carn Brea Ave TR15 139 C5
Carn Brea La TR15 139 C5
Carn Cl TR27 78 E1
Carn Euny Settlement*
TR20 87 C3
Carn Gloose Rd TR19 86 D6
Carn Gwavas Terr TR18 143 D1
Carn Marth La TR16 140 E2
Carn Rock TR10 144 D7
Carn Ros TR19 74 F1
Carn View TR16 80 F6
Carn View Terr TR19 75 A1
Carnarthan Moor TR15 139 C3
Carnarthen Rd TR14 138 E3
Carnarthen St TR14 138 E2
Carncrows St TR26 141 C6
Carne Cross PL24 59 F7
Carne Ct PL26 58 C8
Carne Hill St Dennis PL26 46 C1
Trewoon PL25 58 F4
Carne Mdws TR2 70 F5
Carne View Cl TR14 138 F5
Carne View Rd TR2 71 D6
Carne's Bldgs 10 TR18 143 E4
Carnedon PL14 38 C7
Carnego La TR8 57 B6
Carnellis Rd 7 TR26 141 A5
Carnes Ct TR11 145 C2
Carneton Cl TR8 43 D3
Carnglaze Caverns*
PL14 36 F1
Carnhell Rd TR14,TR27 78 F4
Carninney La TR26 141 C1
Carnkie Com Prim Sch
TR16 139 D2
Carnkief Cnr TR4 55 D4
Carnock Rd PL2 128 D8
Carnon Cres 13 TR3 81 F7
Carnon Terr TR3 81 F6
Carnoustie Dr PL12 122 C2
Carnsew Cl TR10 81 C1
Carnsew Cres TR10 81 C1
Carnsew Mdw TR27 142 A5
Carnsew Rd TR27 142 A5
Carnsmerry PL26 47 C1
Carnsmerry Cres PL25 114 E4
Carnstabba Rd 13 TR26 77 A6
Carntiscoe Workshops
TR27 77 C2
Carnyorth Hill TR19 86 F8
Carnyorth Terr TR19 86 F8
Carolina Gdns PL2 127 F7
Caroline Cl TR27 142 E7
Caroline Pl PL1 148 A2
Caroline Row TR27 142 E7
Carpalla Rd PL26 58 D5
Carpalla Terr PL26 58 D5
Carpenter Rd PL9 135 F8
Carpenter St PL31 109 E5
Carpmael Ave TR8 111 B4
Carracawn Cross PL12 64 D8
Carrack Dhu 37 TR26 141 B6
Carrack Dhu Terr 36
TR26 141 B6
Carrack Gladden TR26 141 D2
Carradale Rd PL6 129 C7
Carrallack Mews TR19 86 E6
Carrallack Terr TR19 86 E5
Carriage Parc TR4 55 D4
Carrick Rd TR11 144 E2
Carrick Way TR2 95 A6
Carrickowel Cres 1
PL25 115 A5
Carrine Rd TR1 69 F3
Carrisbrooke Way PL12 122 B2
Carrnown Gdns TR15 140 D3
Carroll Rd PL5 124 C2
Carron La PL6 121 D1
Carsize La TR27 78 E1
Carter Cl TR7 111 A5
Carteret Rd EX23 104 E5
Carthew Cl
Liskeard PL14 113 D5
St Ives TR26 141 A6
Carthew Ct TR26 141 A6
Carthew La Burras TR13 80 A3
Praze-an-Beeble TR13 79 F2
Carthew Terr TR26 141 A6
Carthew Way TR26 141 A6
Carvath Ho PL25 114 D3
Carvedras Ct 1 TR1 137 C4
Carvosse Est TR20 89 B8
Carvoza Rd TR1 137 D5
Carvynick Cotts TR8 57 A7
Carwin La TR27 78 C5
Carwin Rise
Angarrack TR27 78 C5
Hayle TR27 142 E7
Carwinard Cl TR27 78 C5
Carwinion Rd TR11 93 E3
Carworgie Ct TR9 45 E2
Carworgie Manor Pk
TR8 45 D3
Carworgie Way TR9 45 E2
Carwynnen Cl TR14 79 B3
Casey La PL13 62 D5
Castel Wary Cl TR13 146 B5
Casterills Rd TR13 146 D4
Castle Acre Gdns PL3 129 B5
Castle Bank Gdns PL3 129 B5
Castle Barbican PL7 130 E4
Castle Bldgs PL12 122 D4
Castle Canyke Rd PL31 109 F3
Castle Carey Gdns PL3 129 B5
Castle Cl TR11 145 E3
Castle Ct
Praa Sands TR20 90 C3
Saltash PL12 122 C2
Castle Dr Bodmin PL31 109 F5
Falmouth TR11 145 F2
Praa Sands TR20 90 B3
St Mawes TR2 94 F5
Castle Dyke PL15 106 C6
Castle Dyke La PL1 149 A2
Castle Gdns PL14 113 C6
Castle Gn TR13 146 B5
Castle Hill Helston TR13 146 B5
4 Liskeard PL14 113 C6
Lostwithiel PL22 112 C2
Saltash PL12 122 C1
Castle Hill Ct PL31 109 E5
Castle Hill Gdns PL31 109 F5
Castle Horneck Cl TR18 143 C5
Castle Horneck Rd
TR18 143 C5
Castle Hts PL34 14 C7
Castle La Liskeard PL14 113 C6
Plymouth PL7 130 E4
Castle Mdws
Launceston PL15 106 A4
2 St Agnes TR5 54 D1
Castle Meadows Ct 3
TR5 54 D1
Castle Rd Crowlas TR20 89 A8
Longrock TR20 88 F8
Penzance TR18 143 E7
Tintagel PL34 14 C7
Castle Rise
Plymouth PL3 129 B4
Saltash PL12 122 D1
Truro TR1 137 C5
Castle St Bodmin PL31 109 F5
Launceston PL15 106 C6
Liskeard PL14 113 C6
Looe PL13 117 D3
Plymouth PL1 149 A2
Truro TR1 137 C4
Castle View Longrock TR20 88 F6
Lostwithiel PL22 112 E3
Saltash PL12 122 D1
Tintagel PL34 14 C7
Castle View Cl TR15 140 B6
Castle View Pk TR11 93 D3
Castlehayes Gdns PL7 130 E4
Castlemead Cl PL12 122 D3
Castlemead Dr PL12 122 D3
Castleton Cl PL3 129 A4
Caswarth Terr PL28 107 D5
Catalina Row PL27 31 F3
Catalina Villas PL9 135 A6
Cath of St Mary & St
Boniface PL1 148 B3
Cathcart Ave PL4 129 B2
Cathebedron Rd
Carnhell Green TR14 78 F4
Praze-an-Beeble TR14 79 A3
Cathedral Church of the
Blessed Virgin Mary*
TR1 137 D4
Cathedral La 13 TR1 137 D4
Cathedral St PL1 148 B3
Cathedral View TR1 137 C6
Catherine Cl EX23 104 F4
Catherine Pk PL13 62 E5
Catherine St PL1 148 C2
Catherine's Hill PL15 106 A6
Cattedown Rd PL4 149 C1
Catterick Cl PL5 123 E5
Cattewater Rd PL4 129 B1
Caudledown La PL26 59 C8
Caunter Rd PL14 113 D6
Causeland Sta PL14 51 B2
Causeway The
Falmouth TR11 144 F4
Hayle TR27 142 A4
Causewayhead TR18 143 E5
Causley Cl PL15 106 C7
Cavendish Rd PL4 129 B1
Caxton Gdns PL5 124 C1
Cayforth Flats TR16 67 C6
Cayley Way PL5 123 F2
Cecil Ave PL4 149 C4
Cecil Cotts PL1 148 A3
Cecil St PL1 148 B3
Cedar Ave PL9 135 C5
Cedar Cl
21 Callington PL17 39 F4
Torpoint PL11 126 F2
Cedar Ct Camborne TR14 139 A5
Saltash PL12 122 F2
Cedar Dr PL11 126 F2
Cedar Gr EX23 104 E7
Cedar House Flats TR26 77 E4
Cedarcroft Rd PL2 128 B7
Celandine Gdns PL7 131 C5
Celia Hts PL31 109 F2
Celtic Rd PL17 39 F4
Cemetery Rd PL18 40 F5
Centenary Row Middle
TR14 138 E3
Centenary Row W TR14 138 E2
Centenary St TR14 138 E3
Central Ave PL25 114 E5
Central Cl PL26 58 B4
Central Park Ave PL4 148 C4
Central Rd Holywell TR8 43 B1
Plymouth PL1 148 B1
Central Sq TR7 110 D6
Century Cl Helston TR13 146 D8
St Austell PL25 114 F6
Century Ct TR7 111 C7
Century La TR2 83 F6
Century Sq 7 PL14 38 E4
Ceres Ct EX23 104 E4
Chacewater Hill TR4 69 A3
Chacewater Prim Sch
TR4 69 A3
Chaddlewood Ave PL4 149 B3
Chaddlewood Cl PL7 131 A4
Chaddlewood Ho PL7 131 B5
Chaddlewood Inf Sch
PL7 131 A5
Chaddlewood Prim Sch
PL7 131 A5
Chagford Wlk PL6 129 E8
Chainwalk Dr TR1 137 C6
Challacombe Gdns
TR10 144 C8
Challenger Quay 12
TR11 145 C3
Challgood Cl PL9 135 F5
Challgood Rise PL9 135 F5
Challis Ave TR8 45 A8
Challock Cl PL6 125 D4
Chamberlayne Dr PL7 130 E6
Champion's Ct TR13 146 B6
Chancery Cl TR4 70 D8
Chancery La 23 TR18 143 E5
Chandos Pl 12 PL25 114 C3
Channel Park Ave PL3 129 B5
Channel View
Polruan PL23 116 D2
St Ives TR26 141 A6
Channel View Terr
Plymouth PL4 149 C4
4 Redruth TR15 140 C4
Channon Rd PL12 122 C4
Chantry Ct PL7 130 B5
Chantry La PL13 117 E4
Chantry Pk PL17 39 E4
Chapel Cl Camborne TR14 66 F1
Coad's Green PL15 27 D3
Connor Downs TR27 78 D6
Crantock TR8 110 A3
Gunnislake PL18 40 E5
5 Horrabridge PL20 42 C4
St Just In Roseland TR2 82 F2
Chapel Cnr EX22 8 A5
Chapel Cotts EX23 4 C8
Chapel Cres TR4 56 A2
Chapel Ct
Camborne TR14 138 F4
Padstow PL28 107 D5
Chapel Farm TR14 79 E5
Chapel Field PL25 115 B5
Chapel Gn PL26 59 A1
Chapel Ground PL13 117 C3
Chapel Hill
Camborne, Brea TR14 139 A3
Camborne, Tregajorran
TR15 139 C4
Gweek TR12 92 C2
Hayle TR27 142 C6
Lanner TR16 80 D6
Launceston PL15 106 B5
Newquay TR7 110 D6
Perranporth TR6 55 B4
Polgooth PL26 59 A1
Ponsanooth TR3 81 B4
Porthtowan TR4 68 A5
Redruth TR16 68 A4
St Erth TR27 142 A1
Sticker PL26 58 F1
Truro TR1 137 B4
Chapel La
Bodmin PL31 109 D5
Goldsithney TR20 89 F5
Hayle TR27 142 D6
4 Horrabridge PL20 42 C4
2 Horrabridge PL20 42 C5
Penryn TR10 144 C7
Polruan PL23 116 D2
St Austell PL25 115 C6
St Teath PL30 23 F6
5 Wadebridge PL27 108 B5
Wadebridge, St Mabyn
PL30 34 D8
Chapel Mdw
Buckland Monachorum PL20 41 F3
Perranwell Sta TR3 81 D6
Chapel Park Terr PL15 106 B5
Chapel Pk PL15 106 B5
Chapel Pl Pillaton PL12 53 B7
16 Truro TR1 137 D4
Chapel Point La
PL26 73 C2
Chapel Rd
Camborne TR14 139 A4
Foxhole PL26 58 D5
Heamoor TR18 143 C8
Indian Queens TR9 45 E1
Leedstown TR27 78 E1
2 Par PL24 60 C4
Roche PL26 46 F3
Saltash PL12 122 B3
St Just TR19 86 E6
St Tudy PL30 23 E3
Chapel Row
Praze-an-Beeble TR14 79 B2
2 Redruth TR15 140 B5
Tremar PL14 38 A3
Truro TR1 137 D4
Widegates PL13 63 F8
Chapel Sq Crowlas TR20 89 B8
Mevagissey PL26 73 C3
Troon TR14 79 E5
Chapel St
4 Bere Alston PL20 41 B1
4 Callington PL17 39 F4
Camborne TR14 138 D2
Camelford PL32 105 C4
Grimscott EX23 5 B2
Gunnislake PL18 40 F6
Marazion TR17 89 B5
Mevagissey PL26 73 C3
20 Mousehole TR19 88 C1
9 Newlyn TR18 143 C2
Penzance TR18 143 E5
Plymouth PL4 149 A3
Plymouth,
Mount Wise PL1 127 E2
Probus TR2 71 C6
Redruth TR15 140 B5
St Day TR16 68 D1
St Ives TR26 141 B5
St Just TR19 86 E6
Tavistock PL19 147 B5
Chapel Terr
Camborne TR15 139 D6
Devoran TR3 81 F6
Falmouth TR11 145 B4
Hayle TR27 142 B5
Par PL24 60 B6
9 Porthleven TR13 98 B8
Redruth TR15 140 D2
Redruth, Carn Brae Village
TR15 139 F5
Ruan Minor TR12 103 A5
St Day TR16 68 E1
10 St Mawes TR2 95 A6
Trewellard TR19 86 F8

Chapel Town Cl TR11 ....93 D4
Chapel Way PL3 ....129 A6
Chapeldown Rd PL11 ....127 A2
Chapman Cl PL12 ....122 B3
Chapmans Ope PL1 ......127 D2
Charaton Cross PL14 ....38 F4
Chard Barton PL5 ....124 B3
Chard Rd PL5 ....123 D2
Chard Terr 6 TR11 ......145 A3
Charfield Dr PL6 ....129 A8
Charles Ave TR1 ....139 E6
Charles Bassett Cl 5
  TR13 ....146 C3
Charlotte Cl PL25 ....114 F3
Charlotte St PL2 ....127 C4
Charlton Cres PL6 ......125 A2
Charlton Rd PL6 ....125 A3
Charnhill Cl PL9 ....136 A6
Charnhill Way PL9 ......136 A6
Charter Cl TR13 ....146 C4
Charter Ct TR10 ....144 D7
Charter Way PL14 ......113 E6
Chatsworth Gdns PL25 ..123 F3
Chatsworth Way PL25 ...115 C2
Chaucer Prim Sch PL5 ..124 C2
Chaucer Rd PL19 ....147 D5
Chaucer Way PL5 ....124 C1
Chawleigh Cl PL18 ......40 F5
Chedworth St PL4 ......149 A3
Chegwins Hill PL26 ......58 D5
Chegwin Gdns 6 TR5 ...54 C1
Chegwyns PL26 ....58 D5
Cheltham Sch PL20 .....40 F3
Chellean Mear TR4 .....81 C7
Chellew Rd TR1 ....137 F5
Chelmer Cl PL7 ....131 A5
Chelmsford Pl PL5 ......124 C4
Chelson Gdns PL6 ......125 E3
Cheltenham Pl
  Newquay TR7 ....110 D6
  Plymouth PL4 ....149 B4
Cheney Mill Farm Pk*
  TR27 ....77 E1
Chenhalls Cl PL25 ......77 E2
Chenhalls Rd PL27 .....142 A2
Chenoweth Cl TR14 ....138 D4
Chepstow Ave PL6 .....125 C8
Chequetts Cl 10 PL17 ...39 E4
Cheriton Cl PL24 ....124 A3
Cherrill Gdns PL23 .....104 E7
Cherry Cross PL22 ......12 B7
Cherry Gdns 2 TR18 ...143 E5
Cherry Pk PL7 ....131 A3
Cherry Tree La PL7 ....131 A4
Cherry Tree Mews PL25 .114 D3
Cheshire Dr PL6 ....126 D6
Chester Ct TR7 ....111 A6
Chester Pl 3 PL4 ......128 E4
Chester Rd PL1 ....111 A6
Chesterfield Rd PL3 ....129 B4
Chesterton Cl PL5 .....124 C3
Chesterton Ct PL2 .....108 A6
Chesterton Pl TR7 .....111 A7
Chestnut Ave PL7 .....135 C6
Chestnut Cl
  Callington PL17 ....40 A4
  Falmouth TR11 ....144 F1
  Lamerton PL19 ....30 A4
  Saltash PL30 ....122 D4
  St Tudy PL30 ....23 E3
  Tavistock PL19 ......147 D2
  Torpoint PL11 ....126 F3
Chestnut Gr PL31 .....109 D6
Chestnut Rd PL3 ......128 D7
Chestnut Terr PL19 ....30 A3
Cheviot Rd TR1 ....137 C5
Chichester Cres
  Newquay TR7 ....110 F4
  Saltash PL12 ....122 E1
Chichester Ct PL20 ....42 C4
Chichester Ho PL1 ....148 B2
Childrey Gdns PL6 ....125 C5
Childrey Wlk PL6 ......125 C1
Chili Rd TR15 ....139 D6
Chilton Cl PL6 ....129 B7
Chings Alley 11 PL16 ..106 C6
Chippords Dr PL25 ....114 A3
Chirgwin Ct 22 TR18 ..143 E5
Chirgwin Rd TR1 ......137 E4
Chisholme Ct PL25 ....114 D3
Chisholme Ct PL25 ....114 D3
Chittleburn Cross PL8 .136 E5
Chittleburn Hill PL8 ...136 E5
Chivenor Ave PL5 .....123 D4
Chiverton Cross
  Blackwater TR4 ......68 F5
  Rosudgeon TR20 .....99 F4
Chiverton Greenacres
  TR5 ....68 D8
Chiverton Way TR20 ...96 A4
Chollacott Cl PL19 ....147 C4

Chollacott La PL19 .....147 D3
Chough Cl
  Falmouth TR11 ....144 E4
  Launceston PL15 .....106 E4
Chough Cres PL25 .....73 C4
Choughs Cl TR14 ......138 B3
Christa Ct PL14 ....38 D7
Christian Mill Bsns Pk
  PL6 ....124 E4
Christian Way PL5 ....111 C7
Chubb Dr PL3 ....128 B4
Chudleigh Rd PL4 .....129 A4
Church Cl Lelant TR26 ..77 E4
  Plymouth PL7 ....130 B7
  St Erme TR4 ....56 D1
Church Cove Rd PL12 ..103 A2
Church End PL13 ......117 D3
Church Gate 8 PL14 ...113 C5
Church Hill Calstock PL18 ..43 A3
  Chacewater TR4 .....68 F2
  Crowlas TR20 ....89 A8
  Golant PL23 ....61 B6
  Helston TR13 ....146 C7
  Herodsfoot PL14 .....50 E3
  Hessenford PL11,PL12 ..64 B8
  Milton Combe PL20 ...41 F1
  Penryn TR10 ....144 C8
  3 Penzance TR18 ....143 E4
  Plymouth PL6 ....125 B1
  Port Isaac PL29 ......22 D7
  St Day TR16 ....68 E1
  2 St Mawes TR2 .....95 A6
  Sticker PL26 ....58 F1
  Tavistock PL19 ......147 E2
  Tintagel PL34 ....14 C7
Church Hill Rd PL9 ....135 A6
Church La Bodmin PL31 ..109 E5
  Calstock PL18 ....41 A3
  Camborne TR14 ......138 D3
  Cargreen PL12 ......119 A1
  Flushing TR11 ....145 B8
  Helston TR13 ....146 B6
  Lelant TR26 ....77 E4
  Lostwithiel PL22 .....112 C2
  Mevagissey PL26 ....73 C4
  Padstow PL28 ....107 D5
  Redruth TR15 ....140 A3
  St Columb Minor TR7 ..111 E7
  St John PL11 ....132 B8
  Tavistock PL19 .....147 C5
Church Lea
  Launceston PL15 .....106 A7
  Tavistock PL19 ......147 E2
Church Mdws EX22 ...11 E8
Church Park Ct PL6 ...125 E8
Church Park Mews
  PL27 ....108 B4
Church Park Rd
  Crackington Haven EX23 ..10 C6
  Plymouth PL6 ....125 E8
Church Path EX23 .....104 C5
Church Pk Bodmin PL31 ..109 F5
  Horrabridge PL20 ....42 C4
  Lanjarth PL22 ....70 C4
  St Mellion PL12 ......53 D8
Church Pl Liskeard PL14 ..113 C5
  10 St Ives TR26 .....141 B6
Church Rd
  Camborne, Pool TR15 ..139 B6
  Camborne, Treswithian
    TR14 ....138 B3
  Cury TR12 ....99 A4
  Four Lanes TR16 ....60 A5
  Heamoor TR18 ......143 C7
  Illogan TR16 ....67 E4
  Lanivet PL30 ....47 E7
  Lelant TR26 ....77 E4
  Mabe Burnthouse TR10 ..93 C8
  Madron TR20 ....143 A8
  Mount Hawke TR4 ...68 C6
  Mylor Bridge TR11 ..82 B2
  Pendeen TR19 ....75 F1
  Penponds TR14 .....138 B1
  Penryn TR10 ....144 C8
  Perranarworthal TR3 ..81 D5
  Plymouth, Plymstock PL9 ..130 F4
  Plymouth, Plymstock PL9 ..135 E3
  Saltash PL12 ....122 D2
  Shortlanesend TR4 ..69 F6
  St Austell PL25 .....115 B3
  St Dennis PL26 .....46 C1
  St Tudy PL30 ....23 E3
  Stithians TR3 ....80 F4
  Tideford PL12 ....52 F2

Church St continued
  Padstow PL28 ....107 D5
  Par PL24 ....60 B5
  Par, Tywardreath PL24 ..60 D5
  Plymouth PL3 ....128 A4
  Poughill EX23 ....4 D2
  8 St Austell PL25 ...114 C3
  St Columb Minor TR7 ..111 D7
  St Day TR16 ....68 E1
  St Erth TR27 ....142 A1
  St Germans PL12 ....65 A8
  St Just TR19 ....86 F6
  8 Stratton EX23 ....4 E1
Church St N PL14 .....113 C5
Church St S PL14 .....113 C5
Church Terr Devoran TR3 ..81 F6
  Grampound Road TR2 ..57 E1
  6 St Austell PL25 ...114 C3
Church Town Rd TR16 ..67 F5
Church View St Neot PL14 ..36 F2
  Treburley PL15 ......28 B5
  Walkhampton PL20 ...42 E4
Church View Rd
  Camborne TR14 .....138 F4
  Probus TR2 ....71 D6
Church Way
  Falmouth TR11 ......144 E3
  Plymouth PL5 ....127 B3
  St Cleer PL15 ....17 B2
Church Wlk PL15 ......27 E8
Churchfield Ct TR20 ..89 A8
Churchfields Rd TR8 ..55 D8
Churchill Rd PL19 ....147 D2
Churchill Way PL3 ....128 E6
Churchill Wlk PL22 ...122 E1
Churchlands PL13 .....117 D5
Churchlands Cl PL6 ...125 E7
Churchlands Rd PL6 ..125 E8
Churchtow Wlk PL6 ..129 E8
Churchtown
  Cardinham PL30 .....35 F3
  Gwinear TR27 ......78 D4
  7 Mullion TR12 ......99 A2
  8 St Agnes TR5 .....54 C1
  St Minver PL27 .....22 A4
  St Newlyn East TR8 ..56 B7
Churchtown Mdws PL26 ..58 B4
Churchtown Rd
  Gwithian TR27 ......66 B2
  Phillack TR27 ....142 C7
  Portscatho TR2 .....83 B6
  St Stephen PL26 ....58 B4
Churchtown Vale PL12 ..122 E3
Churchway Madron TR20 ..143 A8
  4 Mawnan PL12 .....122 E3
Chute La PL26 ....85 D5
Chy An Dour TR27 ....142 E7
Chy Hwel TR1 ....137 F6
Chy Kensa Cl TR27 ...142 C5
Chy Nampara 1 TR11 ..145 A4
Chy-An-Cby 10 TR26 ...141 B6
Chy-An-Dour Cl 1 TR26 ..77 A4
Chy-An-Dour Rd TR20 ..90 C3
Chy-an-Gweal Est TR20 ..89 A7
Chy-an-hall Hill TR18 ..143 F8
Chy-an-Mor TR18 .....88 F6
Chyanclare TR18 ......143 D6
Chyanduance Ct TR18 ..143 F8
Chyanduance Terr TR18 ..143 F8
Chyandor Cl PL14 ....60 C4
Chyandour Cl TR26 ...77 A6
Chyandour Cliff TR18 ..143 F6
Chyandour La TR18 ...143 F7
Chyandour Sq TR18 ...143 F7
Chyandour Terr TR18 ..143 F7
Chycoose Parc TR3 ...82 A5
Chycornick Terr TR18 ..143 F8
Chygothow TR13 .....146 B6
Chylan Cres TR7 .....111 E6
Chymeddon TR7 .....110 E6
Chynance Penzance TR18 ..143 D4
  Portreath TR16 .....67 C6
Chynance Dr TR7 ....110 D5
Chynowen La TR8 ....43 D1
Chynowen Parc TR8 ..43 D1
Chynoweth PL26 .....59 C8
Chynoweth Gdns TR18 ..143 F8
Chynoweth La TR20 ..89 A8
Chypons Est TR18 ....76 F3
Chypons Rd TR12 ....99 B3
Chypraze Ct TR14 ...138 B3
Chyreen La
  Carnon Downs TR3 ..81 F8
  Playing Place TR3 ..82 A8
Chyrn Dr PL30 ....24 B3
Chyrose Rd TR16 ....68 D1
Chrysauster Settlement*
  TR20 ....76 D2
Chytodden Terr TR13 ..90 F5
Chytroose Cl TR13 ...146 D8
Chyvelah Ope TR1 ...69 E3
Chyvelah Rd TR3 ....69 E3
Chyvelah Vale TR1 ...69 E3
Chyvellas Cl TR18 ...143 B1
Chyventon Cl TR19 ...97 B6
Chyventon Ho TR15 ..140 B5
Chyverton Cl TR7 ....110 D4
Chywoon Gdns TR15 ..139 D7
Chywoone Ave TR18 ..143 C1
Chywoone Cres TR18 ..143 C1
Chywoone Hill TR18 ..143 C1
Chywoone Pl TR18 ...143 C1
Chywoone Rural Workshops
  TR19 ....87 A5
Citadel Ope 06 PL1 ...149 A2
Citadel Ct PL1 ....149 A2
Citadel Rd E PL1 .....149 A2
Citadel The* PL1 .....149 A1
City Bsns Pk PL3 ....128 A4

City Mus & Art Gal*
  PL4 ....149 A3
City Mus & Art Gal Annexe*
  PL4 ....149 A3
City Rd TR1 ....137 C4
Clairemont Pl 1 PL14 ..38 A3
Clampet La PL12 .....65 E4
Clann La PL30 ....47 E2
Clann Mdws PL30 ....47 F2
Clare Pl PL4 ....149 B2
Clare Terr TR11 ......145 A5
Claremont Cotts 1
  TR11 ....145 A5
Claremont Falls PL13 ..62 E2
Claremont Rd TR15 ..140 B5
Claremont St PL1 ....148 C4
Claremont Terr 3 TR11 ..145 A5
Clarence Ct PL1 .....148 A3
Clarence Pl
  20 Penzance TR18 ...143 E6
  Plymouth, Morice Town
    PL2 ....127 C4
  Plymouth, Stonehouse PL1 ..148 A3
Clarence Rd
  St Austell PL25 .....114 B4
  Torpoint PL11 ....127 B3
Clarence St TR18 ....143 E5
Clarence Terr
  8 Penzance TR18 ...143 E6
  7 Wadebridge PL27 ..108 B5
Clarence Villas TR15 ..140 D6
Clarendon Ho PL1 ....127 F3
Claybourne Ct PL25 ..114 F6
Claylands PL30 ......24 A1
Clayton Pl PL4 ....129 B2
Clayton Rd PL4 ......129 B2
Clear View PL12 ......122 E2
Clearbrook Ave PL5 ..123 E1
Clease Mdws PL32 ...105 C3
Clease Rd PL32 ......105 C4
Clease The PL32 .....105 C3
Cleave Cres EX23 ....4 B8
Cleave The PL30 .....133 B2
Cleaveland PL27 .....108 C4
Cleaverfield Mews
  PL15 ....106 C7
Cleavewell PL27 .....108 C4
Cledma Bank TR27 ..142 A2
Cleers Hill St Dennis PL26 ..46 E1
  Whitemoor PL26 ....58 E8
Cleeve Gdns PL2 ....128 A8
Clegg Ave PL11 .....126 E3
Clemens Cl TR7 .....111 B5
Clemens Rd PL14 ...113 B5
Clemens Way TR27 ..78 D6
Clement Rd PL31 ....131 B5
Clements Rd TR18 ..143 D5
Clemo Rd PL14 ......113 E7
Clevedon Park Ave PL2 ..128 B6
Clevedon Rd TR7 ...110 D5
Cleveland Ave PL13 ..117 D4
Cleveland Rd PL4 ...149 C3
Cles The 4 TR13 ....146 C5
Clifden Cl Mullion TR12 ..99 A1
  Newquay TR7 ....110 E5
Clifden Rd PL23 .....21 D6
Clifden Rd PL25 .....114 F4
Clifden Terr
  Bodmin PL31 ....109 D5
  Lostwithiel PL22 ....112 C2
Cliff Bglws TR27 ....142 A8
Cliff Ct TR11 ....145 B3
Cliff End Pk PL27 ...108 D6
Cliff La Millbrook PL10 ..132 A4
  Mousehole TR19 ....88 D1
  New Polzeath PL27 ..21 D6
Cliff Park Terr PL27 ..99 A8
  Gorran Haven PL26 ..85 D5
  Mevagissey PL26 ...73 C4
  Mousehole TR19 ....88 D2
  Newlyn TR18 ....143 D1
  Newquay TR7 ....110 E6
  Perranporth TR6 ....55 A5
  Plymouth PL1 ....148 B1
  Porthleven TR13 ....99 B8
Cliff Rise PL23 ......116 D2
Cliff St PL26 ....73 C4
Cliff The PL26 ....73 C3
Cliff View Rd PL14 ..138 E4
Cliff View Terr TR14 ..138 E4
Clifford Cl PL5 ....123 E2
Cliftct 3 TR1 ....137 D4
Clifton Ave PL7 .....130 E7
Clifton Cl PL7 ....130 E7
Clifton Cres 10 TR11 ..145 A4
Clifton Gdns 7 TR11 ..137 B4
Clifton Hill 11 TR11 ..143 C2
Clifton Pl
  14 Falmouth TR11 ..145 A4
  Plymouth PL4 ......149 A4
Clifton Rd TR15 .....139 C8
Clifton St PL4 ....149 A4
Clifton Terr
  15 Falmouth TR11 ..145 A4
  Hayle TR27 ....142 A6
  Liskeard PL14 ......113 A5
  18 Newlyn TR18 ...143 C2
  Portscatho TR2 .....83 C2
Clinga Workshops
  TR6 ....54 F4
Clijah Cl TR15 ....140 C2
Clijah La TR15 ....140 D2
Clinton Ave PL4 .....129 A4
Clinton Cl PL25 .....114 D4
Clinton Ct Bude EX23 ..104 C6
  Redruth TR15 ....140 C3
Clinton Dr PL25 .....114 B3
Clinton Pas 4 TR15 ..140 B4

Clinton Rd
  Constantine TR11 ...92 F
  Redruth TR15 ....140 C
Clinton Terr PL10 ...132 F
Clittaford Rd PL6 ...124 F
Clittaford View PL6 ..124 E
Cloake Pl PL4 ....119 A
Clodgey La TR13 ....146 C
Clodgey View 44 TR13 ..146 C
Clodgey Way TR13 ..146 C
Conway 1 PL20 ....42 C
Clos Trevithick TR14 ..138 F
Close Hill TR15 ......140 B
Close The
  2 Bere Alston PL20 ..41 A
  Camelford PL32 .....105 E
  Lanner TR16 ....80 E
  Mylor Bridge TR11 ..82 A
  Penzance TR18 .....143 D
  Saltash PL12 ....122 C
  Trevone PL28 ......20 F
  Truro TR1 ....137 F
Clovelly Rd PL4 .....149 C
Clovelly View PL9 ..135 A
Clover Lane Cl 6 PL35 ..9 C
Clover Rise PL6 .....125 E
Clover Wlk PL12 ....122 C
Clowance Cl PL14 ...127 F
Clowance La PL1 ...127 F
Clowance St PL1 ....127 F
Clyde St PL2 ....127 F
Coach La TR18 ......143 F
Coach House La PL25 ..114 C
Coach House Mews PL9 ..136 B
Coach La TR15 ......140 A
Coaches Cnr TR13 ..90 F
Coachyard Mews PL28 ..107 D
Coad's Green Prim Sch
  PL15 ....27 D
Coast Rd TR4 ....68 A
Coastguard Cotts
  Down Thomas PL9 ..134 F
  Mawnan Smith TR11 ..93 C
  Mullion TR12 ....98 F
  Polperro PL13 ......62 E
  Rosudgeon TR20 ...89 F
Coastguard Cres PL28 ..143 F
Coastguard Hill PL29 ..22 D
Coastguard Ros PL28 ..21 B
Coastguard Sta Flats
  PL13 ....117 C
Coastguard Terr TR2 ..84 B
Coastline Ct TR4 ....44 C
Cobb La PL9 ....135 F
Cobbett Rd PL5 .....124 B
Cobbs Well PL23 ....116 C
Cober Cres TR27 ...78 E
Cobourg St PL1 .....148 C
Cock's Lake La PL12 ..53 D
Cockington Cl PL6 ..125 D
Cockington Wlk PL6 ..125 C
Cocklawelva PL27 ...21 D
Cockwells La TR26 ..77 C
Codford Cres TR14 ..138 E
Coffa Bridge Cl PL22 ..112 D
Coffeelake Mdw PL22 ..112 D
Cogegoes Ind Pk TR14 ..138 A
Cogos Pk TR11 .....82 A
Coinagehall Pl TR18 ..143 F
Coinaghall St
  Helston TR13 ....146 B
  Penzance TR18 .....143 F
Col-Moor Cl TR27 ...142 E
Colborne Rd TR16 ...67 D
Colborne Rd PL6 ...125 A
Coldrenick St PL25 ..123 D
Coldrose Ct TR1 ....137 B
Coldstyle Rd PL14 ..113 C
Coldwind Cross TR3 ..81 D
Cole Moore Mdw PL19 ..147 B
Cole's Cotts PL7 ....130 E
Colebrook Cl TR15 ..140 A
Colebrook La PL7 ...130 E
Colebrook Rd
  Plymouth, Plympton PL7 ..130 E
  Plymouth, St Budeaux PL5 ..123 D
Coleman Dr PL9 .....135 F
Colemans Cross PL15 ..19 C
Colenso Cross TR20 ..89 F
Colenso Pl PL25 ....114 D
Coleridge Ave PL6 ..124 F
Coleridge La PL7 ...28 A
Colesdown Hill PL9 ..130 B
Colesloggett Halt PL30 ..48 E
Colin Campbell Ct 10
  PL1 ....148 B
Colinsey Pl TR18 ....143 D
Colinsey Rd TR18 ..143 D
Coliza Hill PL26 .....59 A
Coll of St Mark & St John
  PL6 ....125 C
Collacombe Cross
  PL19 ....29 F
Collaford Cl PL14 ...131 A
Collan's Cross PL15 ..15 D
College Ave
  Plymouth PL3 ....128 E
  Tavistock PL19 .....147 C
College Cl TR2 ......71 C
College Dean Cl PL6 ..125 C
College Gn Bodmin PL31 ..109 E
  St Austell PL25 .....114 D
College Hill TR10 ...144 C
College La Bodmin PL31 ..109 F
  Plymouth PL4 ......149 A
  Redruth TR15 ....140 E
College of Falmouth The
  TR11 ....145 A4

College Ope TR10 .....144 D7
College Park Pl PL3 ...128 E5
College Rd
  Camelford PL32 .....105 D4
  Plymouth PL2 ......127 E5
College Road Prim Sch
  PL2 ....127 E5
College St TR14 ....138 C3
College View PL3 ......128 E4
College Way PL1 ......69 E3
Collidord Lake Pk* PL14 ..36 E8
Collin Cl PL5 ....123 D1
Collingwood Ave PL4 ..149 C2
Collingwood Rd PL1 ...149 B2
Collingwood Villas 5
  PL1 ....128 A3
Collins Parc TR3 ......80 F3
Collon Field PL22 .....61 D8
Collorian La TR26 .....77 C1
Collygree Parc TR20 ..89 C5
Colne Gdns PL3 ....129 B5
Colroger Cl TR12 ......99 B2
Colston Cl PL6 ....125 B6
Coltness Rd PL9 ....136 B5
Coltsfield Cl PL6 .....129 B8
Colver Cl TR27 ....78 D6
Colvreath Rd TR7 .....105 F6
Colwill Rd PL6 ....125 C3
Colwill Wlk PL6 ....125 F3
Colworth Ave TR11 ....144 F3
Colwyn Rd PL11 ....127 A3
Combe La EX23 ....4 F4
Combley Dr PL6 ....125 D4
Comfort Rd TR11 ......82 A3
Comfort Wartha PL11 ..92 F4
Commercial Hill TR3 ...81 B4
Commercial Ope PL4 ...149 B2
Commercial Pl PL4 ....149 B1
Commercial Rd
  Calstock PL18 ......41 A3
  Hayle TR27 ....142 C6
  Horrabridge PL20 ...42 C4
  10 Mousehole TR19 ..88 C1
  Penryn TR10 ....144 D7
  Plymouth PL4 ......149 B2
  St Keverne TR12 ....101 C4
  6 St Mawes TR2 ....95 A6
Commercial Sq 3 TR14 ..138 D3
Commercial St
  Camborne TR14 .....138 D3
  Gunnislake PL18 ....41 A6
  Plymouth PL4 ......149 B2
Commercial Terr PL28 ..107 D5
Commissioners Rd 1
  PL27 ....108 B5
Common La PL6 ....121 B5
Commons Cl 3 TR12 ...99 A2
Commons Gate PL23 ..13 B8
Commons The TR12 ...99 A2
Comoran Ct TR17 .....89 C5
Compass Dr PL7 ......131 A7
Compass W PL15 ......18 C2
Comprignery Cl TR1 ...137 B5
Compton Ave TR11 ....137 B5
Compton Ave PL3 .....129 A5
Compton CE Prim Sch
  PL3 ....129 A6
Compton Knoll Cl PL3 ..129 A6
Compton Leigh PL3 ...129 A6
Compton Park Rd PL3 ..128 F5
Compton Rd PL7 ......39 E4
Compton Vale PL3 .....129 A5
Congreve Gdns PL5 ...124 C1
Coniston Gdns PL6 ....124 F4
Conker Rd TR27 ......78 C1
Connaught Ave PL4 ...128 F4
Connaught La 2 PL4 ..128 E4
Connor Cl PL14 ....113 D5
Connor Downs Prim Sch
  TR27 ....78 D6
Connor Hill TR27 .....78 D6
Conqueror Dr PL5 ....124 D1
Conrad Rd PL5 ....124 D1
Consols Rd TR16 ......80 F8
Consort Cl PL3 ....128 E7
Constable Cl PL5 .....124 D3
Constance Pl PL1 .....148 A3
Constantine Prim Sch
  TR11 ....92 E4
Constantine St PL4 ...149 A3
Convent Cl PL12 ......122 E3
Conway Cl TR11 ......144 E4
Conway Gdns
  Falmouth TR11 .....144 D4
  Plymouth PL2 ......128 B7
Conway Rd TR11 ......144 D4
Conyngham Ct PL4 ...129 A8
Cooban Ct PL6 ....129 A8
Cook Ct PL12 ....122 B3
Cooks Level PL26 .....95 F5
Cooksland Ind Est PL31 ..35 B2
Cooksland La PL31 ....35 B2
Cooksland Rd PL31 ...35 B1
Cooksley Ct PL1 ......149 A1
Cookworthy Rd PL2 ...127 F6
Coombe Cwn Pk TR14 ..66 F3
Coombe Dean Sch PL9 ..136 A6
Coombe Hill PL26 .....58 C2
Coombe Junction Halt
  PL14 ....51 A6

Coombe La
  Cargreen PL12 ......119 A2
  Crafthole PL11 ......65 B5
  Penzance TR18 ......143 D7
  Plymouth PL5 ....124 D7
  Seaton PL11 ....64 B7
  Truro TR1 ....81 C8
Coombe Park Cl PL10 ..133 A2
Coombe Park La PL5 ..124 A3
Coombe Pk
  Cawsand PL10 ......133 A2
  Penzance TR18 ......143 E6
  Saltash PL12 ....122 F2
Coombe Rd
  Callington PL17 .....39 C4
  Lanjeth PL26 ....58 D3
  Penzance TR18 ......143 E7
  Saltash PL12 ....123 A2
Coombe Sta TR14 .....51 A6
Coombe The
  Crumbleworn PL13 ...62 D2
  Newlyn TR18 ....143 B3
Coombe Vale TR18 ....143 B3
Coombe View
  15 Perranporth TR6 ..55 A4
  Plymouth PL2 ......127 F7
Coombe Way PL5 .....123 E4
Coombes La 9 TR1 ...137 C4
Cooper's La TR13 .....98 C8
Coperage Rd PL26 ...59 A3
Coosebean La TR4 ....137 A5
Copes Gdns TR1 ......137 C5
Copleston Rd PL6 .....124 E5
Coppard Mews PL7 ...130 B6
Copper Beech Way PL6 ..125 C7
Copper Hill PL27 .....142 D6
Copper Terr PL27 .....142 D7
Copperfields PL20 ....42 E5
Coppers Pk PL6 ......125 E7
Coppice Gdns PL5 ....124 E2
Coppice Wood Dr PL6 ..125 C7
Copse Cl PL7 ....130 D4
Copse Rd PL7 ....130 D4
Copse The PL25 ......114 F5
Copshorn Rd PL31 ....109 C7
Copthorne Cross PL15 ..12 B2
Copthorne Gdns PL9 ..135 F5
Corea Terr PL1 ....128 A2
Corfe Ave PL3 ....128 F8
Coringdean Cl PL6 ...125 A5
Cormorant Dr PL25 ..115 A4
Corner Brake PL6 ....125 D7
Corner Gdns EX23 ....4 D1
Corner Pk PL15 ......26 C7
Cornfield Gdns PL7 ..131 B7
Cornhill Rd PL24 .....60 B5
Cornish Beam Engine Mus
  TR15 ....139 C6
Cornish Birds of Prey Ctr
  The * TR9 ....32 D1
Cornish Cres TR1 ....69 F4
Cornish Engines Mus
  TR15 ....139 C6
Cornubia Cl Hayle TR27 ..142 C5
  Truro TR1 ....137 B5
Cornwall Beach PL1 ..127 D2
Cornwall Coll of F & H Ed
  TR15 ....139 B6
Cornwall Coll of F & H Ed
  (Annexe)
  Camborne TR14 .....138 F3
  Camborne TR14 .....139 A4
Cornwall Geological Mus*
  TR18 ....143 E5
Cornwall Maritime Mus*
  TR11 ....145 B4
Cornwall St
  Bere Alston PL20 ....41 B1
  Plymouth PL1 ....148 C3
  Plymouth, Morice Town
  PL1 ....127 D2
Cornwall Terr
  Penzance TR18 ......143 E4
  2 Truro TR1 ....137 C5
Cornwood Rd PL7 ....131 B4
Cornworthy Cl PL2 ...128 A7
Coronation Ave TR14 ..138 E3
Coronation Cl 2 PL17 ..39 F4
Coronation Cotts
  Budock Water TR11 ..144 C2
  Mabe Burnthouse TR10 ..81 C1
  St Keverne TR12 ....101 D4
Coronation Pl
  Helston TR13 ....146 C4
  Plymouth PL5 ....127 E8
Coronation Rd
  10 Callington PL17 ..39 F4
  Hayle TR27 ....142 D5
  1 Illogan TR16 .....67 E4
  Redruth TR15 ....140 D4
Coronation Terr
  Truro TR1 ....137 B4
  Veryan TR2 ....83 D7
  Blackwater TR4 .....68 E5
Coronation Way TR7 ..111 C7
Corondale Rd PL2 ....128 B4
Corporation Rd
  Bodmin PL31 ....109 B4
  Plymouth PL2 ......128 D7
Corsham Cl PL18 .....41 A6
Cort Simmons TR15 ..139 C6
Cort Treloweth TR15 ..139 B6
Corva Cl 1 TR26 .....77 A6
Corva Rd 9 TR26 .....77 A6
Cory Cl EX23 ....10 F6
Cosawes Est TR3 .....81 B4
Cosdon Pl PL6 ....124 F1

Coswinsawsin La TR14 ..79 A5
Cot Hill Plymouth PL7 ..130 B5
  Ponsanooth TR3 ....81 B4
  2 Stratton EX23 ....4 E1
Cot Hill Trad Est PL7 ..130 B6
Cot Hill TR5,TR16 ....67 D4
Cot Wood TR3 ....81 B4
Cotehele Ave
  Plymouth, Keyham PL2 ..127 F5
  Plymouth, Prince Rock PL4 ..149 C2
Cotehele Ho* PL12 ....39 E3
Cotehele Ho* PL12 ....40 F3
Cotehele Quay Mus*
  PL12 ....40 F3
Cotsland Rd TR1 .....137 F5
Cotswold Ave PL26 ...58 E1
Cotswold Cl PL26 ....58 E1
Cott Rd Lostwithiel PL22 ..112 D2
  Lostwithiel PL22 ....112 D4
Cottage Gdn PL15 ....28 B7
Cottage Mews PL7 ...130 E4
Cotton Cl PL7 ....130 F4
Couchwell La PL22 ...112 C2
Coulson's Bldgs 9
  TR18 ....143 E4
Coulson's Pl 4 TR18 ..143 E4
Coulson's Terr 3 TR18 ..143 E4
Coulthard Dr TR13 ...91 A3
Count House La TR26 ..141 C2
Countess Bridge La TR27 ..90 A8
County Cl PL7 ....131 A5
County Rd EX23 ......104 E2
Court Barton Cotts PL9 ..135 C1
Court Barton Mews PL9 ..98 A4
Court Mdw PL13 .....62 B7
Court The Plymouth PL6 ..125 C7
  Saltash PL12 ....122 E1
Court View PL8 ......136 F4
Courtenay Rd PL19 ...147 B6
Courtenay St PL1 ....148 B3
Courtfield Rd PL3 ....128 F5
Courtland Cres PL7 ..130 D7
Courtlands PL12 .....122 E1
Courtlands Cl PL19 ..147 B6
Courtlands Cres 4
  PL25 ....115 A5
Courtlands Sch PL6 ..124 F1
Courtney Cl PL13 ....117 D4
Courtney Rd
  Liskeard PL14 ......113 D6
  St Austell PL25 ....114 B4
Courtyard Cotts TR4 ..70 C6
Courtyard The
  Redruth TR16 ......139 F2
  Truro TR1 ....137 D3
Cove Hill
  Perranarworthal TR3 ..81 D5
  Sennen Cove TR19 ...96 B7
Cove Mdw PL11 ......127 A6
Cove Rd TR19 ....96 C7
Coventry Rd TR11 ...145 B6
Coverack Prim Sch
  TR12 ....101 C1
Coverdale Pl PL25 ...124 C1
Cow Lard Cl PL15 ...106 A4
Cowdray Cl PL12 .....122 E2
Cowdray Terr PL12 ...122 E1
Cowley Rd PL5 ....124 D3
Cowling Gdns PL14 ..51 F6
Cowling Rd 2 TR3 ...81 F7
Cox Park Terr PL18 ..40 C6
Cox Tor Cl 3 PL20 ...42 F3
Cox Tor Rd PL19 ....147 E5
Cox's Cl PL6 ....125 B1
Coxs Mdw EX22 .....4 F7
Coypool Rd PL7 .....130 A6
Crabbs Cl PL15 ......13 F1
Crabtree Cl 3 PL14 ..113 B5
Crabtree Cl PL3 .....129 F5
Crabtree Villas PL25 ..129 E5
Crackston Cl PL7 ....130 B6
Craigie Dr PL1 ......148 A3
Craigmore Ave PL2 ..127 F5
Cramber Cl
  Roborough PL6 .....125 C8
  Tavistock PL19 .....147 B4
Cranberry Rd TR14 ..138 B3
Cranbourne Ave PL4 ..149 C4
Crane Rd Camborne TR14 ..138 F2
  Newlyn TR18 ....143 C3
Cranfield PL7 ....130 C7
Cranfield Rd TR14 ...138 B3
Cranmere Rd PL3 ....129 A6
Crantock St TR7 .....110 D6
Crantock Terr 7 PL2 ..128 A5
Crapstone Terr PL20 ..42 B2
Crashaw Cl PL5 .....124 D3
Craven Ave PL4 .....149 C4
Crawford Rd PL2 ....128 A4
Creakewake Pk PL26 ..58 B4
Creakvose Pk PL26 ..58 B4
Crease La PL19 ......147 A4
Creathorne Rd EX23 ..104 E7
Creaz - An - Bre PL26 ..58 D5
Crediton Wlk PL6 ...129 E8
Creed La PL27 ....22 C5
Creedy Rd PL3 ......129 C5
Creekside View TR2 ..70 F4
Creeping La
  Newlyn TR18 ....143 C3
  Penzance TR18 ......143 C4
Crelake Cl PL19 .....147 B4
Crelake Ind Est 1 PL19 ..147 B4
Crelake Pk PL19 .....147 C4

Crellow Fields TR3 ...80 F3
Crellow Hill TR3 .....80 F3
Crellow La TR3 ......80 F3
Crellow Vale TR3 ....80 F3
Crembling Well TR15 ..139 E6
Cremyll Rd PL11 .....127 B2
Cremyll St PL1 ......134 A8
Crescent Ave PL1 ...148 B2
Crescent Avenue Mews
  PL1 ....148 B2
Crescent Cl Hayle TR27 ..142 C5
  Wadebridge PL27 ...107 E5
Crescent Gdns TR1 ..137 B4
Crescent Pl TR19 ....74 F1
Crescent Rd Bugle PL26 ..47 C1
  Truro TR1 ....137 B4
Crescent Rise
  Constantine Bay PL28 ..20 C1
  Truro TR1 ....137 B4
Crescent The Bude CX23 ..104 D5
  Camborne TR14 .....138 D4
  Carbis Bay TR26 ....77 C4
  Common Moor PL14 ..37 F4
  Crapstone PL20 .....42 B3
  Gunnislake PL18 ....41 A6
  Landrake PL12 ......53 C3
  Lifton PL16 ....19 F4
  Liskeard PL14 ......113 C6
  Looe PL13 ....117 D1
  Newquay TR7 ....110 E6
  Plymouth PL1 ....148 B2
  Porthleven TR13 ....91 B1
  St Ives TR26 ....77 A7
  Truro TR1 ....137 B4
  Wadebridge PL30 ...34 D8
  Widemouth Bay EX23 ..6 F5
Cressbrook Cl PL6 ...125 F2
Cressbrook Dr PL6 ..125 F2
Cressbrook Wlk PL6 ..125 F2
Cresthill Rd PL2 .....128 B7
Creswell Terr TR19 ..86 F7
Cribbage Terr 7 PL31 ..109 D5
Cricket Pk PL26 ......58 B4
Cricketers Hollow PL27 ..21 E3
Crift La PL14 ....51 F7
Criggan Mill Cvn Pk
  TR12 ....102 C7
Crinnick's Hill PL31 ..109 E4
Crinnis Cl PL25 ......115 E3
Crinnis Rd PL25 .....115 B3
Crinnis Wood PL25 ..115 C3
Crinnis Wood Ave PL25 ..115 D3
Crocker's Row PL18 ..41 A6
Crockers Way PL15 ..13 F1
Crockwell St PL31 ...109 E5
Croft Comm TR14 ...79 F5
Croft Parc 3 TR12 ...102 F2
Croft Pk PL6 ....125 C7
Croft Rd PL18 ....143 C4
Croft Row PL26 .....80 B8
Crofthandi PL27 .....21 E3
Crofty Cl TR15 ......139 C5
Cromartie Rd PL4 ...129 B1
Cromer Cl PL6 ......125 A7
Cromer Wlk PL6 ....125 A7
Cromwell Gate PL6 ..125 C7
Cromwell Rd
  Plymouth PL4 ......149 C3
  St Austell PL25 ....114 F3
Crookedor Cl PL9 ...136 A6
Crookedor La PL12 ..65 D5
Crooklets EX23 ......104 C7
Crooklets Rd EX23 ..104 D6
Cross Cl TR7 ....111 A4
Cross Comm TR12 ...102 F2
Cross Gn PL15 ....19 F7
Cross Hill PL27 ......127 E4
Cross La Bodmin PL31 ..109 E5
  Chacewater TR4 ....69 B1
  St Austell PL25 ....114 C3
Cross Lanes
  Cross Lanes TR12 ...99 C4
  Launceston PL15 ...106 C8
  5 Redruth TR15 ....140 B4
Cross Park Ave PL6 ..124 F1
Cross Park Rd PL6 ...73 C4
Cross Park Terr PL26 ..124 F1
Cross Park Way PL6 ..124 F1
Cross Pk
  Buckland Monachorum PL20 ..42 A3
  Crafthole PL11 .....65 B5
Cross St Camborne TR14 ..138 D2
  Hayle TR27 ....142 B6
  Helston TR13 ....146 B6
  Padstow PL28 ......107 D5
  14 Penzance TR18 ..143 E6
  3 Redruth TR15 ....140 B4
  Wadebridge PL27 ...107 D5
  1 Cross Terr PL18 ..40 F5
Cross The
  Camborne PL12 .....138 D3
  St Dominick PL12 ...40 D2
  St Newlyn East TR8 ..56 D8
Crosswalla Fields TR13 ..146 C7
Crosswater EX23 .....2 C1
Crossway PL7 ....130 D7
Crossway Ave PL4 ...129 B3
Crossways TR11 .....144 F2
Crow Pk PL3 ....129 B5
Crowan Prim Sch TR4 ..79 C2
Crowlas Ind Est TR20 ..89 B8
Crown Cl TR7 ....111 A4
Crown Cres TR8 .....56 B7
Crown Gdns PL25 ...125 A1
Crown Hill PL26 .....58 D8
Crown Terr PL26 .....58 D8
Crowndale Ave PL3 ..129 A6

Crownhill Ct PL6 .....124 F2
Crownhill Fort* PL6 ..124 F3
Crownhill Fort Rd PL6 ..124 F3
Crownhill Rd PL5 ....124 C3
Crows-An-Eglos 5 PL26 ..77 A6
Croydon Gdns PL5 ...123 E4
Crozier Rd 6 PL4 ...128 F4
Crun-Melyn Parc TR27 ..142 B4
Cryben TR12 ....92 C1
Crylla Valley Cvn & Camping
  Pk PL12 ....59 D3
Cryon View TR1 ......69 E3
Cubert Prim Sch TR8 ..43 D1
Cuby Rd TR2 ....71 F4
Cuckoo La TR20 .....71 A2
Cuddenbeake Terr PL12 ..65 B8
Cuffe Rd PL3 ....128 C8
Culdrose Manor PL3 ..58 D7
Culdrose Airfield TR12 ..146 E1
Culdrose Cl PL5 .....123 E3
Cullen View TR2 .....71 C6
Culme Rd PL3 ....129 A5
Culroy Flats 8 TR1 ..137 C4
Culver Cl PL6 ....129 A8
Culver Ct PL12 ......122 F2
Culver Rd PL12 .....122 F2
Culver Way PL6 .....129 A8
Culverland Pk PL14 ..113 C7
Culvers Mdw PL15 ..106 B8
Culverwood Cl PL4 ..131 C6
Culverwood Rd PL14 ..113 B8
Culvery The PL27 ...108 B4
Cumberland Rd PL1 ..127 F1
Cumberland St PL1 ..127 E2
Cumble Tor La PL12 ..53 D2
Cundy Cl PL7 ....130 A7
Cundy's La PL26 .....58 D4
Cunliffe Ave PL9 ....135 A6
Cunnack Cl TR13 ....146 C7
Cunningham Rd PL12 ..81 C1
Cunningham Rd PL5 ..124 C8
Cunningham Way PL12 ..122 D3
Curlew Cl TR7 ....110 B5
Curlew Mews PL3 ...129 C4
Curlew Pk Ind Est TR4 ..69 C3
Curnons Rd TR27 ...142 C5
Curnow Sch The TR15 ..140 B6
Curran Hill PL26 .....58 D8
Curtis Rd PL12 ......122 C3
Curtis St PL1 ....56 B7
Curtis VC Ct TR8 ...56 B7
Cury Prim Sch TR12 ..99 A4
Cusgarne Com Prim Sch
  TR8 ....81 C7
Cusgarne Hill TR4,TR16 ..81 B8
Custom House Ct TR18 ..143 F5
Custom House La
  10 Penzance TR18 ..143 E5
  Plymouth PL1 ......148 B1
Customs House Hill
  PL23 ....116 D4
Cutcrew La PL12 .....52 E3
Cutmere Hill PL12 ...52 D3
Cutmere La PL12 ....52 D3
Cuxhaven Way TR20 ..88 F6
Cuxton Mdws PL20 ..41 F3
Cypress Ave PL25 ...115 F4
Cypress Cl PL7 ......131 C5
Cyril Rd TR7 ....137 C5

D

Dabryn Way PL26 ...58 B4
Daglands Hill PL23 ..116 C4
Daglands Rd PL23 ...116 C4
Dairyland Farm World*
  TR8 ....44 F1
Dale Ave PL6 ....129 C7
Dale Cl TR7 ....111 A4
Dale Gdns PL6 ......128 D4
Dale Rd Newquay TR7 ..111 A4
  Plymouth PL4 ......128 D4
Daleswood Rd PL19 ..147 A4
Dalton Gdns PL5 ....123 E3
Damerel Cl PL1 .....127 F2
Dane Rd TR7 ....110 D7
Daniel Cl PL25 ......115 A4
Daniel Pl TR18 ......143 E4
Daniell Cl TR1 ......137 C3
Daniell Rd TR1 .....137 C3
Daniell St TR1 ......137 B3
Daniels La PL25 .....115 B4
Daniels Sail Loft TR10 ..144 D7
Danmore Cl PL34 ...14 C7
Daphne Du Maurier's
  Smuggler's Mus* PL15 ..25 E3
Darite Prim Sch PL14 ..38 A4
Dark La Camelford PL32 ..105 C4
  Liskeard PL14 ......113 D6
  Lostwithiel PL22 ....112 C1
Dark Street La PL7 ..130 E4
Darklake Cl PL6 .....129 F8
Darklake La PL6 ....125 D8
Darklake View PL6 ..125 E8
Darlington Rd PL20 ..88 F6
Darloe La PL13 .....117 C3
Darracott Hill EX39 ..2 C4
Dart Cl Plymouth PL3 ..129 D7
St Giles-On-The-Heath PL15 ..13 F1
Dartington Wlk PL6 ..129 E8
Dartmeet Ave PL3 ..129 B6

Dartmoor View
Plymouth PL4 ....129 C3
Saltash PL12 ....122 E4
Dartmouth Wlk PL6 .129 E8
Darwin Cres PL3 ....129 D5
Dashwood Ho TR11 ..145 A6
Dazbuz Cl TR1 ......137 C6
Dazbuz Ct TR1 ......137 D5
Daucus Cl PL19 .....147 B4
Davenham Cl PL6 ....125 B6
Davey's Cl TR11 ....144 E1
David Cl PL7 ....130 F6
David Penhaligon Way
TR1 ....137 D3
David Southgate Ct TR1 .148 A2
Davy Cl PL11 ....126 F3
Davy Rd PL6 ....125 C4
Davys Row PL14 .....37 E4
Daw's Mdw PL32 ....105 E4
Dawe Cres PL31 ....109 C3
Dawes La Looe PL13 .117 D5
   Millbrook PL10 ...132 E5
   Plymouth PL9 .....136 D7
Dawlish Wlk PL6 ....129 E8
Dawn Rd PL17 ....117 D2
Dawnay Terr PL11 ..65 B5
Daws Cl PL12 ....123 A2
Dawson Cl PL5 ......123 E1
Daymer La PL27 ....221 C4
Daymond Rd PL5 ....123 D2
Dayton Cl PL9 ......124 E3
De Pass Gdns TR11 .145 C3
De Pass Rd TR11 ...145 C2
De-La-Hay Ave PL3 .148 A4
Deacon Dr PL12 ....122 F1
Deacons Gn PL19 ...147 A3
Dean Cross PL9 ....135 E7
Dean Cross Rd PL9 .135 E7
Dean Hill Lostwithiel PL14 .113 B6
   Plymouth PL9 .....135 E7
Dean La PL14 ....113 B6
Dean Park Rd PL9 ..135 D7
Dean Rd PL7 ....130 D6
Dean St PL14 ....113 B5
Dean Terr PL14 ....113 B6
Debden Cl PL5 .....123 D4
Deeble Cl Plymouth PL7 .131 C5
   Threemilestone TR3 .69 C3
Deep La PL7 ....131 C3
Deer Leap PL19 ....147 D4
Deer Park Cl PL19 .147 C5
Deer Park Cres PL19 .147 C5
Deer Park Dr PL3 ..129 D7
Deer Park La PL19 .147 C5
Deer Park Rd PL19 .147 C5
Deer Pk Newquay TR7 .110 D6
   Saltash PL12 .....122 F3
Deerpark Forest Trail*
PL14 ....50 D3
Defoe Cl PL5 ....124 C1
Degibna La TR12,TR13 .146 C2
Delabole Prim Sch PL33 .14 D2
Delacombe Cl PL7 ..130 F7
Delamere Rd PL6 ...129 D2
Delaval Terr PL32 ..105 C3
Delaware Com Prim Sch
   PL18 ....40 F5
Delaware Cotts PL18 .40 F6
Delaware Ct PL18 ..40 F5
Delaware Gdns PL2 .127 F7
Delaware Rd PL18 ..40 F6
Dell Cl TR18 ....143 C3
Dell Mdw PL15 .....18 B8
Dell The Plymouth PL7 .130 A6
   Tavistock PL19 ...147 B6
   Truro TR1 ....137 C5
Denas Water TR2 ...71 A5
Dengie Cl PL7 .....131 B5
Denham Cl PL5 .....124 C2
Dennis Cl PL5 .....127 C7
Dennis La PL28 ....107 D4
Dennis Rd Liskeard PL14 .113 D6
   Padstow PL28 ....107 D5
Dennison Ave PL25 .115 A4
Dennybowl La
   Tideford PL12 ....52 E3
   Tideford PL12 ....52 F2
Denys View TR9 ....45 F2
Deptford Pl PL4 ...149 A4
Derby Rd PL5 ......124 C4
Derby's La PL26 ...85 C5
Dereham Terr PL1 ..137 B4
Derowen Dr TR27 ..142 B3
Derriford Hospl PL6 .125 B4
Derriford Rd PL6 ..125 A3
Derry's Cross PL1 .148 B2
Derwent Ave PL3 ..129 C5
Desborough La PL4 .149 C3
Desborough Rd PL4 .149 C3
Deveral Rd TR27 ...78 D2
Deveron Cl PL7 ....131 A5
Devington Ct TR1 ..137 C4
Devington Hall TR1 .137 C4
Deviock Hill PL11 ..64 C5
Devon Terr PL3 ....128 E5
Devon Tors PL20 ...42 D3
Devon Tors Rd PL20 .42 C3
Devonia Cl PL7 ....130 E7

Devonport High Sch for Boys
   PL1 ....128 A2
Devonport High Sch for Girls
   PL2 ....128 C6
Devonport Hill
   Cawsand PL10 ....133 A2
   Plymouth PL1 .....127 F1
Devonport Leat PL6 .121 B5
Devonport Rd PL3 ..127 F3
Devonport Sta PL1 .127 F3
Devonshire Ho
   Plymouth PL1 .....148 B2
   2 Tavistock PL19 .147 B5
Devonshire St PL4 .149 A3
Devoran Sch TR3 ...81 F6
Diamond Ave PL4 ..149 B4
Diana Cl TR1 ......144 E2
Dickens Rd PL5 ....124 B1
Dickenmoor La PL5 .124 C2
Dickna St PL15 ....13 F1
Dicky La TR3 ......82 D6
Diddies La EX23 ...4 E1
Diddies Rd EX23 ...4 E1
Dieppe Cl PL1 .....127 F2
Digby Gr PL5 ......123 F5
Digey The 25 TR26 .141 B6
Diggory's Field 4 PL14 .38 A3
Dinas Ct PL12 .....64 D5
Dingle Rd TR9 .....45 C6
Dingle Cl PL17 ....28 D1
Dingle Rd
   Plymouth, North Prospect
   PL2 ....127 B6
   Plymouth, Plympton PL7 .130 C6
Dingles Cl TR1 ....81 B4
Dingwall Ave PL5 ..124 E3
Dipper Cl EX23 ....5 A6
Dipper La EX23 ....5 A7
Dirty La PL12 .....122 B5
Discovery Wharf 20 PL4 .149 A2
Distine Cl PL3 ....124 A2
Dithmarschen Way
   PL25 ....114 B2
Dittisham Wlk PL6 .129 E8
Ditton Ct PL6 .....129 A4
Dixon Pl PL2 ......127 F4
Dobbin Cl PL28 ....20 F2
Dobbin La PL28 ....20 F2
Dobbin Rd PL28 ...20 F2
Dobbs La TR1 .....137 A4
Dobell Rd PL25 ...114 E4
Dobwalls Family Adventure
   Pk* PL14 ....50 E8
Dobwalls Prim Sch PL14 .50 E7
Dock La TR18 ......143 F5
Dockacre Rd PL15 .106 C6
Dockey PL15 ......106 C5
Dockray Cl PL6 ...125 D4
Dockyard Halt PL2 .127 E4
Doctor's La PL14 ..113 C6
Doctors Hill
   8 Boscastle PL35 .9 C1
   St Keverne TR12 ..101 C4
Doctors La PL12 ...64 D5
Doddridge Cl PL9 .135 F4
Dodson's Gap TR12 .99 B7
Doidges Farm Cl PL6 .129 B8
Dola La TR20 ......89 E5
Dolbeare Pk (Cvn Pk)
   PL12 ....53 B4
Dolcoath Ave TR14 .138 F3
Dolcoath Cl TR14 ..138 F3
Dolcoath Rd TR14 ..138 F4
Dolgay Post PL27 ..32 A4
Dolphin Cl PL9 ....135 F6
Dolphin Court Rd PL9 .135 F6
Dolphin Ho 4 PL4 .149 A2
Dolphin Sq PL9 ....135 F6
Dolphin Sq PL9 ...22 D7
Dolvin Rd PL19 ....147 C5
Domellick Cnr PL26 .46 B1
Domellick Hill PL26 .46 B1
Doniert's Cl PL14 .113 B5
Donkey La
   Millbrook PL10 ...132 C4
   Portwrinkle PL11 ..65 A4
Donkey Pk PL28 ...31 F8
Donnington Dr PL3 .129 C7
Donnington Rd TR18 .143 C3
Dopps Terr TR15 ..140 C5
Dorchester Ave PL5 .124 D4
Doreema Rd PL9 ...136 C5
Dormy Ave PL3 ....128 F5
Dorset Pk PL15 ....13 A2
Dorsmouth Terr PL7 .130 E4
Doubledois Ind Est PL14 .50 D7
Doubletrees PL24 ..60 B4
Doubletrees Ct 2 PL24 .60 B4
Doubletrees Sch PL24 .60 B4
Douglas Cl PL26 ...47 A3
Douglas Dr PL9 ...136 A6
Douglass Rd PL3 ..129 C6
Doulton Cl PL25 ...115 A4
Dousland Ho PL20 .42 E3
Dousland Rd PL20 .42 E3
Dousland Terr PL20 .42 E3
Dove Gdns PL3 ....129 D7
Dove St 18 TR26 ..141 B5
Dovedale Rd PL2 ..128 A7
Dover Rd PL6 .....125 C3
Down Cl PL12 .....122 C2
Down Park Dr PL14 .147 D4
Down Parks EX23 ..5 B7
Down Rd Plymouth PL7 .131 C5
   Tavistock PL19 ...147 C4
Down The PL20 ....41 C1
Downfield Dr PL7 ..130 F5

Downfield Way PL7 .130 F5
Downfield Wlk PL7 .130 F5
Downgate Gdns PL2 .128 D8
Downham Gdns PL5 .124 C7
Downham Sch PL5 ..124 C7
Downlea PL19 .....147 D4
Downs La PL13 ....117 B3
Downs Lane Pk PL13 .117 B3
Downs Rd PL13 ....117 B3
Downs The PL13 ...117 C3
Downs View Bude EX23 .104 D7
   Looe PL13 ....117 C3
Downside Ave PL6 .124 E7
Downside Cl TR7 ..111 A4
Downstream Cl PL28 .107 C5
Downton Cl PL1 ...148 A4
Dozmere TR3 ......82 C5
Dozmere Cl TR3 ...82 C5
Dracaena Ave
   Falmouth TR11 ...144 F5
   Hayle TR27 ....142 E6
Dracaena Cres TR27 .142 E6
Dracaena Pl TR11 .144 F4
Dracaena View TR11 .144 F5
Drake Cir PL1,PL4 .149 A3
Drake Ct PL4 .....149 B3
Drake Gdns PL19 ..147 C5
Drake Prim Sch PL2 .127 C5
Drake Rd Padstow PL28 .107 C5
   Tavistock PL19 ...147 C6
Drake Villas PL19 .147 A4
Drake's Pk 9 PL20 .41 B1
Drakefield Dr PL12 .123 A3
Drakes Cl PL14 ....124 F4
Drakewalls Gdns PL18 .40 F5
Drakewalls Pl PL18 .40 F5
Drang The TR9 ....45 E1
Drannack La PL27 ..78 D4
Draper Terr 3 PL19 .147 B5
Drax Gdns PL6 ....128 E8
Draycott Terr TR26 .141 C4
Drayton Rd PL5 ...124 C1
Dreysen Cl TR15 ..139 C8
Drift Cl TR20 .....87 F3
Drift La PL14 .....49 F7
Drillfield La 6 TR26 .141 B5
Drinnick Terr PL26 .58 D6
Drive The PL3 ....128 C7
Driving La PL26 ...60 C5
Drogeada Cl PL15 ..27 D3
Droskyn Castle 12 TR6 .55 A5
Droskyn Cl 13 TR6 .55 A5
Droskyn Way TR6 ..55 A5
Druckham Terr PL15 .106 D5
Druid's Lodge TR15 .139 D5
Druid's Rd TR15 ..139 D5
Drummer's Hill PL26 .114 C8
Drummond Cl PL2 .127 F7
Drummond Pl PL1 .127 F3
Drump Rd TR15 ...140 D5
Drunken Bridge Hill
   PL7 ....130 D4
Dryburgh Cres PL2 .127 F6
Dryden Ave PL5 ...124 C1
Drym La Leedstown TR14 .78 F1
   Nancegollan TR14 .91 A8
Drym Rd TR13 .....91 B7
Dualstone Cross EX22 .8 D3
Ducane Wlk PL6 ..129 E8
Duchy Ave TR7 ....111 C7
Duchy Cl PL15 ....106 C7
Duchy Coll PL17 ..28 D1
Duchy Hospl TR1 ..69 C4
Duchy Terr Minions PL14 .38 B6
   Upton Cross PL14 .38 D7
Duck La PL12 .....53 E2
Duck St 6 TR19 ...88 C1
Duckworth St 8 PL28 .128 A4
Ducky La PL12 ....53 C3
Ducky Row PL17 ..40 D4
Dudley Gdns PL6 ..129 B8
Dudley Rd PL7 ....130 B5
Dudman Rd TR1 ...69 F3
Dudnance La TR15 .139 B4
Duke of Cornwall's Light
   Infantry Mus* PL31 .109 F3
Duke St Launceston PL15 .106 B8
   Lostwithiel PL22 ..112 C2
   Padstow PL28 .....107 D5
   Plymouth PL1 .....127 E2
   St Austell PL25 ...114 C3
   Tavistock PL19 ...147 C6
   11 Truro TR1 ......137 D4
Duke's Way TR7 ...111 A5
Dukes Dr PL19 ....41 B4
Duloe Gdns PL2 ...128 D8
Duloe Prim Sch PL14 .51 A1
Dumbarton Terr 7 TR19 .88 C1
Dumfries Ave PL5 .124 D3
Dun Mere Cl 1 PL24 .60 C4
Duncan St PL1 ....127 E1
Duncannon Dr TR11 .144 F4
Dunclair Pk PL3 ..129 D5
Duncombe Ave PL5 .113 D6
Dundas St 4 PL2 ..128 A4
Dunders Hill PL27 .21 D5
Dundonald St PL2 .127 F4
Dungarth Gn PL14 .113 D6
Dungarth Rd PL14 .113 D6
Dunheaved View PL15 .28 B6
Dunheaved Fields PL15 .106 C4
Dunheved Rd
   Launceston PL15 ..106 C5
   Saltash PL12 .....122 F2
Dunkeswell Cl PL2 .127 F8
Dunley Wlk PL6 ...125 C1

Dunmere Rd PL31 ..109 B5
Dunn St 10 PL35 ..9 C1
Dunnet Rd PL6 ....124 D7
Dunraven Dr PL6 ..125 A5
Dunsdon Cross EX22 .5 F3
Dunstan Cl TR10 ..144 C8
Dunstan La PL12 ..40 A1
Dunstanville Terr 12
   TR11 ....145 A5
Dunstone Cl PL9 ..136 E7
Dunstone Cl PL26 .58 C8
Dunstone Ave PL9 .136 A7
Dunstone Dr PL9 ..135 F7
Dunstone La PL9 ..135 F7
Dunstone Prim Sch PL9 .136 A8
Dunstone Rd
   Plymouth, Plymstock PL9 .135 F7
   Plymouth St Budeaux PL5 .123 F3
Dunstone View PL9 .136 A7
Dunstt Hill PL16 ..19 F4
Dunvegan Rd PL10 .144 B8
Dunveth Rd PL27 ..108 A5
Dupath La PL17 ...40 A4
Duporth Bay PL26 .115 A1
Duporth Holiday Village
   PL26 ....115 A1
Duporth Rd PL25,PL26 .115 A2
Dural Cross EX22 ..3 E3
Durban Rd PL3 ....128 D5
Durgan Crossroads TR11 .93 D3
Durgan La TR10 ...144 C8
Durham Ave PL4 ..149 C4
Durley Dene TR26 .77 E4
Durnford St PL1 ..128 A1
Durnford Street Ope
   PL1 ....128 A1
Durning Rd TR5 ...54 C1
Durrant Cl PL1 ...127 E3
Durris Cl PL6 .....125 D4
Durris Gdns PL6 ..125 D4
Durston Rd EX23 ..104 E7
Durwent Cl PL9 ...135 A6
Duson Terr PL15 ..106 C7
Dutson Rd PL15 ..106 C7
Dux Cross EX22 ...8 A4
Duxford Cl PL5 ...123 E5
Dye House Cotts PL14 .36 F2
Dynas-la Rd TR26 .141 B4
Dynevor Cl PL3 ...128 F7

E

Eagle Rd PL7 .....131 C4
Earl's Acre PL3 ...128 C4
Earl's Dr The
   Cawsand PL10 ....133 A1
   Cawsand, Kingsand PL10 .133 B3
   Rame PL10 ....133 A1
Earls Mill Rd PL7 .130 E6
Earls Rise TR7 ....111 B5
Earls Wood Cl PL6 .125 F3
Earls Wood Dr PL6 .125 F3
East Bridge TR4 ..69 A3
East Camps Bay PL11 .64 D4
East Charles St TR14 .138 E2
East Cl TR13 ......146 D7
East Cliff PL13 ...117 D3
East Cliff La TR17 .89 C5
East End TR15 ....140 C6
East Fairholme Rd EX23 .104 F7
East Hill St Austell PL25 .114 D3
East Hill PL15 ....106 B7
East Park Ave PL4 .148 C4
East Pk Pensilva PL14 .38 D7
   Redruth TR15 .....140 D6
East Pool Pk TR15 .139 F6
East Rd Kilkhampton EX23 .5 A6
   Menheniot PL14 ..52 A5
   Quintrell Downs TR8 .44 E3
   Stithians TR3 .....83 F3
East Rosewin Row 10
   TR1 ....137 D5
East St Newquay TR7 .110 E6
   Grampound Road TR2 .71 F6
East Terr TR27 ...142 B6
East View TR15 ...51 F5
East Yeolstone Cross
   EX23 ....3 C2
Eastbourne Cl PL25 .114 E3
Eastbourne Rd PL25 .114 D3
Eastbury Ave PL5 .124 A2
Eastcliff Ave TR4 .68 A7
Eastcliff Avenue No 2
   TR4 ....68 A7
Eastcliffe Rd PL24 .60 C5
Eastcote Cl PL6 ...125 B6
Eastella Rd PL20 ..42 D2
Easterdown Cl PL9 .135 F7
Eastern Ave PL14 .113 D6
Eastern Gn Gulval TR18 .88 E6
   Penzance TR18 ...143 F7
Eastern La TR14 ..138 D4
Eastern Wood Rd PL7 .131 D4
Eastfield Ave PL9 .135 F6
Eastfield Cres PL2 .129 A6
Eastfield Way PL25 .114 F5
Eastlake Ho 5 PL1 .149 A2
Eastlake St PL1 ...149 A3
Eastlake Wlk PL1 .149 A3

Eastwood Pk Ind Est
   TR10 ....144 D7
Eastwood Rd TR10 .144 D7
Ebenezer Pl 12 TR18 .143 C1
Ebrington St PL4 ..149 A3
Eddystone Cl PL3 ..129 C6
Eddystone Pl 13 PL27 .108 B5
Eddystone Rd
   Down Thomas PL9 .135 C1
   St Austell PL25 ...114 E5
   Wadebridge PL27 ..108 B6
Eddystone Rise PL14 .113 D7
Eddystone Road Trad & Ind
   Est PL27 ....108 B6
Eddystone Terr
   Plymouth PL1 .....148 B1
   2 Wadebridge PL27 .108 B5
Eden Cl 11 PL24 ...60 B4
Eden Gdns 18 TR18 .143 C1
Eden Project The*
   PL24,PL26 ....115 D8
Edgar Rd Jacobstow PL23 .11 A6
   Wainhouse Corner EX23 .10 F6
Edgar Terr PL4 ....129 A4
Edgcumbe Ave
   Newquay TR7 .....110 F5
   Plymouth PL1 .....148 A3
Edgcumbe Cl PL18 .41 A6
Edgcumbe Cres PL10 .132 F6
Edgcumbe Ct 13 PL3 .128 A3
Edgcumbe Dr PL19 .147 B6
Edgcumbe Gdns TR7 .110 F6
Edgcumbe Gn PL25 .114 A3
Edgcumbe Park Rd PL3 .128 D6
Edgcumbe Rd
   Lostwithiel PL22 ..112 C2
   Roche PL26 ....46 F3
   Saltash PL12 .....122 C5
   St Austell PL25 ...114 A3
Edgcumbe Terr 1 PL4 ...60 B4
Edgcombe Rd PL12 .40 D2
Edgcumbe Way PL18 .40 E5
Edgcumbe Terr 16 PL20 .41 C1
Edgemoor Cl PL14 .38 A3
Edinburgh Cl PL25 .115 C4
Edinburgh St PL1 .127 E1
Edith Ave PL4 ....149 C4
Edith St PL5 ......123 D1
Edmonton PL27 ...33 B7
Edmund Rd PL15 ..140 B6
Edna Terr PL4 ....149 C3
Ednovean La TR20 .89 E4
Edward Bolitho Ho (Hospl &
   Day Ctr) TR18 ....143 D3
Edward Hain Meml Hospl
   TR26 ....141 B5
Edward St
   Camborne TR14 ..138 F4
   Truro TR1 ....137 C4
Edwards Cl PL7 ...131 B4
Edwards Cres PL12 .122 C2
Edwards Dr PL7 ...131 B5
Edwards Rd Devoran TR3 .81 F6
   St Giles-On-The-Heath PL15 .13 F1
Effingham Cres PL3 .128 D7
Efford Cres PL3 ...129 B6
Efford Down Pk EX23 .104 C5
Efford Farm Bsns Pk
   EX23 ....104 C4
Efford La PL3 .....129 B5
Efford Pathway
   Plymouth PL3 .....129 C6
   Plymouth PL3 .....129 C6
Efford Rd PL3 ....129 B6
Efford Wlk PL3 ...129 B6
Egan's Way PL33 ..14 D2
Egerton Cres PL4 .149 C3
Egerton Pl PL4 ...149 C3
Egerton Rd
   Padstow PL28 ....107 E4
   Plymouth PL4 .....149 C3
Eggbuckland Com Coll
   PL6 ....129 A8
Eggbuckland Rd PL5 .129 A8
Eggbuckland Vale Prim Sch
   PL6 ....129 A8
Eglos Cl TR30 .....129 A3
Eglos Mdw TR11 ..82 A3
Eglos Parc Mullion TR12 .99 A2
Eglos Rd Crowlas TR20 .89 A7
   St Erme TR4 ......69 F6
Eglos View 2 PL35 .9 C1
Egloshayle Rd
   Hayle TR27 ....142 E6
   Wadebridge PL27 ..108 D5
Egloskerry Prim Sch
   PL15 ....18 A5
Egret Cl PL10 .....133 A6
Eight Acre Cl 1 PL7 .131 C5
Elaine Cl PL7 .....130 B5
Elbow La PL13 ....147 C6
Elburton Prim Sch PL9 .136 C7
Elburton Rd PL9 ..136 B8
Eldad Hill PL1 ....148 A3
Elder Cl 3 PL7 ...131 B5
Elderfield Cl 7 PL24 .60 C5
Eleanor Ho PL1 ...148 A2
Elerkey Cl TR2 ...83 F6
Elerkey La TR2 ...83 F6
Elford Cres PL7 ..130 E7
Elford Dr PL9 ....135 C7
Elford Pk PL20 ...42 D2
Elgin Cres PL5 ...124 E3
Elim Ct PL3 ......128 E5
Elim Terr PL3 ....128 E5

Eliot Cl PL15 ....18 C2
Eliot Ct TR7 ....110 F6
Eliot Dr PL12 ....65 B8
Eliot Gdns TR7 ....110 F6
Eliot Rd St Austell PL25 ...114 E4
Truro TR1 ....137 C5
Eliot St PL5 ....127 E8
Elizabeth Cl
Bodmin PL31 ....109 D4
Threemilestone TR3 ....69 C3
Elizabeth Ct 2 PL1 ....149 A2
Elizabeth Pl PL4 ....149 A4
Elizabeth Rd Bude EX23 ...104 F5
St Austell PL25 ....114 E3
Elizabeth Terr TR17 ....89 B5
Elizabethan House (Mus)
The* PL1 ....149 A2
Ellen Cl TR4 ....68 C6
Ellenglaze Ct TR8 ....55 D8
Ellenglaze La TR8 ....55 D8
Ellenglaze Mdw TR8 ....55 D8
Elliot Sq PL11 ....127 B3
Elliot St PL1 ....148 B1
Elliot Terr PL1 ....148 C1
Elliot Terrace La PL1 ....148 C1
Elliott Cl PL12 ....122 D2
Elliott Rd PL4 ....129 B1
Ellis Cl TR27 ....142 C5
Ellis Way TR27 ....142 C5
Elliston Gdns 3 TR13 ....98 C8
Elm Cl Callington PL17 ....39 F4
Camborne TR15 ....139 D6
Newquay TR7 ....110 F4
8 St Columb Major TR9 ....45 D6
Tavistock PL19 ....147 C3
Elm Cotts PL12 ....122 C3
Elm Court Gdns TR1 ....137 D5
Elm Cres PL3,PL4 ....129 A4
Elm Ct TR1 ....137 D5
Elm Dr EX23 ....104 F5
Elm Gr Feock TR3 ....82 C5
Plymouth PL7 ....130 E5
Elm Grove Cotts TR10 ....93 C6
Elm Lea EX23 ....104 F5
Elm Mdw TR3 ....82 C5
Elm Meadow Dr PL13 ...117 D4
Elm Pk PL10 ....133 B6
Elm Rd
Plymouth, Glenholt PL6 ...125 D6
Plymouth, Mannamead
PL4 ....128 D6
Elm Terr 8 Mullion TR12 ....99 A2
St Austell PL25 ....114 C4
Elm Tree Rd PL13 ....117 D4
ElMCroft PL2 ....128 B7
Elmgate Crossways PL12 .65 E8
Elms Close Terr 23
TR18 ....143 C2
Elms The
Perranuthnoe TR20 ....89 D4
Plymouth PL3 ....128 A3
Elmsleigh Rd PL27 ....108 B6
Elmwood Cl PL6 ....125 D5
Elowen Cl TR11 ....144 E2
Elphinstone Rd PL2 ....128 C7
Elwell Rd PL12 ....123 A2
Elwick Gdns PL3 ....129 B5
Embankment La PL4 ....129 B2
Embankment Rd PL4 ....129 B2
Embankment Road La N
PL4 ....129 B2
Emily Gdns PL4 ....149 B4
Emlyn Fields PL25 ....114 F6
Emma Pl PL1 ....128 A1
Emma Place Ope PL1 ....128 A1
Empire Way TR11 ....144 E4
Empress Ave 24 TR18 ....143 E6
Emslie Rd TR11 ....145 C2
Endsleigh Dr PL15,PL19,
PL17 ....28 F5
Endsleigh Gdns 2 PL4 ...149 A4
Endsleigh Park Rd PL3 ..128 D6
Endsleigh Pk EX23 ....7 B6
Endsleigh Pl PL4 ....149 A4
Endsleigh Rd PL9 ....135 C7
Endsleigh Terr PL14 ....113 C6
Energy Ctr* PL33 ....14 F4
Eningdale Rd PL19 ....147 A4
Ennerdale Gdns PL6 ....124 E5
Ennis Cl TR4 ....56 D1
Ennor's Rd TR7 ....110 D6
Enys Cl Carbis Bay TR26 ..141 D1
Truro TR1 ....137 B5
Enys Cotts TR19 ....75 A2
Enys Quay 5 TR1 ....137 D4
Enys Rd Camborne TR14 ..138 D4
Truro TR1 ....137 B5
Enys Redenek TR14 ....138 F5
Epping Cres PL6 ....129 D7
Epworth Cl TR1 ....137 E4
Epworth Terr 4 PL2 ....127 F5
Erdiston Ct EX23 ....104 D6
Ergue-Gaberic Way
EX23 ....104 D5
Eric Rd Calstock PL18 ....41 B3
Plymouth PL4 ....149 C3
Erisey Terr TR11 ....145 B4
Erith Ave PL2 ....127 E7
Erle Gdns PL7 ....130 F3
Erlstoke Cl PL6 ....125 D1
Erme Gdns PL3 ....129 C5
Ermington Terr PL4 ....128 E4
Ernesettle Cres PL5 ....123 E3
Ernesettle Gn PL5 ....123 E4
Ernesettle Jun & Inf Sch
PL5 ....123 F4
Ernesettle La PL5 ....123 D4
Ernesettle Rd PL5 ....123 E3
Erow Glas TR10 ....144 C8
Esmonde Gdns PL5 ....127 B8
Esmonde Rd TR13 ....146 D4
Esperanza Ct TR11 ....144 F6
Esplanade PL23 ....116 C3
Esplanade Rd TR7 ....110 A6
Esplanade The PL1 ....148 C1
Essa Rd PL12 ....122 F2
Essex Dr TR15 ....139 B8
Essex St PL1 ....148 B4
Eston Cl TR10 ....93 C8
Estover Cl PL6 ....125 F5
Estover Com Coll PL6 ...125 D2
Estover Ind Est PL6 ....125 E4
Estover Prim Sch PL6 ...125 D2
Estover Rd PL6 ....125 F4
Estuary View
Falmouth TR11 ....145 B5
Lelant TR26 ....77 E3
Newquay TR7 ....110 D5
Eton Ave PL1 ....148 C4
Eton Pl PL1 ....148 C4
Eton Rd PL25 ....115 A5
Eton St PL1 ....148 C4
Eton Terr 3 PL1 ....148 B3
Euny Cl TR15 ....140 A4
Eureka Vale 3 TR6 ....55 A5
Europa Ct TR8 ....31 C2
Evans Pl PL2 ....128 B5
Evans Way TR20 ....90 C4
Evea Cl TR1 ....69 F3
Evely Ct PL14 ....113 D7
Evelyn Pl PL4 ....149 A4
Evelyn St PL5 ....123 D1
Evenden Ct PL11 ....127 A3
Example Cross PL15 ....27 B6
Exchange St PL1 ....149 A2
Exe Gdns PL3 ....129 C7
Exeter Cl PL5 ....123 D4
Exeter Cl 5 PL15 ....106 C6
Exeter St
Launceston PL15 ....106 C6
Plymouth PL4 ....149 A3
Plymouth PL4 ....149 B2
Exmouth Rd PL1 ....127 F3

F

Factory Cotts PL14 ....51 F5
Fair Cross TR2 ....72 C6
Fair Field TR20 ....89 B8
Fair Park View TR8 ....56 F5
Fair St TR9 ....45 E6
Fair View PL26 ....47 E4
Fair View Terr TR4 ....55 D8
Fairbourne Rd PL25 ....114 F4
Fairfax Rd TR2 ....70 F5
Fairfax Terr 5 PL2 ....127 F4
Fairfield Plymouth PL7 ...130 E7
St Germans PL12 ....65 A8
Fairfield Ave PL2 ....128 C7
Fairfield Cl Lelant TR26 ....77 E4
St Austell PL25 ....115 A4
Fairfield Pk PL15 ....26 C7
Fairfield Pl TR7 ....110 B5
Fairfield Rd Bude EX23 ...104 E5
Falmouth TR11 ....144 F4
Fairfields PL13 ....117 D5
Fairlight PL14 ....113 D5
Fairmantle St TR1 ....137 D4
Fairmead Cl PL12 ....53 E4
Fairmead Mews PL12 ...122 C3
Fairmead Rd PL12 ....122 C2
Fairmeadow TR10 ....144 B7
Fairpark Rd
Liskeard PL14 ....113 C5
Wadebridge PL27 ....108 B5
Fairview Ave PL3 ....129 D5
Fairview Pk TR9 ....45 E2
Fairview Pl TR11 ....145 B4
Fairview Terr TR7 ....110 E6
Fairview Way PL3 ....129 E5
Fairway Saltash PL12 ....122 C2
St Austell PL25 ....115 D3
Fairway The TR11 ....93 C2
Fairways The PL30 ....48 C7
Falcon Terr EX23 ....104 D5
Falmouth Bsns Pk TR11 .144 E3
Falmouth College of Arts
(Tremough Campus)
TR10 ....144 A8
Falmouth College of Arts
(Woodlane Campus)
TR11 ....145 B3
Falmouth Com Sch (Lower)
TR11 ....144 F4
Falmouth Com Sch (Upper)
TR11 ....144 D5
Falmouth Docks Sta
TR11 ....145 D3
Falmouth Hospl TR11 ....144 F4
Falmouth Rd
Helston TR13 ....146 D7
Penryn TR10 ....144 E7
Redruth TR15 ....140 C4
Truro TR1 ....137 C3
Falmouth Town (The Dell)
Sta TR11 ....145 C3
Falmouth Wharves
TR11 ....145 A6
Fanshawe Way PL9 ....135 C6
Faraday Mill Bsns Pk
PL4 ....129 B1
Faraday Rd PL4 ....129 B1
Farm Cl PL7 ....130 C7
Farm La Plymouth PL5 ....124 B2
Saltash PL12 ....122 D1
Farm Town TR15 ....140 C3
Farmer's La PL14 ....50 B6
Farmers Hill PL13 ....117 C4
Farmers Mdw 8 TR18 ....143 C2
Farnley Cl PL6 ....125 B6
Farringdon Rd PL4 ....129 B3
Faugan La TR18 ....143 B1
Faugan Rd TR18 ....143 B1
Faukener Cl TR11 ....144 E4
Fayre View PL12 ....122 B1
Fearnside Way PL12 ....122 C3
Federation Rd PL3 ....129 C4
Fegan Rd PL5 ....123 B1
Feliskirk La TR17 ....89 B6
Felixstowe Ave TR7 ....111 E7
Fellowes Pl PL1 ....128 A2
Fellows La PL1 ....148 A4
Fenten Pk PL12 ....122 F3
Fenteroon Rd PL32 ....105 C2
Fentonluna La PL28 ....107 D6
Fenwick Rd TR11 ....145 B2
Fern Cl PL7 ....131 C5
Fern Lee Terr 19 TR26 ....141 B5
Fern Mdw PL19 ....147 D6
Ferndale Ave PL2 ....127 E7
Ferndale Cl PL6 ....125 D8
Ferndale Rd
Falmouth TR11 ....145 A2
Plymouth PL2 ....127 F7
Ferndale Terr PL14 ....113 B6
Fernhill Rd TR7 ....110 D6
Fernleigh Cres PL27 ....108 C4
Fernleigh Gdns PL27 ....108 C4
Fernleigh Rd
Plymouth PL3 ....128 F5
Wadebridge PL27 ....108 C5
Fernleigh Terr
Gunnislake PL18 ....40 E5
Nanpean PL26 ....58 C6
Fernside Pk PL14 ....38 A3
Fernside Rd TR14 ....138 B1
Ferrers Rd PL5 ....123 E1
Ferretts Cross EX23 ....11 A6
Ferris Town TR1 ....137 C4
Ferris Way PL23 ....116 E2
Ferry La PL11 ....126 D5
Ferry Rd PL1 ....127 E3
Ferry St PL11 ....127 C3
Festival Villas TR3 ....69 D3
Feversham Pl PL7 ....131 B6
Field Cl PL22 ....112 D2
Field Pl TR11 ....93 D3
Field The TR 20 ....76 F2
Fifield Ho PL26 ....58 B4
Fillace La 11 PL20 ....42 C4
Filtrick La TR16 ....139 E1
Finch Cl PL3 ....129 D4
Finches Cl PL9 ....136 C7
Findon Gdns PL6 ....125 D4
Finewell St PL1 ....148 C2
Finn VC Est PL31 ....109 D5
Finnigan Rd PL4 ....129 B1
Finnygook La PL11 ....65 A4
Fir Cl Goonhavern TR4 ....55 D4
Helston TR13 ....146 B7
St Austell PL25 ....114 B3
Fir Gr 8 TR3 ....81 F7
Fircroft Rd PL2 ....128 B7
Firebeacon Cross EX39 ....2 F7
Firs The PL26 ....58 E8
Firsleigh Pk PL26 ....46 F3
First Ave
Plymouth, Billacombe PL9 .135 F8
Plymouth, Stoke PL1 ....128 A2
Fisgard Way PL11 ....126 D3
Fish Mkt PL4 ....149 B2
Fish St 9 TR26 ....141 B6
Fish Strand Hill TR11 ....145 B4
Fish Strand Quay TR11 ..145 B4
Fisher Cl PL27 ....108 D6
Fisher Rd PL2 ....128 A5
Fistral Cl PL11 ....126 F4
Fistral Cres TR7 ....110 A5
Fistral Ct TR7 ....110 A5
Fitzford Cotts PL19 ....147 B4
Fitzroy Rd PL1 ....128 A3
Fitzroy Terr 7 PL1 ....128 A3
Fitzsimmons Cl 6 TR13 .146 C5
Five Fields La TR11 ....145 A5
Five Wells La TR13 ....146 B5
Flamank Pk PL31 ....109 C4
Flambards Village*
TR13 ....146 E4
Flamborough Rd PL6 ....125 A7
Flamborough Way PL6 ..125 A6
Flamsteed Cres PL5 ....123 E1
Flaxmoor Terr PL31 ....109 D5
Fleet St PL2 ....127 E6
Fletcher Cres PL9 ....136 B6
Fletcher Way PL9 ....136 A6
Fletemoor Rd PL5 ....123 E1
Flexbury Ave EX23 ....104 E7
Flexbury Mews EX23 ....104 E7
Flexbury Park Rd EX23 ...104 E6
Flexbury Pk EX23 ....104 E7
Flora Cotts PL1 ....148 B2
Flora Ct PL1 ....148 B3
Flora St PL1 ....148 B2
Florence Hill PL17 ....39 F5
Florence Pl
Falmouth TR11 ....145 B3
Newlyn TR18 ....143 C3
Plymouth PL4 ....149 C3
Florence Rd PL17 ....39 F5
Florence Road Ind Est
PL17 ....39 F6
Florence St PL5 ....123 D1
Florence Terr TR11 ....145 B3
Florida Gdns PL3 ....129 C6
Floyd Cl PL2 ....127 F7
Flushing Sch TR11 ....145 B6
Folders La PL30 ....23 F6
Foliot Ave PL2 ....128 A6
Foliot Rd PL2 ....128 A6
Forbes Cl TR18 ....143 B1
Forbes Rd TR18 ....143 B1
Ford PL22 ....49 E3
Ford Hill PL2 ....128 A5
Ford Park La PL4 ....128 E4
Ford Park Rd PL4 ....128 D4
Ford Prim Sch PL2 ....128 A5
Ford St PL19 ....147 B5
Ford's Row TR15 ....140 B5
Forder Hill PL10 ....132 F1
Forder Hts PL6 ....125 B1
Forder La PL10 ....132 F1
Forder Valley Rd PL6 ....129 D8
Fords Hill TR12 ....100 D7
Fore St Ashton TR13 ....90 E3
Barripper TR14 ....79 B5
Bere Alston PL20 ....41 B1
Bere Ferrers PL20 ....119 F3
Bodmin PL31 ....109 D5
Boscastle PL35 ....9 C1
Bugle PL26 ....47 C1
6 Callington PL17 ....39 E4
Calstock PL18 ....41 A3
Camborne TR14 ....138 D3
Camborne, Beacon TR14 ...138 E1
Camborne, Pool TR15 ....139 B6
Camelford PL32 ....105 D4
Cargreen PL12 ....119 A2
Carharrack TR16 ....80 F8
Cawsand PL10 ....133 A2
Chacewater TR4 ....69 A3
Constantine TR11 ....92 F4
Crumplehorn PL13 ....62 D1
Fowey PL23 ....116 D4
Golant PL23 ....61 B5
Goldsithney TR20 ....89 E5
Grampound TR2 ....72 A7
Grampound Road TR2 ....57 E1
Gunnislake PL18 ....40 F5
Gunnislake PL18 ....41 A6
Hayle TR27 ....142 D6
Herodsfoot PL14 ....50 E3
Lelant TR26 ....77 E4
Lerryn PL22 ....61 C7
Lifton PL16 ....19 F4
Liskeard PL14 ....113 C6
Looe PL13 ....117 C3
Lostwithiel PL22 ....112 C2
Madron TR20 ....88 B7
Marazion TR17 ....89 C5
Mevagissey PL26 ....73 C3
Millbrook PL10 ....132 E5
Milton Abbot PL19 ....29 C6
Mount Hawke TR4 ....68 C6
13 Mousehole TR19 ....88 C1
Nanpean PL26 ....58 D7
Newlyn TR18 ....143 C1
Newquay TR7 ....110 D6
Par PL24 ....60 B5
9 Par, Tywardreath PL24 ...60 D5
Penponds TR14 ....138 B1
Pensilva PL14 ....38 E4
Plymouth, Devonport PL1 ..127 F2
Plymouth, Plympton PL7 ...130 E4
Plymouth, Tamerton Foliot
PL5 ....124 B6
Polgooth PL26 ....59 A1
Polruan PL23 ....116 D2
Port Isaac PL29 ....22 D7
4 Porthleven TR13 ....98 B8
Praze-an-Beeble TR14 ....79 B2
Probus TR2 ....71 C6
Redruth TR15 ....140 B5
Roche PL26 ....46 F2
Saltash PL12 ....122 F2
St Austell PL25 ....114 C3
St Cleer PL14 ....37 F3
St Columb Major TR9 ....45 E6
St Day TR16 ....68 D1
St Dennis PL26 ....58 C8
St Erth TR27 ....142 A1
St Germans PL12 ....65 A8
St Ives TR26 ....141 B6
St Just TR19 ....86 F6
St Stephen PL26 ....58 B4
St Teath PL30 ....23 E7
Sticker PL26 ....58 E1
7 Stratton EX23 ....4 E1
Tintagel PL34 ....14 C7
Torpoint PL11 ....127 B3
Tregony TR2 ....71 F3
Troon TR14 ....79 E5
Foredown Pk PL14 ....38 C3
Forest Ave PL2 ....128 C7
Forest View PL6 ....125 D7
Foresters Rd PL9 ....135 D7
Forge Gdns EX23 ....6 F1
Forge Ind Pk TR14 ....138 E5
Forge La PL12 ....122 C4
Forge The TR3 ....82 A7
Forge Way TR4 ....69 F6
Forlaze Rd PL27 ....21 D2
Formal Ind Pk TR14 ....138 B4
Forrabury Hill 5 PL35 ....9 C1
Forreglos Dr 10 TR17 ....89 C5
Forresters Dr PL6 ....125 D7
Forsythia Dr PL12 ....122 C3
Fort Austin Ave PL6 ....125 C1
Fort Terr PL6 ....124 F3
Fort The PL10 ....133 A1
Fortescue Cl PL26 ....58 D6
Fortescue Pl
Lostwithiel PL22 ....112 D3
Plymouth PL3 ....129 A6
Fortescue Terr PL19 ....147 A6
Forth An Cos TR3 ....81 B4
Forth An Streth TR27 ....142 E7
Forth An Tewennow
TR27 ....142 D7
Forth An Ula TR27 ....142 E7
Forth An Vre TR14 ....139 A3
Forth Coth TR3 ....82 A7
Forth Dall 21 TR16 ....67 E4
Forth Gdns PL3 ....129 D6
Forth Gwedhen TR13 ....146 D8
Forth Kegyn TR15 ....139 B4
Forth Noweth 4 TR3 ....81 F7
Forth Scol
Camborne TR15 ....139 D7
6 Porthleven TR13 ....98 C8
Forth Vean TR13 ....90 E6
Forth-An-Nance TR16 ....67 C6
Forth-An-Praze
Illogan TR15 ....139 D8
St Day TR16 ....68 D1
Forth-An-Ryn TR15 ....140 D4
Forth-An-Tre TR27 ....142 D7
Forthcrom TR12 ....92 C1
Forthnoweth TR15 ....140 B5
Forthvean
Camborne TR14 ....138 D1
Portreath TR16 ....67 C5
Forthvean Cres TR4 ....68 A6
Forthvean Rd TR4,TR16 ....67 F7
Forthveor TR15 ....140 E7
Forthvras TR15 ....139 B8
Fosbrooke Ct 9 PL3 ....128 F6
Foster Dr PL31 ....109 C3
Fosters La PL34 ....14 C7
Fosters Way EX23 ....104 F6
Foulston Ave PL5 ....127 B8
Foundry Gdns PL15 ....106 B6
Foundry Hill TR27 ....142 B4
Foundry La Hayle TR27 ...142 B5
Newlyn TR18 ....143 C2
Foundry Rd
Camborne TR14 ....138 E3
Stithians TR3 ....80 F3
Foundry Row 5 TR15 ....140 B5
Foundry Sq TR27 ....142 B5
Foundry St 6 PL27 ....108 B5
Foundry Terr PL27 ....108 B5
Fountain Ct 27 TR18 ....143 E6
Fountains Cres PL2 ....128 C8
Four Acres Rd TR2 ....83 F6
Four Lanes End TR19 ....88 B1
Four Lanes' End TR19 ....97 F6
Fourgates Est PL14 ....51 F5
Fourlanesend Com Prim Sch
PL10 ....132 F3
Fowey Com Coll PL23 ....116 B4
Fowey Cres 27 PL17 ....39 F4
Fowey Gdns PL3 ....129 D6
Fowey Hospl PL23 ....116 C5
Fowey Mus* PL23 ....116 D4
Fowey Prim Sch PL23 ....116 C4
Fowlfield Row TR13 ....90 F3
Fox Field Cl PL3 ....129 C5
Fox's La TR11 ....145 B3
Foxdown PL27 ....108 D5
Foxes Field TR18 ....88 E6
Foxes La 5 TR19 ....88 C1
Foxglove Cl PL15 ....106 E4
Foxglove Way PL12 ....122 B3
Foxhole La PL26 ....85 D5
Foxhole Prim Sch PL26 ....58 D5
Foxs Yd TR10 ....144 D7
Foxstanton Dr TR10 ....144 D7
Foxtor Cl PL5 ....124 B3
Foxwood Gdns
Plymouth, Plymstock PL9 ..135 F5
Plymouth, Southway PL6 ..124 E5
Foyle Cl PL7 ....131 A5
Fraddam Rd TR27 ....78 D1
Fradgan Pl TR18 ....143 C2
Fradgan The 12 TR18 ....143 C2
Frances St TR1 ....137 C4
Francis La PL27 ....21 D5
Francis Rd PL27 ....21 D5
Francis St PL1 ....148 A3
Frankfort Gate 9 PL1 ....148 B3
Frankland Cl TR11 ....144 F3
Franklin Cl PL27 ....108 D6
Franklyn Cl PL25 ....114 F5
Franklyns Cl PL6 ....125 A4
Franklyns' PL6 ....125 A4
Franwill Terr 15 TR18 ....143 C1
Fraser Pl PL5 ....124 C7
Fraser Rd PL5 ....124 C7
Fraser Sq PL5 ....124 C7
Frederick St E PL1 ....148 B3
Frederick St W 6 PL1 ....148 B3
Fredington Gr PL2 ....128 B6
Freedom Sq PL4 ....149 B4
Freeman Collins Dr
TR11 ....144 F4
Freemans Wharf PL1 ....134 A8
Fremantle Gdns 4 PL2 ....127 F4
Fremantle Pl PL2 ....127 F4
Frenchman's La PL12 ....53 C4
Frensham Ave PL6 ....125 C7
Frensham Gdns PL6 ....125 C7
Freshbrook Cl TR18 ....88 E6
Freshford Cl PL6 ....125 C1
Freshford Wlk PL6 ....125 C1
Freshwater La TR2 ....95 B6

Frewin Gdns PL6 ....125 B6
Friar's La Mullion TR12 ..102 F6
  Ruan Minor TR12 ....103 B5
Friars Wlk PL19 ....147 E2
Friars' La PL1 ....149 A2
Friary Pk PL4 ....149 B3
Friary St PL4 ....149 B3
Frith Rd PL12 ....122 D3
Frobisher App PL5 ....124 E2
Frobisher Dr PL12 ....122 C2
Frobisher Terr 8 TR11 ..145 A5
Frobisher Way
  Tavistock PL12 ....147 B5
  Torpoint PL11 ....126 D3
Frog La PL2 ....71 F3
Frogmore Ave
  Plymouth PL6 ....129 B7
  Plymouth PL6 ....129 B7
Frogmore Ct PL6 ....129 B7
Frogwell Rd PL7 ....39 E4
Frome Cl PL7 ....131 A4
Front Rd PL11 ....64 C4
Frontfield Cres PL6 ....124 E5
Frost Ct TR11 ....144 E5
Fuggoe Croft TR26 ....141 C3
Fuggoe La TR26 ....141 C2
Fullaford Rd PL17 ....40 A4
Fuller Rd TR6 ....55 A5
Fuller-Tre Cl PL26 ....46 F3
Fullerton Rd PL2 ....128 A5
Furland Cl PL9 ....135 C5
Furneaux Ave PL2 ....128 B5
Furneaux Rd PL2 ....128 B6
Furry Way TR13 ....146 B5
Fursdon Cl PL6 ....136 C6
Furse Pk PL5 ....127 C7
Furze Cross EX22 ....8 E5
Furze Gdns EX23 ....2 D1
Furze Hill PL1 ....109 E5
Furze Pk Polruan PL23 ..116 D2
  St Stasey PL27 ....32 D5
  Trelights PL29 ....22 D6
Furzeacre Cl PL7 ....131 A7
Furzedown Terr PL13 ..117 C4
Furzehatt Ave PL9 ....136 A6
Furzehatt Rd PL9 ....136 A6
Furzehatt Rd PL9 ....135 F6
Furzehatt Rise PL9 ....136 A6
Furzehatt Villas PL9 ..135 F6
Furzehatt Way PL9 ....136 A6
Furzehill Rd PL4 ....128 F4

G

Gabriel St 5 TR26 ....141 B5
Gains Cross EX22 ....5 F3
Gainsborough Park Cvn Pk
  PL26 ....58 D5
Galileo Cl PL7 ....130 E6
Gallacher Way PL12 ..122 B3
Galland Rd TR1 ....69 F4
Gallant's Dr PL23 ....116 B3
Galleon Ct TR7 ....110 D4
Gallery La Landrake PL12 .53 A1
  St Germans PL12 ....65 A8
Galligan Cl TR19 ....97 A6
Galligan La TR19 ....97 A6
Gallops The PL12 ....122 D4
Galsworthy Ct PL5 ....124 C2
Galva Rd PL7 ....131 C8
Gander La TR13 ....146 B6
Ganges Cl TR11 ....82 C2
Ganges Rd PL2 ....128 A5
Ganna Park Rd PL2 ....128 D6
Gannel Rd TR7 ....110 E4
Gannel View Cl TR8 ....111 B3
Gannet Dr PL25 ....114 C1
Gara Cl PL9 ....136 B6
Garby La PL5 ....140 C3
Garcia Terr PL15 ....106 D4
Garden Cl PL7 ....131 D5
Garden Ct PL26 ....148 B1
Garden La PL19 ....147 B5
Garden Mdw TR11 ....144 E3
Garden Pk Cl PL9 ....136 C2
Garden St PL2 ....127 E4
Garden Village PL5 ....135 F8
Garden Way PL8 ....111 F3
Gardeners Way PL27 ....32 E6
Gards La PL5 ....123 C2
Garfield Terr PL1,PL3 ..128 A3
Garland PL TR14 ....138 C6
Garlidna 23 TR18 ....143 C6
Garras Com Prim Sch
  TR12 ....99 D3
Garrett St PL10 ....133 A1
Garrick Cl PL3 ....124 C2
Garrison Cl PL1 ....127 E1
Garro La TR12 ....99 A1
Garston Cl PL9 ....136 A8
Garth Morcom PL14 ....113 B5
Garth Rd TR18 ....143 B3
Garth-An-Creet TR26 ....77 A6
Gas Hill TR1 ....137 E2
Gas La 8 TR15 ....140 B4
Gas St TR14 ....138 D3
Gascoyne Cl PL4 ....149 A3
Gascoyne Pl PL4 ....149 A3
Gashouse La PL4 ....149 B2
Gasking St PL4 ....149 A3
Gateway Ct TR27 ....77 E2
Gatewynyack TR12 ....101 C1
Gavercoombe Pk PL34 ..14 C7
Gay's Hill TR12,TR14 ..146 E4

Gays La PL12 ....65 A8
Gdynia Way PL4 ....149 C2
Gear Hill Madron TR20 ..88 C8
  Mawgan TR12 ....99 E8
Gear La TR20 ....88 B8
Gears La
  Goldsithney TR17,TR20 ..89 D6
  Goldsithney TR20 ....89 E5
Geasons La PL7 ....130 E5
Geever Cotts TR19 ....86 FB
Geevor Tin Mine* TR19 ..74 F1
Geevor Tin Mine Mus*
  TR19 ....74 F1
Geffery Cl PL12 ....53 C3
Gendalls Way PL15 ....106 B8
Gennys Cl PL18 ....40 E6
George Ave PL7 ....130 F6
George Cross PL7 ....130 F5
George Downing Ho
  PL6 ....125 A1
George Fox Cl PL15 ....106 A4
George La PL7 ....130 E6
George Pl PL1 ....148 A2
George Sq PL1 ....127 F1
George St Plymouth PL1 ..127 F1
  Truro TR1 ....137 C4
Georges La PL11 ....64 C6
Georges Paddock PL15 ..27 B3
Georgia Cres PL3 ....129 C6
Geraldine Terr PL12 ..122 C1
Germoe Prim Sch TR20 ..90 C6
Gerrans Cl PL25 ....115 B5
Gerrans Hill TR2 ....83 B2
Gerrans Sch TR2 ....83 B1
Gerrans Sq TR2 ....83 B2
Ghost Hill TR12 ....99 E8
Gibbon La PL4 ....149 A3
Gibbons Fields 9 TR12 ..99 A2
Gibbons St PL4 ....149 A3
Gibbs La PL15 ....9 C1
Gibraltar Terr 6 TR12 ..95 A6
Gibralter Sq 8 EX23 ....4 E1
Gibson Way TR18 ....91 B1
Gifford Pl PL3 ....128 D4
Gifford Terrace Rd PL3 ..128 E5
Gig La TR3 ....82 A7
Gilbert Cl PL26 ....58 B4
Gilbert Ct PL7 ....131 B6
Gilbert La PL27 ....128 C5
Gilbert Rd PL31 ....109 F4
Gill Pk PL3 ....129 B5
Gill-An-Creet TR26 ....77 A7
Gillbard Centenary Cl
  PL15 ....106 B5
Gilley La PL26 ....73 A4
Gills Cl TR10 ....144 B6
Gilly Fields TR15 ....140 B3
Gilly Gabben Ind Est
  TR12 ....99 B7
Gilly Hill Curry TR12 ..99 B5
  Plymouth TR15 ....140 C3
Gilly La TR26 ....77 C1
Gilston Rd PL12 ....122 D4
Gilwell Ave PL4 ....136 B7
Gilwell Pl PL4 ....149 A3
Gilwell St PL4 ....149 A3
Gipsy La Helston TR13 ..91 C2
  Liskeard PL14 ....113 A5
Gitchell La Crowlas TR20 ..89 C8
  St Erth TR20 ....77 C1
Glade The PL20 ....42 B2
Gladstone Rd PL30 ....109 C2
Gladstone Terr
  Longrock TR20 ....88 F6
  3 Redruth TR15 ....140 C5
Gladwell Gdns 10 EX23 ..4 D1
Glamis Rd TR7 ....111 B6
Glantis Cres TR9 ....45 E2
Glanville Ave 1 PL19 ..147 B5
Glanville Rd PL19 ....147 B6
Glanville St PL1,PL4 ..148 C3
Glanville Terr PL12 ..122 F3
Glasney Pl TR10 ....144 C7
Glasney Rd TR11 ....145 A5
Glasney Terr TR10 ....144 D7
Glebe Ave PL12 ....122 F3
Glebe Cl Mawgan TR12 ..99 D7
  3 St Columb Major TR9 ..45 E6
Glebe Cres PL27 ....32 D6
Glebe Dr PL26 ....46 F3
Glebe Mdw PL17 ....29 F5
Glebe Parc PL30 ....23 E3
Glebe Pl PL12 ....103 B5
Glebe Row PL27 ....142 D7
Glebe Terr
  Constantine TR11 ....92 F4
  Ruan Minor TR12 ....103 B5
Glebe The
  Camborne TR14 ....138 C3
  Cubert TR8 ....55 D8
  St Mellion PL12 ....53 D8
  Week St Mary EX22 ....11 E8
Glebelands
  Callington PL17 ....39 E5
  Looe PL13 ....117 D5
Glen Dale Cres TR15 ..140 D4
Glen Leigh TR15 ....140 A6
Glen Park Ave PL4 ....148 C4
Glen Park Prim Sch
  PL7 ....131 B5
Glen Pk PL14 ....38 D4
Glen Rd
  Plymouth, Mannamead
    PL3 ....128 F5
  2 Plymouth, Plympton PL7 ..130 F6
  Wadebridge PL27 ....108 B5
Glen Vale TR15 ....139 E6

Glen View Par PL24 ....60 D5
  Penryn TR10 ....144 B8
  Wadebridge PL27 ....108 B4
Glen-Dale Cl PL23 ....115 A5
Glen-Dale Cres PL25 ..115 A5
Glenavon Rd PL3 ....128 E5
Glenburn Cl PL3 ....128 E7
Glendale Cres TR14 ....68 C6
Glendale Terr PL26 ....58 E3
Glendower Rd PL3 ....128 D5
Glendurgan Gdns* TR11 ..93 D2
Gleneagle Ave 4 PL3 ..128 F6
Gleneagle Rd PL3 ....128 F6
Gleneagle Villas St PL3 ..128 F6
Glenfeadon Terr TR16 ....67 C6
Glenfield Cl PL6 ....125 D6
Glenfield Rd PL6 ....125 D5
Glenfield Wdg PL6 ....125 D5
Glenholt Cl PL6 ....125 D6
Glenholt Rd PL6 ....125 D6
Glenhurst Rd 5 PL3 ..128 E6
Glenmoor La TR17 ....89 C6
Glenmore Ave PL2 ....127 F5
Glenmore Terr TR14 ..113 D6
Glennaven Cl PL7 ....131 C6
Glenside Rise PL7 ....130 E6
Glenthorne Rd TR3 ....69 E3
Glentor Rd PL3 ....128 E7
Glenwood Rd PL3 ....128 D4
Globe Vale Cvn Pk TR16 ..68 B3
Globerdon Rd PL14 ....38 E4
Gloucester Ave PL25 ..115 C3
Gloucester Cl PL1 ....148 C3
Gloucester Ct PL1 ....148 C4
Gloucester Pl
  28 Newlyn TR18 ....143 C2
  Plymouth PL1 ....148 C4
Gloucester Rd TR18 ..143 C2
Gloweth View TR1 ....69 E3
Gloweth Villas TR1 ....69 E3
Gluyas The TR11 ....144 E1
Glyn Way TR3 ....69 E3
Glyn Ct 7 TR13 ....146 C5
Glynn Rd Liskeard PL14 ..113 A5
  Padstow PL28 ....107 D5
Goad Ave Plymouth PL4 ..149 C2
Goad Cl PL11 ....126 F3
Godding Gdns PL6 ....124 E6
Godolphin Ave TR17 ....89 B5
Godolphin Cl TR17 ....89 B6
Godolphin Cres TR13 ....90 C6
Godolphin Cross St TR13 ..90 D3
Godolphin Dr TR17 ....89 B6
Godolphin Ho* TR13 ....90 C6
Godolphin Pl TR17 ....89 C4
Godolphin Prim Sch
  TR13 ....90 C6
Godolphin Rd
  Falmouth TR11 ....144 F5
  Helston TR13 ....146 C6
  Longrock TR20 ....88 F6
Godolphin Terr TR17 ....89 B5
Godolphin Way TR17 ..111 E7
Godrevy Cl TR26 ....141 D2
Godrevy Ho TR1 ....69 F4
Godrevy Pk (Cvn Pk)
  TR27 ....66 B1
Godrevy Terr 22 TR26 ..141 B6
Godshank Bglws PL30 ....34 C2
Golden Sands Bglws
  TR27 ....142 E7
Goldfinch Cl PL15 ....106 E4
Goldfinch Cres PL12 ..122 E4
Goldfinch Gr PL12 ....122 D4
Goldmartin Cl TR11 ....93 D3
Goldsmith Gdns PL5 ..124 D3
Goldsworthy Way PL27 ..108 B6
Golf House Rd PL24 ....104 D6
Golf Terr TR7 ....110 C6
Golitha Falls* PL14 ....37 D3
Gonvena Hill PL27 ....108 D6
Goodeve Cl PL9 ....135 E6
Goodmans La PL14 ....38 A4
Goodmartin Sq TR11 ....93 D3
Goodwin Ave PL6 ....125 A6
Goodwin Cres PL2 ....128 A6
Goongumpas La TR16 ....68 E1
Goonhavern Prim Sch
  TR4 ....55 D4
Goonown La TR5 ....54 D1
Goonown Rd
  Goonbell TR5 ....68 D8
  St Agnes TR5 ....54 D1
Goonrea PL13 ....117 D3
Goonrea Cl TR7 ....110 F4
Goonvrea Cl TR7 ....110 F4
Goonvrea Rd TR5 ....54 C1
  Penryn TR10 ....144 B8
Goonwartha Cl PL13 ..117 C4
Goonwartha Rd PL13 ..117 B3
Gooseberry La
  Pensilva PL14 ....38 E4
  Plymouth PL1 ....148 B2
Gooseford La PL11 ....132 C8
Goosewell Hill PL6 ....129 C8
Goosewell Park Rd PL9 ..135 F6
Goosewell Prim Sch
  PL9 ....135 F6
Goosewell Rd PL9 ....135 F6
Goosewell Terr PL9 ..135 F6
Gordon Cl PL22 ....122 D2
Gordon Pl 8 TR9 ....45 E6
Gordon Terr PL4 ....128 E4

Gordons Cl TR3 ....80 F3
Gorran Sch PL26 ....85 B5
Gorse Cl TR7 ....111 A4
Gorsey Cl PL5 ....124 E2
Gorvin Cross EX39 ....3 A6
Goswela Cl PL9 ....135 F5
Goswela Gdns PL9 ....135 F5
Gotch Gdns PL4 ....50 B6
Gothers Rd St Dennis PL26 ..58 C7
  St Dennis, Gathers PL26 ..46 D1
Goudges La PL26 ....58 E8
Gounce The 8 TR6 ....55 A5
Gover Cl TR4 ....44 C6
Gover La TR7 ....110 D6
Gover Rd PL25 ....114 B4
Goverseth Cvn Pk PL26 ..58 D6
Goverseth Hill PL26 ....58 D6
Goverseth Rd PL26 ....58 D6
Goverseth Terr PL26 ..58 D6
Gower Ridge Rd PL9 ..135 D6
Goyne's Field TR4 ....68 A7
Gracca Terr PL26 ....47 C1
Grade-Ruan Sch TR12 ..103 B5
Grafton Rd PL4 ....128 E4
Graham Ave PL25 ....114 E4
Graham Rd Redruth TR15 ..140 C5
  Redruth TR15 ....140 D8
Grainge Rd PL6 ....125 A1
Grampound Rd Village CE
  Sch TR2 ....57 E1
Grampound Road Ind Est
  TR2 ....57 E1
Grampound-with-Creed CE
  Sch TR2 ....72 A7
Granby Ct PL1 ....127 E2
Granby Gn PL1 ....127 E2
Granby Pl PL1 ....127 E2
Granby St PL1 ....127 E2
Granby Way PL1 ....127 E2
Grand Hotel Rd PL1 ..148 B1
Grand Par PL1 ....148 B1
Grange Cotts PL7 ....130 F4
Grange Rd Helston TR13 ..146 B5
  Plymouth PL7 ....131 A4
  Yelverton PL20 ....42 C3
Granite Way PL17 ....39 F4
Grannery Ct EX23 ....104 D5
Granny's Gn PL31 ....109 E3
Granny's La TR6 ....55 A4
Grant's Ct PL25 ....114 C3
Grant's Wlk 4 PL25 ..114 C3
Grantham Ct PL7 ....130 B4
Grantley Gdns PL3 ....129 A5
Granville Terr EX23 ..104 D5
Grasmere Cl PL6 ....124 E5
Grasmere La PL14 ....38 B5
Grass Valley Pk PL31 ..109 F1
Grassendale Ave PL2 ..127 F7
Grassmere Way PL12 ..122 D4
Gratton Cross EX23 ....42 D2
Gratton La PL20 ....42 D2
Gravesend Gdns PL11 ..127 B3
Gravesend Wlk PL5 ..123 D4
Gray Cres PL5 ....127 C8
Graybridge Rd PL20 ....42 C4
Great Berry Rd PL6 ....124 F1
Great Charles Cl PL26 ..58 B4
Great Churchway PL9 ..136 A7
Great Mdw PL14 ....36 F2
Great Mis Tor Cl 5 PL20 ..42 C3
Great Orchard Cl 4 PL7 ..131 C5
Great Pk 4 PL7 ....130 C5
Great Western Commercial
  Village PL22 ....112 D2
Great Western Rd PL1 ..148 B1
Great Wheat Seton
  TR14 ....138 F6
Great Woodford Dr PL7 ..130 B6
Greatfield Rd PL3 ....129 B7
Greatlands Cres PL2 ..128 A6
Greatlands Pl PL2 ....128 A6
Greatwood TR11 ....82 C3
Grebe Cl PL7 ....130 F5
Greeb Way TR20 ....89 D4
Green Acre PL15 ....28 A5
Green Ct Feock TR3 ....82 C5
  Truro TR1 ....137 B3
Green Cres TR13 ....146 D7
Green Hill Lamerton PL19 ..30 A3
  St Martin TR12 ....100 D6
  Tavistock PL17 ....147 B5
  Wadebridge PL27 ....108 E5
Green Hill Terr TR12 ..100 D6
Green Hill Villas PL27 ..108 E5
Green La Bodmin PL31 ..109 F2
  Boscastle PL35 ....9 C1
  Cawsand PL10 ....133 A2
  Crantock TR8 ....43 D3
  Fowey PL23 ....116 C5
  Gwithian TR27 ....66 B2
  Lelant TR26 ....77 B6
  Marazion TR17 ....89 B6
  Penryn TR10 ....144 B8
  Porthleven TR13 ....91 B1
  Portholland TR2 ....84 D6
  Redruth, Wheal Rose TR16 ..68 C4
  Rock PL27 ....21 D2
  Ruan Minor TR12 ....103 A2
  Tavistock PL19 ....147 F7
  Truro TR1 ....137 B3
  Veryan TR2 ....83 F6
  Yelverton PL20 ....42 C1
Green La The PL27 ....108 E5
Green La W PL17 ....39 F4
Green Lane Cl TR10 ..144 B8
Green Lane Hill TR14 ..138 F8
Green Lane Vean TR15 ..140 B5

Green Mdws PL32 ....105 C3
Green Park Ave PL4 ....128 D4
Green Park Rd PL9 ....135 E6
Green Pk PL10 ....133 A2
Green St Penzance TR18 ..143 E4
  Truro TR1 ....137 D5
Green The Bridgerule EX22 ..8 A4
  Carnon Downs TR3 ....82 A6
  Cawsand PL10 ....133 A1
  8 Horrabridge PL20 ....42 C4
  Liskeard PL14 ....113 B5
  Meavy PL20 ....127 F6
  Milton Combe PL20 ....120 B7
  Nancegollan TR13 ....91 A1
  Plymouth PL7 ....135 E1
  Probus TR2 ....71 C6
  Saltash PL12 ....122 E1
  St Martin TR12 ....100 D6
  6 Trevnon PL25 ....59 D2
Greenacres Bodmin PL30 ..34 C2
  Plymouth PL9 ....135 F6
Greenbank
  Connor Downs TR27 ....78 C2
  1 Penzance TR18 ....143 E3
  Polruan PL23 ....116 C2
Greenbank Ave PL4 ....149 A4
Greenbank Cl TR12 ....57 E6
Greenbank Cres TR7 ....111 C5
Greenbank La PL14 ....113 C1
Greenbank Rd
  Devoran TR3 ....81 F6
  Liskeard PL14 ....113 C1
  Plymouth PL4 ....149 B4
Greenbank Terr
  1 Callington PL17 ....39 F5
  Plymouth PL4 ....149 A4
  9 Yelverton PL20 ....42 C3
Greenbanks Ct PL27 ....21 E1
Greendale Pd PL2 ....128 A5
Greendale Rd 8 TR12 ..102 F2
Greenfield Rd PL12 ..122 D2
Greenfield Terr TR16 ....67 D6
Greenfields Cl TR11 ....93 D3
Greenhill Cl PL19 ....30 B3
Greenhill Ct PL9 ....135 C5
Greenland PL10 ....132 F1
Greenlees Dr PL2 ....131 B6
Greenmarket The 7
  TR18 ....143 E4
Greens The Sennen TR19 ..96 C1
  Sennen Cove TR19 ....86 B6
Greensplat Rd PL26 ....114 A4
Greensway Rd PL19 ..147 C2
Greenway Ave PL7 ....130 A6
Greenway Cl 3 PL20 ..42 C4
Greenwich Cl PL12 ....122 F1
Greenwich Pl 1 PL19 ..137 B8
Greenwich Cres TR3 ....81 D1
Greenwich Hill TR3 ....81 D1
Greenwich Rd TR3 ....81 D1
Greenwood Cres TR3 ..81 D1
Greenwood Park Cl PL7 ..131 B6
Greenwood Park Rd
  PL7 ....131 B6
Greenwood Rd TR10 ..144 A6
Gregor Rd TR1 ....137 F
Gregory's Ct 10 PL31 ..109 F2
Gregory's Mdw PL15 ..106 F7
Grenfell Ave PL12 ....122 D4
Grenfell Gdns PL12 ..122 C4
Grenfell St 11 TR19 ....89 E5
Grenifer Rd TR15 ....139 C1
Grenna La TR3 ....81 D1
Grenofen Cl PL19 ....42 A4
Grenville Cl TR12 ....57 E6
Grenville Cres TR11 ..144 F7
Grenville Ct
  Plymouth PL7 ....131 C5
  2 St Austell PL25 ....114 C2
Grenville Dr
  8 St Agnes TR5 ....54 D1
  Tavistock PL19 ....147 B5
Grenville Mdws PL22 ..112 C2
Grenville Pk PL20 ....42 D7
Grenville Rd
  Falmouth TR11 ....145 A5
  Helston TR13 ....146 D7
  Lostwithiel PL22 ....112 D2
  Padstow PL28 ....107 C4
  Plymouth PL4 ....149 C2
  Truro TR1 ....137 B5
Grenville Road La S
  PL4 ....129 B2
Grenville Wlk PL13 ....62 D2
Gresham Cl
  Newquay TR7 ....110 F4
  Plymouth TR7 ....124 C2
Greys Terr 1 TR16 ....140 F3
Greystoke Ave PL6 ....129 B8
Gribbas Cl TR3 ....80 F2
Gribben Cl PL25 ....114 E6
Gribben Rd PL25 ....114 E6
Griffin Way PL9 ....136 C8
Griffins The PL14 ....113 D6
Griggs Cl PL7 ....131 B6
Griggs Hill TR27 ....77 E3
Grimscott Est EX23 ....5 B2
Grimstone Terr PL20 ..42 B2
Grist La TR27 ....78 C5
Grizedale Rd PL6 ....129 C7
Grose Hires Cres 10 PL26 ..59 D2
Grose Mdws PL26 ....58 B4
Grosvenor Ave TR7 ....110 E6
Grosvenor Cotts 1 PL4 ..128 F4
Grosvenor Pl PL25 ....114 B4

Grosvenor Rd PL6 .....124 F2
Grove Cotts TR2 .....57 C1
Grove Dr 3 PL14 .....51 A7
Grove Hill
  Mawnan Smith TR11 .....93 D3
  St Mawes TR2 .....95 A6
Grove La TR20 .....89 F5
Grove Park Ct PL14 .....113 B4
Grove Pk Par PL24 .....60 C6
  Tavistock PL19 .....147 D5
  Torpoint PL11 .....126 E3
Grove Pl
  6 Falmouth TR11 .....145 C3
  Padstow PL28 .....107 D5
Grove Rd Par PL24 .....115 F6
  St Austell PL25 .....114 B4
Grove The
  Plymouth, Plymstock PL9 .....135 D8
  Plymouth, Stoke PL3 .....128 A4
Grovehill Cres TR11 .....145 A5
Grovehill Dr TR11 .....145 B3
Grovehill Ho TR11 .....145 B3
Grylls Parc TR13 .....146 B6
Grylls Pk PL13 .....62 A7
Sue The 8 TR13 .....96 D8
Guildford Ct PL5 .....124 E3
Guildford Rd TR27 .....142 E7
Guildford Road Ind Est
  TR27 .....142 E6
Guildford St PL4 .....149 A3
Guildhall La PL12 .....122 C2
Guildhall Sq PL1 .....148 C2
Guineaport Parc PL27 .....108 C5
Guineaport Rd PL27 .....108 C5
Guipavas Rd PL7 .....39 F4
Gulland Rd PL27 .....21 D6
Gully's Ct PL26 .....58 B8
Gulval Almshouses
  TR18 .....143 F8
Gulval Com Prim Sch
  TR18 .....88 E6
Gulworthy Cotts PL19 .....41 B7
Gulworthy Cross PL19 .....41 B7
Gulworthy Prim Sch
  PL19 .....41 B7
Gun Hill Rd TR8 .....43 B1
Gunnislake Prim Sch
  PL18 .....40 F6
Gunnislake Rural Workshops
  PL18 .....40 F5
Gunpool La 3 PL35 .....9 C1
Gunrogget Rd PL20 .....90 A7
Gurlyn Hill TR20 .....90 A7
Gurnard Wlk PL3 .....129 C6
Gurney Ct Bude EX23 .....104 E7
  Torpoint PL11 .....126 F3
Gurney's La 2 TR14 .....138 D3
Gurnick Est TR18 .....143 B2
Gurnick Rd TR18 .....143 B1
Gurnick St 23 TR19 .....88 C1
Gustavus Rd TR14 .....138 D3
Gustory Rd TR8 .....43 D3
Guy Miles Way PL5 .....124 B3
Gwallon La TR17 .....89 C6
Gwallon Rd PL25 .....114 E5
Gwarnick Rd TR1 .....137 B4
Gwarth An Drae TR13 .....146 C8
Gwarth An Ore TR27 .....142 E8
Gwavas Bglws 4 TR18 .....143 C1
Gwavas La PL18 .....88 C2
Gwavas Rd TR18 .....143 C1
Gwavas St 10 TR18 .....143 E6
Gweal Darras TR10 .....81 C1
Gweal Goldas TR27 .....142 E8
Gweal Wartha TR13 .....146 B8
Gweal-an-Top PL25 .....140 D5
Gweal-an-Top Inf Sch
  TR15 .....140 C5
Gwealdues TR13 .....146 B7
Gwealfolds Rd TR13 .....146 C7
Gwealla Warren
  TR13 .....146 B7
Gwedhenek TR18 .....143 C7
Gweek Dr Gweek TR12 .....92 C1
  Rawgan TR12 .....99 D8
Gweek La TR13 .....92 A3
Gwel An Garrek 2 TR12 .....99 A1
Gwel An Wheal TR14
Gwel An Wheal Cres
  TR26 .....141 A4
Gwel Avon Bsns Pk
  PL12 .....122 D4
Gwel Lewern TR18 .....108 E6
Gwel Marten Flats TR26 .....141 E2
Gwel Mengleth PL27 .....108 D5
Gwel Trencrom TR27 .....142 B3
Gwel-an-mor
  Marazion TR17 .....89 C5
  St Austell PL25 .....115 A5
  Trenance TR8 .....31 C2
Gwel-An-Nans Cl 2
  PL18 .....113 B5
Gwel-An-Scol TR13 .....82 C5
Gwel-Mor TR19 .....75 A1
Gwel-Tek TR27 .....142 D8
Gwelamor Cl TR26 .....141 D2
Gwelanmor Rd TR26 .....141 D2
Gwelavon Cl PL27 .....108 D5
Gwelenys Rd 3 TR19 .....88 C1
Gwel-An-Nans TR7 .....71 C6
Gwelmeneth Pk 6 PL14 .....38 A3
Gwelmor TR14 .....138 E2
Gwendra La PL26 .....58 E8
Gwendroc Cl TR1 .....137 D3
Gwendroc House Mews
  TR1 .....137 D3

Gwendrona Cl TR13 .....146 D8
Gwendrona Way TR13 .....146 D8
Gwennap Pit 8 TR16 .....140 F4
Gwindra Ind Est PL26 .....58 C3
Gwindra Rd PL26 .....58 B4
Gwinear Com Prim Sch
  TR27 .....78 E4
Gwinear La TR27 .....78 E4
Gwinear Rd TR27 .....78 E5
Gwithian Cl PL11 .....126 F4
Gwithian Rd
  Connor Downs TR27 .....78 D6
  Gwithian TR27 .....66 C1
Gwithian Sands Chalet Pk
  TR27 .....66 B1
Gwyn Rd PL4 .....149 C4
Gwythian Way TR6 .....55 A4
Gyllyng Hall TR11 .....145 B3
Gyllyng St TR11 .....145 B4
Gyllyngvase Hill TR11 .....145 B2
Gyllyngvase Rd TR11 .....145 C2
Gyllyngvase Terr TR11 .....145 C2

H

Haddington Rd PL2 .....127 F4
Haddon Way PL25 .....115 D3
Hain Pl 8 TR18 .....143 E7
Hain Wlk TR26 .....141 C4
Halcyon Ct PL2 .....128 A6
Halcyon Rd PL2 .....128 A6
Haley Barton 4 PL2 .....128 A5
Halgavor Pk PL31 .....109 F1
Halgavor Rd PL30,PL31 .....109 D2
Halgavor View PL31 .....109 F2
Halifax Rd PL27 .....31 F3
Halimote Rd PL26 .....58 C8
Hall Loft Flats 2 TR26 .....141 B6
Hall Rd PL26 .....58 C8
Hall Terr PL23 .....116 E5
Hallan Vean TR19 .....96 A6
Hallane Rd PL25 .....115 A6
Hallaze Rd PL26 .....59 D7
Hallerton Cl PL6 .....125 E2
Hallett Cl PL12 .....122 B3
Hallett Way EX23 .....104 F7
Halloon Ave TR8 .....58 C7
Halley Gdns PL25 .....123 E1
Halloon Ave TR9 .....45 E2
Halt Rd Goonhavern TR4 .....55 D6
  St Newlyn East TR8 .....56 B7
Halvarras Pk TR3 .....82 B8
Halvarras Rd TR3 .....82 B8
Halveor Ct TR3 .....45 C6
Halveor La TR19 .....45 C6
Halwin La TR13 .....92 B8
Halwin Prim Sch TR13 .....92 C8
Halwyn Cl 4 PL3 .....81 F7
Halwyn Hill TR8 .....110 A3
Halwyn Pl TR1 .....137 B4
Halwyn Rd TR1 .....110 A3
Harwell Cl 6 PL3 .....148 B3
Ham Cl PL2 .....128 B8
Ham Dr PL2 .....128 B8
Ham Gn PL2 .....128 A7
Ham Green Ct PL2 .....128 A7
Ham Green La PL2 .....128 A7
Ham Ho PL2 .....128 A8
Hamble Cl PL3 .....129 D7
Hamble Ct PL3 .....129 D7
Hamilton Ct TR27 .....142 B4
Hamilton Gdns PL4 .....128 D4
Hamilton Rd TR11 .....145 D3
Hammill's Cl 13 TR13 .....98 C8
Hammils Dr 15 TR13 .....98 C8
Hamoaze Ave PL5 .....127 D8
Hamoaze Pl PL1 .....127 D2
Hamoaze Rd PL11 .....127 B2
Hampton Sch PL4 .....149 A3
Hancock Cl PL6 .....124 D6
Hancock La 14 TR2 .....95 A6
Hangmans Wlk TR11 .....145 A1
Hannaford Rd PL16 .....119 F3
Hannafore Rd PL13 .....117 C3
Hannafore Rd PL13 .....117 D2
Hanover Cl
  10 Perranporth TR6 .....55 A5
  Plymouth PL3 .....129 B5
Hanover Ct
  Camborne TR14 .....138 E4
  16 Penzance TR18 .....143 E6
  3 Plymouth PL1 .....149 A2
Hanover Ho EX23 .....4 D4
Hanover Pk TR9 .....45 F2
Hanover Rd PL3 .....129 C4
Hanson Dr PL23 .....116 C3
Hanson Rd PL14 .....113 D6
Harbour Ave
  Plymouth PL4 .....149 A2
  Plymouth, Camels Head
  PL5
Harbour Ct
  Falmouth TR11 .....145 B4
  15 Penzance TR18 .....143 E5
  Portreath TR16 .....67 C6
Harbour Ct Flats
  Portreath TR16 .....83 C2
Harbour Lights 11 TR18 .....143 C1
Harbour Par PL4 .....60 C4
  Portleven TR13 .....98 B8
  Wadebridge PL27 .....108 C5
Harbour St PL11 .....127 B2
Harbour Terr
  Portreath TR11 .....145 B5
  Portreath TR16 .....67 C6

Harbour View
  Fowey PL23 .....116 C4
  Hayle TR27 .....142 B5
  Marazion TR17 .....89 C5
  Penryn TR10 .....144 B8
  Plymouth PL9 .....135 A7
  6 Porthleven TR13 .....98 B8
  Saltash PL12 .....122 E2
  Truro TR1 .....137 E3
Harbour View Cres
  TR18 .....143 E6
Harbourside 13 TR13 .....98 B8
Harcourt Cl TR1 .....69 F3
Hardisworthy Cross EX39 .....2 E7
Hardy Cres PL5 .....124 E1
Hardy Ho TR3 .....80 F3
Harebell Cl PL12 .....122 D4
Harefield Cres TR14 .....138 D4
Hareston Cl PL7 .....131 B3
Harewood Cl PL7 .....130 C5
Harewood Cres PL5 .....124 B2
Harewood Rd PL18 .....41 A3
Hargood Terr 2 PL2 .....127 F4
Hargreaves Cl PL5 .....123 F2
Harlech Cl PL3 .....129 A7
Harleigh Rd PL31 .....109 E3
Harleigh Terr PL31 .....109 E3
Harlyn Barton PL28 .....20 D1
Harlyn Cotts PL28 .....20 D2
Harlyn Rd PL28 .....20 D1
Harmer Ct PL31 .....109 D6
Harmony Cl
  Redruth TR15 .....140 B6
  Roche PL26 .....46 F3
Harmony Mdw PL26 .....46 F3
Harmony Rd PL26 .....46 F3
Harmony Terr
  4 Illogan TR16 .....67 C4
  Truro TR1 .....137 E2
Harnorlen Rd PL2 .....127 E4
Haroldsleigh Ave PL5 .....124 E2
Harriet Gdns PL7 .....130 B6
Harris Cl PL17 .....39 F6
Harris Cl 11 Penryn TR10 .....144 C7
  Plymouth PL9 .....135 B6
Harrison Gdns TR15 .....139 C7
Harrison St 7 PL2 .....127 F4
Harrison Terr TR1 .....137 B4
Harrowbarrow Sch PL17 .....40 D4
Harrowbeer La PL20 .....42 C3
Hartland Cl PL6 .....125 A7
Hartland Rd PL29 .....22 E7
Hartland Terr EX23 .....104 D6
Hartley Ave PL3 .....129 A6
Hartley Cl PL3 .....129 A6
Hartley Park Gdns PL3 .....128 F6
Hartley Rd PL3 .....128 E6
Hartmeade PL14 .....62 B6
Hartwell Ave PL9 .....136 D7
Harvenna Cl TR9 .....45 E1
Harvey Ave PL4 .....129 B1
Harvey Rd TR1 .....137 D2
Harvey St PL11 .....127 B3
Harvey's Way TR27 .....142 C5
Hatch's Hill TR27 .....78 C5
Havelock Terr PL2 .....127 F3
Haven Ct TR27 .....142 C5
Haven Pk PL14 .....39 A2
Haven Rd EX23 .....10 C6
Hawarden Cotts PL4 .....149 C4
Hawkesley Dr PL6 .....129 B1
Haweswater Cl PL6 .....125 D8
Hawk's Tor Dr PL15 .....27 B7
Hawke Rd PL13 .....146 D4
Hawke Way 9 PL5 .....127 A8
Hawkers Ave PL4 .....149 A2
Hawkinge Gdns PL5 .....123 E4
Hawkins Cl PL6 .....125 A5
Hawkins Ct 7 PL18 .....143 D5
Hawkins Dr PL7 .....110 E5
Hawkins Rd
  Padstow PL28 .....107 C5
  Penzance TR18 .....143 D5
Hawkins Way 7 PL11 .....145 A4
Hawks Pk PL12 .....122 C2
Hawthorn Ave
  Bude EX23 .....104 E4
  Torpoint PL11 .....126 F3
Hawthorn Cl Bude EX23 .....104 E4
  Plymouth PL9 .....135 C5
  Plymouth, Woolwell PL6 .....125 D7
  Redruth TR15 .....140 B6
  St Austell PL25 .....114 F6
  12 St Columb Major TR9 .....45 D6
Hawthorn Pk PL19 .....147 C2
Hawthorn Way
  Plymouth PL3 .....129 B7
  Threemilestone TR3 .....69 C3
Hawthorns PL12 .....122 D2
Haxter Cl PL6 .....121 B1
Hay La Looe PL13 .....117 C4
  Sherlock PL11 .....65 B6
Haydon Gr PL5 .....123 C1
Haye La PL17 .....39 E5
Haye Rd Callington PL17 .....39 D4
  Plymouth PL7,PL9 .....130 C1
Haye Rd S PL9 .....136 C7
Hayes Rd PL9 .....135 C7
Hayle Com Sch TR27 .....142 D5
Hayle Ind Pk TR27 .....142 F6

Hayle Rd TR27 .....78 C1
Hayle Sta TR27 .....142 B5
Hayle Terr TR27 .....142 B5
Hayman Way TR11 .....144 E5
Hayne Corfe Gdns TR1 .....137 A4
Hayston Pl PL14 .....148 B4
Haytor Cl PL5 .....124 B3
Hazel Cl Plymouth PL6 .....125 B6
  St Austell PL25 .....115 A6
Hazel Dr PL9 .....136 C7
Hazel Gr Plymouth PL9 .....136 C7
  Yelverton PL20 .....42 D3
Hazel Rd PL19 .....147 C2
Hazelmead PL14 .....113 B5
Hazelwood Cres PL13 .....136 D7
Hazelwood Dr PL6 .....125 D8
Hazelwood Rd PL17 .....39 F4
Hea Cl TR18 .....143 C7
Hea Cotts 5 TR18 .....143 C7
Hea Rd TR18 .....143 C7
Heabrook Parc 2 TR18 .....143 C7
Headland Cl TR26 .....141 E2
Headland Ct TR26 .....141 E2
Headland Pk PL4 .....149 A4
Headland Rd
  Carbis Bay TR26 .....141 E2
  Newquay TR7 .....110 C2
Headleigh Rd TR7 .....110 F5
Headon Cross EX23 .....11 A5
Healy Cl 9 PL2 .....127 F4
Healy Pl PL2 .....127 F4
Heamoor Com Prim Sch
  TR18 .....143 B6
Heanton Terr
  Millbrook PL10 .....132 E6
  Redruth TR15 .....140 C4
Heanton Villas TR15 .....140 C4
Hearl Rd PL12 .....122 B3
Heath Terr PL18 .....40 F5
Heather Cl
  Heamoor TR18 .....143 B7
  Tavistock PL19 .....147 D4
Heather La TR27 .....77 C2
Heather Mdw TR9 .....45 E1
Heather Way TR20 .....89 F4
Heatherdell Gdns TR26 .....141 E1
Heathers The PL6 .....125 D7
Heathfield Gdns TR15 .....140 E7
Heathfield Pk PL20 .....42 D3
Heathfield Rd PL4 .....129 B3
Heathlands Bsns Pk
  PL14 .....113 C5
Heathlands Ind Est 8
  PL14 .....113 C5
Heathlands Rd PL14 .....113 C5
Heavitree Rd PL10 .....133 A2
Hedgerow Cl PL6 .....125 E8
Hedgerows The PL12 .....122 B3
Hedingham Cl PL7 .....131 C4
Hedingham Gdns PL5 .....125 B7
Helca Dr PL13 .....141 C3
Hele Cross PL15 .....13 E3
Hele Gdns PL7 .....131 C5
Hele La PL6 .....121 F2
Hele's Sch EX23 .....7 A6
Hele's Terr PL4 .....129 B2
Helebridge Rd EX23 .....7 B6
Helena Cl 7 PL6 .....59 D7
Helland Rd PL31 .....109 E6
Hellescott Way TR13 .....146 D8
Hellescott Rd PL15 .....146 C4
Hellesvean Cl 3 TR26 .....77 A6
Hellesveor Cl TR26 .....77 A6
Helleur Cl PL24 .....60 B4
Helman Tor View PL31 .....109 E2
Helnoweth Cotts TR18 .....143 F8
Helnoweth Gdns TR18 .....143 F8
Helnoweth Rd TR18 .....143 F8
Helscott Rd EX23 .....7 A6
Helston Com Hospl
  TR13 .....146 D3
Helston Mus* TR13 .....146 B5
Helston Rd* TR10 .....144 C8
Helston Sch & Com Coll
  TR13 .....146 C7
Hembal Cl 5 PL25 .....59 A3
Hembal La PL25 .....59 A3
Hembal Rd 4 PL25 .....59 A3
Hemerdon Mts PL7 .....131 A6
Hemerdon La PL7 .....131 C8
Hemerdon Way PL7 .....130 D6
Hen Wythva TR14 .....138 E2
Henders Cnr 6 PL3 .....128 F6
Henderson Pl PL2 .....127 F6
Hendra Barton TR1 .....137 B5
Hendra Cl Ashton TR13 .....90 E3
  Stithians TR3 .....80 E4
Hendra Cl Truro TR1 .....137 C5
Hendra Gdns PL15 .....106 B5
Hendra Holiday Pk TR8 .....111 C3
Hendra La Ashton TR13 .....90 D2
  Truro TR1 .....137 C5
Hendra Parc PL14 .....113 C7
Hendra Pk PL15 .....106 B5
Hendra Prazey PL26 .....58 B8
Hendra Rd St Dennis PL26 .....58 C8
  Stithians TR3 .....80 E4
  Truro TR1 .....137 C5
Hendra Terr TR3 .....80 E4
Hendra Tor View PL15 .....26 C7
Hendra Vale PL15 .....106 A4
Hendra Vean
  Carbis Bay TR26 .....141 E1
  Truro TR1 .....137 B5
Hendras Ct TR26 .....141 E2
Hendras Parc TR26 .....141 D2

Hendrawna La TR6 .....55 B4
Hendwell Cl PL6 .....124 E6
Henfor Cl 12 TR17 .....89 C5
Henfor Mews 6 TR17 .....89 C5
Henfor Terr 18 TR17 .....89 C5
Henfordh Grange PL14 .....113 A6
Hengar La PL30 .....23 F3
Henley Cl TR4 .....68 C6
Henley Cres TR4 .....68 C6
Henley Dr
  Mount Hawke TR4 .....68 C6
  Plymouth PL5 .....124 C7
Henliston Dr TR13 .....146 D4
Henry Scott Tuke Ho 5
  .....145 A4
Hensbury La PL20 .....119 F4
Henscol TR16 .....80 D6
Henscol Vale PL14 .....113 A6
Henshorn Ct TR13 .....146 C7
Hental 8 TR6 .....55 A4
Henterverne Cvn & Camping
  Pk EX23 .....10 C5
Henver Cl TR27 .....78 E3
Henver Gdns TR27 .....78 E3
Henver La TR4 .....56 A3
Henver Rd TR7 .....111 B7
Henvor Cl TR15 .....140 D6
Henvor Terr TR15 .....140 C7
Henwood Cres TR7 .....111 C7
Herbert Pl PL1 .....127 E4
Herbert St PL2 .....127 E4
Hereford Rd PL5 .....124 B5
Heritage Ct PL12 .....122 C3
Herland Hill TR27 .....78 D4
Herland Rd TR13 .....90 E6
Hermes Cl TR13 .....146 D5
Hermes Rd TR13 .....146 C5
Hermitage Rd
  Plymouth PL3 .....128 E5
  Roche PL26 .....46 F3
Heron Cl Millbrook PL10 .....132 F6
  Tresillian TR2 .....70 D6
Heron Way TR1 .....137 E1
Herons Ct 7 TR18 .....55 A5
Herring Cl PL14 .....113 D7
Herring Rd PL14 .....113 D7
Herschel Gdns PL5 .....123 E1
Hersham Cross EX23 .....5 B2
Hertland Wlk PL2 .....128 A7
Hessary Dr PL6 .....121 C1
Hessary Ho PL14 .....113 D6
Hessary View
  Saltash PL12 .....122 E4
  Tavistock PL19 .....147 D4
Hessenford Rd PL13,PL11 .....64 B6
Hetling Cl PL1 .....148 B3
Hewer's Row PL4 .....149 A3
Hewitt Cl PL14 .....122 C1
Hexham Pl PL2 .....128 A8
Hexton Hill Rd PL9 .....135 B6
Heybrook Ave PL5 .....123 D1
Hgher Boskerris TR26 .....141 D1
Hibernia Rd PL3 .....146 D1
Hibernia Terr PL5 .....127 E8
Hichens La TR11 .....145 A5
Hichens Rd TR13 .....146 D4
Hick's La PL14 .....149 A2
Hickory Dr PL7 .....131 B5
Hicks Cl TR2 .....71 C6
Hidden Valley Adventure
  Pk* PL15 .....18 A3
High Cross Lanivet PL30 .....47 F5
  Porth Navas TR11 .....93 A4
  12 St Columb Major TR9 .....45 D6
  Truro TR1 .....137 D4
High Cross St PL25 .....114 C4
High Field Rd TR4 .....68 C6
High Lanes Cubert TR8 .....55 E8
  Hayle TR27 .....142 B5
High St Boscastle PL35 .....9 D1
  Camelford PL32 .....105 C3
  Chacewater TR4 .....68 F3
  Delabole PL33 .....14 D3
  Falmouth TR11 .....145 B5
  Launceston PL15 .....106 C6
  Padstow PL28 .....107 D5
  Penzance TR18 .....143 E5
  8 Plymouth PL1 .....149 A2
  Plymouth, Stonehouse PL1 .....128 A2
  Probus TR2 .....71 C6
  St Ives TR26 .....141 B6
  St Keverne TR12 .....102 E6
High Street & Waterloo
  Street Flats PL1 .....128 A1
High Street Ind Est PL26 .....58 D3
High Trip La
  Dawson Dr PL17 .....39 F7
  Kelly Bray PL17 .....40 A8
Highbank Cl PL19 .....147 A4
Highburrow 24 TR13 .....146 C5
Highburrow La TR15 .....139 C5
Highbury Cl PL7 .....131 B7
Highbury Cres PL7 .....130 D7
Highclere Gdns PL25 .....125 B8
Highcliffe PL27 .....21 D5
Higher Albion Row TR16 .....80 F8
Higher Anderton Rd
  PL10 .....132 F5
Higher Beech Terr
  PL13 .....117 C4
Higher Bodinnel Rd
  PL31 .....109 C7
Higher Bojewna 14 TR6 .....55 A4
Higher Bore St PL31 .....109 C5
Higher Bridge Pk PL27 .....108 D5

Higher Broad La TR12 ....139 D7
Higher Bugle Bugle PL26 ...47 C1
  Stenalees PL26 ....59 C8
Higher Burrow Cl TR26 ...141 A4
Higher Chapel St PL13 ....117 D3
Higher Church St PL7 ......142 D6
Higher Churchway PL9 ...136 A7
Higher Cleaverfield
  PL15 ....106 C7
Higher Compton Rd
  PL3 ....128 E5
Higher Cotts TR2 ....57 C1
Higher Cross La PL32 ......105 E4
Higher Daws La PL15 ....18 E2
Higher East St TR9 ....45 E6
Higher Efford Rd PL3 .....129 B5
Higher Elms PL27 ....21 F3
Higher Fernleigh Rd
  PL27 ....108 C4
Higher Fore St
  Marazion TR17 ....89 C5
  Redruth TR15 ....140 C5
Higher Gln Pk PL14 ....38 D4
Higher Goongumpas La
  TR16 ....68 F1
Higher Green St TR18 .....143 D1
Higher Gwavas Rd
  TR18 ....143 D1
Higher Kelly PL18 ....41 A3
Higher La Ashton TR13 ....90 E3
  Mawgan TR12 ....99 D7
  Plymouth PL1 ....148 C2
  Wadebridge PL27 ....108 C4
  Wadebridge PL27 ....108 E5
Higher Larigan La PL14 ..143 D4
Higher Lavorrick PL26 .....73 C4
Higher Lidden Rd TR18 ...143 C3
Higher Lux St PL14 ....113 C6
Higher Market St
  Looe PL13 ....117 D3
  Penryn TR10 ....50 E7
Higher Mdw PL14 ....50 E7
Higher Medrose PL33 ....14 E3
Higher Middle Hill PL14 ..38 D4
Higher Mount Ambrose La
  TR15 ....140 D6
Higher Mowles PL3 ....129 B6
Higher Newham La TR1 ..137 D2
Higher Park Cl PL7 ....131 B3
Higher Park Stenak TR16 .80 F8
Higher Pengegon TR14 ..138 F2
Higher Penponds Rd
  TR14 ....79 B5
Higher Peverell Rd
  TR18 ....143 E7
Higher Polsue Way TR2 ...70 F5
Higher Port View PL12 ...122 F2
Higher Pumpfield Row
  TR15 ....139 B6
Higher Rd Breage TR13 ....90 F3
  Pensilva PL14 ....38 D4
Higher Redannick TR1 ....137 B3
Higher Row TR13 ....90 D3
Higher Silver Hill TR11 ..134 C6
Higher Stennack PL26 ....141 A5
Higher Stennack Cotts
  TR26 ....141 A5
Higher Stert Terr PL4 ....149 C3
Higher Tamar Terr PL18 ..41 A7
Higher Terr TR3 ....81 B4
Higher Tower Rd TR7 .....110 C6
Higher Tregenna St
  TR26 ....141 C3
Higher Trenaverne TR3 ...81 B4
Higher Tremena PL35 .....114 C4
Higher Tresavean Terr
  TR16 ....80 E6
Higher Trewidden St
  TR26 ....141 B4
Higher Trezaise PL26 ......47 A1
Higher Tristram PL27 ......21 D5
Higher Vicarage La
  TR12 ....99 A1
Higher Well La TR13 ....146 C6
Higher Well Pk PL26 ....73 C3
Higher West End PL26 .....73 C6
Higher Whiterock PL27 ..108 B5
Higher Woodford La
  PL7 ....130 C7
Higher Woodside PL5 .....114 A4
Highermoor Cross EX22 ...5 E1
Hightown TR1 ....69 F3
Hightown Pk PL12 ....53 C3
Highwell Cl TR7 ....111 A4
Highfield Ave
  St Austell PL25 ....114 C4
  15 St Columb Major TR9 ..45 D6
Highfield Cl
  Plymouth PL3 ....129 C5
  St Austell PL25 ....114 C4
Highfield Est 3 PL14 ....38 E4
Highfield Park Rd PL15 ..106 A5
Highfield Pk PL12 ....122 B3
Highfield Prim Sch PL3 ..129 C5
Highfield Rd
  Camelford PL32 ....105 C3
  Falmouth TR11 ....144 F4
Highfield Rd Ind Est
  PL32 ....105 C3
Highgate Hill 1 TR9 ....45 E1
Highglen Dr PL7 ....131 B7
Highgrove PL15 ....27 A6
Highland Pk
  Penryn TR10 ....144 B8
  Redruth TR15 ....140 C5

Highview TR4 ....68 E5
Highview Cl PL14 ....38 A2
Highview Cres TR4 ....68 E5
Highway PL14 ....50 B6
Highway La TR15 ....140 D7
Higman Cl PL14 ....50 F2
Hilgrove Rd TR7 ....111 A6
Hill Church TR4 ....68 F2
Hill Cl Heamoor TR18 .....143 B7
  Plymouth PL7 ....130 D4
  St Breward PL30 ....24 B3
Hill Crest PL3 ....128 E5
Hill Gdns PL12 ....119 C2
Hill Hay Cl PL23 ....116 A4
Hill Head TR10 ....146 D6
Hill La PL3 ....128 E5
Hill Park Cres
  Plymouth PL4 ....149 A4
  St Austell PL25 ....114 A2
Hill Park Mews PL4 ....149 B4
Hill Path PL5 ....123 F5
Hill Rd PL27 ....108 C5
Hill Rise PL27 ....108 C5
Hill St St Padstow PL28 ..107 D5
  Plymouth PL1 ....149 A3
Hill Top Crest PL5 ....123 E2
Hill View PL20 ....41 F3
Hillcrest Helston TR13 ...146 C7
  Shortlanesend TR4 ....69 F6
Hillcrest Ave TR4 ....137 A5
  St Columb Major TR9 ......45 E6
Hillcrest Dr PL7 ....131 A4
Hillcrest Rd TR27 ....142 D6
Hilldale Rd PL9 ....135 E6
Hilldean Cl PL5 ....124 C7
Hillhead TR2 ....95 A6
Hillhead Gdns PL32 ....105 D4
Hillhead Rd TR11 ....144 C5
Hillocks The PL11 ....141 A4
Hillpark Cotts PL15 ....106 D6
Hillsborough 2 PL4 ....128 F4
Hillsborough Cross EX22 ..8 D7
Hillsdunne Rd PL3 ....128 E6
Hillside
  Grampound Road TR2 ......57 E1
  Portreath TR16 ....67 C6
  St Austell PL25 ....115 B3
Hillside Ave Par PL24 .....60 B4
Hillside Rd
  Plymouth PL4 ....128 D4
  Saltash PL12 ....122 F3
Hillside Bglws TR13 ....90 F5
Hillside Cl PL20 ....41 F3
Hillside Cres PL9 ....135 E6
Hillside Ct Angarrack TR27 .78 C5
  Bodmin PL31 ....109 C5
Hillside Gdns PL22 ....112 C2
Hillside Ind TR14 ....140 B4
Hillside Mdw TR14 ....140 D7
Hillside Parc TR20 ....88 B7
Hillside Pk PL31 ....109 D5
Hillside Terr
  Carharrack TR16 ....80 E8
  Downderry PL11 ....64 C5
  Liskeard PL14 ....117 D4
  8 Redruth TR15 ....140 C5
Hillson Cl PL27 ....22 E7
Hillsview PL13 ....62 D2
Hilton Ave PL5 ....124 D1
Hilton Rd EX23 ....7 B6
Hingston Cl PL6 ....129 A8
Hirmandale Rd PL5 ....123 F3
Hobart St PL1 ....148 A2
Hobbacott La EX23 ....7 B6
Hobbs Cres PL12 ....122 D2
Hockens La PL23 ....116 C2
Hookders Way PL12 ....119 A2
Hodge Cl PL27 ....122 C2
Hoe App PL1 ....148 C2
Hoe Cl PL1 ....148 C1
Hoe La PL1 ....148 C1
Hoe St PL1 ....148 C2
Hoe The PL1 ....148 C2
Hoegate Cl PL1 ....148 C2
Hoegate PI PL1 ....148 C2
Hoegate St PL1 ....149 A2
Hogarth Cl PL9 ....136 B6
Hogarth Wlk PL9 ....136 B6
Holborn PI PL7 ....130 E6
Holborn St PL4 ....149 B2
Holcombe Dr PL9 ....135 F5
Holcroft Cl PL12 ....122 D2
Holdsworth St PL4 ....148 B4
Hole Cross PL20 ....39 D7
Holebay Cl PL9 ....136 A5
Hollabury Rd EX23 ....104 F7
Hollacombe Brake PL7 ..136 C1
Holland Rd
  Plymouth, Chaddlewood
  PL7 ....131 D5
  Plymouth, Peverell PL3 ..128 E6
  Plymouth, Plymstock PL9 .135 F6
  Widegates PL13 ....63 A2
Hollies Rd PL15 ....106 A7
Hollong Pk PL11 ....65 E5
Hollow's Terr TR27 ....142 E7
Holloway Gdns PL9 ....136 A5
Hollowgater La PL11 ......126 D2
Hollows The PL9 ....136 B8
Holly Cl TR3 ....69 C3
Holly Ct PL6 ....129 E7
Holly Park Cl PL5 ....124 A5

Holly Park Dr PL5 ....124 A5
Holly Pk TR14 ....138 B3
Holly Terr 3 TR18 ....143 C7
Hollycroft Rd PL3 ....129 A7
Hollywell Bay Fun Pk*
  TR8 ....43 C1
Hollywood Terr PL1 ....148 A3
Holman Ave TR14 ....138 C4
Holman Cl PL2 ....128 C8
Holman Rd PL14 ....113 E6
Holman's PI 1 TR13 ....98 C8
Holman's Terr TR16 ....80 E5
Holmans Bldgs PL12 ......127 D2
Holmans Mdw PL15 ....19 C1
Holmbush Arch Rd
  PL25 ....115 B3
Holmbush Hill PL27 ....39 F7
Holmbush Ind Est PL25 .115 B4
Holmbush Rd PL25 ....115 C4
Holmer Down PL6 ....125 D7
Holmes Ave PL3 ....129 B5
Holmwood Ave PL9 ....135 E5
Holne Chase PL6 ....125 B7
Holnicote Rd EX23 ....104 E5
Holt Cres TR7 ....110 D5
Holtwood Rd PL6 ....125 D6
Holwell Cl PL9 ....136 A5
Holy Cross RC Prim Sch
  PL4 ....149 A3
Holyrood PI PL1 ....148 C2
Holyway Cross PL15 ....18 A1
Holywell Cl TR3 ....82 B8
Holywell Rd Cubert TR8 ..55 C8
  Holywell TR8 ....43 B1
  Liskeard PL14 ....110 F6
  Newquay TR7 ....43 A2
  Playing Place TR3 ....82 B8
Home Farm Rd PL9 ....135 E8
Home Park (Plymouth Argyle
  Fc) PL2 ....128 C5
Home Pk Ave PL3 ....128 E6
Home Park Rd PL12 ....123 A3
Home Pk Landrake PL12 ..53 C3
  Plymouth PL2 ....127 F4
Home Sweet Home Terr
  PL14 ....149 C2
Homefield Pk PL31 ....109 F3
Homer Park La S PL9 .....135 C5
Homer Park Rd PL28 ....20 F2
Homer Pk Plymouth PL9 .135 C5
  Saltash PL12 ....122 D3
Homer Rise PL9 ....136 B7
Home Water Pk PL6 ....58 B4
Homeyard Homes The
  TR2 ....83 F6
Honcray PL9 ....135 D8
Honey St PL31 ....109 E5
Honeysuckle Cl
  Plymouth PL6 ....125 E7
  Saltash PL12 ....122 D4
Honicknowle Gn PL5 ......124 B2
Honicknowle La PL5 ....124 B1
Honicombe Cnr PL17 ....40 E5
Honicombe Manor Holiday
  Village PL17 ....40 E5
Honiton Wlk PL5 ....124 B4
Hood Hill TR14 ....79 A6
Hood Hill PL7 ....135 C5
Hooe La PL9 ....135 C5
Hooe Prim Sch PL9 ....135 B5
Hooe Rd PL9 ....135 C5
Hooksbury Ave PL7 ....131 B3
Hooper Cl PL14 ....113 C8
Hooper La PL14 ....127 C3
Hooper St PL11 ....127 C3
Hoopers Cl PL12 ....53 C3
Hoopers La PL12 ....116 B2
Hope Terr PL17 ....110 D6
Hopton Cl PL6 ....128 F8
Horn Cross Rd PL9 ....135 E7
Horn Cross Rd PL9 ....135 E7
Horn La PL9 ....135 E7
Horn Lane Flats PL9 ....135 E7
Hornapark Cl PL16 ....19 F3
Hornbrook Gdns PL6 ......124 D6
Hornby St 2 PL2 ....127 F4
Hornchurch La PL5 ....123 E4
Hornchurch Rd PL5 ....123 E5
Hornick Hill PL26 ....58 E4
Horrabridge Prim Sch
  PL20 ....42 C4
Horse & Jockey La 1
  TR13 ....146 C5
Horse Whim Dr PL25 .....115 B5
Horsepool La PL11 ....65 B6
Horsepool Rd
  Connor Downs TR27 ....78 E6
  Sheviock PL11 ....65 B6
Horseshoe Cl PL26 ....47 A3
Horsewell La PL20 ....42 B3
Horswell Cl PL7 ....131 B5
Horton Cross EX22 ....3 F3
Hosford Cl PL9 ....136 A4
Hosken's Mdw TR19 ....97 A6
Hosking's Row TR15 ......140 B4
Hospital Rd
  Plymouth PL4 ....149 B4
  Stratton EX23 ....7 B6
Hotham PI PL1 ....148 A4
Houldsworth Rd PL27 ....135 C7
Houndiscombe Rd PL4 ..128 E4
Hounster Dr PL10 ....132 D4
Hounster Hill PL10 ....132 D4

Housecraft Ct 7 PL4 ......149 A2
Housel Bay Rd TR12 ......102 F2
Houseman Cl PL5 ....124 B3
Housman Cl PL5 ....124 B3
How St PL4 ....149 A2
Howard Cl Plymouth PL5 .123 F2
  Saltash PL12 ....122 D3
  Tavistock PL19 ....119 F4
Howard La EX23 ....7 C8
Howard Rd PL9 ....135 E8
Howards Way EX23 ....104 D5
Howe Downs TR14 ....79 A2
Howell's Rd 1 EX23 ....4 E1
Hudson Cross EX22 ....5 E4
Hudson Rd PL27 ....31 F3
Hughville St TR14 ....138 D4
Hugus Rd TR3 ....69 D3
Hull's La TR11 ....145 C3
Humber Cl PL3 ....129 D6
Humphrey's Cl PL14 ....37 F7
Humphry Davy La TR27 .142 D5
Humphry Davy Sch The
  TR18 ....143 E6
Hungerford Rd PL2 ....128 B5
Hunkin Cl TR1 ....137 C5
Hunter Cl PL6 ....124 F2
Hunters's Oak PL20 ....41 D2
Huntersfield TR14 ....138 F7
Huntingdon Gdns PL5 ...124 D4
Huntley PI PL3 ....129 C4
Hunts Crossing* PL15 ....18 C5
Hurdon Rd PL15 ....106 D2
Hurdon Way PL15 ....106 C3
Hurdwick Rd PL19 ....147 A5
Hurland Rd TR1 ....137 D3
Hurlers The PL14 ....38 E2
Hurrabrook Cl PL6 ....128 D2
Hurrabrook Gdns PL6 ....125 E2
Hurrell Cl PL4 ....124 D6
Hurrell Ct PL3 ....129 C5
Hursley Bsns Pk PL6 .....121 D1
Hurst Cl PL9 ....135 F5
Hustyns PL27 ....33 D3
Hutchings Cl PL6 ....124 D6
Huthnance Cl TR1 ....137 C4
Hutton Hts TR1 ....69 F3
Huxham Cl PL6 ....129 A8
Huxley Cl PL7 ....130 E7
Hyde Park Jun & Inf Schs
  PL3 ....128 E5
Hyde Park Rd PL3 ....128 E5

I

Idless La TR4 ....69 F6
Ilbert Cotts PL7 ....130 E4
Ilbert St PL1 ....148 B4
Illogan Downs TR15 ....139 B8
Illogan Pk 3 TR16 ....67 E4
Illogan Sch TR16 ....67 D5
Ince Cl PL11 ....126 F4
Inchkeith Rd PL6 ....124 F7
Indian Queens Com Prim Sch
  TR9 ....45 E1
Indian Queens Workshops
  TR9 ....45 F1
Infirmary Hill TR1 ....137 C4
Ingra Rd PL3 ....129 A6
Ingra Tor Cl 2 PL20 ....42 C3
Ingra Wlk PL6 ....125 B8
Innes Ho PL1 ....148 B3
Inny Cl PL17 ....39 F4
Inny Vale Holiday Village
  PL32 ....16 A5
Inow Terr TR11 ....93 A2
Instow Wlk PL5 ....124 B4
Inswell Cl PL19 ....147 A6
Insworke Cl PL10 ....133 A6
Insworke Cres PL10 ....132 F6
Insworke Pl PL10 ....133 A6
Interdene PL3 ....128 E7
Ipswich Cl PL5 ....124 C4
Iron Mine La PL20 ....42 E3
Isacombe Oaks PL27 ......39 F6
Island Cres TR7 ....110 E6
Island Lanes PL31 ....109 F3
Island Rd 6 TR26 ....141 B6
Island Sq 8 TR26 ....141 B6
Islington Wharf TR10 ....144 D8
Ivanhoe Rd PL5 ....123 D2
Ivey Terr PL11 ....113 D7
Ivy Cotts PL18 ....40 F6
Ivy La TR18 ....143 C5
Ivydale Rd PL5 ....106 B6
Ivydale Rd PL4 ....128 F4
Ivydene Flats TR7 ....111 D7

J

Jack Bice Cl PL14 ....113 E5
Jack La TR18 ....143 C2
Jack Stephens Est
  TR18 ....143 D6
Jack's La PL11 ....132 B8
Jackett's Stps TR11 ....145 B5
Jackman's Mdw PL10 ....133 A3
Jacks Cl TR10 ....144 D7
Jackson Cl PL5 ....127 F4
Jackson PI PL2 ....127 F4
Jackson Way PL12 ....122 E3
Jacob's Ladder TR1 ....145 B4
Jacobstow Com Prim Sch
  EX23 ....11 A3
Jago Ave PL11 ....127 B3
Jago Cl PL31 ....109 B3
Jake's La TR4 ....69 A3
Jamaica St PL4 ....143 C7

Jamaica Terr 13 TR18 ....143 C7
Jame's Cross EX23 ....2 C2
James Cl PL9 ....136 B6
James PI Plymouth PL4 ..148 C4
  Truro TR1 ....137 D4
James Rd PL19 ....147 E2
James St Plymouth PL4 ..148 C4
  Plymouth, Mount Wise PL1 .127 E1
Jane's Ct TR11 ....145 B5
Jasmine Gdns
  Plymouth, Chaddlewood
  PL7 ....131 B5
  Plymouth, Glenholt PL6 ..125 E6
Jasper Parc PL14 ....37 F3
Jays Cres PL15 ....19 C6
Jean Cres PL3 ....129 B6
Jeanne Rees Ct 9 PL14 .113 B5
Jedburgh Cres PL2 ....128 A8
Jeffery Cl PL6 ....124 D6
Jelbert Way TR18 ....88 E6
Jellicoe Rd PL5 ....124 E1
Jenkins Cl PL9 ....136 A5
Jenkins Ct TR7 ....110 E6
Jenkins Terr 5 TR15 ......140 C5
Jennings Rd TR10 ....144 A6
Jennings Rd TR18 ....143 C5
Jenns Cross EX22 ....5 F3
Jennycliff La PL9 ....135 A4
Jennys Combe Cl PL9 ....135 F4
Jephson Rd PL4 ....129 B3
Jericho La TR27 ....142 D3
Jeryon Cl PL25 ....114 E6
Jessops PL7 ....130 D7
Jethan Dr TR14 ....138 B4
Jetty St PL26 ....73 C2
Jewel's Cross EX22 ....7 F6
Jewell's Terr TR16 ....80 B5
Jinkin Ave PL4 ....149 B4
John Ellis Ct TR27 ....142 C5
John Kitto Com Coll
  PL5 ....124 B3
John La PL4 ....148 C4
John Sparke Ho 9 PL1 ..149 A2
John's Cl PL6 ....127 C5
  Truro TR1 ....137 C4
John's Cnr TR20 ....89 F5
Johns Pk TR15 ....140 B6
Johnson Cl 2 PL20 ....41 B3
Johnson Pk PL18 ....41 A1
Jon Davey Dr TR16 ....140 C7
Jopes Cl 2 PL14 ....38 A3
Jordan La
  Horrabridge PL20 ....42 C5
  Walkhampton PL20 ....42 D6
Jorys Mdw PL30 ....23 E3
Joseph's Ct 10 TR6 ....55 A5
Joseph's La TR18 ....143 C8
Jubilee Bglws 10 TR18 ..143 C12
Jubilee Cl Duloe PL14 .....51 A3
  Kilkhampton EX23 ....5 A6
Jubilee Cotts PL12 ....53 C2
Jubilee Hill PL13 ....62 D5
Jubilee Mdw PL25 ....115 C9
Jubilee Pl TR14 ....138 E3
Jubilee Rd
  Falmouth TR11 ....145 A3
  Pensilva PL14 ....38 D4
  Plymouth PL5 ....123 F2
  Threemilestone TR3 ....69 C2
  Wadebridge PL27 ....108 C5
Jubilee St TR7 ....110 D6
Jubilee Terr
  Bodmin PL31 ....109 B5
  Goonhavern TR4 ....146 C9
  Helston TR13 ....146 C6
  Plymouth PL4 ....129 B2
Julian St PL4 ....149 C2
Julian Wlk PL6 ....125 E6
Jump Cl PL6 ....121 C7
Juniper Way PL7 ....131 B5

K

Karenza Ct TR26 ....141 E3
Kathleaven St PL5 ....123 D2
Kay Cl PL7 ....130 F2
Kay Cres PL31 ....109 B3
Kay Gdns PL27 ....108 E5
Kea Com Prim Sch TR3 ...70 A1
Keason Est PL14 ....39 A2
Keason Hill PL12 ....53 C4
Keast Cl 3 TR9 ....45 E1
Keast Rd PL26 ....58 C7
Kedlestone Ave PL5 ....124 A1
Keeble Pk TR3 ....81 E6
Keep The PL12 ....122 C2
Kehelland Village Sch
  TR14 ....66 F2
Keigwin PI TR19 ....88 C3
Kellaway Pk TR13 ....146 D6
Kelley Rd TR11 ....144 E3
Kellivith TR3 ....82 B3
Kellow Hill PL13 ....62 D5
Kellow Rd PL14 ....62 D5
Kellow Pk PL26 ....58 C5
Kelly Cl TR15 ....127 C5
Kelly Coll PL19 ....34 C8
Kelly Pk PL30 ....34 C2
Kelvin Ave PL4 ....149 C2
Kelwyn Ct TR26 ....141 C5
Kemp Cl TR1 ....137 D2
Kemp's Cl 7 TR5 ....54 C2
Kempe Cl PL2 ....127 F7
Kempton Terr PL11 ....127 B2
Kemyell PI PL2 ....127 E5
Kendal Gn TR2 ....57 C1

endal Pl PL5 .....124 E4
enidjack TR26 ...141 E1
enilworth Rd PL2 ...128 B7
enley Gdns PL5 ...123 F4
enmare Dr PL7 ...131 A5
enn Cl PL5 ...124 B3
enna Pk TR1 ...69 F3
ennall Pk TR3 ...81 B4
ennall Vale TR3 ...81 B4
ennall Vale Sch TR3 ...81 B4
ennedy Cl TR15 ...139 B8
ennel Hill PL7 ...130 C4
ennel Hill Cl PL7 ...130 C4
ennerley Terr TR2 ...95 A6
ennet Cl PL3 ...129 B6
ensa Way PL7 ...78 E6
ensey Pl 3 PL15 ...106 C6
ensey View PL15 ...106 D5
ensington Rd 3 PL4 ...149 B4
ensington Rd PL4 ...149 B4
enstella Rd TR18 ...143 C2
ent Ave PL25 ...115 D3
ent Cl PL26 ...58 C8
ent Rd PL2 ...127 F4
enwyn Church Rd TR1 ...137 B6
enwyn Cl Bude EX23 ...104 D7
Truro TR1 ...137 B6
enwyn Hill TR1 ...137 B6
enwyn Pk PL30 ...23 B2
enwyn Rd Truro TR1 ...137 B7
Truro TR4,TR1 ...137 A7
enwyn St TR1 ...137 C4
enython La TR19 ...86 F7
eppel St PL2 ...127 F4
eppel St 3 PL2 ...127 F4
eppel Terr 3 PL2 ...127 F4
er St PL1 ...127 E1
er St Ope PL1 ...127 E2
erensa Gdns PL5 ...68 D8
erensa Gn TR11 ...144 E5
errgilliack Rd TR11 ...144 A5
erley Gr TR1 ...69 A3
erley Hill TR1 ...69 A3
erley Vale TR1 ...69 A3
ernhunn Ct PL31 ...109 D6
ernick Gdns TR10 ...144 A6
ernick Rd TR10 ...144 A6
ernick Road Ind Est TR10 ...144 A7
ernow Cl Bodmin PL31 ...109 F5
orpoint PL11 ...126 E3
Vadebridge PL27 ...108 B5
ernow Cres EX23 ...104 E4
ernow Ct Newquay TR7 ...110 E6
orpoint PL11 ...126 E3
ernow Mill* PL12 ...52 E1
erryk Lowen TR14 ...138 F5
erris Gr TR1 ...137 B5
ersbrook Cross PL17 ...27 F2
ersey La PL11 ...145 C2
ersey Rd TR11 ...145 B7
eryor Cl PL25 ...114 F3
estle Dr TR1 ...69 F3
estral Way 10 TR16 ...67 E4
estrel Cl Plymouth PL6 ...125 D8
3 Porthleven TR13 ...98 B8
eswick Cres PL6 ...125 D5
everal Gdns PL11 ...64 B5
everal La PL11 ...64 B5
ew Cl TR1 ...137 C4
ew Noweth TR14 ...138 D2
ew Pendra TR19 ...97 A6
ew Wean TR26 ...141 C3
eyes Cl PL1 ...127 A2
eyham Barton RC Prim Sch
PL2 ...127 E6
eyham Rd PL2 ...127 E4
eyham St PL2 ...127 E8
eyham Sta PL2 ...127 E8
nyber Cl PL11 ...63 A8
bbiscombe Terr PL14 ...63 A8
dwelly Cl PL7 ...131 C4
el Pl PL3 ...129 D5
halion Woodlands
PL24 ...60 C5
Iknampton Jun & Inf Sch
EX23 ...104 D5
larney Springs Leisure
Pk* PL23 ...3 B1
latree Cross EX22 ...8 F7
llerton Rd EX23 ...104 E5
lliacourt TR3 ...82 A7
lliers Ct TR15 ...139 C7
lliersfield TR15 ...139 C6
lligrew Ave PL12 ...122 D1
lligrew Gdns TR4 ...70 D8
lligrew Rd 3 PL4 ...149 C3
lligrew Rd PL14 ...113 D6
lligrew St TR11 ...145 A4
llivose Gdns TR14 ...138 C5
llivose Rd TR14 ...138 D1
llyvarder Way PL25 ...115 B6
lmar Cl PL14 ...37 F3
lmar Rd PL14 ...113 E6
lmar Way PL14 ...37 F3
lminorth Wood*
PL13 ...117 A5
ln Cl Mevagissey PL26 ...73 C4
Plymouth PL5 ...127 C8
lm Mdws TR12 ...92 C1
lna La PL12 ...53 A2
lworthy Hill PL19 ...147 C6
lworthy Rd PL19 ...147 C6
mber Ct TR11 ...145 B2

Kimberley Ct TR7 ...110 D6
Kimberley Foster Cl
TR1 ...65 B5
Kimberley Park Rd
TR11 ...145 A4
Kimberley Pk PL14 ...38 A3
Kimberley Rd PL14 ...145 A4
Kimberly Ct TR7 ...110 D6
Kimberly Rd PL6 ...125 B1
Kiming EX23 ...104 E4
King Arthurs Terr PL34 ...14 C7
King Charles Prim Sch
TR1 ...145 A3
King Edward Cres TR7 ...110 D7
King Edward Rd PL12 ...122 F2
King George V Meml Wlk
TR27 ...142 C6
King St Bude EX23 ...104 E5
Gunnislake PL18 ...41 A6
Millbrook PL10 ...132 E5
Newquay TR7 ...110 D6
Plymouth PL1 ...148 B3
Redruth TR15 ...140 B5
Tavistock PL19 ...147 B6
Torpoint PL11 ...127 C3
Truro TR1 ...137 C4
King's Ave Falmouth TR11 ...144 F4
St Austell PL25 ...114 D3
King's Hill EX23 ...104 E3
King's Hill Ind Est
EX23 ...104 F3
King's Rd Camborne TR14 ...138 D4
Penzance TR18 ...143 D5
Plymouth PL1 ...128 A2
King's St PL22 ...112 C8
King's Tamerton Rd PL5 ...123 F2
Kingfisher Cl PL6 ...125 E6
Kingfisher Dr PL25 ...115 A4
Kingfisher Gdns PL6 ...125 E6
Kings Cross EX39 ...2 E5
Kings Ct PL1 ...128 A3
Kings Hill Cl EX23 ...104 E4
Kings Hill Mdw EX23 ...104 E3
Kings Mead ...21 E3
Kings Rd Marazion TR17 ...89 B5
Plymouth, Devonport PL1 ...127 F2
Plymouth, West Park PL5 ...123 F3
3 St Mawes TR2 ...95 A6
Kings Sch PL3 ...128 E6
Kingsland Gardens Cl
PL3 ...128 E6
Kingsley Ave PL11 ...127 B2
Kingsley Cl TR1 ...69 E3
Kingsley Cove TR4 ...68 A7
Kingsley Ct TR9 ...57 E8
Kingsley Meade TR8 ...111 B5
Kingsley Rd PL4 ...128 E4
Kingsley Terr TR1 ...67 C6
Kingsmill Rd PL13 ...146 F5
Kingsmill Rd PL12 ...122 C5
Kingston Cl PL7 ...131 A5
Kingston Dr PL7 ...131 B5
Kingston Rd PL17 ...28 E1
Kingsway PL10 ...132 D4
Kingsway Gdns PL6 ...124 F3
Kingswear Cres PL6 ...125 B1
Kingsway Park Ave
PL3 ...128 D6
Kingswood Rd PL18 ...41 A6
Kinnaird Cres PL6 ...124 F7
Kinnear Cres PL6 ...124 F7
Kinross Ave PL4 ...129 A4
Kinsale Rd PL5 ...123 E3
Kinsman Est PL31 ...109 C3
Kinterbury Rd PL5 ...127 B8
Kinterbury Terr PL5 ...149 A2
Kinver Cl PL6 ...125 D4
Kipling Gdns PL5 ...124 D2
Kirby Cl TR1 ...137 A4
Kirby Terr PL4 ...148 C4
Kirkdale Gdns PL2 ...128 B7
Kirkella Rd PL20 ...42 D2
Kirkland Cl PL6 ...125 C7
Kirkstall Cl PL2 ...128 A8
Kirkwall Rd PL5 ...124 C1
Kirland Bower PL30 ...48 B7
Kirton Pl PL3 ...129 B5
Kit Hill Cres PL5 ...127 C8
Kitley Way PL5 ...123 E1
Kitter Dr PL9 ...136 A5
Kitts Ct 17 TR18 ...143 E5
Kleinfontein Terr PL14 ...38 D4
Knapmedown PL15 ...11 B1
Knapps Cl PL9 ...136 C6
Knave-Go-By TR4 ...79 D5
Kneele Gdns PL3 ...128 E8
Knight's Mdws TR3 ...81 F7
Knighton Rd PL4 ...149 C3
Knighton Terr 3 PL20 ...42 C5
Knighton Cl PL25 ...59 E6
Knights Cl PL34 ...14 C7
Knights Hill PL6 ...137 B6
Knights Way PL15 ...140 D7
Knill Cl PL26 ...141 C2
Knill Cross PL10 ...132 E5
Knoll Pk TR1 ...137 D4
Knoll The PL7 ...130 B6
Knowland Cl PL1 ...127 F3
Knowle Ave PL6 ...127 E6
Knowle Cl PL26 ...58 C8
Kyl Cober Parc PL17 ...28 E1
Kynance Cl PL11 ...126 F4
Kynance Ho PL7 ...69 E4
Kynance Terr 7 TR12 ...102 F2

L

La Rochelle TR12 ...98 F1
La Vague TR3 ...82 C5
Labernum Terr EX23 ...5 A6
Laburnum Cl TR11 ...144 F5
Laburnum Cotts PL14 ...147 C6
Laburnum Dr TR11 ...144 F5
Lacey Cl TR14 ...79 E5
Ladock Rd Ladock TR2 ...57 C1
Probus TR2 ...71 C7
Lady Modifords CE Prim Sch
PL20 ...42 E4
Lady St TR18 ...146 B5
Ladysmith Cl PL4 ...149 C4
Ladysmith Pl PL4 ...129 B3
Ladywell PL28 ...107 D5
Ladywell Pl PL4 ...149 B3
Laflouder Fields TR12 ...99 A2
Laflouder La TR12 ...99 A2
Lafrowda Terr TR19 ...86 F6
Laguna Cl TR15 ...140 B5
Laira Ave PL3 ...129 D4
Laira Bridge Rd PL4 ...129 B1
Laira Green Prim Sch
PL3 ...129 C4
Laira Park Cres PL4 ...129 B4
Laira Park Pl PL4 ...129 B4
Laira Park Rd PL4 ...129 B4
Laira Pl PL4 ...149 C2
Laira St PL4 ...149 C3
Laity La TR26 ...77 C4
Laity Rd TR11 ...144 F5
Laity Wk PL6 ...124 D6
Lake La Dousland PL20 ...42 E3
Liskeard PL14 ...113 D5
Lake Mews PL10 ...132 E5
Lake Rd PL9 ...135 B6
Lake View PL12 ...53 C8
Lake View Cl PL5 ...124 B6
Lakeside PL19 ...147 B6
Lakeside Cl PL6 ...125 D8
Lakeview Dr PL5 ...124 B5
Lalebrick Rd PL9 ...135 B5
Lamanva Cl 10 TR16 ...67 E4
Lamanva Rd 9 TR16 ...67 E4
Lamb Pk 3 PL24 ...60 C7
Lamb's Barn PL12 ...116 B4
Lambert Rd PL5 ...124 B6
Lambert Terr 4 TR11 ...145 A5
Lambhay Hill PL1 ...149 A1
Lambhay St PL1 ...149 A1
Lambourne Ave 7 TR5 ...54 D1
Lambs La TR11 ...144 E5
Lamellion Hospl PL14 ...113 B5
Lamellyn Dr TR1 ...69 F3
Lamellyn Rd PL14 ...60 B4
Lamerhooe Cross PL19 ...29 C1
Lamerhooe Dr
Horsebridge PL19 ...29 C1
Luckett PL19 ...40 C8
Lametton Cl PL5 ...124 B3
Lametton Gn PL14 ...51 B4
Lamledra Hill PL26 ...85 D5
Lamorna Cl PL4 ...73 B3
Lamorna Ct TR16 ...67 D6
Lamorna Dr 11 PL17 ...39 F4
Lamorna Pk 12 PL17 ...39 F4
Lamorna Pk PL11 ...126 E4
Lamorran Gn 3 TR6 ...55 A4
Lampen Rd PL14 ...36 F2
Lana Cotts EX22 ...13 C7
Lanadwell St PL28 ...107 D5
Lanaton Rd PL10 ...144 A8
Lancashire La TR20 ...89 F5
Lancaster Cres PL27 ...31 F3
Lancaster Gdns PL5 ...124 C4
Lanchard La PL14 ...113 B5
Lanchard Rd PL14 ...113 B5
Lanchard Rise PL14 ...113 B5
Land's End (St Just)
Aerodrome TR19 ...86 F3
Landaviddy La PL13 ...62 D2
Lander Cl TR1 ...137 D3
Lander Rd PL12 ...122 F3
Landeryon Gdns 9
TR18 ...143 D5
Landithy PL20 ...143 A8
Landlake Cross PL15 ...28 A8
Landlake Rd PL15 ...106 B2
Landrake Cl PL5 ...127 C8
Landreath Pl PL24 ...60 B5
Landreyne Cl PL15 ...18 D8
Lands End 3 TR19 ...96 A5
Lands End PT TR19 ...97 A6
Lands Pk PL9 ...135 F7
Landulph Cross PL12 ...118 F1
Landulph Gdns PL5 ...127 C8
Landulph Sch PL12 ...118 F1
Lane End Cross PL19 ...29 D2
Lane Reddin Terr 10
TR18 ...143 D5
Lanepark La EX39 ...2 D5
Lang Gr Plymouth PL7 ...136 C2
Tavistock PL19 ...147 D5
Lang Rd PL14 ...113 B6
Langage Cross PL7 ...131 F6
Langage Ind Est PL7 ...131 D4
Langage Pk PL7 ...131 C4
Langage Science Pk
PL7 ...131 D5
Langarth Cl TR3 ...69 D4
Langdale Cl PL6 ...125 D1
Langdale Gdns PL6 ...125 D1
Langdon Cross PL15 ...18 D8

Langdon Ct PL9 ...136 B6
Langdon Down Way
PL11 ...126 E3
Langerwell Cl PL12 ...122 C3
Langerwell La PL12 ...122 C3
Langfords Mdw 4 PL35 ...9 F1
Langham Pl PL4 ...149 C3
Langhill Rd PL3 ...128 C5
Langley Cl PL6 ...125 A7
Langley Com Inf Sch
PL6 ...125 A6
Langley Cres PL6 ...124 F7
Langmead Cl PL6 ...129 C8
Langmead Rd PL6 ...129 C8
Langmore Cl PL6 ...129 A7
Langorran Rd TR14 ...138 B3
Langreek Bglws PL13 ...62 C2
Langreek Rd PL13 ...62 C2
Langstone Rd PL2 ...128 C7
Langstone Terr PL2 ...128 C7
Langton Rd
Falmouth TR11 ...145 A6
3 Wolverton PL20 ...42 C3
Langton Terr 3 TR11 ...145 A5
Langurroc Rd TR8 ...110 A3
Langurtho Rd PL23 ...116 A4
Langweath East TR12 ...99 D7
Langweath Gdns TR27 ...77 E3
Langweath La TR12 ...99 D7
Langwedh TR11 ...67 D4
Lanhenver Ave TR7 ...110 E5
Lanherne Ave TR8 ...45 A8
Lanhenvere Parc 4
TR12 ...101 C4
Lanhydrock Ho* PL30 ...48 D6
Lanhydrock Rd PL4 ...129 B2
Lanhydrock View PL31 ...109 D3
Lanivet Com Prim Sch
PL30 ...47 E7
Lanjowan TR13 ...146 B6
Lankelly La PL23 ...116 A4
Lanlivery Com Prim Sch
PL30 ...48 D2
Lanlovie Mdw TR8 ...55 D8
Lanmoor Est TR16 ...80 D6
Lannarth Glas TR16 ...67 D4
Lanner Cl TR16 ...140 E1
Lanner Gn TR16 ...140 E1
Lanner Hill TR16 ...140 E1
Lanner Moor Terr TR16 ...80 D6
Lanner Prim Sch TR16 ...80 D6
Lanner Sq TR16 ...80 D6
Lannowth Rd TR18 ...143 F6
Lanoweth TR10 ...81 D2
Lanreath Farm & Folk Mus*
PL13 ...62 B8
Lanreath Prim Sch PL13 ...62 A8
Lansallos St 3 PL23 ...62 D1
Lansdown Ct EX23 ...104 D5
Lansdown Rd Bude EX23 ...104 D5
Wadebridge PL27 ...108 B5
Lansdowne Cl TR18 ...143 E5
Lansdowne Ct TR18 ...143 B5
Lansdowne Dr TR18 ...143 C4
Lansdowne Rd
Callington PL17 ...39 E4
Falmouth TR11 ...145 C3
Penzance TR18 ...143 C5
Plymouth PL6 ...124 F1
Lantallack Cross PL12 ...53 A2
Lanuthhorne Est TR27 ...77 F1
Lanwithan Cl PL22 ...112 D2
Lanwithan Rd PL22 ...112 C2
Lanxon Cres PL30 ...48 C2
Lanyon Ct PL14 ...37 F3
Lanyon Rd TR13 ...146 C6
Lappa Valley Steam Rly*
TR8 ...56 C7
Lapthorn Cl PL9 ...135 C7
Larch Cl PL12 ...122 C3
Larch Dr PL6 ...125 E7
Larcombe Rd PL25 ...115 A6
Largan Hill TR18 ...143 D4
Larigan Cres TR18 ...143 D4
Larigan Rd TR18 ...143 D4
Lark Hill PL2 ...128 A6
Larkhall Rise PL3 ...129 B5
Larkham Cl PL7 ...130 C6
Larkham La PL7 ...130 C6
Latham Cl PL6 ...129 A7
Latimer Cl PL7 ...131 B5
Latimer Wlk PL6 ...124 E7
Launcells Cross EX23 ...5 C7
Launceston
Castle* PL15 ...106 C6
Launceston Cl
Bodmin PL31 ...109 F4
Plymouth PL6 ...125 B7
Launceston Coll PL15 ...106 C4
Launceston Com Prim Sch
PL15 ...106 C4
Launceston Hospl PL15 ...106 C5
Launceston Rd
Bodmin PL31 ...35 B1
Callington PL17 ...39 E6
Launceston Ret Pk
PL15 ...106 B6
Launceston Sta PL15 ...106 B6
Launceston Steam Rly*
PL15 ...106 B6

Ken – Lif 163

Law Wlk PL6 ...124 D6
Lawn Cl 2 PL7 ...131 C5
Lawn Stps TR11 ...145 B4
Lawn The Par PL24 ...60 B5
Tavistock PL19 ...147 D6
Lawns The Plymouth PL5 ...124 E1
Torpoint PL11 ...127 A2
Lawrence House Mus*
PL15 ...106 C6
Lawrence Rd
Plymouth PL9 ...135 A6
St Agnes TR5 ...54 C1
Lawry Cl 6 PL14 ...113 B5
Lawson Gr PL9 ...135 C7
Lawson Cl TR7 ...110 B5
Lea Way EX23 ...104 F6
Leader Rd TR7 ...111 E7
Leander Way PL5 ...124 D2
Leanway PL12 ...122 E2
Leap Pk TR3 ...69 C3
Leas The TR1 ...137 E5
Leat Cl PL20 ...42 E3
Leat Rd Lifton PL16 ...19 F3
Pendeen TR19 ...75 A1
Leat The 3 EX23 ...4 E1
Leat View PL12 ...122 E3
Leat Wlk Plymouth PL3 ...128 E6
Roborough PL6 ...121 D1
Leatfield PL26 ...73 C3
Leatfield Dr PL6 ...124 F4
Leather Cl PL6 ...124 E4
Leather Tor Cl 4 PL20 ...42 C3
Leats The TR1 ...137 C4
Leatside PL6 ...121 C1
Leaves Yd PL3 ...129 B7
Lebrunick Cross PL15 ...28 D8
Ledgate La PL7 ...131 F8
Ledra Cl TR12 ...103 A4
Ledrah Gdns PL25 ...114 C3
Ledrah Rd PL25 ...114 B3
Leedstown Com Prim Sch
TR27 ...78 E1
Legion La 3 PL24 ...60 C5
Legis Wlk PL6 ...125 A8
Leigh Ct PL6 ...129 A8
Leigh La Halt PL12 ...53 D6
Roborough PL6 ...121 D2
Leigham Ct PL1 ...148 B2
Leigham Inf & Jun Schs
PL6 ...125 C1
Leigham St PL1 ...148 B2
Leigham Terrace La
PL1 ...148 B2
Leighton Rd PL3 ...128 F8
Lelant Mdws TR26 ...77 E4
Lelant Saltings Sta PL26 ...77 E3
Lelant Sta TR26 ...77 E4
Lemellen Gdns PL30 ...23 B2
Lemin Parc TR27 ...78 E3
Lemin's Ct TR15 ...140 B5
Lemon Hill TR11 ...82 A3
Lemon Hill Gdns TR11 ...82 A3
Lemon La TR1 ...137 C4
Lemon Quay TR1 ...137 C4
Lemon Row TR1 ...137 D3
Lemon St
St Keverne TR12 ...101 C4
Truro TR1 ...137 D4
Lemon Terr TR1 ...137 B8
Lender La 5 PL17 ...99 A2
Lendewednack Prim
Sch TR12 ...102 F2
Lendra La PL17 ...39 D4
Lerryn CE Prim Sch PL22 ...61 D8
Lerryn View PL27 ...61 C8
Lerwick Rd PL27 ...31 F3
Lescudjack Cres TR18 ...143 E6
Lescudjack Rd TR18 ...143 E6
Lescudjack Terr TR18 ...143 E6
Lesingey La PL20 ...88 A5
Leskinnick Pl 15 TR18 ...143 D6
Leskinnick St TR18 ...143 E6
Leskinnick Terr TR18 ...143 E6
Leslie Ct TR13 ...146 B6
Lesnewth 18 PL24 ...60 B4
Lester Cl PL3 ...129 B6
Lestraynes La TR10 ...92 E8
Lethlean Cl TR27 ...142 D7
Lethlean La TR27 ...142 D7
Levant Beam Engine*
TR19 ...74 E1
Levant Cl TR19 ...86 F8
Levant Rd TR19 ...86 F8
Leverlake Rd EX23 ...6 F4
Levine View TR11 ...144 E1
Lewannick Cl PL15 ...27 B7
Lewannick Com Prim Sch
PL15 ...27 B7
Lewarne Cres TR7 ...111 C7
Lewarne Rd TR7 ...111 C8
Lewes Gdns PL5 ...124 C4
Lewis Way PL25 ...114 E6
Lewman Cl TR2 ...71 C6
Lewman Rd TR2 ...71 C6
Ley La PL20 ...119 D6
Leypark Dr PL6 ...125 E2
Leypark Wlk PL6 ...125 E2
Leys La TR17 ...89 B5
Liberator Row 4 PL7 ...31 F3
Lidden Cl TR18 ...143 C3
Lidden Cres TR18 ...143 C3
Lidden Rd TR18 ...143 C3
Liddicoat Rd PL22 ...112 B8
Lifeboat Hill 32 TR26 ...141 B6
Lifton Prim Sch PL16 ...19 F4

Lifton Rd PL4 ....149 C2
Liftondown Cross PL16 ...19 D4
Lightgate Hill PL12 .....137 E2
Lighthouse Hill TR16 ....67 C6
Lighthouse La PL26 .....85 C5
Lighthouse Rd TR12 ....102 F2
Lilac Cl PL9 ....135 C5
Lime Tree Way PL15 .....27 D4
Limerick Pl PL4 ....149 C3
Limes La PL14 ....113 B5
Limes The PL6 ....128 C2
Limetree Rd PL3 ....128 D7
Lincoln Ave PL4 ....149 C4
Lincoln Row 6 PL27 ....31 F3
Linden Ave TR7 ....110 C5
Linden Cres TR7 ....110 C5
Linden Terr PL4 ....149 C3
Lingard Cl PL14 ....113 A6
Lingfield Ave PL26 .....58 E1
Linhay Cl PL25 ....115 D6
Link Cl TR11 ....144 F4
Link Rd PL15 ....106 B3
Linkadells PL7 ....130 D6
Linketty La PL7 ....130 D6
Linketty La E PL6 .....125 A1
Linketty La W PL6 .....128 F8
Links View EX23 ....104 F6
Linley Cl PL25 ....69 D3
Linnet Ct PL12 ....122 C2
Linton Cl PL5 ....124 C8
Linton La EX39 ....2 E5
Linton Rd PL12 ....124 C7
Linton Sq PL5 ....124 C8
Lippell Dr PL9 ....135 E6
Lipson Ave PL4 ....149 C4
Lipson Com Coll PL4 ...129 C4
Lipson Cres PL4 ......149 B3
Lipson Rd PL4 ....149 A4
Lipson Terr PL4 ......149 C4
Lipson Vale PL4 ......149 C4
Lipson Vale Prim Sch
  PL4 ....129 A4
Liscawn Terr PL11 .....127 B3
Liscombe Cl PL18 .....144 C2
Lishaperhill Cross EX22 ...5 E2
Liskeard (Looe Branch) Sta
  PL14 ....113 B4
Liskeard Hill PL14 .....36 F2
Liskeard Inf Sch PL14 ...113 B6
Liskeard Jun Sch PL14 ...113 A6
Liskeard Rd
  Callington PL17 ......39 E4
  Saltash PL12 ....122 B3
Liskeard Sch & Com Coll
  PL14 ....113 C7
Liskeard Sta PL14 .....113 B4
Liskeard Town Mus*
  PL14 ....113 C6
Liskerrett Rd PL17 ....113 D5
Liskey TR6 ....55 A4
Liskey Hill TR6 ....55 A4
Liskey Hill Cres 1 TR6 ...55 A4
Lister Gr PL7 ....128 F4
Lister Cl PL7 ....130 F6
Lister Hill 10 TR11 ....145 A4
Lister St TR11 ....145 A3
Listowel Dr PL13 ......117 D7
Listry Rd TR7 ....110 E5
Litchaton Cres PL7 ....130 B7
Litchaton Way PL7 .....130 B7
Litchfield Cl PL7 ......131 B6
Little Ash Gdns PL5 ....123 E1
Little Ash Rd PL5 ......123 B1
Little Bodieve Holiday Pk
  PL27 ....108 D7
Little Bridge Pk PL27 ...108 D6
Little Butts PL9 ....135 E6
Little Castle St 7 TR1 ...137 C4
Little Dean PL14 ......113 A5
Little Dinas PL28 .....107 E4
Little Dock La PL5 ....122 E3
Little Down La PL6 ....121 E3
Little Down Pk TR7 ....111 A4
Little Fancy Cl PL6 ....125 C7
Little Gilly Hill 3 TR15 ...140 C4
Little Gwargwartha TR16 ...82 A5
Little La Cawsand PL10 ...133 A2
  Hayle TR27 ....142 E7
  Staddiscombe PL9 ....135 D3
Little Laney PL13 ......62 D1
Little Mdw PL12 ....103 A4
Little Mill La PL27 ....77 E2
Little Oaks TR10 ......144 B6
Little Orch PL12 ....53 C3
Little Point Cres PL10 ...132 F5
Little Stark Cl PL26 ....58 B4
Little Treloweth TR15 ...139 B6
Little Trelyn PL12 .....21 E2
Little Trethewey Est
  TR19 ....96 E4
Little Trethigga TR8 ...111 F2
Little Woburn Cl PL15 ...106 C4
Littlebridge Mdw EX22 ...8 A5
Littleton Pl PL2 ......127 E7
Littlewood Cl PL7 .....131 A4
Lizard Cl PL6 ....124 F7
Lizard Head La TR12 ...102 E2
Lizard Nature Reserve The*
  TR12 ....100 F2
Lizard Wlk PL6 ....125 A7
Llawnroc Cl TR14 .....138 E2
Llewellyn Cl PL32 .....105 C3

Lloyds Rd TR12 ....103 A2
Loatmead Cross EX22 ...3 E3
Lockeridge Rd PL20 ....41 B1
Lockington Ave PL3 ...128 F7
Locks Wlk PL1 ....127 E1
Lockyer Ct PL1 ....148 C2
Lockyer Mews PL19 ...147 C6
Lockyer Rd PL3 ....128 E5
Lockyer St PL1 ....148 C2
Lockyer Terr PL12 ....123 A3
Lockyers Quay PL4 ...149 B2
Lodenek Ave PL28 ....107 D4
Lodge Dr TR1 ....137 F6
Lodge Gdns PL6 ......122 F1
Lodge Hill PL14 ......113 A3
Lodge La PL8 ....136 F5
Lodge Way TR9 ....45 F2
Loe Bar Rd TR13 .....146 B7
Loe Valley Rd TR13 ...146 B7
Lofoten Cl PL1 ....127 E2
Loftus Gdns PL5 ......123 C2
Loggans Cl TR27 .....142 E8
Loggans Rd Hayle TR27 ...142 F8
  Phillack TR27 ....142 E8
Loggans Way TR27 ....142 E8
Lollabury Rd PL12 ....122 E3
Long Acre PL12 ....122 B4
Long Barn The TR20 ...89 D8
Long Cross PL29 .....22 C6
Long Down Gdns PL6 ...125 E3
Long La Crowlas TR20 ...89 A7
  High Street PL26 ......58 C4
  St Erth TR20,TR27 ....89 E8
Long Lanes TR20 .....89 F7
Long Ley PL12 ....129 B6
Long Mdw PL7 ....130 D7
Long Moor TR12 ......103 A5
Long Orch PL20 ....41 B1
Long Park Cl PL5 .....135 F5
Long Park Dr PL6 ....125 D7
Long Park Rd PL12 ...122 D2
Long Rd PL12 ....122 B4
Long Row TR19 ....88 B1
Long Rowden PL3 ....128 E6
Long Terrace Cl 6 PL7 ...131 C5
Long-A-Row Cl EX23 ...10 C6
Longacre
  Harrowbarrow PL17 ...40 C4
  Plymouth PL7 ....130 B7
Longbridge Cl EX22 ...6 D5
Longbridge Rd
  Plymouth, Laira PL3 ...129 C4
  Plymouth, Longbridge PL6 ...129 C2
Longbrook Barton PL7 ...130 D5
Longbrook St PL7 .....130 F4
Longcause PL7 ....130 F4
Longcause Com Specl Sch
  PL7 ....130 F4
Longcoombe La PL13 ...62 D3
Longdowns Trad Est
  TR10 ....81 A1
Longfield PL14 ....144 E4
Longfield Cl 1 PL17 ...39 F4
Longfield Dr PL32 ....105 C3
Longfield Pl PL3 .....149 B4
Longfield Rd PL32 ....105 C3
Longfield Villas PL9 ...135 D6
Longhouse La PL27 ...21 E3
Longlands PL9 ....135 D8
Longlands PL12 ......122 B1
Longman's La 1 TR9 ...39 E4
Longmeadow Cl PL7 ...130 E7
Longmeadow Rd PL12 ...123 E3
Longpark Dr EX23 ......6 F5
Longpark Rd PL5 .....114 F5
Longrock Bsns Pk TR20 ...88 F6
Longrock Ind Est TR20 ...88 F6
Longstone Ave PL6 ...125 A6
Longstone Cl TR26 ...141 E1
Longstone Hill TR26 ...141 E1
Longview Rd PL12 ....122 D3
Longview Terr PL13 ...129 B7
Longwood Cl PL7 .....131 A4
Longwool Mdw EX23 ...7 B6
Looe Aquarium* PL13 ...117 C3
Looe Bay Holiday Pk
  PL13 ....117 F8
Looe Com Sch PL13 ...63 F5
Looe Hill Looe PL13 ...63 F5
  Seaton PL13,PL11 ....64 A5
Looe Prim Sch PL13 ...117 D4
Looe St PL4 ....149 A2
Looe Sta PL13 ....117 C4
Lookout The TR11 ....145 B5
Looseleigh Cl PL6 ....125 A4
Looseleigh La PL6 ....124 F5
Looseleigh Pk PL6 ....124 F5
Lopes Dr PL6 ....121 C1
Lopes Rd Dousland PL20 ...42 E3
  Plymouth PL2 ....128 B6
Lopwell Cl PL6 ....124 F5
Lord Louis Cres PL9 ...134 F6
Lords Mdw TR2 ....71 F3
Lorrimore Ave PL2 ....127 F5
Loscombe Cl TR16 ....80 A5
Loscombe La TR16 ....80 A5
Loscombe Rd TR16 ...139 C1
Lost Gdns of Heligan*
  PL26 ....73 B5
Lostwithiel Sta* PL22 ...112 D2
Lostwithiel Mus* PL22 ...112 C2
Lostwithiel Rd PL30,PL31 ...48 C2
Lostwithiel Sch PL23 ...116 C4
Lostwood Rd PL25 ....114 E4

Lotherton Cl PL7 .....131 B3
Loughboro Rd PL5 ....123 C1
Love La Bodmin PL31 ...109 F5
  Hayle TR27 ....88 C1
  Mousehole TR19 .....96 B8
  Penryn TR10 ....144 D8
  Penzance PL8 ....143 C4
  Saltash PL12 ....122 E2
  8 St Ives TR26 ....141 B6
Lovell Rd PL3 ....128 F6
Lovely La PL12 ....65 A8
Loveny Cl PL14 ....36 F2
Loveny Rd PL14 ....36 F2
Lovibond Wlk PL27 ...108 C5
Low Lee Rd TR19 .....88 D1
Lowen Ct 7 TR1 ......137 D4
Lowen Way TR3 ....69 C3
Lowenac Ct PL14 .....78 B6
Lowenac Gdns TR14 ...138 C2
Lowenek Cl TR11 .....144 E5
Lower Anderton Rd
  PL10 ....132 F5
Lower Aylmer Sq 12
  PL25 ....114 C3
Lower Barncoose TR15 ...139 F6
Lower Biteford Cross
  EX39 ....3 A6
Lower Bore St PL31 ...109 D5
Lower Boscawell Parc
  TR19 ....74 F1
Lower Broad La TR15, ...139 C8
Lower Cardrew La TR15 ...140 B6
Lower Castle Rd TR2 ...95 A5
Lower Chapel St PL13 ...117 D3
Lower Church St TR27 ...142 D6
Lower Clicker Rd PL14 ...51 F4
Lower Compton Rd PL3 ...128 F5
Lower Coronation Terr 9
  PL17 ....39 E4
Lower East St 1 TR9 ...45 E6
Lower Eastcliff TR4 ...68 A7
Lower Elms PL27 ......21 F3
Lower Fairfield PL12 ...65 A8
Lower Farm Rd PL7 ...131 C5
Lower Fore St PL12 ...123 A2
Lower Glen Pk PL14 ...113 C6
Lower Goongumpas La
  TR16 ....68 F1
Lower Green St TR18 ...143 E5
Lower Greenbanks PL27 ...21 E2
Lower Gurnick Rd TR18 ...143 B3
Lower Hill TR13 ......146 C6
Lower Hillside PL14 ...50 B6
Lower Hugus Rd TR3 ...69 C3
Lower Kelly PL18 .....41 A3
Lower La Mawgan TR12 ...99 D7
  8 Plymouth PL1 ......149 A2
Lower Lux St 3 PL14 ...113 C6
Lower Market St
  Looe PL13 ....117 D3
  Penryn TR10 ....144 C7
Lower Mdw TR9 ....69 A3
Lower Merritts Hill 1
  TR16 ....67 E4
Lower Middle Hill PL14 ...38 E4
Lower Molinnis PL26 ...47 D2
Lower Parc TR12 .....92 C2
Lower Park Dr PL9 ....135 F4
Lower Pengegon TR14 ...138 F3
Lower Peverell Rd TR18 ...143 E7
Lower Pk TR2 ....70 F5
Lower Polstain Rd TR3 ...69 D3
Lower Port View PL12 ...122 F2
Lower Pumpfield Row
  TR15 ....139 B6
Lower Rd PL11 ....64 C4
Lower Redannick TR1 ...137 C4
Lower Ridings PL7 ....131 C6
Lower Rosewin Row 9
  TR1 ....137 D5
Lower Row PL10 ......133 A2
Lower Saltram PL9 ...135 E7
Lower Sq TR22 ....11 E8
Lower St Looe PL13 ...117 D3
  Plymouth PL4 ....149 A3
Lower Tamar Terr PL18 ...41 A7
Lower Terr TR3 ....81 B4
Lower Tregoniggie
  PL26 ....59 A1
Lower Tywarnhayle 11
  TR6 ....55 B7
Lower Well La TR13 ...146 C6
Lower Well Pk PL26 ...73 C3
Lower Wesley Terr TR14 ...38 D4
Lower Woodside PL25 ...114 A4
Lower Yonder St PL4 ...149 B3
Lowertown Cl PL12 ...53 C3
Lowertown La TR14 ...146 C7
Lowery Cross PL20 ...42 F4
Lowley Rd PL15 ......18 E2
Lucas Cl PL11 ....109 E3
Lucas La PL7 ....130 D6
Lucas Terr PL4 ....129 B2
Lucknow Rd PL31 .....48 DB
Ludgvan Com Prim Sch
  TR20 ....89 B8

Lundy Cl PL6 ....124 F7
Lundy Dr EX23 ....10 C6
Lundy Rd PL27 ....22 E7
Lusart Dr 8 TR11 .....102 F2
Lusty Glaze Rd TR7 ...111 A7
Lutsford Cross EX39 ...3 A6
Lutyens Fold PL19 ....29 C6
Luxmore Cl PL6 ......125 E1
Luxon Dr TR7 ....110 F6
Luxstowe Dr 1 PL14 ...113 C6
Luxstowe Gdns PL14 ...113 C6
Luxulyan Rd PL24 ....115 F7
Luxulyan Sch PL30 ...48 A1
Luxulyan Sta PL30 ....47 F1
Lych Cl PL9 ....135 A6
Lychgate Dr TR1 .....137 C6
Lyd Gdns PL12 ....124 D2
Lydcot Wlk PL6 ......125 A1
Lydcott Cl PL13 ....63 F8
Lydcott Cres PL13 ....63 F8
Lydford Park Rd PL3 ...128 D5
Lydia Way PL14 ......149 B4
Lympne Ave PL5 .....123 F5
Lyn Terr 8 TR18 ......143 C1
Lyn-Meynel TR15 .....140 C4
Lynbridge Ct 5 PL19 ...147 B5
Lyndhurst Ave PL25 ...115 A4
Lyndhurst Cl PL2 .....128 C6
Lyndhurst Rd PL2 ....128 C6
Lyndon Cl PL12 ......122 D4
Lyndrick Rd PL3 .....128 E7
Lynes Cotts 2 PL14 ...51 A7
Lynher Cl PL15 ....27 B3
Lynher Dr PL12 ......122 F1
Lynher St PL5 ....123 D2
Lynher View PL17 ....38 E8
Lynher Way
  28 Callington PL17 ...39 F4
  North Hill PL15 ....27 A4
Lynmouth Cl PL7 .....130 C8
Lynstone Rd EX23 ...104 D4
Lynwood Ave PL7 ....130 B6
Lynwood Cl PL31 ....109 E4
Lynwood Cotts 1 TR19 ...88 C1
Lynwood Flats TR13 ...91 A1
Lyons Rd PL25 ....115 B4
Lytton Pl PL25 ....114 F4

M

Mabbots Ct TR18 .....143 F6
Mabe Com Prim Sch
  PL10 ....81 C1
Mabena Cl PL30 ......34 C8
Macadam Rd PL14 ...149 C1
Macaulay Cres PL5 ...124 C1
Macey St PL11 ....127 C3
Mackenzie Pl PL5 ....123 C2
Madden Rd PL1 ......127 F2
Maddever Cres PL14 ...113 C5
Maddock Cl PL7 .....131 A4
Maddock Dr PL7 .....131 B4
Madeira Dr EX23 ......6 F5
Madeira Rd PL1 ......149 A1
Madeira Wlk TR11 ...145 A2
Madeirs Villas 1 PL20 ...42 C5
Madford La PL15 .....106 C5
Madge Ct PL19 ......147 B6
Madge La PL19 ......147 B6
Madison Terr PL27 ...142 E7
Madison Vean PL27 ...142 E7
Madron Rd TR18 .....143 C2
Maen Valley Pk TR11 ...144 D1
Maenporth Est TR11 ...93 E4
Maenporth Rd TR11 ...93 E4
Maer Down Rd EX23 ...104 D8
Maer La PL23 ....104 D8
Magdalen Gdns PL7 ...130 F3
Magnificent Music Machines
  Mus* PL14 ....51 C3
Magnolia Cl PL7 .....131 B5
Magor Ave TR14 ......79 C5
Maida Vale Terr PL4 ...128 F4
Maiden St 1 EX23 ....4 A1
Maidenwell Rd PL7 ...130 C5
Maidstone Pl PL5 ....123 E4
Main Rd Crumplehorn PL13 ...62 D2
  Downderry PL11 .....64 C5
Main St TR18 ....143 C7
Maine Gdns PL2 .....127 F7
Mainstone Ave PL4 ...149 C2
Maitland Dr PL3 .....128 F8
Maker La PL10 ....133 B4
Maker Rd PL11 ......127 A2
Maker View TR3 .....128 B4
Malabar Rd PL1 ......69 F3
Mallard Cl PL7 ....130 F5
Malmesbury Cl PL2 ...128 B8
Malory Cl PL5 ....124 D2
Malpas Rd TR1 ....137 E2
Malt House Cl PL17 ...142 D6
Malt House Gdns 2
  TR18 ....143 C2
Malt House The 3
  TR18 ....143 C2
Malthouse La PL17 ...89 C5
Man Of War View 11
  TR12 ....102 F2
Manaccan Prim Sch
  TR12 ....101 A8
Manadon Cl PL5 .....124 E1
Manadon Dr PL5 .....124 E1
Manadon Hill PL5,PL6 ...124 E1
Manadon Vale Prim Sch
  PL5 ....124 D2
Manaton Cl PL13 ....146 D8
Manby Gdns PL5 .....123 F5

Mandeley Cl PL33 .....14 E
Manewas Way TR7 ...111 B
Manfield Way PL25 ...115 D
Manifold Gdns PL3 ...129 C
Manley Cl PL14 ....113 B
Manley Ct PL14 ......113 B
Manley Rd PL14 .....113 B
Manley Terr 5 PL14 ...113 B
Mannamead Ave PL3 ...128 E
Mannamead Rd PL3 ...128 E
Manor Bourne Rd PL9 ...135 C
Manor Cl Blisland PL30 ...35 C
  Crackington Haven EX23 ...10 E
  Falmouth TR11 ......144 E
  Heamoor TR18 ......143 B
  Helston TR13 ....146 E
  St Austell PL25 ......114 E
  Tavistock PL19 ......147 E
Manor Cotts TR11 ....145 E
Manor Cotts TR14 ....144 E
Manor Crs 1 TR2 ......95 A
Manor Dr TR26 ....141 C
Manor Farm PL20 ......42 E
Manor Farm Cl 7 TR20 ...89 F
Manor Gdns
  Camelford PL32 ......105 C
  Horrabridge PL20 .....42 E
  Plymouth PL1 ....148 B
  Redruth TR15 ....140 D
Manor La PL13 ....113 D
Manor Park Cl PL7 ...130 A
Manor Park Dr PL7 ...131 A
Manor Pk Dousland PL20 ...42 E
  Roche PL26 ....51 A
  Saltash PL12 ....122 C
Manor Pl TR18 ....143 E
Manor Rd Bude EX23 ...104 E
  Camborne TR14 ......138 C
  Carharrack TR16 ......80 E
  Falmouth TR11 ......144 E
  Newquay TR7 ....110 F
  Plymouth PL9 ....135 C
  Tavistock PL19 ......147 E
Manor St PL1 ....148 A
Manor View PL24 .....60 E
Manor Way
  Heamoor TR18 ......143 E
  Helston TR13 ....146 E
Manse Rd 4 TR3 ......81 E
Manson Cl PL26 ....58 E
Manston Cl PL5 ......127 D
Mantle Gdns PL5 ....127 E
Maple Ave PL11 .....127 A
Maple Cl Bodmin PL31 ...109 E
  8 Callington PL17 .....39 E
  Plymouth PL6 ....125 C
  8 St Columb Major TR9 ...45 E
  Tavistock PL19 ......147 C
Maple Gr
  Plymouth, Mutley PL4 ...128 E
  Plymouth, Plympton PL7 ...130 E
Maple Way PL6 ......125 D
Marazion Prim Sch TR17 ...89 E
Marazion Town Mus*
  TR17 ....89 E
Marbein Cotts TR8 ...44 E
Marchant's Cross PL20 ...42 E
Marchant's Way PL20 ...42 E
Marconi Cl TR13 .....146 E
Marcus Hill TR7 ......110 E
Marcwheal 6 TR19 ...88 E
Mardon Cl PL6 ....125 E
Marett Rd PL5 ....123 E
Margaret Ave PL25 ...115 E
Margaret Cres PL31 ...109 E
Margaret Gdns PL27 ...108 E
Margaret Pk PL3 .....128 E
Margaret Pl TR11 ....144 E
Margate La PL30 ......35 E
Marhamchurch CE Prim Sch
  EX23 ....7 E
Maria's La TR19 ......96 E
Maribou Cl PL28 ......31 E
Marina Rd PL5 ....123 E
Marina Terr 7 PL4 ....128 E
Marine Cres 5 TR11 ...145 E
Marine Ct Falmouth TR11 ...145 E
  7 Perranporth TR6 ...55 E
Marine Dr Looe PL13 ...117 E
  Torpoint PL11 ....127 E
Marine Dr Looe PL13 ...117 C
  Widemouth Bay EX23 ...95 C
Marine Par TR2 ....95 C
Marine Rd PL9 ....135 E
Marine Terr Boscastle PL35 ...9 C
  6 Penzance TR18 ....143 E
Maristow Ave PL2 ....127 E
Maritsov Cl PL6 ......124 E
Market Ave PL1 ......148 E
Market Bldgs TR27 ...142 E
Market Cl PL28 ....31 E
Market Hill PL25 .....114 E
Market House Arc 8
  PL15 ....106 E
Market House Rd TR18 ...143 E
Market Jew St TR18 ...143 E
Market Pl
  Camelford PL32 ......105 E
  Helston TR13 ....146 E
  Marazion TR17 ......89 E
Padstow PL28 ....107 D
Penzance TR18 ......143 E
8 St Columb Major TR9 ...45 E
  St Ives TR26 ....141 E
  Week St Mary EX22 ...11 E
Market Rd Plymouth PL7 ...130 E
  Tavistock PL19 ......147 C
Market Sq Callington PL17 ...39 E
  Hayle TR27 ....142 E
  Plymouth PL1 ....148 E

Mar – Mor 165

arket Sq *continued*
St Day TR16 68 D1
St Just TR19 86 F6
arket St Bodmin PL31 109 E5
Cawsand PL10 133 A2
Devoran TR3 81 F6
Falmouth TR11 145 B4
Fowey PL23 116 D4
Hayle TR27 142 D6
9 Launceston PL15 106 C6
Liskeard PL14 113 C6
Plymouth PL1 128 A1
6 St Austell PL25 114 C3
St Just TR19 86 F6
3 Stratton EX23 4 E1
Tavistock PL19 147 C5
arket Strand
Falmouth TR11 145 B4
Padstow PL28 107 D5
7 Redruth TR15 140 B5
31 St Ives TR26 141 B6
arket Way
Plymouth PL1 148 C3
5 Redruth TR15 140 B4
arks Dr PL31 109 E3
arkwell La PL12 53 C1
arlborough Ave TR11 145 A3
arlborough Cl
1 Falmouth TR11 145 A3
Saltash PL12 122 F1
arlborough Cres TR11 145 A3
arlborough Ct 5
TR11 145 A3
arlborough Gr 2
TR11 145 A3
arlborough Prim Sch
PL1 127 E2
arlborough Rd
Falmouth TR11 145 B3
Plymouth PL4 149 A4
arlborough Row PL1 127 E2
arlborough Sch TR11 145 A3
arlborough St PL1 127 E2
arlborough Way PL26 58 E1
arldon Cl PL5 124 B3
arlow Gdns PL9 135 F5
arriotts Ave TR14 138 B4
arrowbone Slip PL4 149 B2
arryat Gdns PL5 124 E1
arsh Cl PL6 129 F6
arsh La Angarrack TR27 142 F7
Calstock PL18 41 A3
Hayle TR27 142 E7
arsh Mills PL6 129 F7
arsh Mills Pk PL6 129 F6
arsh Mills Ret Pk PL6 129 E7
arshall Ave PL27 108 D5
arshall Cl Roche PL26 46 F3
Tavistock PL19 147 D2
arshall Rd
Bodmin PL31 109 D3
Bodmin, Nanstallon PL30 34 C2
Plymouth PL7 130 A5
Tavistock PL19 147 D2
arshallen Rd TR4 68 C6
arshalls Way PL29 22 D6
arshfield View PL11 64 B5
arshlands PL27 34 A6
artin Cl TR15 140 D5
artin La
Plymouth, Barbican PL4 149 A2
Plymouth, Millbay PL1 148 B2
artin Sq 6 PL17 39 F4
artin St PL1 148 B2
artin's Ct 2 PL31 109 D5
artin's La TR15 139 C8
artins Cl PL14 113 E7
artinvale Ave TR15 140 E7
artinvale Parc TR15 140 E7
artlesham Pl PL5 123 F4
artyn's Cl TR4 55 D4
ary Dean Ave PL5 124 C7
ary Dean Cl PL5 124 C7
ary Dean's CE Prim Sch
PL5 124 C7
ary Moon Cl PL12 53 B7
ary Newman's Cottage*
PL12 123 A2
ary Seacole Rd PL1 148 A3
aryland Cotts PL30 34 C5
aryland Gdns PL2 127 F7
arythorne Rd 15 PL20 41 B1
asefield Gdns PL5 124 B1
asons Row PL18 40 F6
asterman Rd PL2 127 F4
atela Cl 10 TR13 98 C8
atthews Way PL14 51 F6
audlin Cl PL14 113 D5
audlins La PL19 147 A5
aunsell Cl PL2 127 F7
aurice Ct PL7 130 F4
awes Ct PL18 40 D5
awgan TR12 99 D6
awgan Cross TR12 99 D7
awgan-in-Pydar Com Prim
Sch TR8 45 A8
awnan Village CE Prim Sch
TR11 93 D3
axwell Rd PL4 135 B8
axworthy Cross PL15 12 B4
ay Gdns TR16 80 D6
ay La PL13 117 F5
ay Terr PL4 149 B3
aybank Rd PL4 149 C3
aybrook Dr PL12 122 D3
ayers Way PL9 135 D6
ayfair Cres PL6 125 B1
ayfield Cl Bodmin PL31 35 B2

Mayfield Cl *continued*
Port Isaac PL29 22 E7
St Austell PL25 115 A4
Mayfield Cres TR7 110 E5
Mayfield Dr
Port Isaac PL27 22 E7
Roche PL26 47 A3
Mayfield Rd
Falmouth TR11 144 F4
Newquay TR7 110 E5
Port Isaac PL29 22 E7
Mayflower Cl
18 Bere Alston PL20 41 B1
Plymouth PL9 135 F7
Mayflower Dr PL2 128 B5
Mayflower St PL1 148 C3
Maymear Terr PL30 23 E3
Mayna Parc PL15 18 B8
Maynard Pk PL20 41 B1
Maynarde Cl PL7 131 B5
Mayne Cl PL15 106 B7
Maynes Row TR14 139 A5
Mayon Farm TR19 96 B6
Mayon Green Cres TR19 96 B7
Mclean Dr PL26 58 D5
Mead Cnr EX39 2 D4
Mead Hos The TR18 143 F8
Mead The PL7 130 D7
Meadfoot Terr PL4 128 F5
Meadow Brook PL19 147 A4
Meadow Cl Gloweth TR1 69 E3
Newquay TR7 111 A4
Plymouth PL7 131 D4
Polruan PL23 116 D2
Saltash PL12 122 F3
St Austell PL25 114 F6
St Stephen PL26 58 B4
Meadow Ct
Mevagissey PL26 73 C3
Wadebridge PL27 34 C8
Meadow Dr Bude EX23 104 F6
Camborne TR14 138 C4
Looe PL13 117 D5
Par PL24 115 F5
Saltash PL12 122 D4
Meadow Flats 27 TR26 141 B6
Meadow La TR1 137 D3
Meadow Pk
7 Liskeard PL14 113 B5
Plymouth PL9 135 C5
Trewoon PL25 59 A3
Meadow Pl PL31 109 D4
Meadow Rd PL13 62 A7
Meadow Rise
1 Penwithick PL26 59 D7
Plymouth PL7 131 A4
12 St Columb Major TR9 45 E6
Meadow St PL26 73 C3
Meadow Terr PL14 37 F3
Meadow The Illogan TR16 67 D4
Truro TR1 137 B5
Meadow View
Camborne TR14 138 E1
8 Goldsithney TR20 89 E5
St Minver PL27 21 F3
Meadow View Rd PL7 130 D5
Meadow Villas 8 TR18 143 C1
Meadow Way
Plymouth PL7 130 D7
St Issey PL27 32 E6
Meadow Wlk PL23 116 D2
Meadowbank TR11 82 A3
Meadowbank Rd TR11 145 A6
Meadowfield Pl PL7 131 B3
Meadowhead PL27 108 C4
Meadowlands PL6 125 D7
Meadows The
St Dennis PL26 58 C8
St Dominick PL12 40 D2
St Teath PL30 23 E7
Torpoint PL11 126 E4
Meadowside
Launceston PL15 106 A4
Newquay TR7 111 A4
Plymouth PL9 135 F7
St Austell PL25 115 C6
Whitstone EX22 12 B8
Meadowside Cl
Hayle TR27 142 A3
St Kew Highway PL30 23 B2
Meadowside Rd TR11 144 F2
Meadowside Rise PL26 58 D6
Meadowsweet Pk PL12 122 D6
Meadway Looe PL13 117 E4
Saltash PL12 122 E1
St Austell PL25 114 F5
Mearwood La TR11 144 F4
Meaver Rd TR12 99 B1
Meavy Ave PL5 124 E2
Meavy Bourne PL20 42 D2
Meavy CE Prim Sch PL20 42 F2
Meavy La PL20 42 D2
Meavy Villas PL20 42 D2
Meavy Way Plymouth PL5 124 E2
Tavistock PL19 147 D5
Meddon Cross
Edistone EX39 3 C5
Welcombe EX39 3 C4
Meddy's Row PL14 39 A2
Medland Cres PL6 124 D6
Medland Gdns PL25 114 C4
Medlyn Ct TR13 146 B5
Medrose St PL33 14 E3
Medrose Terr 22 TR18 143 E6
Medrow PL15 27 A8
Medway Pl PL3 129 D6
Meeks Row PL18 41 A6
Melbourne Cotts PL1 148 B3

Melbourne Gn 2 PL1 148 B3
Melbourne Pl PL1 148 B4
Melbourne Rd PL14 113 B5
Melbourne St PL1 148 B3
Melbourne Terr 17
TR18 143 C7
Mellanear Cl TR27 142 B4
Mellanear Rd TR27 142 B3
Mellanvrane La TR7 110 F4
Melliars Way EX23 104 F6
Melrose Ave PL2 128 C8
Melrose Terr 6 TR9 45 E1
Melvill Cres TR11 145 B3
Melvill Ct TR11 145 B2
Melvill La TR11 145 B2
Melvill Rd TR11 145 C2
Melville Pl 1 PL2 128 A5
Melville Rd Plymouth PL2 128 A5
Threemilestone TR3 69 D3
Melville Terr PL22 112 C2
Mena Park Cl PL9 136 B7
Mena Park Rd PL9 136 B7
Menabilly Cl PL17 39 E3
Menabilly Rd PL25 114 E6
Menacuddle Hill PL25 114 C4
Menacuddle La PL25 114 C4
Menadue Ct TR27 78 E3
Menage St TR13 146 C5
Menague PL27 21 E3
Menakarne TR16 80 F8
Menallack Cheese Farm*
TR10 93 A6
Meneage Cotts 2 TR13 146 C5
Meneage Ho 3 TR13 146 C5
Meneage Parc TR13 146 C5
Meneage Rd TR13 146 C4
Meneage St TR13 146 C5
Meneage Villas PL25 114 B3
Menear Rd PL25 115 A6
Menefreda Way PL27 22 A4
Meneth TR12 92 C1
Meneth Rd TR14 138 F2
Menhay View TR11 144 C3
Menhaye Gdns TR15 139 D7
Menheniot Cres PL15 18 D5
Menheniot Prim Sch
PL14 52 A5
Menheniot Sta PL14 51 F4
Menhinick Cl PL12 53 C3
Menhyr Dr TR26 141 C2
Menna La TR2 57 E5
Mennaye Ct TR18 143 D4
Mennaye Rd TR18 143 D4
Merafield Cl PL7 130 B5
Merafield Dr PL7 130 C4
Merafield Farm Cotts
PL7 130 B4
Merafield Rd PL7 130 B4
Merafield Rise PL7 130 C4
Merchants House (Mus)*
PL1 148 C2
Merchants Quay PL15 18 E2
Meredith Rd PL2 128 C6
Meres Valley TR12 99 A2
Meridian Ho PL4 149 A3
Merlin Cl PL6 125 E8
Merlins Way PL34 14 D7
Mermaid Ct TR7 111 C8
Merrick Ave TR1 137 E6
Merrifield Cl TR1 137 B5
Merrifield Cross EX22 7 F4
Merrill Pl TR11 145 A3
Merritts Hill TR16 67 E4
Merritts Way TR15 139 C7
Merrivale Rd
Plymouth, Ham PL2 128 B7
Plymouth, Honicknowle
PL5 124 B3
Merrivale View Rd PL20 42 E3
Merry Mit Mdw TR11 144 C3
Mersey Cl PL3 129 D6
Merther Cl TR13 91 B4
Messack Cl TR11 144 E2
Metha Pk TR8 56 C7
Metha Rd TR8 56 C7
Methleigh Bottoms TR13 91 A1
Methleigh Parc TR13 91 A1
Mevagissey Aquarium*
PL26 73 C3
Mevagissey Com Prim Sch
PL26 73 C4
Mevagissey Ho TR1 69 E4
Mevagissey Mus* PL26 73 C3
Mews Ct PL14 51 F5
Mews The Par PL24 60 B5
3 Penzance TR18 143 E6
Plymouth, Devonport PL1 128 A3
Plymouth, Stonehouse PL1 148 A3
Mexico La TR27 142 C7
Mexico Terr TR27 142 C8
Michael Rd PL3 129 A5
Michaelstow Holiday Village
PL30 23 F5
Michell Ave TR7 110 E6
Michigan Way PL3 129 C6
Mid Churchway PL9 136 A7
Mid Cornwall Bsns Ctr
PL25 115 E4
Mid Moor PL14 38 B6
Middle Down Cl PL9 136 A5
Middle Market St PL13 117 D3
Middle Rd TR15 140 E7
Middle Rosewin Row 8
TR1 137 D5
Middle Row TR13 90 E3
Middle St Padstow PL28 107 D5
Port Isaac PL29 22 D7
Middle Wharf PL26 73 C3

Middlefield Rd PL6 124 D6
Middlefield Cl PL12 122 B2
Middlegates 5 TR5 54 D1
Middleton Cres TR7 110 F4
Middleton Wlk PL5 123 D4
Middletons Row 6
TR15 140 C5
Middleway PL24 60 B5
Middlewell Parc PL27 108 B4
Midella Rd PL20 42 D2
Midway Dr TR1 137 E5
Midway Rd PL31 109 A5
Miers Cl PL5 127 C8
Mildmay St PL4 149 A4
Mile End TR12 102 F4
Milehouse Rd PL2 128 A5
Miles Mitchell Ave PL6 125 A1
Miles Mitchell Village
PL6 125 A1
Milford La PL5 124 B5
Military Rd
Millbrook PL10 132 C3
Plymouth PL3 129 E6
Rame PL10 64 C2
St Mawes TR2 95 B4
Mill Ball Hill EX23 10 B7
Mill Bridge PL1 148 A3
Mill Cl Porthleven TR13 91 A1
Wadebridge PL27 108 E5
Mill Cotts TR13 146 A6
Mill Ford Sch PL5 123 F4
Mill Gdns PL22 112 C2
Mill Hill Crumplehorn PL13 62 D1
Lelant TR27 77 E3
Lostwithiel PL22 112 D2
St Just In Roseland TR2 82 F3
Mill La Camelford PL32 105 D5
Coad's Green PL15 27 C1
Grampound TR2 72 A7
Helston TR13 146 B6
19 Mousehole TR19 88 C1
Porthleven TR13 91 A1
St Breward PL30 24 B3
St Germans PL12 65 A8
Torpoint PL11 127 A2
Tregony TR2 71 F3
Truro TR3 137 C1
Mill Pool 15 TR19 88 C1
Mill Rd Millbrook PL10 133 A5
Padstow PL28 107 D5
Penponds TR14 79 B5
Perranporth TR6 55 B4
Tideford PL12 52 F2
Mill Rd Est PL12 52 F2
Mill Sq PL28 107 D5
Mill St PL31 109 E5
Mill View Gdns PL10 132 F5
Mill View Rd PL10 132 F5
Milladon La PL12 64 D8
Millbank Mdw TR27 78 E1
Millbay Rd PL1 148 A2
Millbrook CE Sch PL10 132 E5
Millendreath Holliday Vill
PL13 117 F5
Millenium Appartments
TR10 81 D2
Millennium Way TR13 146 D8
Miller Bsns Pk PL14 113 B4
Miller Ct PL1 148 A2
Miller Way PL6 125 E3
Millet Cl TR17 89 D5
Millfield TR18 88 E6
Millham La PL22 112 E3
Millhill PL19 30 B1
Millhouse Pk PL11 127 A2
Millpond Ave TR27 142 B4
Millpool PL22 112 F3
Millpool Head PL10 132 E4
Millpool Rd PL10 133 A6
Mills Rd PL1 127 F2
Mills' St TR16 68 E1
Milltown Gdns PL15 18 E6
Millway Pl PL9 135 D8
Millwood Dr PL6 125 E1
Milne Pl PL1 127 F3
Milton Abbott Sch PL19 29 D5
Milton Cl PL5 124 D2
Milton Cres PL19 147 D5
Milton Ct Plymouth PL4 129 B1
Plymouth PL4 149 C2
Minack Theatre* TR19 96 E2
Mine Hill PL14 51 F6
Mine La PL30 47 E7
Mineral Tramways Discovery
Ctr TR15 139 B4
Miners Ct TR6 55 A4
Miners Row TR15 140 C5
Miners Way PL14 113 D7
Minerva Cl PL7 131 A6
Minions Row PL14 38 B6
Minnie Pl TR11 145 B3
Minorca La PL26 47 D2
Minses Cl PL9 136 C7
Minster Ave EX23 104 F4
Minster Mdw TR12 101 A8
Minster Terr TR12 101 A8
Minton Cl PL25 115 A4
Mirador Pl PL4 129 C3
Misterton Cl PL9 136 B8
Mitchell Cl 3 TR12 102 F2
Mitchell Ct 11 TR1 137 D5
Mitchell Hill TR1 137 D5
Mitchell Hill Terr 4
TR1 137 D5
Mitchell La
Camborne TR14 138 E3
Mitchell TR8 56 E5

Mitchell Rd
Camborne TR14 138 C3
St Austell PL25 114 F4
Mitchell's Boatyard
PL26 73 C2
Mithian Jun & Inf Sch
TR5 54 E1
Mitre Ct 15 Plymouth PL1 149 A2
Tavistock PL19 147 A3
Modbury Cl PL5 124 B3
Modus La PL26 58 E1
Modyford Wlk PL20 41 F3
Mohun's Cl PL19 147 C4
Mohun's Pk PL19 147 C3
Molenick La PL12 52 E3
Molesworth Ct 4 PL27 108 B5
Molesworth Rd
Plymouth, Plympton PL7 130 C6
Plymouth, Stoke PL1,PL3 128 A3
Molesworth St
Tintagel PL34 14 C7
Wadebridge PL27 108 B5
Molesworth Terr PL10 132 F5
Molinnis PL26 47 C2
Molinnis Rd PL26 47 C2
Mollison Rd PL5 123 E2
Molyneaux Pl 10 PL1 127 F3
Monastery Cl TR12 101 D4
Mongleath Ave TR11 144 E3
Mongleath Cl TR11 144 E3
Mongleath Rd TR11 144 E3
Monica Wlk PL4 149 B4
Monks Hill PL15 28 C4
Monks Park Cotts PL15 106 D6
Monksmead PL19 147 A4
Monmouth Gdns PL5 124 C4
Monmouth La PL22 112 D2
Montacute Ave PL5 124 B2
Montague Ave TR15 140 A6
Monterey Cl EX23 104 E4
Monterey Gdns TR1 137 E5
Montgomery Cl PL12 122 D3
Montgomery Rd 2 PL26 59 D7
Montpelier Jun & Inf Schs
PL2 128 B6
Montpelier Rd PL2 128 C7
Monument Rd TR13 146 B5
Monument St PL1 127 E1
Monument Way PL31 109 C4
Moon La PL4 149 A3
Moon St PL4 149 A3
Moonrakers TR26 141 D2
Moonsfield 5 PL17 39 F4
Moor La PL5 123 E1
Moor Parc TR12 100 D6
Moor St TR14 138 D3
Moor View Bodmin PL31 109 F2
Plymouth, Keyham PL2 127 F5
Plymouth, Laira PL3 129 C4
Torpoint PL11 127 B3
Moor View Terr
Plymouth PL4 128 E4
Yelverton PL20 42 D2
Moorcroft Cl PL9 136 A7
Moorfield PL16 19 F4
Moorfield Ave 4 PL6 129 C7
Moorfield Rd
Camborne TR15 139 C6
St Giles-On-The-Heath PL15 13 F1
Moorlan Mdws PL26 47 A3
Moorland Ave PL7 130 F6
Moorland Cl
Liskeard PL14 113 D7
Pendeen TR19 74 F1
Yelverton PL20 121 D8
Moorland Ct
1 St Austell PL25 114 C3
Yelverton PL20 42 C2
Moorland Dr PL7 130 E6
Moorland Gdns PL7 130 F6
Moorland Rd
Indian Queens TR9 45 F2
Launceston PL15 106 A4
Par PL24 60 C4
Plymouth PL7 130 E5
St Austell PL25 114 C3
Moorland View
Linkinhorne PL17 39 B6
Liskeard PL14 113 D7
Plymouth, Derriford PL6 125 A5
Plymouth, Plymstock PL9 136 B7
Saltash PL12 122 F4
Moorland Way PL18 40 F5
Moorlands La PL12 122 C4
Moorlands Trad Est
PL12 122 C4
Moorview Terr PL14 38 D7
Morcom Cl PL25 115 A5
Moresk Cl TR1 137 D5
Moresk Gdns TR1 137 D5
Moresk Rd TR1 137 D5
Moreton Ave PL6 124 F1
Morice Sq PL1 127 E2
Morice St PL1 127 E2
Morice Town Prim Sch
PL2 127 E4
Morla La TR15 140 A6
Morlaix Ave TR1 137 D3
Morlaix Dr PL6 125 B4
Morleigh Cl PL25 114 F3
Morley Cl PL7 130 A5
Morley Ct PL1 148 B3
Morley Dr PL20 42 A2
Morley View Rd PL7 130 C6
Morrab Ct TR7 110 F6

Morrab Pl 34 TR18 ....143 C6
Morrab Rd
  Camborne TR14 ....138 C3
  Penzance TR18 ....143 E5
Morrab Terr 35 TR18 ...143 E5
Morrish Pk PL9 ....135 F6
Morshead Rd PL6 ....124 F2
Mortain Rd PL12 ....122 D2
Mortimore Cl PL12 ....122 D2
Morvan Trad Est PL25 ...114 F3
Morven Rd PL26 ....114 C5
Morview Rd PL13 ....63 F8
Morwell Gdns PL2 ....128 A6
Morwellham Quay *
  PL9 ....41 B4
Morwenna Gdns TR6 .....55 B5
Morwenna Rd EX23 ....2 D1
Moses Cl PL6 ....124 E7
Moses Ct PL6 ....124 E7
Mosquito Cres 3 PL27 ...31 F3
Moss Side Ind Est PL17 ..39 F4
Moss Terr PL23 ....116 D3
Mostyn Ave PL14 ....129 A4
Mote Pk PL12 ....122 C3
Mothecombe Wlk PL6 ...125 E1
Moulton Cl PL7 ....131 B5
Mount Agar Rd PL4 ....81 F7
Mount Ambrose TR15 ...140 E7
Mount Batten Waterside Pk
  PL9 ....134 F7
Mount Bennett Rd 8
  PL24 ....60 D5
Mount Bennett Terr 4
  PL24 ....60 D5
Mount Camel PL32 ....105 C4
Mount Carbis Gdns
  TR15 ....140 C3
Mount Carbis Rd TR15 ...140 D3
Mount Charles Jun & Inf Sch
  PL25 ....114 F3
Mount Charles Rd PL25 ..114 F4
Mount Cres PL24 ....60 C4
Mount Edgcumbe Country
  Pk * PL10 ....133 E6
Mount Edgcumbe Terr
  TR11 ....145 B4
Mount Folly TR27 ....142 C6
Mount Gould Ave PL4 ...129 B2
Mount Gould Cres PL4 ..129 B3
Mount Gould Hospl PL4 ..129 B3
Mount Gould Rd PL4 .....129 B3
Mount Gould Way PL4 ...129 B3
Mount Hawke Chalet Pk
  TR4 ....68 B6
Mount Hawke Com Prim Sch
  TR4 ....68 C6
Mount House Sch PL19 ..147 E7
Mount Lidden TR18 ....143 C4
Mount Pleasant
  Bodmin PL3 ....109 E5
  Boscastle PL35 ....9 D1
  Falmouth TR11 ....144 E1
  Hayle TR27 ....142 E4
  Lelant TR26 ....77 E3
  Millbrook PL10 ....132 E5
  Newlyn TR18 ....143 C4
  Par PL24 ....60 B6
  Plymouth PL5 ....124 B2
  St Ives TR26 ....141 A6
Mount Pleasant Cl TR14 .138 E1
Mount Pleasant Gdns
  TR27 ....142 C6
Mount Pleasant Pl PL22 .112 C3
Mount Pleasant Rd
  Camborne TR14 ....138 D1
  11 Porthleven TR13 .....98 B8
  Threemilestone TR3 .....69 D3
Mount Pleasant Terr
  TR15 ....140 E7
Mount Pleasure TR14 ....138 E1
Mount Prospect Terr
  TR18 ....143 C3
Mount Rd PL24 ....60 C4
Mount St Mevagissey PL26 ..23 C3
  Penzance TR18 ....143 E6
  Plymouth, Mount Wise PL1 127 E1
  Plymouth, Mutley PL4 ....149 A4
Mount Stamper Rd
  PL25 ....114 D7
Mount Stephens La
  TR11 ....144 F4
Mount Stone Rd PL1 .....134 A8
Mount Street Prim Sch
  PL4 ....149 A4
Mount Tamar Cl PL5 .....123 E2
Mount Tamar Sch PL5 ...123 E2
Mount Tavy Rd PL19 .....147 E6
Mount Terr 9 PL24 ....60 B6
Mount View Lane TR28 ...111 B3
  Madron TR20 ....88 A7
Mount View Cotts TR20 ...89 A7
Mount View Terr
  5 Marazion TR17 ....89 C5
  2 Newlyn TR18 ....143 C3
Mount Whistle Rd TR14 ..138 F7
Mount Wise
  Launceston PL15 ....106 C5
  Newquay TR7 ....110 A7
Mount Wise Cotts TR7 ...110 E5
Mount Wise Ct PL1 ......127 F1
Mount Wise Prim Sch
  PL1 ....127 E1
Mount's Bay Bsol Flts
  TR18 ....88 E6
Mount's Bay Sch TR18 ..143 B7

Mount's Bay Terr 21
  TR13 ....98 C8
Mount's Rd 20 TR13 .....98 C8
Mountbatten Cl
  Plymouth PL9 ....135 D6
  St Columb Minor TR7 ...111 E7
Mountbatten Rd 6 PL26 ..59 D7
Mountbatten Way PL9 ...135 E6
Mountfield Terr 6 PL24 ..60 C4
Mountlea Dr PL24 ....60 B4
Mounts Bay Rd PL18 ....143 C4
Mounts Bay Terr TR13 ...90 D3
Mountstephen Cl PL25 ..114 B3
Mourne Villas PL9 ....135 F8
Mousehole Com Prim Sch
  TR19 ....88 C1
Mousehole La TR19 ....88 C1
Mowbray Mews PL32 ....10 B2
Mowhay Cl TR7 ....111 A4
Mowhay La 8 PL17 ....39 E4
Mowhay Mdw
  St John PL11 ....132 B8
  Wadebridge PL27 ......108 B4
Mowhay Rd
  Plymouth PL5 ....123 F1
  Plymouth PL5 ....124 A2
Moyle Rd PL28 ....107 E4
Mr Potter's Mus of
  Curiosity * PL15 ....25 E3
Mudge Way PL7 ....130 E5
Mudges Terr PL18 ....41 A6
Mulberry Cl PL6 ....125 E7
Mulberry Dr PL19 ....147 E5
Mulberry Gr PL4 ....145 B5
Mulberry Quay TR11 ....145 B5
Mulberry Rd PL12 ....122 E1
Mulgrave St PL1 ....148 C2
Mullet Ave PL3 ....129 C4
Mullet Cl PL3 ....129 C4
Mullet Rd PL3 ....129 C4
Mullion Cl PL11 ....126 F1
Mullion Comp Sch TR12 ..99 B1
Mullion Cove TR12 ....102 B7
Mullion Jun & Inf Sch
  TR12 ....99 A1
Mundys Field TR21 ......103 A5
Murdoch Cl
  Redruth TR15 ....140 B6
  Truro TR1 ....137 E6
Murdock Rd PL11 ....126 F3
Murrey Villas TR19 ......86 E6
Murtons Terr TR16 ....68 E7
Mus of Witchcraft * PL35 .9 C2
Museum of Submarine
  Telegraphy * TR19 ......96 E3
Mutley Cl PL4 ....149 A4
Mutley Plain PL4 ....148 C4
Mutley Plain La PL4 .....128 E4
Mutley Rd PL3 ....128 E5
Mutton Cove PL1 ....127 E3
Mutton Row TR10 ....144 C8
My Lords Rd TR9 ....57 E8
Mylor Cl PL2 ....128 D8
Mylor Com Prim Sch
  TR11 ....82 A3
Myrtle Cl PL20 ....42 E3
Myrtle Ct PL26 ....73 C3
Myrtles Ct PL12 ....122 D4
Myrtleville PL2 ....128 C6
Mythyon Ct 4 TR18 .....143 C7

Nailzea Ho PL13 ....117 D2
Nalder's Ct 6 TR1 ....137 C4
Nampara Ct 4 TR6 ......55 A4
Nancarrows PL22 ....122 C2
Nancealverne TR18 ......143 D6
Nancealverne Sch TR18 .143 C6
Nanceddon Farm TR18 ...89 A8
Nancegollan Ind Est
  TR13 ....91 B7
Nancemere Rd TR1 ......137 D6
Nancherrow Hill TR19 ....86 F6
Nancherrow Row TR19 ...86 F6
Nanclidra Sch TR 26 .....76 F3
Nangitha Cl TR11 ....144 C3
Nangitha Terr TR11 ......144 C3
Nanhayes Row TR8 ......56 B7
Nanjivey Pl 8 TR26 .....141 A5
Nanjivey Terr 9 TR26 ...141 A5
Nanpean Prim Sch PL26 .58 D6
Nanpusker Cl TR27 ......142 E6
Nanpusker Rd TR27 .....78 C4
Nans Kestenen TR13 ....146 B5
Nansale Ct TR7 ....111 A6
Nansavallon Rd TR1 ......69 F3
Nanscober Pl TR13 ....146 B8
Nansloe Cl TR13 ....146 D4
Nansloe Com Prim Sch
  TR13 ....146 C4
Nansmelyon Rd TR22 ....99 A1
Nanstallon Com Prim Sch
  PL30 ....34 C1
Nanterrow La TR27 ....66 D1
Nanturras Parc TR20 .....89 E5
Nanturras Row TR20 .....89 E5
Napier St PL1 ....127 F3
Napier Terr PL4 ....128 E4
Narkurs Cross PL11 .....64 D7
Narrow La Saltash PL12 ..122 C7
  Summercourt TR8 ....57 C8
Narrowcliff PL7 ....111 A7
Nash Cl PL7 ....131 A5

Nathan Cl TR7 ....111 B5
National Marine Aquarium *
  PL4 ....149 A2
National Seal Sanctuary
  The * TR12 ....92 C1
National Seal Sanctuary
  Visitor Ctr * TR12 ....92 D1
Navy Inn Ct 10 TR18 ....143 C1
Neal Cl PL7 ....131 B6
Neath Rd PL4 ....149 C4
Neeham Rd TR8 ....56 B7
Nelson Ave PL1 ....127 F3
Nelson Gdns 5 PL1 ......127 F3
Nelson St PL4 ....149 C4
Nelson Terr PL6 ....125 E6
Nepean St 1 PL2 ....127 F5
Neptune Ave PL27 ....31 F3
Neswick St PL1 ....148 B3
Neswick Street Ope
  PL1 ....148 A3
Nethercott Cross EX21 ...13 F7
Netherton Rd PL20 ....42 A3
Netherton Terr PL20 .....42 A3
Nettell's Hill TR15 ....140 B5
Nettlehayes PL9 ....136 D7
Netton Cl PL9 ....136 B6
Nevada Cl PL3 ....129 D6
Nevada Hill 8 PL18 ......143 C7
Nevada St TR18 ....143 C7
Nevada Villas 8 PL26 ....60 C4
New Barn Hill PL7 ....130 F3
New Bglws PL30 ....36 B3
New Bridge St 1 TR1 ....137 D4
New Connection St 4
  TR14 ....138 D3
New Cotts
  Gunnislake PL18 ....41 A6
  Kilkhampton EX23 ....5 A6
New Ct TR11 ....145 B4
New Cut TR15 ....140 B5
New Dairy La TR17 ....89 C6
New George St PL1 ....148 C3
New Hill Est TR2 ....72 A7
New Hos TR14 ....139 B3
New La TR15 ....140 E7
New Launceston Rd
  PL19 ....147 A5
New Mills Farm Pk *
  PL15 ....18 C4
New Mills La TR1 ....137 A6
New Molinnis PL26 ....47 C2
New Northernmays 2
  PL15 ....106 C6
New Park Rd
  Plymouth PL7 ....131 A4
  Wadebridge PL27 ......108 C5
New Passage Hill PL1 ...127 E3
New Pk Horrabridge PL20 ..42 C4
  Wadebridge PL27 ......108 C4
New Pottery Rd
  Illogan TR16 ....67 F5
  Redruth TR16 ....140 A7
New Rd Barripper TR14 ...79 B5
  Bere Alston PL20 ....41 B2
  Boscastle PL35 ....9 C2
  Callington PL17 ....39 E4
  Camborne TR14 ....139 B3
  Cawsand PL10 ....133 A1
  Cawsand, Kingsand PL10 ..133 B2
  Lifton PL16 ....19 F4
  Liskeard PL14 ....113 B5
  Newlyn TR18 ....143 C3
  Perranporth TR6 ....55 B4
  Port Isaac PL29 ....22 D7
  Roborough PL6 ....121 D2
  Ruan Minor PL12 ....103 A4
  Saltash PL12 ....122 E3
  St Columb Major TR9 ....45 E1
  St Hilary TR20 ....89 F6
  St Just TR19 ....86 F6
  Stithians TR3 ....80 F3
  Stratton EX23 ....4 D1
  Summercourt TR8 ......57 D7
  Tregony TR2 ....71 F4
  Truro TR1 ....79 E4
New Road Cl PL10 ....133 A2
New Road Hill PL23 ......116 C4
New Road Terr PL12 .....53 C3
New Row Gweek TR12 ....92 C1
  Mylor Bridge TR11 ......82 A3
  Nanclidra TR 20 ....76 F2
  Redruth TR16 ....139 E8
  Summercourt TR8 ....57 B6
New St Bugle PL26 ....47 C1
  Falmouth TR11 ....145 B4
  Millbrook PL10 ....132 E5
  Padstow PL28 ....107 D5
  Penryn TR10 ....144 D7
  Penzance TR18 ....143 E5
  Plymouth PL1 ....149 A2
  Troon TR14 ....79 E4
New Town La TR18 ......143 E5
New Windsor Terr 11
  PL1 ....148 A4
New Wood Cl PL6 ....125 E8
New Zealand Ho PL3 ....128 B4
Newacott Cross EX22 ....7 F5
Newbridge Hill PL18 .....41 A6
Newbridge La TR1,TR3 ...69 F3
Newbridge Way TR1 .....69 F3
Newbury Cl PL5 ....124 B5
Newcastle Gdns PL5 .....124 B5
Newham Est TR1 ....137 D3
Newham Ind Est TR1 ....137 D2
Newham La
  Helston TR13 ....146 A7
  Lostwithiel PL22 ....49 A1
Newham Rd TR1 ....137 E2

Newhouses PL17 ....38 E8
Newlyn Art Gall * TR18 ..143 C3
Newlyn Rd TR19 ....97 B6
Newlyn Sch TR18 ....143 C1
Newman Rd
  Plymouth PL5 ....123 E2
  Saltash PL12 ....122 F3
Newmills * PL15 ....118 D4
Newnhall Ind Est PL7 ...130 F7
Newnham Ind Est PL7 ...130 F6
Newnham Rd PL7 ....130 F7
Newnham Way PL7 ......130 F6
Newport PL12 ....65 A8
Newport Cl 12 PL17 .....39 F4
Newport Ind Est PL15 ...106 C6
Newport Sq PL15 ....106 B7
Newport St
  Millbrook PL10 ....132 E5
  Plymouth PL1 ....128 A1
Newport Terr 3 PL17 ....39 F4
Newquay Airport TR8 ....44 F8
Newquay Hospl TR7 ......110 F5
Newquay Jun Sch TR7 ...110 F6
Newquay Rd
  Goonhavern TR4 ....55 C4
  St Columb Major TR9 ....45 D6
Newquay Sta TR7 ....110 F6
Newtake Rd PL19 ....147 E2
Newton Cl PL4 ....123 E2
Newton Ct PL14 ....50 E8
Newton Gdns PL5 ....123 E2
Newton Pk 18 TR2 ....95 A6
Newton Rd St Mawes TR2 ..95 B6
Newton Sq PL3 ....60 F3
Newtown La TR17,TR20 ..89 F7
Nicholas Ave TR16 ....80 A5
Nicholas Parc 3 TR8 .....48 C4
Nicholas Rd PL5 ....124 E2
Nicholson St PL6 ....126 B5
Nicolls Flats PL16 ....106 B5
Nightingale Cl PL9 ....136 C8
Nilch Pk PL12 ....122 D2
Nine Maidens Com Prim Sch
  TR16 ....80 A4
Nine Oaks PL10 ....42 F3
No Go By Hill TR19 ....86 F7
No Mans' Land Rd TR11 ..93 D5
Nook The PL19 ....147 D6
Norfolk Cl PL3 ....129 C5
Norfolk Rd
  Falmouth TR11 ....145 B4
  Plymouth PL3 ....129 C5
Norman Cotts PL15 ......106 C7
Norman's Way PL30 .....23 E3
Normandy Hill PL5 ....123 B2
Normandy Way
  Bodmin PL31 ....109 F2
  Camborne TR14 ....138 F3
  Plymouth PL5 ....123 C2
North Cl EX23 ....5 A6
North Cliff 12 TR19 ......88 C1
North Cnr PL12 ....53 A3
North Cornwall Mus & Gall *
  PL32 ....105 C4
North Dimson PL18 ......40 F6
North Down Cres PL2 ...127 F6
North Down Rd PL2 ......127 F6
North Down Rd PL2 ......128 B6
North Grange Ind Est
  TR3 ....81 F6
North Hill Blackwater TR4 ..68 F5
  Carharrack TR16 ....80 F8
  Chacewater TR4 ....68 F3
  Plymouth PL4 ....149 A4
North Hill Pk PL25 ......114 D4
North Moor Cross EX22 ...3 F3
North Orchard Cl 1
  TR20 ....89 C5
North Par
  Camborne TR14 ....145 A6
  Falmouth TR11 ....145 E5
  Penzance TR18 ....143 E5
  Portscatho TR2 ....83 B2
North Parade Rear
  TR14 ....138 D3
North Park Villas PL12 ..122 C4
North Pethwerin Prim Sch
  PL15 ....12 B1
North Pl 15 TR18 ....141 B6
North Pool Cl TR15 ......139 C7
North Pool Rd TR15 ......139 C7
North Prospect Prim Sch
  PL2 ....128 A7
North Prospect Rd PL2 ..128 A6
North Quay Hayle TR27 ..142 B6
  Padstow PL28 ....107 D6
North Quay Hill TR7 .....110 D7
North Quay Par PL28 ....107 D6
North Rd Camborne TR14 .138 D3
  Goldsithney TR20 ....89 E5
  Landrake PL12 ....53 C3
  Lifton PL16 ....19 F4
  Looe PL13 ....117 C3
  Pentewan PL26 ....73 C6
  Redruth TR16 ....140 E1
  Saltash PL12 ....122 F3
  St Teath PL30 ....23 E7
  Torpoint PL11 ....127 B3
  Whitemoor PL26 ....58 E8
  Yelverton PL20 ....42 C3
North Rd E PL4 ....148 C4
North Rd W PL1 ....148 B4
North Roskear Rd TR14 ..138 F5
North Row TR19 ....86 F6
North St Fowey PL23 ....116 D4
Newham Rd TR1 ....137 E2

North St continued
  Lostwithiel PL22 ....112 C2
  Marazion TR17 ....89 B5
  14 Mousehole TR19 .....88 C3
  Par PL24 ....60 C5
  Plymouth PL4 ....149 A3
  Redruth TR15 ....140 B6
  St Austell PL25 ....114 C4
  Tavistock PL19 ....147 C5
North Terr
  2 Penzance TR18 ......143 E4
  Whitemoor PL26 ....58 E8
  12 St Ives TR26 ....141 B5
North View Ave PL13 ....117 D4
North View TR8 ....111 F4
North Weald Gdns PL5 ..123 E5
Northampton Cl PL5 .....124 B5
Northcott Mouth Rd
  EX23 ....104 F8
Northesk St PL2 ....128 A4
Northey Cl TR4 ....69 F6
Northey Rd PL31 ....109 D4
Northfield Cl TR16 ....68 E1
Northfield Dr TR1 ....137 D3
Northgate Pl 1 TR18 ....106 C6
Northolt Ave PL5 ....123 D4
Northumberland St TR27 .127 E8
Northumberland Terr
  PL1 ....148 B3
Norton Ave PL4 ....149 C4
Norwich Ave PL5 ....124 B5
Notre Dame Cl PL6 ......124 F5
Notre Dame Ho PL1 .....148 B3
Notre Dame RC Sch
  PL6 ....124 F5
Notte St PL1 ....148 C2
Notter Mill Holiday Village
  PL12 ....53 D4
Novorossisk Rd PL6 .....125 E2
Noweth Pl TR11 ....144 E5
Nunnery Hill PL26 ....72 F7
Nurseries The TR1 ....144 D5
Nursery Cl 11 Par PL24 ..60 D5
  Plymouth PL5 ....124 B7
  Truro TR1 ....77 E3
Nut La TR27 ....77 E3
Nut Tree Hill PL12 ....65 B8

O

Oak Apple Cl PL12 ....122 D4
Oak Ave PL26 ....40 A1
Oak Dr 8 Liskeard PL14 ..113 B5
  Plymouth PL6 ....129 D6
Oak Ford PL30 ....48 C2
Oak La Truro TR1 ....69 E4
  Whitstone EX22 ....7 F1
Oak Park Rd PL14 ....113 A6
Oak Rd St Tudy PL30 ....23 E2
Oak Ridge PL16 ....147 C2
Oak Tree Cl PL25 ....115 B3
Oak Tree Cres PL14 .....124 F1
Oak Tree Pk PL6 ....147 C3
Oak Tree Pk PL6 ....125 D6
Oak Vale TR2 ....72 A7
Oak Way TR1 ....137 D5
Oakapple Cl PL7 ....130 B7
Oakcroft Rd PL2 ....128 B6
Oakdene Rise PL9 ....135 F6
Oakdene Villas 7 TR9 ...45 E2
Oakey Orch PL17 ....40 D4
Oakfield PL15 ....27 D3
Oakfield Cl PL7 ....131 C6
Oakfield Pl PL4 ....129 B3
Oakfield Rd
  Falmouth TR11 ....144 F5
  Plymouth PL7 ....130 C6
Oakfield Terrace Rd
  PL4 ....129 B3
Oakham Rd PL5 ....124 B5
Oakhill PL30 ....47 C6
Oakland Pk TR11 ....144 D5
Oaklands PL19 ....147 D2
Oaklands Bsns Pk PL13 ..63 D8
Oaklands Cl PL6 ....125 D7
Oaklands Dr PL12 ....122 D2
Oaklands Gn PL12 ....122 D3
Oaklands Ind Est PL14 ..113 E6
Oaklands Rd PL14 ....113 E6
Oakleigh Terr TR7 ......110 F6
Oakridge PL12 ....53 C2
Oaks The
  Quintrell Downs TR8 .....111 F3
  St Austell PL25 ....114 B3
Oakwood Cl PL6 ....125 D2
Oakwood Pk PL31 ....109 F4
Oates Rd Helston TR13 ..146 C4
  Marazion TR17 ....89 C5
  Plymouth PL2 ....128 B6
Ocean Cres 22 TR13 ....98 C2
Ocean Ct Porthtowan TR4 ..68 A1
  Plymouth PL1 ....133 F4
Ocean St PL2 ....127 E6
Ocean View
  Indian Queens TR9 ....45 E1
  Polruan PL23 ....116 D3
  Porthleven TR13 ....98 B8
Ocean View Rd EX23 ....104 D2
Ocean View Terr PL26 ...141 A6
Octagon St PL1 ....148 B3
Octagon The PL1 ....148 B3
Okehampton Cl PL7 .....131 B6
Old Barn Ct TR7 ....110 E6
Old Barns The PL14 .....49 A8
Old Boat Yard The PL28 .107 E4
Old Boys Sch TR16 ......67 E7

Old Brewery Yd 4
Old Bridge St TR1 ....143 E5
Old Callywith Rd PL31 ....35 B2
Old Canal Cl EX23 ....7 B6
Old Carnon Hill TR3 ....81 F6
Old Chapel Way PL10 .....132 F6
Old Chough TR7 ....111 C7
Old Church Rd TR11 ....93 E2
Old Coach Rd
    Lanivet PL26,PL30 ....47 D6
    Playing Place TR3 ....82 B8
    Truro TR3 ....70 A1
Old Coastguard Cotts
PL11 ....65 A4
Old Corn Mill The TR12 ...92 C1
Old Dairy The PL3 ....129 B6
Old Drovers Way EX23 ....4 E1
Old Exeter Rd PL19 ....147 D7
Old Falmouth Rd TR1 ....137 C1
Old Farm Rd PL5 ....127 C8
Old Ferry Rd PL12 ....123 A3
Old Foundry Cl TR19 ....86 F6
Old Foundry The PL19 ...147 D6
Old George St PL1 ....148 C2
Old Grammer School Ct
PL22 ....112 C2
Old Greystone Hill PL15,
PL19 ....28 F6
Old Guildhall Mus*
PL12 ....117 D3
Old Hill Falmouth TR11 ...144 F6
    Grampound TR2 ....72 A7
    Helston TR13 ....146 A6
Old Hill Cres TR11 ....144 F5
Old La PL26 ....46 F3
Old Laira Rd PL3 ....129 C4
Old Launceston Rd
PL19 ....147 B6
Old Laundry The PL1 .....148 A3
Old Lawn School La
PL25 ....114 B3
Old Market Pl PL31 ....109 C4
Old Mill Cl PL15 ....27 B3
Old Mill Ct PL7 ....130 E5
Old Mill La Camborne TR14 .78 F6
    Penponds TR14 ....79 A6
Old Mine La PL18 ....40 E6
Old Nursery Cl TR13 ....91 A1
Old Orchard Cl EX23 ....7 B6
Old Park Rd PL3 ....128 D6
Old Paul Hill TR18 ....143 C2
Old Plymouth Rd PL3 .....129 E5
Old Portreath Rd
    Illogan TR16 ....67 F5
    Redruth TR15 ....67 F4
Old Post Office* PL18 ....14 C7
Old Post Office Hill 8
EX23 ....4 E1
Old Pound PL26 ....58 E6
Old Priory PL7 ....130 D5
Old Priory Jun Sch PL7 ..130 D5
Old Quarry Rd PL20 ....42 A3
Old Quay La PL12 ....65 B8
Old Rd Boscastle PL35 ......9 C2
    Liskeard PL14 ....113 A6
Old Rectory Dr TR9 ....45 E6
Old Roselyon Cres PL24 ..60 C5
Old Roselyon Rd PL24 ......60 C4
Old School Cl PL27 ....21 F3
Old School Ct
    Padstow PL28 ....107 D5
    Wadebridge PL27 ....108 B5
Old School La PL30 ....34 D4
Old School Rd PL5 ....127 C8
Old Schoolhouse The
TR11 ....145 B4
Old Smithy Cl 4 TR17 .....89 C5
Old Smithy Gdns EX39 .....2 C1
Old Station Rd
    Horrabridge PL20 ....42 C4
    Liskeard PL14 ....51 A7
Old Station The PL20 ....42 C4
Old Tannery Bsns Pk The 4
PL4 ....149 A4
Old Town Hall The PL24 ...60 B5
Old Town St PL1 ....148 C3
Old Tram Rd TR3 ....82 A5
Old Vicarage Cl TR3 ....80 F4
Old Vicarage Gate TR2 ..142 A1
Old Vicarage Pl 11 PL25 ..114 C3
Old Warleigh La PL5 ....124 B7
Old Well Gdns TR10 ......144 C8
Old Wharf The PL4 ....135 C7
Old Woodlands Rd PL5 .124 D3
Oldlands Ct PL6 ....125 B6
Oliver Ct PL12 ....40 A1
Oliver's Terr TR13 ....146 C5
Olivey Pl TR11 ....82 A3
Olivia Ct TR4 ....109 B4
Omaha Rd PL31 ....109 F3
Onslow Rd PL2 ....128 C7
Ope's Ct TR11 ....145 B5
Opie's Row TR16 ....80 B5
Opie's Terr TR16 ....80 A5
Opies La PL11 ....109 C5
Orange La TR26 ....141 A6
Orch The TR7 ....111 B7
Orchard Ave PL6 ....129 E7
Orchard Cl Helston TR13 .146 B7
    3 Plymouth PL6 ....131 C5
    Poughill EX23 ....4 D2
    St Austell PL25 ....114 E4
    St Giles-On-The-Heath PL15 .13 A1
    St Mellion PL12 ....53 C8
    Tavistock PL19 ....41 D8
    Tideford PL12 ....52 F2
    Truro TR1 ....69 F3

Orchard Cotts PL19 ....30 B3
Orchard Cres PL9 ....135 C7
Orchard Ct PL4 ....149 B4
Orchard Dr PL18 ....14 C7
Old Lamerton PL19 ....30 A3
    Penzance TR18 ....143 C2
Orchard Gr PL25 ....114 B4
Orchard Ho 11 TR18 .....143 C2
Orchard La TR13 ....93 B1
Orchard Pl 18 TR18 ....143 C2
Orchard Rd PL2 ....128 C7
Orchard Terr 18 TR18 ...143 C2
Orchard The
    Gunnislake PL18 ....41 A6
    Lerryn PL22 ....61 D8
    North Petherwin PL15 ....18 A8
    St Erth TR27 ....77 E2
Orchard Vale TR11 ....144 F6
Orchard Way 6 TR20 ......89 E5
Ordnance St PL1 ....127 E2
Orduff PL20 ....147 A5
Oregon Way PL3 ....129 D6
Oreston Prim Sch PL9 ...135 C7
Oreston Rd PL9 ....135 C8
Orion Dr PL27 ....31 F3
Osborne Parc TR13 ....146 B7
Osborne Rd PL3 ....128 A3
Osborne Villas
    10 Falmouth TR11 ....145 C3
    2 Plymouth PL3 ....128 A3
Osprey Gdns PL9 ....136 C7
Otterham Com Prim Sch
PL32 ....10 C2
Otterham Pk PL32 ....16 A8
Ottery Cotts PL19 ....30 A2
Ottery Park Ind Est PL19 ..30 A2
Outland Rd PL2 ....128 C7
Overdale Rd PL2 ....128 A7
Overton Gdns PL3 ....128 E5
Overton Villas PL15 ......106 C5
Owen Sivell Cl PL14 ....28 A3
Oxford Ave PL3 ....128 E5
Oxford Gdns PL3 ....128 E5
Oxford Pl PL1 ....148 C3
Oxford St PL1 ....148 C3
Oxford Terr 4 PL1 ....148 B3
Oxland Rd TR16 ....67 E5

P

Paardeberg Rd PL31 ....48 D8
Packet La TR20 ....89 F5
Packington St PL2 ....128 A4
Packsaddle TR10 ....81 D2
Packsaddle Cl TR10 ....81 D2
Paddock Cl Plymouth PL9 .135 E5
    Saltash PL12 ....122 D4
Paddock The
    Helston, Gwealfolds TR13 .146 C7
    Helston, Lowertown TR13 .146 D8
    Redruth TR15 ....140 D2
Padstow Harbour Ind Est
PL28 ....107 C4
Padstow Jun & Inf Sch
PL28 ....107 C4
Padstow Workshop Units
PL28 ....107 C4
Page's Cross PL26 ....106 D4
Paiges Farm PL15 ....135 C1
Painton Water EX39 ....3 A8
Palace Rd PL25 ....114 D4
Palace St PL1 ....149 A2
Palm Ct TR1 ....137 C2
Palmers Terr PL34 ....14 C6
Palmers Way PL7 ....108 D6
Palmerston St PL1 ....148 A4
Pannier La PL6 ....141 C2
Pannier Mkt TR7 ....147 C5
Panson Cross PL15 ....13 E3
Par Gn PL24 ....60 C4
Par La PL24 ....60 B4
Par Moor Rd
    Par PL24,PL25 ....60 B3
    St Austell PL24, PL25 ......115 F4
Par Sta PL24 ....60 C5
Parade Bsns Pk 4 PL19 ..147 B4
Parade Ope PL1 ....149 A2
Parade Pass 20 TR18 ......89 E5
Parade Rd PL5 ....124 A3
Parade Sq PL22 ....112 D2
Parade St PL1 ....149 A2
Parade The Helston TR13 .146 C5
    Liskeard PL14 ....113 C6
    Lostwithiel PL22 ....112 D2
    Millbrook PL10 ....132 E5
    Milton Abbot PL19 ....29 C6
    Mousehole TR19 ....88 C1
    Truro TR1 ....137 E4
Paradise Park (Wildlife
Conservation Sanctuary)*
TR27 ....142 A4
Paradise Pk EX22 ....7 F1
Paradise Rd Boscastle PL35 .9 C1
    Plymouth PL1 ....128 A2
Parc An Gate TR19 ....88 C1
Parc An Manns TR11 ....93 D3
Parc An Yorth TR19 ....86 F8
Parc Bean Terr TR26 ......141 A6
Parc Behan Cl TR2 ....83 F6
Parc Bowen TR13 ....92 A3
Parc Browse 8 TR12 ......102 F2
Parc Eglos Helston TR13 ..146 B6
    St Merryn PL28 ....31 F8
Parc Eglos Sch TR13 .....146 C6

Parc Enys TR12 ....99 B4
Parc Erissey Ind Est
TR16 ....68 A3
Parc Fer EX23 ....4 E1
Parc Godrevy TR7 ....110 C5
Parc Holland TR13 ....146 D8
Parc Ledden TR13 ....146 C6
Parc Ledrak TR13 ....146 B8
Parc Letta TR18 ....143 C7
Parc Mellan TR18 ....143 D7
Parc Merys TR2 ....83 B2
Parc Monga Rd TR11 ....92 F3
Parc Morrep TR20 ....90 B3
Parc Owles TR20 ....141 D2
Parc Peneglos TR11 ....82 A3
Parc Shady TR26 ....144 C1
Parc Stephney TR11 ......144 C2
Parc Vean PL30 ....34 C1
Parc Venton Cl TR14 ......138 F7
Parc Villas TR18 ....143 C7
Parc Wartha Ave TR18 ...143 D6
Parc Wartha Cres TR18 .143 D6
Parc-Abnac TR20 ....88 B7
Parc-An-Bal Ct TR14 ......138 E4
Parc-An-Bre Dr PL26 ......58 D8
Parc-an-Cady Est TR19 ...97 A6
Parc-An-Challow TR10 ...144 B8
Parc-An-Creet TR26 ....77 A7
Parc-An-Dillon Rd TR2 ....83 B2
Parc-An-Dower TR13 ......146 C6
Parc-An-Forth 6 TR26 .....77 A6
Parc-An-Gwarry 7 TR3 ....81 F7
Parc-An-Ithan 5 TR12 ....102 F2
Parc-An-Maen TR13 ....98 C8
Parc-An-Peath TR19 ....97 A6
Parc-An-Stamps 4
TR26 ....77 A6
Parc-Askell Cl TR12 ....98 E5
Parc-Bracket St TR14 ....138 D3
Parcandowr TR2 ....57 E1
Pargolla Rd TR7 ....110 F6
Park An Gonwyn TR26 ...141 A6
Park An Gorsaf TR14 .....138 D2
Park Ave
    Plymouth, Devonport PL1 .127 E3
    Plymouth, Plymstock PL9 .135 D7
    St Ives TR26 ....141 A6
Park Cl Illogan TR15 ....139 B8
    Nancegollan TR13 ....91 B7
    Plymouth PL7 ....130 B7
Park Cnr TR18 ....143 E5
Park Cres Falmouth TR11 .145 A4
    Helston TR13 ....146 B5
    Plymouth PL7 ....135 C7
    Ponsanooth TR3 ....81 B4
Park Dr PL21 ....109 B4
Park Enskellaw 6 TR12 ...99 A2
Park Fenton TR11 ....113 D5
Park Gwyn PL26 ....58 B4
Park Hill TR11 ....145 A4
Park Ho PL25 ....114 C4
Park La
    Bere Alston PL20 ....41 B1
    Bugle PL26 ....47 C1
    Camborne TR14 ....138 E4
    Falmouth TR11 ....145 A4
    Plymouth PL7 ....135 C7
    Ponsanooth TR3 ....81 B4
    Redruth TR15 ....140 C4
    St Austell PL25 ....114 C3
    St Dominick PL12 ....44 D7
    Torpoint PL11 ....127 B3
    Wadebridge PL27 ....108 B5
    Whitemoor PL26 ....58 E8
Park Rd Hos PL22 ....63 D3
Park Rise TR11 ....145 A4
Park St PL3 ....128 A4
Park Stenak TR16 ....80 F8
Park Street Ope PL3 ....128 A4
Park Terr TR11 ....145 A4
Park The Penryn TR10 ....144 B7
    Tregony TR2 ....71 F4
Park View Liskeard PL14 .113 C6
    Plymouth PL4 ....149 C3
    Pyworthy EX22 ....8 E5
    Summercourt TR8 ....57 B7
    Truro TR1 ....137 C3
Park View Cl TR3 ....82 A7
Park View Rd TR7 ....110 D5
Park View Terr PL27 ....108 B5
Park Way PL25 ....114 F5
Park Wise TR10 ....144 C8
Park Wood Rise PL6 ....19 F4
Parka Rd TR9 ....45 E2
Parkancreeg 9 TR2 ....83 F6
Parkenbutts TR7 ....111 D7
Parkengue Vean TR2 ....71 D6
Parkengue TR10 ....144 A7
Parkenhead La PL28 ....20 F2

Parker Cl PL7 ....130 B5
Parker Rd PL2 ....128 B6
Parker's Gn PL18 ....40 F6
Parkesway PL22 ....112 D2
Parkfield Dr PL6 ....125 F1
Parkins Terr 7 TR1 ....137 D5
Parklands PL26 ....58 C7
Parklands Cl TR7 ....111 D6
Parknoweth TR12 ....56 B6
Parkryn Rd 4 TR19 ....88 C1
Parkside PL2 ....127 F5
Parkside Com Tech Coll
PL10 ....127 E3
Parkstone La PL7 ....130 F6
Parkvedras Ho 5 TR1 ....137 B4
Parkvedras Terr TR1 ......137 B4
Parkventon PL26 ....47 C2
Parkway Cl TR4 ....109 C7
Parkway Ho PL27 ....21 F3
Parkway Ind Est The
PL6 ....129 C7
Parkway The PL3,PL5,
PL6 ....124 B1
Parkwood Cl PL6 ....121 B2
Parkwood Ct PL19 ....147 D6
Parkwood Rd
    Tavistock PL19 ....147 D6
    Tavistock PL19 ....147 E7
Parkwoon PL26 ....46 F3
Parnell Cl PL6 ....129 A8
Parr La PL14 ....149 B2
Parr St PL4 ....149 B2
Parsonage Ct PL16 ....19 F4
Parsons Ct PL9 ....136 A4
Parsons Rd PL27 ....39 C6
Partreyns PL19 ....30 A3
Pascoe Ct TR3 ....69 D4
Pasley St PL2 ....127 E4
Pasley St E PL2 ....127 E4
Passage Hill TR11 ....82 A3
Passage St PL23 ....116 B5
Passage St PL23 ....116 D5
Passmore Cl
    Blackwater TR4 ....68 E5
    Liskeard PL14 ....113 D6
Passmore Edwards Hospl
PL14 ....113 B6
Pathfields EX23 ....104 E5
Pathway Fields The
TR27 ....142 C5
Patna Pl PL1 ....148 A3
Patterdale Cl PL6 ....125 D3
Patterdale Wlk PL6 ....125 D3
Pattinson Cl PL6 ....125 E2
Pattinson Dr PL6 ....125 F2
Paul's Row TR11 ....137 D5
Paul's Terr TR1 ....137 D5
Pauley Rd PL6 ....109 B4
Paulls Row 4 PL15 ....140 C5
Paviland Grange 6 PL1 .128 A3
Pavilion Pk TR14 ....138 F4
Pavlova Cl PL14 ....113 C5
Paviova Ct PL14 ....113 C5
Paynter Wlk 2 PL7 ....131 B5
Paynter's Cross PL12 ......53 E7
Paynter's Lane End Est
TR16 ....67 D4
Paynters La TR16 ....67 E4
Peacock Ave PL11 ....127 A3
Peacock Cl PL7 ....130 F7
Peacock La PL4 ....149 A2
Pearce's La 12 TR26 ......141 A5
Pearce's Row 8 PL24 ......60 C4
Pearn Cotts 2 PL3 ....128 F6
Pearn Gdns PL3 ....129 A7
Pearn Rd PL3 ....129 A7
Pearn Ridge PL3 ....129 A7
Pearson Ave 8 PL4 ....128 F4
Pearson Rd PL4 ....128 F4
Pedlars Cl PL15 ....18 B8
Pedn-Moor Cross EX22 ...13 E4
Pedn-an-Dria PL27 ....21 F3
Pedn-vyr La 1 TR12 ....99 A1
Pednandrea TR19 ....86 F6
Pednolva Wlk TR26 ....141 B5
Peek Moor Cross EX22 ...13 E4
Peel St PL1 ....128 A1
Peguarra Cl PL28 ....20 E1
Peguarra Ct PL28 ....20 E1
Pelean Cross TR3 ....81 B5
Pelham Cl 1 TR11 ....145 C5
Pellew Cl
    7 Falmouth TR11 ....145 A5
    Padstow PL28 ....107 C5
Pellew Cres TR11 ....146 C4
Pellew Rd TR11 ....145 A4
Pellor Fields TR13 ....90 F3
Pellor Rd TR13 ....90 F3
Pelynt Prim Sch PL13 ......62 D6
Pelyn Cl PL14 ....51 A7
Pembrey Wlk PL5 ....124 D3
Pembroke Cl 2 PL24 ......60 C4
Pembroke La PL1 ....127 F1
Pembroke St
    Plymouth PL1 ....127 F1
    Plymouth PL1 ....127 E1
Pembroke Terr
    Plymouth PL1 ....127 E1
    Plymouth PL1 ....127 F1
Pemros Rd PL5 ....123 C1
Pen Brea Cl TR2 ....95 B6
Pen Hallow Cl TR4 ....68 D5
Pen Porth Ave TR26 ....77 A7
Pen Tor Rd PL20 ....35 C8
Pen y Bryn PL27 ....108 D6
Pen-An-Gwel TR26 ....141 A4
Pen-Eglos 6 TR11 ....93 D2
Pen-Tye TR27 ....78 E3
Penair Cres TR1 ....70 D4

Penair View TR1 ....137 F4
Penally Cl PL35 ....9 D2
Penally Hill PL35 ....9 D2
Penally Terr PL35 ....9 C2
Penalverne Ave TR18 .....143 D5
Penalverne Cres TR18 ...143 D5
Penalverne Dr TR18 ....143 D5
Penalverne Pl TR18 ....143 D5
Penameyne Ct 5 TR26 ...141 B6
Penare Gdns 2 TR18 ......143 E6
Penare Rd TR18 ....143 E6
Penare Terr TR18 ....143 E6
Penarrow Cl TR11 ....144 E2
Penarrow Rd TR11 ....145 C8
Penarth PL13 ....117 B3
Penarth Rd TR11 ....145 A5
Penarwyn Cres TR18 .....143 B7
Penarwyn Rd PL24 ....60 B4
Penarwyn Woods 6
PL24 ....60 B4
Penbeagle Cl PL26 ....77 A6
Penbeagle Cres 8 TR26 ...77 A6
Penbeagle La TR26 ....77 A6
Penbeagle Terr 7 TR26 ...77 A6
Penbeagle Way TR26 .....141 A4
Penberthy Cross TR20 ....89 F7
Penberthy Rd
    Helston TR13 ....146 C5
    Portreath TR16 ....67 D6
Penbothidno TR13 ....92 F3
Penbrea Rd TR18 ....143 E7
Penbugle La PL31 ....109 E7
Pencair Ave PL11 ....126 B2
Pencalenick Sch TR1 ....70 E4
Pencantol TR4 ....81 C7
Pencarn Parc TR16 ....80 A5
Pencarrick Cl TR1 ....137 B6
Pencarrow* PL30 ....34 D6
Pencarrow Cl PL17 ....39 E3
Pencarrow Rd 13 TR16 ....67 E4
Pencavo Hill PL12 ....53 A3
Pencreber Rd 8 PL20 ......42 C4
Pendale Sq TR1 ....137 B4
Pendarves Flats TR18 ....143 D6
Pendarves Rd
    Camborne TR14 ....138 C1
    Falmouth TR11 ....144 F4
    Penzance TR18 ....143 D6
    Truro TR1 ....137 C6
Pendarves St
    Camborne TR14 ....138 F4
    Camborne, Beacon TR14 .138 F1
    Troon TR14 ....79 E4
Pendarves View TR14 ....138 C1
Pendean Ave PL14 ....113 B6
Pendean Cl PL14 ....113 B6
Pendean Ct PL14 ....113 B6
Pendean Dr PL14 ....113 B6
Pendeen Cl Plymouth PL6 .124 F6
    Threemilestone TR3 ....69 D3
Pendeen Cres
    Plymouth PL6 ....125 A6
    Truro TR1 ....69 D3
Pendeen Ho TR1 ....69 A4
Pendeen Lighthouse Mus*
TR19 ....75 A1
Pendeen Pk TR13 ....146 C8
Pendeen Prim Sch TR19 ..75 A1
Pendeen Rd
    Porthleven TR13 ....91 B1
    Threemilestone TR3 ....69 D3
    Truro TR1 ....137 E3
Pendennis Castle*
TR11 ....145 E2
Pendennis Cl
    Penzance TR18 ....143 E7
    Plymouth PL3 ....128 F8
    Torpoint PL11 ....126 F3
Pendennis Pl TR11 ....145 D3
Pendennis Rd TR7 ....143 F7
Pendennis Rd
    Falmouth TR11 ....145 D3
    Looe PL13 ....117 C4
    Penzance TR18 ....143 E6
Pendennis Rise TR14 .....145 D3
Pender's La TR15 ....140 B5
Pendilly Ave PL11 ....126 F2
Pendour Pk PL22 ....112 C2
Pendower Ct TR2 ....83 D5
Pendower Rd Looe PL13 .117 E4
    Veryan TR2 ....83 F6
Pendower Terr TR14 ....138 E1
Pendra Loweth TR11 ......144 C1
Pendragon Cres TR7 ......111 A5
Pendragon Ho PL11 ....145 D3
Pendragon Rd PL14 ....113 D6
Pendray Gdns PL14 ....50 F7
Pendrea Cl TR18 ....138 F5
Pendrea Ct TR18 ....138 F5
Pendrea Pl TR18 ....143 F7
Pendrea Rd TR18 ....143 F7
Pendrea Wood PL6 ....69 F3
Pendrim Rd PL13 ....117 D4
Pendruccombe Ct PL15 ..106 D5
Penforth TR14 ....138 E2
Pengannel Cl TR7 ....110 D4
Pengarrock Hill TR12 ....101 D5
Pengarth 11 TR5 ....54 D1
Pengarth Cl TR1 ....137 C2
Pengarth Rd TR11 ....145 A3
Pengarth Rise TR11 ....145 A3
Pengegon Moor TR14 ....138 F2
Pengegon Parc TR14 .....138 F2
Pengegon Way TR14 .....138 F2

168 Pen – Pol

Pengelly
24 Callington PL17 39 F4
Delabole PL33 14 E2
Pengelly Cl PL11 126 F5
Pengelly Cross
Godolphin Cross TR27 90 F7
Wadebridge PL27 108 C1
Pengelly Hill PL11 127 A5
Pengelly Pk PL11 126 F5
Pengelly Pl TR11 144 E5
Pengelly Way TR3 69 D3
Pengellys Row TR14 139 A5
Pengeron Ave TR14 138 F7
Pengersick Est TR20 90 C3
Pengersick La TR20 90 C3
Pengersick Parc TR20 90 C3
Pengover Cl PL14 113 D6
Pengover Gn PL14 51 E8
Pengover Hts PL14 113 D6
Pengover Parc TR15 140 C6
Pengover Pk PL14 113 D6
Pengover Rd PL14 113 E6
Pengrowyn PL26 59 D6
Pengwarras Rd TR14 138 C3
Pengwel 16 TR18 143 C2
Penhale Cl PL14 37 F3
Penhale Est TR15 140 B6
Penhale Gdns TR9 57 D8
Penhale Mdw PL14 37 F3
Penhale Rd
Barripper TR14 79 A4
Carnhell Green TR14 78 F4
Falmouth TR11 144 F1
Penwithick PL26 59 D7
Penhaligon Cl TR15 140 D4
Penhaligon Ct TR1 137 E5
Penhaligon Way PL25 114 F4
Penhall La TR4 68 C6
Penhallow TR15 139 B8
Penhallow Cl TR2 83 C5
Penhallow Ct TR7 111 C7
Penhallow Parc PL33 14 D2
Penhallow Rd TR7 111 C7
Penhalls Way TR3 82 B8
Penhalt Farm Holiday Pk
EX23 6 E3
Penhaven Cl TR8 56 B7
Penhaven Ct TR7 110 E6
Penhellaz Hill TR13 146 B6
Penhellaz Rd TR13 146 B6
Penhole Cl PL15 27 D3
Penina Ave TR7 110 F4
Peninsular Pk PL12 122 C4
Penjerrick Hill
Budock Water TR11 144 C1
Falmouth TR11 93 E5
Penkenna Cl EX23 10 C6
Penkernick Cl TR18 143 B1
Penkernick Way TR9 45 E6
Penknight La PL22 112 A2
Penlea Rd TR10 144 B8
Penlean Cl TR15 140 D7
Penlee Cl
13 Callington PL17 39 F4
Praa Sands TR20 90 C3
Tregony TR2 71 F4
Penlee Cotts PL10 64 C2
Penlee Gdns PL3 128 A4
Penlee Ho TR1 69 E4
Penlee House Gall & Mus*
TR18 143 E5
Penlee Manor Dr TR18 143 E4
Penlee Pk PL11 126 E4
Penlee Pl 4 PL4 128 F4
Penlee Rd PL3 128 A4
Penlee St 11 TR18 143 E6
Penlee Villas TR3 82 B8
Penlee Way PL3 128 B4
Penlu Ho TR14 138 F5
Penluke Cl TR16 80 A5
Penlyne Woodland Trail*
PL22 112 E5
Penmare Cl TR27 142 E7
Penmare Terr TR27 142 E7
Penmayne Parc TR16 140 F1
Penmayne Villas PL27 21 E3
Penmead Rd PL33 14 E2
Penmelen PL32 105 C4
Penmeneth TR13 146 F8
Penmenner Est 7 TR12 101 C4
Penmenner Rd TR12 102 F2
Penmere Cl
Helston TR13 146 B7
Penzance TR18 143 E7
Penmere Cres TR11 144 F3
Penmere Ct 4 TR11 145 A3
Penmere Dr TR7 110 C5
Penmere Hill 7 TR11 145 A3
Penmere Pl
3 Falmouth TR11 145 A3
Penzance TR18 143 E7
Penmere Rd
Penzance TR18 143 E7
St Austell PL25 115 A4
Penmere Sta TR11 144 F3
Penmerrin Ct TR7 110 E5
Penmeva View PL26 73 C3
Penmorvah TR11 82 A2
Penmorvah Pl TR14 138 E2
Penmorvah Rd TR1 137 F6
Penn An Drea TR13 146 D8
Pennance Hill TR11 93 F5
Pennance Ho TR11 145 A2
Pennance La TR16 140 F1
Pennance Parc TR16 140 F1
Pennance Rd
Falmouth TR11 145 A2
Lanner TR16 80 E7
Redruth TR16 140 F1
Pennance Terr TR16 140 F1
Pennard Villas PL27 33 B5
Pennkarn Parc PL33 14 E3
Pennor Dr PL25 114 D3
Penny's La PL9 136 D6
Pennycomequick Hill
PL1,PL3 148 B4
Pennycross Cl PL2 128 D8
Pennycross Park Rd
PL2 128 C7
Pennycross Prim Sch
PL2 128 C8
Pennygillam Ind Est
PL15 106 A4
Pennygillam Way PL15 18 E2
Pennys La PL24 115 F5
Penoweth TR11 82 A2
Penpol Ave TR27 142 C5
Penpol Hill Crantock TR8 110 B4
Devoran TR3 82 B6
Penpol Rd TR27 142 B5
Penpol Terr TR27 142 B5
Penpol Vean TR27 142 C5
Penponds Rd TR13 91 A1
Penponds Sch TR14 79 B5
Penpons Cl TR18 143 C4
Penpont Rd TR15 140 D6
Penpont View PL15 26 C7
Penquite Dr PL31 109 F5
Penrice Com Coll PL25 115 A3
Penrice Hospl (Maternity & Gastric) PL26 114 F1
Penrice Parc PL25 115 A3
Penrith Cl PL6 125 D3
Penrith Gdns PL6 125 D3
Penrith Wlk PL6 125 D3
Penrose Ct TR14 138 F7
Penrose Parc TR13 91 B1
Penrose Rd
Falmouth TR11 145 A4
Helston TR13 146 C6
Penrose St PL1 148 B3
Penrose Terr TR18 143 F6
Penrose Villas 5 PL4 128 F4
Penrose Walks* TR12, TR13 98 D8
Penruan La TR2 95 B6
Penryn Coll TR10 144 B7
Penryn Com Inf Sch
TR10 144 B7
Penryn Jun Sch TR10 144 B8
Penryn St TR15 140 B4
Penryn Sta TR10 144 B8
Penscombe Cross PL15 28 C6
Penscott La PL26 114 C1
Pensilva TR6 55 A4
Pensilva Prim Sch PL14 38 E5
Pensilva Rd TR1 137 E6
Pensilva Rural Workshop
PL14 38 E4
Penstowe Rd EX23 5 A6
Penstrasse Pl 1 PL24 60 D5
Penstraze Bsns Ctr TR4 69 A5
Penstraze La PL26 47 A4
Pensylva PL25 114 E3
Pentalek Rd TR14 138 D1
Pentamar St PL2 127 E4
Pentargon Rd 1 PL35 9 C1
Pentewan Hill PL26 73 D6
Pentewan Rd PL25, PL26 59 C1
Pentidna La TR27 66 B2
Pentillie PL26 73 C4
Pentillie Gdns 14 PL17 39 E4
Pentillie Rd
Bere Alston PL20 41 B1
Plymouth PL4 128 E4
Pentillie Way PL26 73 C4
Pentillis Cres PL4 128 D4
Pentire Ave TR7 110 A5
Pentire Cres TR7 110 B5
Pentire Ct TR7 110 B5
Pentire Gn TR8 43 D3
Pentire Rd Newquay TR7 110 C5
Penryn TR10 144 B8
Torpoint PL11 126 F3
Pentland Cl PL6 124 F7
Pentor Ct PL30 35 C8
Pentour 3 PL24 60 B4
Pentowan Rd TR27 142 E8
Pentre Ct EX23 4 D4
Pentreath Cl TR18 143 D7
Pentreath La Lizard TR12 102 F2
Praa Sands TR20 90 B3
Pentreath Terr TR16 80 E7
Pentrevah Rd 8 PL26 59 D7
Pentyre Ct PL4 149 C4
Pentyre Terr PL4 149 C4
Penvale 4 PL14 38 E4
Penvale Cl TR14 79 B5
Penvale Cres TR10 144 B8
Penvale Ct 8 TR11 145 A4
Penvale Dr TR10 144 B8
Penvean La TR11 144 E5
Penventinnie La TR1 69 E4
Penventinue La PL23 116 B7
Penventon Terr
Redruth TR15 140 A4
Redruth, Four Lanes TR16 80 B6
Penventon Wlk TR13 146 B5
Penview Cres TR13 146 B5
Penvorder Cotts PL30 24 B2
Penvorder La PL30 24 B2
Penware Parc TR14 138 C1
Penwarne Cl TR14 138 F7
Penwarne La PL26 73 C3
Penwarne Rd TR11 93 D5
Penwartha TR12 101 B2
Penwartha Cl
Constantine TR11 92 F3
St Columb Minor TR7 111 D7
Penwartha Ct TR11 92 F3
Penwartha Rd
15 Illogan TR16 67 E4
Perranporth TR6 55 B4
Penwartha Vean 14 TR16 67 E4
Penwerris Ct TR11 145 A6
Penwerris La TR11 145 A6
Penwerris Rd TR1 69 F3
Penwerris Rise TR20 90 B3
Penwerris Terr 10 TR11 145 A5
Penwethers La TR1 69 F3
Penwinnick Cl 9 TR5 54 C1
Penwinnick Parc 4 TR5 54 D1
Penwinnick Rd
St Agnes TR5 68 D8
St Austell PL25 114 B3
Penwith Bsns Ctr TR20 88 F6
Penwith Cl TR26 141 A4
Penwith Coll TR18 143 D7
Penwith Rd TR26 141 A4
Penwith St 12 TR18 143 E6
Penwithhick Rd PL26 59 D7
Penwithian Cl TR27 142 E6
Penwithick Pk 6 PL26 59 D7
Penworth Cl PL15 106 C5
Penwyth TR12 92 C1
Penzance Inf Sch TR18 143 E7
Penzance Rd
Helston TR13 146 A6
St Buryan TR19 87 E1
Pepo La TR2 72 A7
Pepper Cl PL12 40 C2
Pepper La PL9 136 D7
Pepper St PL19 147 C6
Peppers Ct PL12 40 C2
Peppers Hill Cl PL15 18 F7
Peppers Park Rd PL14 113 E6
Peppersfield Row TR13 90 F3
Pepys Pl PL5 124 E1
Percuil View TR2 95 B6
Percy Davy Cl TR6 55 A5
Percy St PL5 123 D1
Percy Terr PL4 129 A4
Pergolla Ct TR7 110 F6
Perhaver Pk PL26 85 D5
Perhaver Way PL26 85 D5
Periwinkle Dr PL7 131 C5
Permarin Rd TR10 144 C8
Perran Cl TR3 81 F6
Perran Crossroads TR20 89 E5
Perran Sands Holiday Ctr
TR6 55 B6
Perran View Holiday Park
TR5 54 E2
Perran-ar-worthal Com Prim Sch TR3 81 D6
Perrancombe Garden Ct
TR6 55 A4
Perranporth Cl PL5 123 E4
Perranporth Jun & Inf Sch
TR6 55 A4
Perranwell Rd TR4 55 D4
Perranwell Sta TR3 81 E6
Perryman Cl PL7 130 E7
Perseverance Cotts 1
PL7 130 E7
Peryn Rd PL19 147 A5
Peter Hopper's Hill PL5 120 C2
Peter's Cl PL9 136 C7
Peter's Park La PL5 123 E1
Peters Hill PL26 58 E4
Peters Park Cl PL5 123 E1
Peters Row TR19 75 A1
Petersfield Cl PL3 129 B6
Petes Pl 24 TR26 141 B5
Petherick Creek Holiday Bglws PL27 32 C7
Petherick Rd EX23 104 E7
Pethericks Mill EX23 104 E4
Pethick Cl PL6 124 D6
Pethill Cl PL6 125 F2
Pethybridge Dr PL31 109 B3
Peverell Park Rd PL3 128 D6
Peverell Rd
Penzance TR18 143 E7
7 Porthleven TR13 98 C8
Peverell Terr
Plymouth PL3 128 D5
Porthleven TR13 98 B8
Pew Tor Cl
Tavistock PL19 147 E5
3 Yelverton PL20 42 C3
Phernyssick Rd PL25 114 F6
Philgray Cl TR27 142 E7
Philip Cl PL9 136 A6
Philip Gdns PL9 135 F6
Phillack Hill TR27 142 D7
Phillimore St 3 PL2 127 F4
Phoenix Cl 9 PL20 42 C4
Phoenix St PL1 148 A2
Piala Pl TR27 142 E7
Pick Pie Dr PL6 125 E8
Pickard Way EX23 104 D7
Pickering Villas TR4 69 A3
Picketts Yd TR10 144 D7
Pier La PL10 133 A1
Pier St PL1 148 B1
Pigmeadow La PL14 113 C6
Pike Rd PL3 129 D5
Pike St PL14 113 C6
Pike's Hill TR11 145 B3
Pikes Hill PL23 116 C4
Pilchard Works The*
TR18 143 C3
Pilgrim Cl PL2 128 B6
Pilgrim Ct 11 PL20 41 B1
Pilgrim Dr PL20 41 B1
Pilgrim Prim Sch PL1 148 B3
Pilgrims Way TR27 78 C1
Pill La PL12 122 E4
Pillar Wlk PL6 124 E7
Pillars Cl TR8 56 F5
Pillars Rd Flushing TR11 145 B8
Mylor Bridge TR11 82 A2
Pillmere Dr PL12 122 D4
Pilot Cotts PL28 21 B4
Pin La PL1 149 A2
Pinch Hill EX23 7 B7
Pinder Ct PL19 147 B5
Pine Cl TR13 146 D5
Pine Ct Par PL24 115 F6
Perranwell Sta TR3 81 D6
Pine Lodge Gdns*
PL25 115 D4
Pine Rd TR18 143 B4
Pine Trees Camp Site*
TR12 99 F5
Pine View PL18 41 A6
Pinewood Cl PL7 130 F6
Pinewood Dr PL6 125 E7
Pinewood Flats PL27 21 D5
Pink Moors TR16 68 D1
Pinslow Cross PL15 19 C8
Pipers Cl PL15 18 E2
Pit Mdw TR11 144 E3
Pitick Terr TR11 145 B6
Pitland Cnr PL19 30 D4
Pits La PL10 64 B2
Pityme Bsns Ctr PL27 21 F3
Pityme Farm Rd PL27 21 F3
Pityme Ind Est PL27 21 F3
Pixieland Fun pk* EX23 5 A6
Pixon La PL19 147 B4
Pixon Trad Est 2 PL19 147 B4
Pizza 14 TR26 141 B6
Place de Brest PL1 148 C3
Place Parc TR7 111 D7
Place Rd PL23 116 C4
Place View PL23 116 C4
Place View Rd 15 TR2 95 A6
Plaidy La PL13 117 E4
Plaidy Park Rd PL13 117 E4
Plain-An-Gwarry TR15 140 B5
Plaistow Cl PL5 123 E2
Plaistow Cres PL5 123 E2
Plaistow Hill Inf Sch
PL5 123 E2
Plas Newydd Terr PL31 109 E3
Plash Mdw PL30 35 C8
Platt The PL27 108 C5
Pleasant Pl 15 TR18 143 C7
Pleasant Terr TR19 86 E6
Pleasure Hill Cl PL9 135 D8
Plestin Cl PL15 106 C7
Pleyber Christ Way
PL22 112 C2
Plintona View PL7 130 E7
Plougastel Dr PL12 122 E3
Plough Ct TR10 81 C2
Plough Gn PL12 122 C3
Plumer Rd PL6 124 F2
Plym Cres PL19 147 D5
Plym St PL4 149 A3
Plym Valley Rly* PL7 130 A7
Plym View Prim Sch
PL3 129 D6
Plymbridge Gdns PL7 130 C7
Plymbridge La PL6 125 B4
Plymbridge Rd
Plymouth, Estover PL6 125 E5
Plymouth, Mainstone PL6 125 F2
Plymouth, Plympton PL7 130 C7
Plymouth PL6 125 A4
Plymouth City Airport
PL6 125 C5
Plymouth Coll PL4 128 E4
Plymouth Coll of Art & Design PL4 149 A3
Plymouth Coll of Art & Design (Sutton Annexe)
PL4 149 A3
Plymouth Coll of F Ed
PL1 128 A2
Plymouth Coll of F Ed (Annexe) PL1 148 C4
Plymouth Coll Prep Sch
PL3 128 E6
Plymouth Dome Discovery Ctr* PL1 148 C1
Plymouth High Sch for Girls
PL4 149 A4
Plymouth International Bsns Pk PL6 125 A3
Plymouth Nuffield Hospl The
PL6 125 B4
Plymouth Pavilions PL1 148 B2
Plymouth Rd
Liskeard PL14 113 D5
Plymouth PL7 130 B6
Tavistock PL19 147 B5
Plymouth Road Ind Est
PL19 147 C3
Plymouth Sta PL1,PL4 148 C4
Plympton Hill PL7 130 F3
Plympton Hospl PL7 130 D5
Plympton St Mary CE Inf Sch
PL7 130 D5
Plympton St Maurice Prim Sch PL7 130 F3
Plymstock Rd PL9 135 D7
Plymstock Sch PL9 135 F
Plymtree Dr PL7 130 C
Poad's Trust PL14 51 F
Pocklington Rise PL7 130 E
Pocohontas Cres 4 TR9 45 E
Pode Dr PL7 131 B
Point Curlew Country Holiday Est PL28 31 F
Point Rd TR3 82 A
Polapit Tamar PL15 19 A
Polbathic Rd TR15 140 C
Polbreen Ave TR5 54 C
Polbreen La TR5 54 C
Poldark Gdns 7 PL24 60 B
Poldark Mine Heritage Complex* TR13 92 A
Poldark Rd 12 TR16 67 E
Poldhu Cl TR26 141 D
Poldhu Rd Liskeard PL14 113 D
Mullion TR12 99 A
Poldice La TR16 68 E
Poldice Terr TR16 68 E
Poldrea PL24 60 D
Poldrissick Hill PL12 53 C
Poldrissick La PL12 53 C
Poldue Cl TR15 140 D
Polean La PL13 117 B
Polecoverack La TR12 101 C
Polgarth Camborne TR15 139 C
Newlyn TR18 143 B
Polgarth Cl TR26 141 D
Polgine Cl TR14 79 E
Polgine La TR14 79 E
Polglase Wlk TR4 70 D
Polglaze Cl TR18 143 D
Polglist PL26 58 D
Polgoon Cl TR18 143 C
Polgooth Cl TR15 140 D
Polgover Way 5 PL24 60 B
Polgrain Rd TR14 138 F
Polgrean Pl PL24 60 B
Polhigay Terr TR16 80 C
Polhorman La TR12 99 A
Police Ho TR11 145 B
Polisken Way TR4 56 D
Polkerris Rd TR16 80 F
Polkirt Hill
Gorran Haven PL26 73 B
Mevagissey PL26 73 C
Polkyth Rd PL25 114 F
Pollard Cl Plymouth PL9 135 B
Saltash PL12 122 B
Pollard Rd 7 PL17 39 F
Pollards Cl
Goonhavern TR4 55 D
Pensilva PL14 38 E
Pollards Way PL12 122 E
Polmark Dr PL28 20 D
Polmarth Cl PL25 114 F
Polmassick Vineyard*
PL26 72 E
Polmear Ct 9 PL27 108 B
Polmear Hill PL24 60 E
Polmear Parc PL24 60 D
Polmear Rd Par PL24 60 D
St Austell PL25 114 F
Polmeere Ho TR18 143 E
Polmeere Rd TR18 143 E
Polmena La PL22 112 E
Polmennor Dr TR26 141 D
Polmennor Rd
Falmouth TR11 144 F
Heamoor TR18 143 C
Polmenor Downs N TR14, TR27 78 F
Polmenor Downs S TR14 78 F
Polmeor Cl TR26 141 D
Polmewan Flats PL26 59 A
Polmor Rd TR20 89 B
Polmorla Mews 10 PL27 108 B
Polmorla Rd PL27 108 B
Polmorla Wlk PL27 108 C
Polperro Heritage Mus*
PL13 62 E
Polperro Model Village*
PL13 62 D
Polperro Prim Sch PL13 62 E
Polperro Rd PL13 117 B
Polpey La PL24 60 D
Polruan Cl TR26 77 C
Polruan Com Prim Sch
PL23 116 D
Polruan Ct TR1 137 E
Polruan Rd
Redruth TR15 140 D
Truro TR1 137 E
Polruan Terr PL1 148 A
Polscoe Rd PL22 112 F
Polsethow TR10 144 B
Polstain Cres TR3 69 D
Polstain Rd TR3 69 D
Polstain Villas TR3 69 D
Polsue Way TR2 70 F
Poltair Ave PL25 114 E
Poltair Cl TR18 143 C
Poltair Com Sch & Sports Coll PL25 114 D
Poltair Ct PL25 114 E
Poltair Dr TR10 144 B
Poltair Hospl TR20 143 B
Poltair Rd Penryn TR10 144 B
St Austell PL25 114 D
Poltair Terr 7 TR18 143 C
Poltamar PL15 106 D
Poltesco La TR12 103 B
Poltisko Rd TR10 144 B
Poltisko Terr TR10 144 B
Poltreen Cl TR26 141 D

Polurrian Rd TR12 .....99 A1
Polvarth Est TR2 .....95 B6
Polvarth Rd 95 A6
Polvean Cross PL14 .....51 A1
Polvean Terr PL14 .....51 A1
Polvellan Terr PL13 .....117 C4
Polvelyn Parc TR27 .....142 E7
Polventon Cl
  Falmouth TR11 .....144 E4
  Heamoor PL18 .....143 C7
Polventon Parc 6 TR12 .....101 C4
Polvillion Rd PL23 .....116 B4
Polweath Cl TR18 .....143 E7
Polweath Rd TR18 .....143 E7
Polwhaveral Terr TR11 .....145 A5
Polwheal Rd TR14 .....138 F6
Polwhele House Sch TR14 .....70 C6
Polwhele Rd
  Newquay TR7 .....111 A3
  Truro TR1 .....137 F6
Polwhithen Dr TR26 .....141 C1
Polwhithen Gdns TR26 .....141 C1
Polwithen Rd
  Falmouth TR11 .....145 A4
  Penryn TR10 .....144 B7
  Penzance TR18 .....143 D5
Polwrath Terr PL14 .....38 A1
Polwyn Cl TR18 .....143 B7
Polyear Ct PL26 .....59 A1
Polzeath Ct PL27 .....21 D6
Polzeath Gdns PL28 .....128 D8
Pomphlett Cl PL9 .....135 D8
Pomphlett Farm Ind Est PL9 .....129 E1
Pomphlett Gdns PL9 .....135 D8
Pomphlett Prim Sch PL9 .....135 E8
Pomphlett Rd PL9 .....135 E8
Pond La TR15 .....140 A6
Pond Lanes End TR15 .....140 B6
Pond View Terr PL26 .....58 D5
Pond Wlk TR27 .....142 D7
Pondbridge Hill 1 .....113 C5
Pondfield Rd PL22 .....123 B3
Pondhu Cres PL25 .....114 B3
Pondhu Jun & Inf Sch PL25 .....114 B2
Pondhu Rd PL25 .....114 C3
Ponds Hill TR19 .....75 B1
Poniou La TR20 .....88 F6
Poniou Rd TR20 .....88 F6
Poniou Way TR20 .....88 F6
Ponsandane Farm Mews TR18 .....143 F7
Ponsandane Cotts TR11 .....144 F6
Ponsharden Ind Est TR11 .....144 E6
Ponsmere Ct 3 TR6 .....55 A5
Ponsmere Rd TR6 .....55 A5
Ponsonby Rd PL3 .....128 B4
Ponstantial Hill TR12 .....99 D7
Ponsvale TR3 .....81 B4
Pontsmill Rd PL24 .....60 C6
Pool Hall PL14 .....51 F5
Pool Ind Est TR15 .....139 C5
  TR15 .....139 B6
Pool St PL31 .....109 E5
Pool's Ct TR27 .....142 D6
Poole Park Rd PL5 .....127 C8
Poplar Cl PL2 .....131 B5
Poplar Terr PL14 .....145 B7
Poplars Ct 9 TR6 .....55 A5
Porcupine Rd PL24 .....60 C6
Pordenack Cl TR19 .....86 B8
Porfell Animal Land* PL14 .....50 A2
Porhan Gn TR11 .....144 E6
Pork St TR12 .....100 D6
Porsham Cl PL6 .....121 B1
Porsham La PL5 .....124 E8
Porspoder Pl PL10 .....133 A2
Port Isaac Com Prim Sch PL29 .....22 E7
Port La TR15 .....27 B2
Porthyan Rd PL13 .....117 C3
Porteous Cl PL1 .....127 E2
Porter Way PL12 .....122 C3
Porth Bean Ct TR7 .....111 C7
Porth Bean Rd TR7 .....111 C7
Porth Par TR7 .....111 C8
Porth Sawle Flats TR2 .....83 B2
Porth View TR7 .....95 B6
Porthcollum La TR27 .....78 A1
Portheast Cl PL26 .....85 C5
Portheast Way PL26 .....85 C5
Porthellow Vineyard* TR12 .....101 D5
Porthras Cross TR19 .....75 A1
Porthras Terr TR19 .....75 A1
Porthras Villas TR19 .....75 A1
Porthwidden Studios TR26 .....141 C6
Porthia Cl TR26 .....141 A4
Porthia Cres TR26 .....141 A4
Porthia Rd TR26 .....141 A4
Porthilly La PL27 .....21 D2
Porthilly View PL27 .....107 E6
Porthkerris Water Sports Ctr* TR12 .....101 E5
Porthleven Jun & Inf Sch TR13 .....91 B1
Porthleven Rd TR13 .....146 A5
Porthmellon Gdns PL17 .....39 F4
Porthmeor Hill TR26 .....141 A6

Porthmeor Rd
  St Austell PL25 .....115 A3
  6 St Ives TR26 .....141 B6
Porthmeor Sq 21 TR26 .....141 B6
Porthminster Terr 28 TR26 .....141 B5
Porthpean Beach Rd PL26 .....59 G1
Porthpean Rd PL25, PL26 .....114 F2
Porthrepta Rd TR26 .....141 E1
Portisco Cl TR1 .....137 E3
Portland Cl PL14 .....113 D7
Portland Ct 9 PL1 .....127 F3
Portland Gdns PL14 .....144 F4
Portland Pl 22 TR19 .....88 C1
Portland Pl E PL4 .....149 A4
Portland Pl W PL1 .....127 F3
Portland Sq
  Plymouth PL4 .....148 C4
  Plymouth PL4 .....149 A4
Portland Square La N PL4 .....149 A4
Portland Terr PL14 .....113 C7
Portland Villas PL4 .....148 C4
Portmellon Pk PL26 .....73 C7
Portreath Com Prim Sch TR16 .....67 D6
Portuan Rd PL13 .....117 C2
Portway Cl PL9 .....136 D7
Posses La PL7 .....88 E6
Possession La PL12 .....53 C3
Post Box Row TR14 .....139 B3
Post Office Row PL26 .....58 D7
Potters La PL35 .....9 C1
Potters Way PL7 .....130 C5
Pottery Est PL10 .....132 E6
Pottery Rd PL1 .....127 F2
Poughill Rd EX23 .....104 F7
Poultney Cl PL7 .....131 A5
Pound Dean PL14 .....113 A5
Pound Hill PL22 .....53 C3
Pound La Bodmin PL31 .....109 E6
  Stoke Climsland PL17 .....28 E1
  Threemilestone TR3 .....69 E1
Pound Pk PL14 .....51 F5
Pound Rd PL20 .....42 B3
Pound St Liskeard PL14 .....113 C6
  Plymouth PL1 .....134 A8
Pound's Cross PL6 .....120 E2
Poundfield Cl 2 EX23 .....4 D1
Poundfield Hill 1 EX23 .....4 D1
Poundfield La EX23 .....4 D1
Pounds Park Rd
  1 Bere Alston PL20 .....41 B1
  Plymouth PL3 .....128 C7
Pounds Pk PL12 .....122 F3
Poundstock Cl PL30 .....35 F3
Powderham Rd PL3 .....128 F7
Powis Gdns PL5 .....124 B2
Powisland Dr PL6 .....125 A5
Praed's La TR27 .....89 C5
Praze Mdw TR10 .....144 C8
Praze Rd Newquay TR7 .....111 B7
  Porthleven TR13 .....91 B1
  Praze-an-Beeble TR14 .....79 F2
Praze The TR10 .....144 C8
Praze-an-Creet TR26 .....77 A2
Praze-an-Cronor TR5 .....45 E5
Prazegooth La TR12 .....103 A4
Predannack Rd AF PL12 .....99 A1
Preeze Cross PL30 .....35 C6
Prestonbury Cl PL6 .....125 B7
Prevenna Rd 2 TR19 .....88 C1
Prideaux Cl PL12 .....122 C5
Prideaux Pl* PL28 .....107 C6
Prideaux Rd PL24 .....60 B6
Pridham La PL2 .....128 D7
Pridmouth Rd PL25 .....114 E6
Priestacott Pk EX23 .....4 D4
Priesthood Terr PL10 .....132 E5
Priestley Ave PL5 .....123 E2
Primitive Row PL14 .....139 A5
Primrose Cl
  Camborne TR14 .....138 B4
  6 Goldsithney TR20 .....89 E5
  Roche PL26 .....47 A3
  Torpoint PL11 .....126 E4
Primrose Gdns
  Illogan TR16 .....67 D6
  Tavistock PL19 .....147 E4
Primrose Hill TR20 .....89 E5
Primrose La 4 TR20 .....89 E5
Primrose Rd EX23 .....104 F5
Primrose Terr
  Newlyn TR18 .....143 D1
  Portreath TR16 .....67 D6
  Tresillian TR2 .....70 F5
Primrose Valley TR26 .....141 C4
Primrose Way
  Launceston PL15 .....106 C4
  Lewannick PL15 .....27 A6
Prince Charles Cl PL15 .....106 C7
Prince Charles Pk PL25 .....114 E5
Prince Charles Rd PL25 .....114 E5
Prince Maurice Ct PL4 .....149 B3
Prince Maurice Rd PL4 .....128 F4
Prince Philip Rd PL5 .....106 C7
Prince Rock Prim Sch PL4 .....129 B2
Princes Rd PL6 .....125 E6
Princes Row PL14 .....38 B6
Princes Sq PL13 .....117 C3
Princes St Bude EX23 .....104 D6
  Looe PL13 .....117 C3

Princes St continued
  Penzance TR18 .....143 E5
Princess Ave
  Plymouth, Plymstock PL9 .....135 E6
  Plymouth, West Park PL5 .....124 A3
Princess Cres PL9 .....135 E6
Princess Ct 18 PL18 .....143 E5
Princess Parc TR9 .....45 E1
Princess Rd PL14 .....38 E4
Princess St Plymouth PL1 .....148 C3
  St Just TR19 .....86 E6
Princess Street Ope PL1 .....148 C2
Princess Terr 8 PL14 .....38 E4
Princess Villas PL17 .....28 B1
Princess Way PL1 .....148 C2
Priors Cl 10 TR26 .....77 A6
Priors Row TR13 .....90 D3
Priory Cl Par PL24 .....60 C5
Priory Cotts PL15 .....106 B6
Priory Dr PL7 .....130 D5
Priory Gdns PL19 .....147 D3
Priory La PL15 .....106 B6
Priory Lawn Terr PL3 .....129 A6
Priory Mews PL7 .....130 D5
Priory Rd Bodmin PL31 .....109 F4
  St Austell PL25 .....114 C4
  St Columb Minor TR7,TR8 .....111 F7
Priory Ridge PL7 .....130 D5
Priory Wlk PL15 .....106 B6
Prislow Fields PL14 .....144 E2
Prislow La TR11 .....144 E2
Probus Com Prim Sch TR2 .....71 C6
Promenade The PL1 .....148 C1
Prospect Cl TR27 .....142 D6
Prospect Gdns TR11 .....137 E6
Prospect La PL12 .....122 C3
Prospect Pl Ashton TR13 .....90 E3
  Falmouth TR11 .....145 B5
  Hayle TR27 .....142 D6
  Helston TR13 .....146 C5
  Mevagissey PL26 .....73 C4
  Penzance TR18 .....143 E5
  Plymouth PL1 .....148 B2
  6 Porthleven TR13 .....90 B8
  6 Truro TR1 .....137 D5
Prospect Row
  Ashton TR13 .....90 D3
  Plymouth PL1 .....127 E1
Prospect St PL4 .....149 A3
Prospect Terr
  Gunnislake PL18 .....41 A6
  Gunnislake, St Ann's Chapel PL18 .....40 E5
  Mevagissey PL26 .....73 C4
Prospect Wlk PL12 .....122 C3
Prosper Cl PL26 .....47 A2
Prosper Hill TR27 .....66 B1
Prosper Rd PL26 .....47 A2
Prouse Cres PL2 .....128 C8
Prouse Rise PL12 .....122 C3
Prout's La PL27 .....78 D6
Prouts Ct 6 PL15 .....106 C6
Prouts Way PL15 .....18 C2
Providence Pl
  Calstock PL18 .....41 A3
  Plymouth PL1 .....128 A3
Providence St 4 PL4 .....149 A4
Provis Rd TR18 .....143 C4
Prynne Cl PL1 .....148 B3
Puckator La PL14 .....38 A2
Puggis Hill TR14 .....138 A5
Pulla Cross PL14 .....81 B6
Putnam Cl PL14 .....113 D5
Pydar Cl TR7 .....111 A3
Pydar Mews 8 TR1 .....137 C4
Pydar St TR1 .....137 C5
Pym St Plymouth PL1 .....127 F3
  Tavistock PL19 .....147 C6
Pyramid Ct PL25 .....58 F4
Pyworthy CE Prim Sch EX22 .....8 E5

Q

Quakers Rd TR4,TR3 .....81 B6
Quant Pk PL19 .....147 C6
Quarry Cl EX23 .....104 E7
Quarry Cotts
  Plymouth PL1 .....148 A3
  Plymouth, Honicknowle PL5 .....124 B2
Quarry Cres PL15 .....106 A4
Quarry Gdns TR18 .....143 D5
Quarry Hill
  Falmouth TR11 .....145 B4
  Gulval TR18 .....88 B7
Quarry House Flats TR1 .....137 E3
Quarry La Gunnislake PL18 .....40 F4
  Landrake PL12 .....53 D3
  Launceston PL15 .....106 B2
  Paul TR19 .....88 B1
  St Germans PL12 .....65 A8
Quarry Park Ave PL9 .....135 D7
Quarry Park Rd
  Newquay TR7 .....110 F5
  Plymouth, Peverell PL3 .....128 F5
  Plymouth, Plymstock PL9 .....135 D7
Quarry Park Terr PL31 .....109 C4
Quarry Rd Pensilva PL14 .....38 A6
  Perranporth TR6 .....55 B4
Quarry St St Germans PL12 .....65 A8
  Torpoint PL11 .....127 C3
Quarterdeck The PL1 .....134 A8
Quay Hill Falmouth TR11 .....145 C4
  Penryn TR10 .....144 D7
Quay La PL12 .....53 D1
Quay Mews 3 TR1 .....137 D4
Quay Rd Crumplehorn PL13 .....62 D1
  Devoran TR3 .....81 F6
  Landrake PL12 .....53 A2
  Looe PL13 .....117 C3
  Mylor Bridge TR11 .....82 B4
  St Agnes TR5 .....54 C2
  St Austell PL25 .....115 B2
  St Germans PL12 .....65 B8
  Tideford PL12 .....52 F2
Quay St Falmouth TR11 .....145 C4
  Looe PL13 .....117 C3
  Lostwithiel PL22 .....112 C2
  8 Mousehole TR19 .....88 C1
  Penzance TR18 .....143 E4
  St Ives TR26 .....141 C6
  Truro TR1 .....137 D4
Quay The Pentewan PL26 .....73 C6
  Penzance TR18 .....143 F5
  Plymouth PL4 .....135 C7
  St Just TR19 .....86 E6
Quay Wlk 4 TR11 .....145 C4
Queen Anne Gdns TR11 .....144 E3
Queen Elizabeth Rd PL15 .....106 C7
Queen Mary Ct TR1 .....145 B2
Queen Mary Rd TR11 .....145 B2
Queen St Bude EX23 .....104 D6
  Goldsithney TR20 .....89 E5
  Lostwithiel PL22 .....112 C2
  Penzance TR18 .....143 E5
  Plymouth PL1 .....127 D2
  St Just TR19 .....86 E6
Queen Terr PL17 .....40 C4
Queen's Cres PL31 .....109 B3
Queen's Ct 5 TR18 .....143 C5
Queen's Gate
  Plymouth, Lipson PL4 .....149 A4
  Plymouth, Stoke PL3 .....148 A4
Queen's Gate Mews PL4 .....149 A4
Queen's Gate Villas PL4 .....149 A4
Queen's Rd PL4 .....149 A4
Queen's St 24 TR18 .....143 E5
Queen's Way
  2 Goldsithney TR20 .....89 E5
  Hayle TR27 .....142 E7
Queens Cl
  5 Indian Queens TR9 .....45 E1
  Plymouth PL6 .....125 A8
Queens Ct PL27 .....108 C4
Queens Rd Plymouth PL5 .....123 F3
  St Austell PL25 .....114 E3
Quenchwell Rd TR3 .....81 F7
Quethiock CE Prim Sch PL14 .....52 C7
Quillet Rd TR18 .....143 B3
Quilver Cl PL26 .....85 D5
Quimperle Way PL14 .....113 C5
Quintrell Downs Sta TR8 .....111 F3
Quintrell Gdns TR8 .....111 E3
Quintrell Rd TR7,TR8 .....111 E5

R

Rabys Row TR16 .....140 F8
Race Hill
  Launceston PL15 .....106 C5
  Truro TR1 .....81 C8
Race Hill Terr PL15 .....106 C5
Rachel's Way PL27 .....45 E6
Radcliffe Cl PL6 .....124 F2
Radford Ave PL4 .....129 B1
Radford Dr PL10 .....132 D4
Radford Park Dr PL9 .....135 D6
Radford Park Rd PL9 .....135 D6
Radford Rd PL1 .....148 B1
Radford View PL9 .....135 D6
Radland Cross PL12 .....40 C3
Radnor Cl PL31 .....109 F4
Radnor Hall PL4 .....149 A3
Radnor Pl PL4 .....149 A3
Radnor Rd Redruth TR16 .....140 D8
  Redruth TR16 .....68 D3
Radnor St PL4 .....149 A3
Ragan Ct TR10 .....144 C8
Raginnis Hill 24 TR19 .....88 C1
Raglan Gdns PL1 .....127 F2
Raglan Rd PL1 .....127 F2
Raglan Rd PL1 .....127 F2
Railway Cotts
  Camborne TR14 .....139 A3
  Falmouth TR11 .....145 D3
  6 Plymouth, Ford PL2 .....127 F6
  Plymouth, Keyham PL2 .....127 F6
  Tavistock PL19 .....147 E3
Railway Cres PL14 .....38 A4
Railway Terr
  Bodmin PL31 .....109 B5
  Carharrack TR16 .....80 F8
Railway Villas TR15 .....139 F7
Rainham Cl TR15 .....139 C8
Rainy Fields Cl PL28 .....107 D5

Rainyfields PL28 .....107 D5
Raleigh Cl PL28 .....107 C4
Raleigh Ct PL7 .....131 B6
Raleigh Pl 16 TR11 .....145 A4
Raleigh Rd PL28 .....107 C5
Raleigh St PL1 .....148 B3
Raleigh's St PL1 .....148 B3
Ralph's Ct PL19 .....147 B5
Ramage Cl PL6 .....125 F3
Rame Croft TR10 .....82 B1
Rame La Cawsand PL10 .....132 F1
  Rame PL10 .....64 B2
Rame View PL13 .....117 E5
Ramehead Cotts PL10 .....64 B1
Ramehead La PL10 .....64 B1
Ramillies Ave PL5 .....124 A4
Ramoth Way TR6 .....55 B5
Randwick Park Rd PL9 .....135 D7
Ranelagh Mews PL31 .....109 D5
Ranelagh Rd PL25 .....114 F4
Ransum Way PL19 .....147 B4
Raphael Cl PL9 .....136 A5
Raphael Dr PL9 .....136 A5
Raphael Rd PL13 .....62 C1
Rapson Rd PL14 .....113 D6
Rashleigh Ave
  Plymouth PL7 .....130 F7
  Saltash PL12 .....122 D3
Rashleigh Ct PL25 .....115 C3
Rashleigh Gdns PL25 .....116 A4
Rashleigh Mews PL25 .....115 A3
Rashleigh Pl PL25 .....114 F4
Rashleigh Vale TR1 .....137 E4
Ratcliffes La PL13 .....146 A5
Rattle St PL26 .....85 D5
Rawley La TR7 .....110 E5
Rawlin Cl PL6 .....129 D8
Rawlings La PL23 .....116 D5
Raymond Rd PL14 .....130 D6
Reading Way PL7 .....131 C5
Raynham Rd PL3 .....128 B4
Reading Wlk PL5 .....124 C4
Readymoney Rd PL23 .....116 B3
Reawla La TR27 .....78 E3
Rebecca Cl PL24 .....60 B6
Recreation Rd PL2 .....128 C7
Rectory Gdns TR14 .....138 C2
Rectory Rd
  Camborne TR14 .....138 C2
  Lanivet PL30 .....47 F6
  Plymouth PL1 .....127 E2
  St Buryan TR19 .....97 B6
  St Dennis PL26 .....46 B1
  St Stephen PL26 .....58 B4
Rectory Terr TR1 .....137 C5
Red La Bugle PL26 .....47 C2
  Rosudgeon TR20 .....89 F5
Redannack D 2 TR12 .....99 A2
Redannack N 1 TR12 .....99 A2
Redannick Cres TR1 .....137 B3
Redannick La TR1 .....137 B4
Redbrooke Rd TR14 .....138 E2
Redbrooke Terr TR14 .....138 E2
Reddicliff Cl PL9 .....135 D5
Reddicliff Rd PL9 .....135 D5
Reddington Rd PL3 .....129 B7
Redfern Ct 2 TR26 .....141 B5
Redhill Cl PL5 .....123 E4
Redinnick Gdns 3 TR18 .....143 E4
Redinnick Pl TR18 .....143 D4
Redinnick Terr 1 TR18 .....143 E4
Redmoor Cl
  Kelly Bray PL17 .....39 E6
  Tavistock PL19 .....147 A7
Redmoor Rd PL17 .....39 D6
Redruth Cl PL5 .....124 A5
Redruth Com Sch TR15 .....140 A5
Redruth Highway TR15 .....140 E7
Redruth Rd TR13 .....146 D7
Redruth Sta TR15 .....140 C5
Redvale Rd PL30 .....23 C4
Redvers Gr PL7 .....130 E4
Redvers Hts TR15 .....140 B3
Redwing Dr PL6 .....125 D8
Redwood Cl EX23 .....104 D5
Redwood Dr PL7 .....131 B5
Redwood Gr EX23 .....104 E5
Reeds Pk PL22 .....112 E3
Reen Hill TR6 .....55 B4
Reens Cres TR18 .....143 C7
Reens Rd TR18 .....143 C7
Reeves Cl TR13 .....91 B1
Regal Ct PL12 .....122 F2
Regent St 21 TR18 .....143 E5
Regent Sq PL4 .....149 A3
Regent Terr
  Penzance TR18 .....143 E4
  2 St Just TR19 .....86 E6
Reigate Rd PL9 .....135 E8
Relistian La PL27 .....78 E3
Relistian Pk TR27 .....78 E3
Relubbus Hill TR20 .....90 A6
Relubbus La TR20 .....90 A6
Rendle St Delabole PL33 .....14 E3
Rendle Street PL1 .....148 B3
Rendlesham Gdns PL6 .....125 E3
Renney Rd PL9 .....135 C1
Rennie Ave PL5 .....123 C1
Renoir Cl PL9 .....136 A6
Renown St PL2 .....127 E6
Reperry Cross PL30 .....47 C4
Research Way PL6 .....125 C4
Reservoir Cres PL9 .....136 B7

Reservoir La ❸ PL3 ....128 F6
Reservoir Rd
  Plymouth, Hartley PL3 ....128 F6
  Plymouth, Plymstock PL9 ..136 B7
Reservoir Way PL7 ....136 B7
Reskadinnick Rd TR14 ..138 B4
Resolution Ho PL4 ....149 B3
Respryn Cl PL14 ....113 D6
Respryn Rd PL31 ....48 D8
Restormel Castle*
  PL22 ....112 C5
Restormel Ind Est PL22 ..112 D2
Restormel Rd Looe PL13 ..117 D4
  Lostwithiel PL22 ....112 C4
  Newlyn TR18 ....143 C3
  Plymouth PL4 ....148 C4
Restormel Terr
  Falmouth TR11 ....145 B3
  Plymouth PL4 ....148 C4
Restronguet Hill TR11 ..82 B4
Reswythen Wlk TR14 ..138 F7
Retallack Gdns ❸ TR20 ..89 E5
Retallick Mdws PL25 ..115 B5
Retanna Cvn Pk TR13 ..92 D7
Retanning La PL26 ....58 E1
Retreat The
  Chacewater TR4 ....69 A3
  Plymouth PL3 ....129 B7
  St Columb Major TR9 ..45 E6
Revel Rd PL3 ....129 A6
Revell Park Rd PL7 ....130 D6
Reynolds Gr PL5 ....127 C8
Reynolds Rd PL7 ....130 D6
Rheola Gdns PL6 ....125 D3
Rhind St PL31 ....109 E5
Rhodes Cl PL7 ....130 E7
Rhubarb Hill TR8 ....43 B1
Rhude Cross EX23 ....5 B3
Rialton Hts TR7 ....111 E7
Rialton Rd TR7,TR8 ....111 E6
Ribble Gdns PL3 ....129 D7
Rice La PL26 ....85 C5
Richard Lander Sch TR1 ..69 F3
Richards Cres 69 F3
Richards Ct ❺ PL31 ..109 D5
Richards Row PL3 ....128 F7
Richards Terr PL10 ..132 E5
Richmond Hill TR1 ....137 B4
Richmond Pl
  ❹ Truro TR1 ....137 B4
  ❹ St Ives TR26 ....141 B6
Richmond Rd Pelynt PL13 ..62 D6
  Plymouth PL6 ....125 A2
Richmond St
  Heamoor TR18 ....143 C7
  Penzance TR18 ....143 E6
Richmond Terr
  Buckland Monachorum PL20 ..41 F3
  Truro TR1 ....137 B4
Richmond Way TR26 ..141 D1
Richmond Wlk PL1 ....127 F1
Rick Mdw PL15 ....18 E6
Rickard St PL26 ....59 A1
Ride The PL7,PL9 ....129 D2
Ridge Cross PL9 ....136 A3
Ridge Ho PL4 ....129 A4
Ridge Park Ave PL4 ..128 D4
Ridge Park Rd PL7 ....130 E5
Ridge Pk PL7 ....130 E5
Ridge Rd PL7 ....130 E3
Ridgegrove Hill PL15 ..106 D6
Ridgegrove La PL15 ..106 C7
Ridge Mill TR18 ....143 E8
Ridgevale Cl TR18 ....143 F8
Ridgevale La TR18 ....143 F8
Ridgeway
  ❸ Perranporth TR6 ....55 A5
  Plymouth PL7 ....130 D5
  Plymouth PL7 ....130 F5
  Probus TR2 ....71 C6
  Saltash PL12 ....122 D1
Ridgeway Sch PL7 ....130 E5
Ridgewell Terr TR9 ....57 E8
Ridgewood Cl PL26 ..114 F1
Riga Terr PL3 ....129 D8
Rigdale Cl PL6 ....129 D1
Ringmore Way PL5 ..124 B3
Ringway Flats ❽ PL31 ..109 D5
Ringwell Holiday Pk TR3 ..81 F7
Rinsey La TR13 ....90 D2
Risdon Ave PL4 ....129 B1
Rivendell PL27 ....108 C4
River Cl Saltash PL12 ..122 D5
  Tavistock PL19 ....147 D6
River St Mevagissey PL26 ..73 C3
  Portscatho TR2 ....83 B2
  Truro TR1 ....137 C4
River View Flushing TR11 ..145 B7
  Gunnislake PL18 ....41 C2
  Lerryn PL22 ....61 C7
  Plymouth PL4 ....129 B1
  Saltash PL12 ....122 F3
  Tresillian TR2 ....70 E4
River View La PL4 ....129 B1
Riverford Cl PL6 ....125 D7
Rivers The PL12 ....122 E1
Riverside Angarrack TR27 ..78 C4
  Lanivet PL30 ....47 E7
  Launceston PL15 ....106 B7
  Lelant TR26 ....77 E4
  Padstow PL28 ....107 E5
Riverside Ave PL7 ....130 A5
Riverside Bsns Pk PL1 ..127 E3
Riverside Cl ❶ PL20 ..42 C4
Riverside Cott PL12 ....122 C1
Riverside Cres TR7 ....110 A5
Riverside Ct PL22 ....112 C2
Riverside Ho TR1 ....137 D1
Riverside Holiday Pk
  TR8 ....111 B1
Riverside Mews PL12 ..123 A3
Riverside Pl
  Plymouth PL1 ....127 D2
  ❸ Wadebridge PL27 ..108 B5
Riverside View TR1 ..137 E3
Riverside Wlk PL15 ..124 B6
Riverview TR11 ....145 A6
Riviera Apartments
  TR26 ....141 D2
Riviera Est TR1 ....70 D1
Riviera La TR2 ....95 A6
Riviera Chalet Camp
  TR27 ....142 A7
Riviere Sands Holiday Pk
  TR27 ....142 B8
Riviere Towans TR27 ..142 B7
Roach's Row TR16 ....139 D1
Robartes Cl ❻ TR1 ..137 C4
Robartes Gardens Flats
  PL25 ....114 E4
Robartes Gdns PL25 ..114 E4
Robartes Jun Sch PL31 ..109 D4
Robartes Pl PL25 ....114 E5
Robartes Rd
  Bodmin PL31 ....109 D4
  Newquay TR7 ....110 F5
  St Dennis PL26 ....58 C8
Robartes Terr
  ❽ Illogan TR16 ....67 E4
  Lostwithiel PL22 ....112 C3
Robeclave Cl PL7 ....131 C6
Robert Adams Cl PL7 ..130 B5
Robert Eliot Ct PL25 ..114 B3
Robert Hichens Rd
  TR11 ....145 A5
Roberts Ave PL11 ....127 B3
Roberts Rd PL27 ....127 D8
Robin Dr PL15 ....106 E4
Robins Cl ❸ PL24 ....60 B6
Robins Way PL9 ....135 E8
Roborough Cl PL6 ....125 B5
Roborough Down La
  PL6 ....121 F5
Roborough La PL5 ....124 D8
Robyns Cl PL7 ....131 B5
Roche Prim Sch PL26 ..46 F2
Roche Rd Bugle PL26 ..47 C2
  Stenalees PL26 ....59 C7
Roche Sta PL26 ....47 A4
Rochester Rd ❶ PL4 ..128 E4
Rochford Cres PL5 ..123 F5
Rock Cl TR14 ....138 F2
Rock Close Ho TR27 ..142 A1
Rock Gdns PL9 ....129 D1
Rock La PL31 ....109 C4
Rock Rd Newlyn TR18 ..143 C3
  St Minver PL27 ....21 E2
Rock Terr Heamoor TR18 ..143 C7
  Plymouth PL7 ....130 D5
Rock Twrs PL13 ....117 D2
Rock Vale Parc PL26 ..47 A3
Rock Villas PL27 ....21 D2
Rockfield Ave PL6 ..124 F6
Rockham Gdns PL27 ..21 F3
Rockhead St PL33 ....14 E3
Rockhill PL7 ....124 C7
Rockingham Rd PL3 ..129 A5
Rockland Villas PL14 ..145 D3
Rockwood Rd PL6 ....125 E8
Rocky Hill PL19 ....147 B5
Rocky La Praa Sands TR20 ..90 C6
  St Agnes TR5 ....54 C2
  Treworlas TR2 ....83 D5
Rocky Park Ave PL9 ..135 E8
Rocky Park Rd PL9 ..135 E8
Rodda Cl PL18 ....41 A7
Rodda's Rd TR4 ....66 A3
Roddick Way ❸ PL7 ..131 C5
Rodings The PL14 ....51 F5
Rodney St PL2 ....127 F6
Rodwell Cl TR15 ....140 D5
Rodwill Cl TR27 ....78 C1
Roeback Villas PL13 ..145 D3
Roekindale Cl TR15 ..139 D6
Roeselare Ave PL11 ..127 A3
Roeselare Cl PL11 ....127 A3
Rogate Dr PL6 ....125 D4
Rogate Wlk PL6 ....125 D4
Rogers Dr PL12 ....122 D4
Roland Bailey Gdns
  PL19 ....147 A6
Rollis Park Cl PL9 ....135 C8
Rollis Park Rd PL9 ....135 C8
Rolston Cl PL6 ....124 D6
Roma Cl TR7 ....111 C7
Roman Bridge PL13 ..62 D1
Roman Dr PL31 ....109 F2
Roman Rd PL5 ....123 E2
Roman Way PL5 ....123 E2
Romilly Gdns PL7 ....130 B5
Romney Cl PL5 ....124 E3
Rona Cl TR27 ....142 B5
Ronald Terr PL2 ....127 F5
Ronsdale Cl PL9 ....135 D8
Rope Wlk
  Mount Hawke TR4 ....68 C6
  Padstow PL28 ....107 D5
Rope Wlk The
  ❸ St Ives TR26 ....141 B6
  ❾ St Mawes TR2 ....95 A6
Ropehaven Cl PL25 ..114 E6
Ropehaven Rd PL25 ..114 E6
Roper Ave PL9 ....136 C7
Ropewalk Ct ❷ TR11 ..145 C3
Ropewalk Rd TR3 ....137 C1
Ropewalk The TR18 ..143 C4
Rorkes Cl PL7 ....131 C5
Ros Lyn TR26 ....141 C1
Roscadghill Parc ❶
  TR18 ....143 C7
Roscadghill Rd TR18 ..143 C6
Roscarrack St TR13 ..139 B8
Roscarrack Cl TR11 ..144 E2
Roscarrack Rd TR11 ..144 D1
Roscarrock Hill PL29 ..22 D7
Rose Cotts
  Camborne TR14 ....138 E3
  Plymouth PL6 ....129 B8
  Stithians TR3 ....80 F3
Rose Eglos TR11 ....144 C2
Rose Eglos Cl TR11 ..144 C2
Rose Gdns PL6 ....125 E6
Rose Hill Alltarnun PL15 ..26 C8
  Fowey PL23 ....116 C4
  Port Isaac PL29 ....22 D7
  Porthtowan TR4 ....68 A6
  Redruth TR15 ....140 B5
  Sticker PL26 ....58 F1
Rose Hill Cl PL22 ....112 B2
Rose Hill Rd PL24 ....60 B5
Rose Hill Terr PL17 ..41 A3
Rose Hill Touring Pk
  TR4 ....68 A6
Rose La ❷ TR26 ....141 B6
Rose Mdw TR3 ....80 F3
Rose Mdws TR4 ....54 D3
Rose Mullion Gdns PL17 ..39 F5
Rose Row TR15 ....140 A5
Rose Terr Gunnislake PL18 ..40 F5
  ❷ Penzance TR18 ....143 E6
Rose Valley TR19 ....75 B2
Roseannon TR11 ....93 D3
Rosebery Ave PL4 ..149 C4
Rosebery La PL4 ....149 C4
Rosebery Rd PL4 ....149 C4
Rosecliston Pk TR8 ..110 E1
Rosecott Pk EX23 ....5 A6
Rosecraddoc Holiday Village
  PL14 ....38 B2
Rosecraddoc Lodge Holiday
  Bglws PL14 ....38 A2
Rosecraddoc View PL14 ..38 A2
Rosedale Ave PL2 ....128 D7
Rosedale Gdns PL31 ..35 B2
Rosedale Rd TR1 ....137 A5
Rosedown Ave PL2 ..128 A7
Rosehill Ladock TR2 ..57 C1
  Lanivet PL30 ....47 C6
  Marazion TR17 ....89 B5
  Mylor Bridge TR11 ....82 A2
Rosehill Gdns TR18 ..143 B6
Rosehill Mdw TR18 ..143 B6
Roseip Cl PL6 ....125 E7
Roseland Cnr TR2 ....69 A3
Roseland Cres TR2 ....71 F3
Roseland Est TR2 ....95 A7
Roseland Gdns
  Bodmin PL31 ....109 E6
  Redruth TR15 ....140 D6
  Veryan TR2 ....83 F6
Roseland Pk TR14 ..138 D4
Roseland Terr TR4 ....55 F2
Roselands Rd PL31 ..109 F6
Roseledden Parc TR13 ..146 B7
Roseline Est TR3 ....80 D1
Roselyon PL24 ....60 C5
Roselyon Sch PL24 ....60 C4
Rosemellen Terr PL14 ..113 B4
Rosemellin TR14 ....138 E4
Rosemellin Com Prim Sch
  TR14 ....138 E4
Rosemullion Gdns TR14 ..138 F7
Rosemullion Ho TR11 ..69 E4
Rosemundy TR5 ....54 D1
Roseannon La TR15 ..139 B8
Roseannon Rd TR15 ..139 C8
Roseteale TR18 ....143 D4
Rosevale Cres TR14 ..138 C4
Rosevale Gdns PL30 ..59 F8
Rosevalley TR3 ....69 D3
Rosevean Cl TR14 ....138 E3
Rosevean Ave TR14 ..138 E3
Rosevean Ct ❸ PL3 ..128 F6
Rosevean Gdns TR14 ..138 E3
Rosevean Ho ❻ PL3 ..128 F6
Rosevean Rd TR18 ..143 E6
Rosevear Rd PL26 ....47 C1
Rosevears Cl TR14 ..138 A5
Roseware Pl PL9 ....136 A6
Rosevin Row TR11 ..137 D5
Rosewall Cotts ❻ TR26 ..141 A5
Rosewall Terr ❺ TR26 ..141 A5
Rosewarne TR13 ....91 A1
Rosewarne (Trng Ctr)
  TR14 ....138 D5
Rosewarne Cl TR14 ..138 D4
Rosewarne Gdns TR14 ..138 D4
Rosewarne Manor Holiday
  Village TR27 ....78 F5
Rosewarne Mdws TR14 ..138 D5
Rosewarne Mews TR14 ..138 D4
Rosewarne Rd
  ❶ Camborne TR14 ....138 D3
  Carnhell Green TR27 ....78 F4
Rosewarne Terr TR14 ..138 D5
Rosewin Row ❸ TR9 ..45 E6
Rosewin Row TR9 ....45 E6
Rosewood Cl PL9 ....135 F5
Roseworthy Hill TR14 ..78 F6
Roskear TR14 ....138 E4
Roskear Fields TR14 ..138 E4
Roskear Parc TR14 ....138 F5
Roskear Rd TR14 ....138 E3
Roskear Sch TR14 ....138 F3
Roskilling TR13 ....146 D7
Roskilling Wartha TR13 ..146 D7
Roskilly Cotts TR19 ..88 C7
Roskilly's Open Farm*
  TR12 ....101 D3
Roskrow Cl TR16 ....80 A5
Roskruge Cl TR11 ....146 D8
Rospannel La PL26 ....58 F8
Rosparvah Gdns TR18 ..143 C7
Rospeath Cres PL2 ..128 D8
Rospeath La TR20 ....89 C7
Ross St PL2 ....127 E4
Rossett Gdns PL31 ....35 B1
Rosslyn Park Rd PL3 ..128 D5
Rossventon TR4 ....69 A1
Rostalek PL30 ....24 B2
Rothbury Cl PL6 ....125 E4
Rothbury Gdns PL6 ..125 D4
Rothesay Gdns PL5 ..124 D3
Rougemont Cl PL3 ....129 B7
Rough La TR3 ....81 B4
Rough St TR16 ....80 C6
Roughtor Dr PL32 ....105 C3
Roughtor Rd
  Camelford PL32 ....15 D1
  Helstone PL32 ....24 F8
Round Ring TR10 ....144 D8
Round's La PL14 ....14 D7
Roundhayes Farm Cotts
  EX23 ....10 C5
Rous Rd PL12 ....40 C2
Row La PL5 ....123 E2
Row The PL12 ....53 B7
Rowan Cl Bodmin PL31 ..109 B4
  Tavistock PL19 ....147 C3
Rowan Ct PL12 ....122 C2
Rowan Way PL6 ....125 E7
Rowans The Bude EX23 ..104 E4
  Lifton PL16 ....19 F4
  St Mellion PL12 ....53 C8
Rowden St PL3 ....128 E5
Rowdown Cl PL7 ....131 D4
Rowe St
  Plymouth PL1,PL4 ....148 C3
  Torpoint PL11 ....127 B3
Rowe's La PL13 ....146 E8
Rowena Terr Pz PL26 ..58 D5
Rowland Cl PL9 ....135 E5
Rowse Gdns PL18 ....41 A3
Royal Cornwall Hospl
  TR1 ....69 E4
Royal Cornwall Mus*
  TR1 ....137 C4
Royal Eye Infmy PL4 ..128 E4
Royal Navy Ave PL2 ..127 F6
Royal Par PL1 ....148 C2
Royal William Rd PL1 ..134 A8
Royale Ct TR18 ....143 F6
Roydon Cl PL15 ....106 B8
Roydon La PL15 ....106 B8
Roydon Rd PL15 ....106 B8
Ruby Terr PL13 ....92 B8
Rudyerd Wlk PL3 ....129 D6
Rufford Cl PL2 ....128 A7
Rule Cross EX23 ....2 E2
Ruminella View TR12 ..103 A4
Rundle Ct PL14 ....113 B4
Rundles Ct TR1 ....137 E3
Runnymede Ct PL6 ..125 E2
Rush Park Terr PL18 ..40 F7
Ruskin Cres PL5 ....124 E2
Ruskin Ct TR9 ....45 D5
Russell Ave PL3 ....129 C7
Russell Cl Gunnislake PL18 ..41 A7
Russell Ct Plymouth PL1 ..148 C2
Russell Court Gdns
  PL19 ....147 B6
Russell Pl Plymouth PL1 ..148 C2
  Tavistock PL19 ....147 B6
Russell Pl PL1 ....148 B4
Russell St
  ❼ Liskeard PL14 ....113 C5
  Tavistock PL19 ....147 C5
Russell Way ❶ TR10 ..144 C7
Russet Wood PL5 ....123 F4
Rutger Pl PL1 ....148 A4
Ruthern Valley PL30 ..34 A1
Ruthven Cl PL6 ....128 F8
Ruthy's La PL28 ....107 D5
Rutland Rd PL4 ....128 F4
Rydal Cl PL6 ....125 D2
Ryder Rd PL2 ....127 F4
Rydon La EX22 ....8 F7
Rye Hill Ponsanooth TR3 ..81 B4
  Saltash PL12 ....122 C2
Rylands Terr PL30 ....24 B3

S

Saffron Cl PL23 ....116 B4
St Agnes Mus* TR5 ....54 D1
St Agnes Prim Sch TR5 ..54 D1
St Albans Pk PL20 ....42 C4
St Ambrusca Rd TR8 ..110 A4
St Andrew St
  Millbrook PL10 ....132 E5
  Plymouth PL1 ....148 C3
St Andrew's CE Prim Sch
  PL20 ....41 F3
St Andrew's CE Prim Sch
  PL1 ....148 C3
St Andrew's Cross ❶
  PL1 ....148 C3
St Andrew's Pl PL10 ..133 A2
St Andrew's Rd PL24 ....60 F4
❷ Stratton EX23 ....4 D1
St Andrews Ct
  Cawsand PL10 ....133 A1
St Andrew's Terr PL24 ..60 F4
St Andrews Cl
  ❷ Bere Alston PL20 ....41 A6
  Ponsanooth TR3 ....81 B4
  Saltash PL12 ....122 E2
St Andrews Rd PL19 ..147 D5
St Ann's Hill EX23 ....104 F4
St Anne's Rd
  Newquay TR7 ....111 C6
  Plymouth PL6 ....125 B6
  Saltash PL12 ....122 E2
❸ Trewoon PL25 ....59 A1
St Annes TR11 ....93 B3
St Annes Cl EX22 ....7 A2
St Annes Pl ❾ PL24 ....60 F4
St Anta Rd TR26 ....141 B5
St Anthony Way TR11 ..145 A5
St Aubyn Ave PL2 ....127 F6
St Aubyn Est TR14 ....79 F1
St Aubyn Rd PL2 ....127 F6
St Aubyn St PL1 ....127 F1
St Aubyn's Rd TR1 ....137 D4
St Aubyn's Vean TR1 ..137 D4
St Aubyn's Terr TR20 ..89 E5
St Austell Coll PL25 ..114 D5
St Austell Hospl PL25 ..114 C2
St Austell Row ❷ TR2 ..95 A6
St Austell St
  Summercourt TR8 ....57 C7
  Truro TR1 ....137 D4
St Austell Sta PL25 ..114 B3
St Barnabas Hospl PL12 ..122 F3
St Barnabas Terr PL1 ..148 A4
St Benedicts Cl ❸ PL24 ..60 D6
St Benets Cl PL30 ....47 E7
St Blazey Rd PL24 ....60 C6
St Boniface Cl PL2 ....128 C6
St Boniface Dr PL2 ..128 C6
St Boniface Prim Sch
  PL1 ....148 B3
St Boniface's RC Coll
  PL5 ....124 C1
St Breaca Cl TR13 ....91 A4
St Breock Prim Sch
  PL27 ....108 B6
St Breward Prim Sch
  PL30 ....24 E2
St Bridget Ave PL6 ..124 F2
St Budeaux Ferry Rd Sta
  PL5 ....127 C2
St Budeaux Foundation Jun
  Sch PL5 ....123 F2
St Buryan Prim Sch TR19 ..96 F6
St Buryan Prim Sch TR19 ..97 F6
St Carantoc Way TR8 ..43 D1
St Catherine's Castle*
  PL23 ....116 B2
St Catherine's CE Prim Sch
  PL15 ....106 A7
St Clare Flats PL14 ..113 C5
St Clare St TR18 ....143 C2
St Cleer Dr PL27 ....108 C3
St Cleer Prim Sch PL14 ..38 A4
St Cleer Rd PL14 ....113 C5
St Clement St ❶ TR1 ..137 D4
St Clement's Cl TR1 ..137 E3
St Clement's Hill TR1 ..137 E4
St Clement's Terr ❸
  TR1 ....137 D4
St Clements Parc TR1 ..137 E3
St Clements Terr ❸
  TR19 ....88 C2
St Columb Major Com Prim
  Sch TR9 ....45 E6
St Columb Major Ind Est
  TR9 ....45 D6
St Columb Minor Prim Sch
  TR7 ....111 D7
St Columb Road Ind
  Workshops TR9 ....45 C3
St Columb Road Sta TR9 ..45 D3
St Crewenna Terr TR27 ..78 E4
St Cuthbert Cl PL25 ..106 B8
St Cuthbert's Rd TR7 ..110 D7
St Cyriac PL30 ....47 F7
St David's Rd PL19 ..147 C3
St Davids Cl EX23 ....104 F4
St Day & Carharrack Com
  Prim Sch TR16 ....68 E3
St Day Rd Redruth TR15 ..140 C7
  Redruth TR16 ....140 E6
St Dennis Prim Sch PL26 ..58 C7

St Dominic Cl PL31 ....109 E5
St Dominic Sq 4 TR1 .....137 C4
  9 Penzance TR18 ....143 E6
  5 Truro TR1 ....137 C4
St Dominick CE Sch
  PL12 ....40 D2
St Dunstan's Abbey Sch
  PL1 ....148 A3
St Dunstan's Terr PL4 .....149 C3
St Edmunds La PL28 ....107 D5
St Edward Gdns PL6 ....125 B1
St Edward's CE Prim Sch
  PL6 ....125 C1
St Eia TR26 ....141 C6
St Elizabeth Cl PL7 ....133 D7
St Elvan Cres TR13 ....91 A1
St Enodoc Cl PL27 ....108 D6
St Erme with Trispen Com
  Prim Sch TR4 ....70 D8
St Erth Com Prim Sch
  TR27 ....142 A1
St Erth Hill TR27 ....77 F1
St Erth Ind Est TR27 ....77 E2
St Erth Prac TR27 ....77 E2
St Erth Sta TR27 ....77 E2
St Eval Pl PL5 ....123 E4
St Fimbarrus Rd PL23 ....116 C3
St Francis CE Prim Sch
  TR11 ....144 E3
St Francis Cl PL5 ....124 B3
St Francis Rd TR19 ....45 E2
St Francis St 8 TR18 .....143 E6
St Gabriel's Ave PL3 ......128 D5
St George's Arc TR11 ......145 B4
St George's Ave PL2 ....128 C7
St George's CE Prim Sch
  PL1 ....148 A1
St George's Cres 9 TR1 ...109 C4
St George's Hill TR6 ....55 A4
St George's Pk PL12 ......112 C3
St George's Rd
  Hayle TR27 ....142 C5
  Looe PL13 ....117 D4
  Newquay TR7 ....110 D5
  Saltash PL12 ....122 E3
  Truro TR1 ....137 B5
St George's Terr
  Perranporth TR6 ....54 F4
  Plymouth PL2 ....127 E4
St Georges Cl Looe PL13 ..117 D2
  2 Plymouth PL2 ....127 F4
St Georges Hill Cl 13
  TR6 ....55 A4
St Georges Rd
  Nanpean PL26 ....58 D6
  Saltash PL12 ....122 D3
St Germains Rd PL7 ....39 F3
St Giles Dr PL27 ....108 C6
St Giles Mews PL27 ......108 C6
St Giles on the Heath Prim
  Sch PL15 ....13 F1
St Gluvias Pk TR10 ....144 D8
St Gluvias St TR10 ....144 D7
St Golder Rd PL4 ....143 B3
St Helens Wlk PL5 ....124 C5
St Henry St 4 TR18 ....143 E6
St Hilary Prim Sch TR20 ..89 F6
St Hilary Terr PL4 ....149 C5
St Ive Rd PL14 ....38 E4
St Ives Bay Chalet & Cvn Pk
  TR27 ....78 B6
St Ives Bay Holiday Pk
  TR27 ....78 B6
St Ives Holiday Village
  TR20,TR26 ....77 C3
St Ives Jun & Inf Sch
  TR26 ....141 A5
St Ives La TR27 ....66 B1
St Ives Mus* TR26 ....141 C6
St Ives Rd Lelant TR26 ...141 D1
  Pendeen TR19 ....75 A1
  St Ives Sch TR26 ....141 B3
  St Ives Sta TR26 ....77 B7
St James Ct
  Plymouth PL1 ....148 B2
  Torpoint PL11 ....127 B3
St James Pl TR13 ....146 B6
St James Rd PL11 ....127 B2
St James' Pl E PL1 ....148 B2
St James' Wlk PL1 ....148 B2
St James's Terr TR18 .....143 E5
St James's Terr TR10 ....144 B7
St John's Bridge Rd
  PL4 ....149 B2
St John's Cl
  Helston TR13 ....146 A6
  Millbrook PL10 ....132 E5
St John's Ct
  7 Falmouth TR11 ....145 A4
  Hayle TR27 ....142 D6
St John's Dr PL9 ....135 B6
St John's RC Prim Sch
  TR14 ....138 C2
St John's Rd
  Helston TR13 ....146 B6
  Horrabridge PL20 ....42 C4
  Millbrook PL10 ....132 F6
  Newquay TR7 ....110 D5
  Plymouth PL4 ....149 B2
  Plymouth,Turnchapel PL9 .135 A6
St John's Sq 5 Hayle TR27 .142 D6
  Plymouth PL4 ....149 B2
St John's Terr
  Devoran TR3 ....81 F6
  Pendeen TR19 ....75 A1

St John's Terr continued
  8 Penzance TR18 ....143 E6
St Johns PL19 ....147 C5
St Johns Ave PL19 ....147 C5
St Johns Cl PL6 ....125 C4
St Johns Ct 7 TR18 ....143 E6
St Johns Gdns TR11 .....145 B6
St Johns La PL11 ....132 B8
St Johns Rd
  Launceston PL15 ....106 B4
  Plymouth PL4 ....149 C2
  St Johns Wlk TR26 ......77 A7
St Joseph's Cl PL6 ....124 F1
St Joseph's RC Prim Sch
  PL1 ....127 C2
St Joseph's Rd PL15 .....106 B8
St Joseph's Sch PL15 ...106 B7
St Jude's Rd PL4 ....149 B2
St Julian's Cotts PL10 ...133 E7
St Julitta PL30 ....48 A1
St Just Prim Sch TR19 ....86 E6
St Keri Ct PL5 ....18 A5
St Keverne Pl PL2 ....128 D8
St Keverne Prim Sch
  TR12 ....101 D4
St Keverne Rural Workshops
  TR12 ....101 C3
St Kew Com Prim Sch
  PL30 ....22 F3
St Keyne Cl TR1 ....137 C6
St Keyne Sta PL14 ....51 C3
St Lawrence Mews PL4 ..149 A4
St Lawrence Rd
  Bodmin PL30,PL31 ....109 A4
  Plymouth PL4 ....149 A4
St Leo Pl PL2 ....127 E4
St Leonard's La
  Launceston PL15 ....106 B8
  Plymouth PL4 ....149 C2
St Leonards PL31 ....109 C5
St Levan Cl 8 TR17 ....89 C5
St Levan Com Prim Sch
  TR19 ....96 E5
St Levan Rd
  7 Marazion TR17 ....89 C5
  Plymouth PL2 ....127 E5
St Mabyn Holiday Pk
  PL30 ....34 E8
St Madderns CE Prim Sch
  TR20 ....143 A8
St Margarets Holiday Pk
  PL26 ....59 A1
St Margarets La PL26 .....59 A1
St Margarets Rd PL7 .....130 B7
St Mark's Sch TR23 ....2 C2
St Marks Rd PL6 ....125 D5
St Marnach's PL13 ....62 B8
St Marnach's Rd PL13 ....62 B8
St Martin's Ave PL3 ......128 D7
St Martin's CE Prim Sch
  PL4 ....113 D5
St Martin's Cl TR14 ......138 C2
St Martin's Cres TR14 ...138 C2
St Martin's Rd PL13 .....117 D6
St Martin's Terr TR14 ....138 C4
St Martin-in-Meneage Prim
  Sch TR12 ....100 D6
St Martins Cl
  Lewannick PL15 ....27 B7
  Looe PL13 ....117 D6
St Martins Rd EX23 ....7 B8
St Marwenne CE EX23 ....7 B6
St Mary St PL1 ....148 A2
St Mary's PL13 ....117 D3
St Mary's CE Prim Sch
  TR18 ....143 E4
St Mary's CE Sch TR1 ...137 C6
St Mary's Cl PL31 ....109 C4
St Mary's Cres PL31 .....109 C4
St Mary's Ct TR7 ....110 D5
St Mary's Gdns PL31 .....109 C4
St Mary's Mews 10
  TR1 ....137 D4
St Mary's Terr 4 TR1 ....137 C5
St Maryhaye PL19 ....147 A5
St Marys Cl PL27 ....107 D5
St Marys Ct PL7 ....130 D5
St Marys Rd PL24 ....60 B4
St Matthews Hill PL27 ...108 D5
St Maurice Mews PL7 ...130 E4
St Maurice Rd PL7 ....130 E3
St Maurice View PL7 .....131 B4
St Mawes Prim Sch TR2 ..95 A6
St Mawes Terr 8 PL2 .....127 F5
St Mawgan Cl PL31 ....109 F5
St Mellans Terr 1 TR1 .....99 A1
St Meriadoc CE Inf Sch
  TR14 ....138 C2
St Meriadoc CE Jun Sch
  TR14 ....138 B2
St Meriadoc Rd TR14 ....138 C3
St Merryn Holiday Village
  PL28 ....31 F7
St Merryn Prim Sch PL28 .108 C4
St Sulien Luxulyan PL30 ...60 A8

St Mewan Com Prim Sch
  PL26 ....59 A2
St Mewan La PL25,PL26 ..59 A3
St Michael Ave PL2 ....127 F5
St Michael CE Prim Sch
  TR13 ....146 C5
St Michael's Cl
  Hayle TR27 ....142 B4
  Plymouth PL1 ....122 E1
St Michael's Cotts 11
  TR18 ....143 E5
St Michael's Ct 7 PL1 ...127 F3
St Michael's Hospl
  TR27 ....142 B4
St Michael's Mount*
  TR17 ....89 B4
St Michael's Rd
  Newquay TR7 ....110 D5
  Perranporth TR6 ....55 A4
  Ponsanooth TR3 ....81 C4
  9 Stratton EX23 ....7 B6
St Michael's St TR18 ....143 E6
St Michael's Terr
  Penzance TR18 ....143 D6
  Plymouth PL4 ....148 C4
  43 Plymouth,Devonport
  PL1 ....127 A2
St Michaels Cl PL15 .....19 C1
St Michaels Ct
  Mawnan Smith TR11 ......93 D3
  12 Penzance TR18 ....143 E5
St Minver House Holiday Pk
  PL27 ....22 A3
St Minver Sch PL27 ......21 F3
St Modwen Rd PL6 ....129 F7
St Moritz Cl PL27 ....21 D5
St Nazaire App PL1 ......127 E2
St Nazaire Cl PL1 ....127 E2
St Neot Com Prim Sch
  PL14 ....36 F2
St Newlyn East Prim Sch
  TR8 ....56 B7
St Nicholas Cl TR6 ....78 C6
St Nicholas St 1 TR26 ...141 B6
St Nicholas Pk PL22 .....112 B3
St Nicholas St
  Bodmin PL31 ....109 E4
  18 Truro TR1 ....137 C4
St Nonna's Cl PL15 ....26 C8
St Olaf's Rd 18 EX23 .....7 A5
St Pancras Ave PL2 ......128 D8
St Paternus Ct PL15 .....26 C8
St Paul St PL1 ....134 A8
St Paul's RC Prim Sch
  PL5 ....123 D1
St Pauls Cl PL3 ....129 D4
St Pauls Com Prim Sch
  TR18 ....143 D6
St Peter Cl PL7 ....130 F4
St Peter's CE Jun Sch
  PL19 ....147 D5
St Peter's Hill TR18 ......143 C1
St Peter's RC Prim Sch
  PL5 ....124 B5
St Peters Rd PL11 ....145 B7
St Peters CE Prim Sch
  PL1 ....148 A3
St Peters Ct PL1 ....148 A3
St Peters Rd
  Plymouth PL5 ....124 C2
  3 Stratton EX23 ....4 E1
St Peters Way TR18 ....98 C3
St Pol-de-Leon View
  TR19 ....88 C2
St Rumon's CE Inf Sch
  PL19 ....147 C4
St Sampson's Terr PL23 ..61 B5
St Sampsons Cl 6 PL24 ..60 D5
St Saviour's Hill PL23 ...116 D2
St Saviour's La PL28 ....107 D6
St Silien TR18 ....143 B5
St Simon's La PL4 ....129 B3
St Smithwick Way TR11 ..145 C3
St Stephen Churchtown Prim
  Sch PL26 ....58 E4
St Stephen Rd PL7 ....130 F3
St Stephen St PL1 ....127 F1
St Stephen's Hill
  Launceston PL15 ....106 B7
  Saltash PL12 ....122 C1
St Stephen's Pl PL7 .....130 E5
St Stephen's Rd PL12 ...122 D2
St Stephens Com Prim Sch
  Launceston PL15 ....106 B8
  Saltash PL12 ....122 D2
St Stephens Ct PL15 ....106 B7
St Stephens Rd PL26 .....58 E1
St Sulien Luxulyan PL30 ...60 A8

St Sulien continued
  Luxulyan PL30 ....48 A1
St Teresa Ho PL4 ....149 A3
St Therese Cl 20 PL17 ....39 F4
St Therese's Ct PL1 ......127 F2
St Thomas Cl PL7 ....130 F3
St Thomas Hill PL15 .....106 B6
St Thomas Rd PL15 ......106 B6
St Thomas St TR10 ......144 D7
St Thomas' Rd TR7 ......110 F5
St Tinney Farm PL32 ......10 D1
St Treath Com Prim Sch
  PL30 ....23 E7
St Tudy Com Prim Sch
  PL30 ....23 E3
St Uny Cl Sch TR26 .....141 D1
St Uny Cl TR26 ....77 E3
St Uny Cres TR15 ....139 F5
St Vincent St PL2 ....127 E4
St Warren St 7 TR18 ....143 E6
St Wenn Prim Sch PL30 ..46 D7
St Winnols Pk PL13 ......117 D4
St Winnow Barton Farm
  Mus* PL22 ....61 A8
St Winnow CE Sch PL22 .112 F2
Salamanca St PL11 ......127 B3
Salisbury Ope PL11 ......128 B5
Salisbury Rd
  Plymouth PL4 ....149 C4
  Truro TR1 ....137 B4
Salisbury Road Jun Sch
  PL4 ....149 C3
Salmon Row 3 TR1 ......137 D4
Salt Cellar Hill 10 TR13 .146 D8
Salt Mill PL12 ....122 F4
Saltash Bsns Pk PL12 ...122 C4
Saltash Coll PL12 ....122 D2
Saltash Com Sch PL12 ..122 E1
Saltash Ctr (Coll of F Ed)
  PL12 ....122 D1
Saltash La PL28 ....112 A2
Saltash Rd Callington PL17 .39 F4
  Plymouth PL3 ....148 C4
  Plymouth,Keyham PL2 ....127 E6
Saltash Sta PL12 ....123 A2
Saltbox Cl PL1 ....82 A2
Saltbox Rd TR11 ....82 A2
Saltburn Rd PL5 ....123 C1
Saltings Cl TR26 ....77 E3
Saltings The TR26 ....77 D4
Saltram Ho* PL7 ....130 E5
Saltram Terr PL7 ....130 E5
Salts Mdw PL14 ....50 B6
Sampford Gdns PL20 .....42 C5
Sampford Terr 7 PL20 ...42 C5
Sampson Cl PL14 ....40 D6
Sampson Gdns TR1 ......81 B4
Sampson Way TR3 ....69 D3
Sampys Hill TR11 ....93 D3
Samuel Bone Cl PL14 ...113 D6
Sanctuary Cl TR14 ....138 C2
Sanctuary La
  Helston TR13 ....146 C6
  13 Stratton EX23 ....4 E1
Sanctuary Lane Flats
  TR13 ....146 C6
Sand Bay TR11 ....145 C2
Sand Cl PL6 ....41 A6
Sand La TR11 ....145 C2
Sand-Bay Holiday Flats 2
  TR6 ....55 A5
Sandbank Holiday Flats
  TR27 ....66 B1
Sandercock Cl PL1 ....127 F7
Sandfield Cres TR14 ....138 C2
Sandford Rd PL9 ....135 F8
Sandhole Cross EX39 .....2 D8
Sandhurst Terr 1 TR1 ...137 C5
Sandon Wlk PL6 ....125 A1
Sandows La 15 TR26 ....141 A5
Sandpiper Rd PL3 ....128 B6
Sandplace Halt PL13 .....63 B8
Sandplace Rd PL13 ......117 C6
Sandra Way PL31 ....109 C5
Sandy Cl PL14 ....51 B3
Sandy Cove Travel Lodge
  TR4 ....68 A6
Sandy Ct TR8 ....31 B2
Sandy Hill PL25 ....114 F4
Sandy Hill Com Prim Sch
  PL25 ....114 F4
Sandy La Harlyn PL28 ...20 D5
  Redruth TR15,TR16 ....140 D5
  Trevone PL28 ....20 F2
Sandy Rd Plymouth PL7 .131 C4
  Porthtowan TR4 ....68 A7
Sandyacres Hayle TR27 ..78 B6
Sandygate PL14 ....51 B3
Sandyhills PL27 ....21 E2
Sandylake La PL22 ......112 F3
Sandymouth Bay Holiday Pk
  EX23 ....4 C5
Sango Ct PL10 ....132 F6
Sango Rd PL11 ....127 A2
Saracen Cl PL14 ....144 C7
Saracen Cres TR10 ......144 C7
Saracen Ho 5 TR10 ......144 C7
Saracen Pl TR10 ....144 C7
Saracen Way TR10 ....144 C7
Sarah Ct PL20 ....41 B1
Sarah's Cl PL28 ....107 D4
Sarah's Gate PL27 ....32 C7
Sarah's La PL28 ....107 D4
Sarah's Mdw PL28 ....107 D4

Sarah's View PL28 ....107 D4
Sarahs Cl PL28 ....107 D4
Sargents Mdw EX23 ......2 D1
Sarum Cl PL3 ....128 F7
Saunders La PL11 ....65 A5
Saunders Wlk PL6 ....124 D6
Savage Rd PL6 ....127 D7
Savoy Bldg 8 PL25 .....114 C3
Sawles Rd
  St Austell PL25 ....114 B2
  St Austell PL25 ....114 D2
Sawmills La TR16 ....68 D3
Sawrey St PL1 ....148 A2
Sawyers Ct TR13 ....92 A6
Scarlett's Well Rd PL31 .109 B5
Scarletts Well Pk PL31 ..109 C5
Scarletts Well Rd PL31 ..109 C5
Scarne Ind Est PL15 .....106 C3
Scholar's La PL13 ....91 C3
Scholars Cl PL14 ....38 F2
School Cl Par PL24 ....60 B4
  Plymouth PL7 ....130 D7
  St Columb Minor TR7 ....111 E6
  Tavistock PL19 ....147 D5
School Dr PL6 ....125 D7
School Hill Golant PL23 ..61 B5
  Herodsfoot PL14 ....52 A6
  Lanjeth PL26 ....58 E4
  Mevagissey PL26 ....73 C4
Padstow PL28 ....107 D5
  Perranwell Sta TR3 ......81 D6
  Shortlanesend TR4 ....69 F6
  South Petherwin PL15 ...27 E8
  St Buryan TR19 ....96 E5
  St Keverne TR12 ....101 D4
  St Keverne, Porthallow
  TR12 ....101 D6
  St Neot PL14 ....36 F2
School La
  Budock Water TR11 ......144 C3
  Gulval TR18 ....88 E6
  Jacobstow EX23 ....11 A6
  Marazion TR17 ....89 C5
  Plymouth PL7 ....130 E4
  Polruan PL23 ....116 D2
  Redruth TR15 ....140 D5
  St Austell PL25 ....115 C6
  St Erth TR27 ....142 A1
  Troon TR14 ....79 E4
  Truro TR1 ....137 C3
School Rd Breage TR13 ..90 F3
  Landrake PL12 ....53 C3
  Pensilva PL14 ....38 E5
  Summercourt TR8 ....57 F7
  Whitchurch PL19 ....147 D2
School Wlk PL27 ....108 D6
Sclerder La PL13 ....63 E4
Scoble's Terr TR1 ....70 D1
Sconner Rd PL11 ....127 A3
Scoria Cl TR10 ....68 D3
Scorrier St TR16 ....68 E1
Scott Ave PL5 ....127 C8
Scott Cl 9 PL14 ....38 F2
Scott Hospl PL2 ....128 A6
Scott Rd PL2 ....128 B6
Scowbuds TR14 ....138 F5
Scrations La PL22 ....112 C2
Screech Owl Sanctuary*
  TR9 ....46 A3
Sea Ct TR7 ....142 D6
Sea Rd PL25 ....115 D2
Sea View PL18 ....40 E5
Sea View Ave PL4 ....149 C4
Sea View Cotts PL26 ....73 C3
Sea View Cres 11 TR2 ...95 A6
Sea View Pl TR26 ....141 C6
Sea View Rd
  Falmouth TR11 ....145 B2
  12 St Mawes TR2 ....95 A6
Sea View Terr
  Camborne TR14 ....138 E2
  Helston TR13 ....146 B6
  8 Newlyn TR18 ....143 C1
  Par PL24 ....60 B6
  11 Penwithick PL26 ......59 D7
  Plymouth PL4 ....149 B4
  Redruth TR15 ....140 C5
  26 St Ives TR26 ....141 B5
Seabank TR11 ....145 B2
Seacroft Rd PL5 ....123 C2
Sealife Ctr* TR7 ....110 D6
Seaspray Leisure Flats
  TR11 ....68 A7
Seaton Ave PL4 ....128 E4
Seaton Bsns Pk PL6 ....125 B3
Seaton La PL4 ....128 E4
Seaton Pk PL11 ....64 B5
Seaton Pl PL2 ....127 F5
Seaton Way PL20 ....42 A2
Seaview Cotts TR11 .....145 B5
Seaview Terr
  Sennen Cove TR19 ......96 C7
  Summercourt TR8 ....57 E6
Seawell Rd EX23 ....104 F7
Second Ave
  Plymouth, Billacombe PL9 .130 A1
  Plymouth, Devonport PL1 .128 A2
  Plymouth, Weston Mill PL2 .127 E7
Sedgemoor Ctr (St Austin
  Coll) PL25 ....114 C4
Sedley Way PL5 ....124 D3
Sefton Ave PL4 ....128 B3
Sefton Cl PL4 ....149 C4
Segrave Rd PL2 ....128 B6
Seiners Ct 10 TR6 ....55 A4

Selkirk Pl PL5 . . . . .124 E2
Selsden Cl PL9 . . . . .136 C6
Sendall's Way PL6 . . . . . . .124 F4
Seneschall Pk TR13 . . . . .146 D8
Sennen Cl PL11 . . . . .126 F4
Sennen Dr PL2 . . . . .127 E5
Sennen Prim Sch TR19 . . .86 E1
Sentry Cl PL27 . . . . .32 D6
Sergeants Hill TR4 . . . . . . .68 F3
Serpell Cl PL6 . . . . .124 E6
Serpells Mdw PL15 . . . . . . .17 F1
Sethnoe Way PL13 . . . . . . .91 A3
Seton Gdns TR14 . . . . . . .138 B4
Seven Stars La PL5 . . . . . .124 C6
Seven Trees Ct PL4 . . . . . .149 B4
Severn Pl PL3 . . . . .129 C5
Sewell Ct PL3 . . . . .128 E5
Seymour Ave
  Newquay TR7 . . . . .110 E6
  Plymouth PL4 . . . . .149 B4
Seymour Cl TR3 . . . . .69 C3
Seymour Dr PL3 . . . . .128 F5
Seymour Mews PL4 . . . . .149 C4
Seymour Pk PL3 . . . . .129 A5
Seymour Rd
  Plymouth, Mannamead
  PL3 . . . . .128 F5
  Plymouth, Plympton PL7 . .130 C6
Seymour St PL4 . . . . .149 A3
Shackleton Cres ☑ PL7 . .31 F3
Shackleton Dr TR7 . . . . . . .111 B5
Shaft Downs La TR27 . . . . . .78 F3
Shaftesbury Cotts PL4 . . .149 A4
Shaftesbury Ct ☑ PL4 . . .149 A4
Shakespeare Rd PL5 . . . . .124 C2
Shaldon Cres PL5 . . . . . . .123 E3
Shallowford Cl PL6 . . . . . .129 C8
Shallowford Rd PL6 . . . . .129 C8
Shapleys Gdns PL9 . . . . . .136 A5
Shapters Rd PL4 . . . . .149 C2
Shapters Way PL4 . . . . . . .135 B8
Sharaman Cl PL25 . . . . . . .115 A5
Sharlands Rd PL23 . . . . .7 B6
Sharon Way PL6 . . . . .125 A5
Sharpitor Row PL20 . . . . . .42 E4
Sharrose Rd PL9 . . . . .135 B5
Shaw Way PL9 . . . . .135 A7
Shearwood Cl PL7 . . . . . . .130 C6
Sheep Fair Mdw ☑ PL17 . .39 F4
Sheepstor Rd PL6 . . . . . . .125 D1
Sheila's Ct TR26 . . . . .141 D1
Shelburne Ct TR11 . . . . . .144 F3
Shelburne Rd TR11 . . . . . .144 F3
Shell Cl PL6 . . . . .125 E1
Shelley Ave PL7 . . . . .147 D6
Shelley Rd PL25 . . . . .115 A4
Shelley Way PL5 . . . . .123 D1
Shepherd's La PL4 . . . . . . .149 B2
Sherborne Cl PL9 . . . . .136 A6
Sherford Cres
  Plymouth, Elburton PL9 . .136 C7
  Plymouth, West Park PL5 .124 A3
Sherford Rd PL9 . . . . .136 D7
Sherford Wlk PL9 . . . . .136 C7
Sheridan Rd PL5 . . . . .124 C1
Sherrell Pk PL20 . . . . .41 B1
Sherril Cl PL9 . . . . .135 F4
Sherwell La PL4 . . . . .149 A4
Sherwood Dr PL31 . . . . . . .109 C5
Shewock La PL11 . . . . .65 B5
Shilla Pk PL22 . . . . .24 A8
Shilson Terr PL15 . . . . .106 C5
Shipley Wlk PL6 . . . . .125 A1
Shire Horse Farm & Carriage
  Mus The* TR16 . . . . .79 F5
Shires Adventure Pk*
  PL27 . . . . .32 D4
Shirley Gdns PL5 . . . . .124 C1
Shoemakers Row PL13 . . . .63 B7
Shoot Row TR15 . . . . .140 C5
Shop Hill ☑ TR17 . . . . .89 C5
Shop Pk PL4 . . . . .38 A2
Shoreline TR7 . . . . .111 B8
Shores La PL27 . . . . .21 E3
Short Cotts PL11 . . . . .127 A3
Short Cross Mews TR4 . . . .68 C6
Short Cross Rd TR4 . . . . . . .68 C6
Short Park Rd PL3 . . . . .128 D5
Shortacross PL14 . . . . .38 A2
Shortlands EX22 . . . . .8 E5
Shortlanesend Prim Sch
  TR4 . . . . .69 F6
Shortwood Cres PL9 . . . . .136 A7
Shrewsbury Rd PL5 . . . . . .124 C4
Shrubberies Hill TR3 . . . . .98 C8
Shute Hill Breage TR13 . . . .90 F3
  Helston TR13 . . . . .146 C6
  Lostwithiel PL22 . . . . .112 C2
  Mawnan Smith TR11 . . . . .93 D3
  Pelynt PL13 . . . . .62 D5
Shute La Penryn TR10 . . . .144 C8
  Pensilva PL14 . . . . .38 E4
  ☑ Porthleven TR13 . . . . . . .98 B8
Shute Mdw TR10 . . . . .144 C7
Shute Park Rd PL9 . . . . . . .135 F6
Shutta Rd PL13 . . . . .117 C4
Sidings The PL3 . . . . .14 E2
Sidney Terr ☑ TR5 . . . . . .140 C5
Silvanus Jenkin Ave
  PL14 . . . . .113 C5
Silver Birch Cl PL6 . . . . . .125 C7
Silver Ct ☑ TR15 . . . . .140 B4
Silver Hill TR3 . . . . .81 D6

Silver St
  Bere Ferrers PL20 . . . . . . .120 A3
  Saltash PL12 . . . . .123 A2
Silver Terr PL10 . . . . .133 A6
Silver Way TR3 . . . . .69 C3
Silverdale Cl TR7 . . . . .110 E6
Silverdale Rd TR11 . . . . . . .145 A2
Silvershell Rd PL29 . . . . . . .22 D7
Silvershell View PL29 . . . . .22 D7
Simon Cl PL9 . . . . .135 E6
Simpsons Cts ☑ TR18 . . .143 E5
Singlerose Rd PL26 . . . . . . .59 C7
Sir James Smith's Sch
  PL32 . . . . .105 C4
Sir John Hunt Com Coll
  PL5 . . . . .124 D4
Sir Robert Geffery's CE Prim
  Sch PL12 . . . . .53 C3
Sir Williams Morles
  Almshouses PL12 . . . . . .65 A8
Sisley Com Prim Sch
  TR13 . . . . .91 B5
Sithney Common Hill
  TR13 . . . . .91 C2
Sithney Old Hill TR13 . . . .146 A6
Sithney St PL5 . . . . .123 C2
Skandale Gdns PL6 . . . . . .129 D8
Skardon Pl PL4 . . . . .149 A4
Skerries Rd PL6 . . . . .124 F7
Skidden Hill ☑ TR26 . . . .141 B5
Skinnard La PL6 . . . . .40 F5
Skitches Cnr EX23 . . . . .4 D1
Skyburriowe La TR12 . . . . .99 C6
Skylark Rise PL6 . . . . .125 E8
Slade Cl PL9 . . . . .136 A6
Slade Park Rd PL14 . . . . . . .38 E5
Slades La ☑ TR10 . . . . . . .144 C7
Slades Rd PL25 . . . . .114 E5
Slatelands Cl PL7 . . . . .131 B3
Slipway PL27 . . . . .21 D2
Smallack Cl PL6 . . . . .124 F2
Smallack Dr PL6 . . . . .124 F2
Smallridge La EX23 . . . . .4 F1
Smeaton Sq PL3 . . . . .129 D6
Smith's Cotts PL13 . . . . . . .113 C6
Smithfield Cl TR8 . . . . .111 B3
Smithfield Dr PL12 . . . . . . .122 B3
Smithick Hill TR11 . . . . . . .145 B4
Smiths Way PL12 . . . . .122 B3
Smithy Cl PL12 . . . . .122 C4
Smithy Ct PL32 . . . . .105 D3
Smithy La TR3 . . . . .81 F7
Smugglers Row TR11 . . . . .145 B5
Snell Dr PL12 . . . . .122 B3
Snow's Pas TR11 . . . . .145 B4
Snowdrop Cress PL15 . . . .106 C4
Socotra Dr PL14 . . . . .59 A3
Solar Row ☑ TR1 . . . . . . .137 D5
Somer Ct PL11 . . . . .145 B4
Somerset Pl ☑ PL25 . . . . .128 A4
Somerset Pl L1 . . . . .128 A4
Somerset Place La ☑
  PL3 . . . . .128 A4
Somerville Rd TR6 . . . . .55 A4
Sonamerg Cl TR18 . . . . . . .143 C2
Soper's Hill PL5 . . . . .120 E1
South Cliff ☑ TR19 . . . . . . .88 C1
South Coombe La PL7 . . . . .39 F8
South Down Rd PL2 . . . . . .128 B6
South Downs TR15 . . . . . . .140 D2
South Dr TR14 . . . . .138 E8
South East Cornwall
  Discovery Ctr* PL13 . . . .117 C4
South Harbour TR10 . . . . .144 D7
South Hill
  Plymouth, Hooe PL9 . . . . .135 C5
  Plymouth, Stoke PL1 . . . . .128 A3
South Hill Rd PL17 . . . . .39 E5
South Park ☑ TR18 . . . . . .143 E5
South Par ☑ TR18 . . . . . . .143 E5
South Park Ct TR15 . . . . . .140 A4
South Petherwin Com Prim
  Sch PL15 . . . . .27 E8
South Pk Jacobstow EX23 . .11 A6
  Redruth TR15 . . . . .139 F6
  ☑ St Columb Major TR9 . . .45 E6
South Pl TR19 . . . . .86 E6
South Place Folly ☑
  TR18 . . . . .143 E4
South Place Gdns TR19 . . . .86 E6
South Quay PL28 . . . . .107 D5
South Quay Hill TR7 . . . . . .110 D6
South Rd Goldsithney PL20 .89 E5
  Stithians TR3 . . . . .80 F3
South Roskear Terr
  TR14 . . . . .138 F4
South St Fowey PL23 . . . . . .116 D4
  Grampound Road TR2 . . . . .57 E2
  Lostwithiel PL22 . . . . .112 C2
  St Austell PL25 . . . . .114 C3
South Terr
  Camborne TR14 . . . . .138 D2
  ☑ Penzance TR18 . . . . . .143 E4
South Towan TR4 . . . . .68 A6
South View
  ☑ Harrowbarrow PL20 . . . .42 C4
  Liskeard PL14 . . . . .113 D7
  Penryn TR10 . . . . .144 C8
South View Cl PL7 . . . . . . .130 D7
South View Parc TR4 . . . . . .68 A6

South View Pk PL7 . . . . . . .130 D7
South View Terr
  Blackwater TR4 . . . . .68 C5
  Nancegollan TR13 . . . . .91 B7
  Plymouth PL4 . . . . .149 C1
Southbourne Rd PL25 . . . .114 E2
Southcliff TR11 . . . . .145 C2
Southcott Mdws EX23 . . . . .11 A6
Southdown Cl PL26 . . . . . . .58 E1
Southdown Rd
  Millbrook PL10 . . . . .133 A6
  Sticker PL26 . . . . .58 E1
Southdown Terr PL10 . . . .133 A6
Southella Rd PL20 . . . . .42 D2
Southern Cl PL2 . . . . .127 F7
Southern Rd PL2 . . . . .127 F7
Southern Terr PL4 . . . . . . .128 F4
Southern Way PL27 . . . . . .108 C5
Southernway PL9 . . . . .136 A8
Southfield Cl PL22 . . . . . . .112 C3
Southfield Rd EX23 . . . . . . .104 E5
Southfields EX22 . . . . .8 E5
Southfields Pl ☑ TR26 . . .141 A5
Southgate Ave PL9 . . . . . . .135 E4
Southgate Cl PL9 . . . . .135 E4
Southgate St
  Launceston PL15 . . . . .106 C5
  Redruth TR15 . . . . .140 C3
Southlea Terr TR3 . . . . .80 F3
Southleigh Hill ☑ TR1 . . .137 C4
Southleigh Mews ☑
  TR1 . . . . .137 C4
Southpark Rd PL24 . . . . .60 C5
Southside Ope ☑ PL4 . . . .149 A2
Southside St PL1 . . . . .149 A2
Southview Dr PL31 . . . . . . .109 E5
Southview Rd PL24 . . . . .60 B5
Southview Terr ☑ TR19 . . . .88 C1
Southway PL6 . . . . .124 F6
Southway Com Coll PL6 . .124 F6
Southway Dr PL6 . . . . .124 E6
Southway La
  Plymouth, Southway PL6 . .125 B6
  Plymouth, Tamerton Foliot
  PL6 . . . . .124 C6
Southway Prim Sch PL6 . .124 E6
Southwell Rd PL6 . . . . .124 E1
Sovereign Ct PL7 . . . . .130 C5
Spar La TR15 . . . . .139 B4
Sparco Ct TR10 . . . . .93 C8
Sparkatown La PL20 . . . . . .42 E3
Sparke Cl PL7 . . . . .131 B4
Sparkwell CE Prim Sch
  PL7 . . . . .131 F8
Sparnon Cl Redruth TR15 . .140 C4
  St Austell PL25 . . . . .114 B4
Sparnon Cross TR15 . . . . . .90 F5
Sparnon Ct TR15 . . . . .140 C4
Sparnon Pl ☑ TR15 . . . . . .140 C4
Sparnon Terr ☑ TR15 . . . .140 C4
Sparry La TR16 . . . . .80 F8
Spaven Mor TR14 . . . . .138 C2
Spear's Terr PL11 . . . . .144 F1
Speares The PL12 . . . . .122 B2
Speech La TR3 . . . . .81 C4
Speedwell Cl Bude EX23 . .104 F5
  Millbrook PL10 . . . . .132 E5
Speedwell Cres PL6 . . . . . .129 B7
Speedwell Wlk PL6 . . . . . .129 B7
Spencer Gdns PL12 . . . . . .122 F1
Spencer Rd PL9 . . . . .135 E8
Spernen Cl TR26 . . . . .141 C1
Spernen Wyn Rd TR11 . . .145 B2
Spicers La ☑ EX23 . . . . .4 E1
Spinaker Quay PL9 . . . . . .134 F7
Spinney The PL7 . . . . .131 A4
Spire Ct PL3 . . . . .129 B5
Spire Hill Pk PL12 . . . . . . .122 C2
Spires The TR1 . . . . .137 C6
Spirit of the West (Theme
  Pk)* TR9 . . . . .45 E2
Spitfire Row PL27 . . . . .31 F3
Sportsmans Rd PL32 . . . . .105 C3
Spring Hill PL19 . . . . .147 B5
Spring Pk PL6 . . . . .125 E7
Springfield PL2 . . . . .83 B2
Springfield Ave PL6 . . . . . .136 B6
Springfield Cl
  Dobwalls PL14 . . . . .50 E7
  Lostwithiel PL22 . . . . .112 D2
  Phillack TR27 . . . . .142 D7
  Plymouth PL7 . . . . .136 B7
  St Austell PL25 . . . . .59 A1
Springfield Dr PL3 . . . . . . .128 A4
Springfield La PL7 . . . . . . .136 B7
Springfield Pk
  Barripper TR14 . . . . .79 B5
  Mylor Bridge TR11 . . . . . . .82 A3
  Wadebridge PL13 . . . . .63 E7
Springfield Rd ☑ TR19 . . . .45 E6
Springfield Rd
  Falmouth TR11 . . . . .144 E5
  Goldsithney TR20 . . . . .89 E5
  Liskeard PL14 . . . . .113 E6
  Looe PL13 . . . . .117 D5
  Newquay TR7 . . . . .110 F6
  Plymouth PL9 . . . . .136 B6
Springfield Way
  Roche PL26 . . . . .46 F3
  Threemilestone TR3 . . . . . .69 C3
Springfields Fun Pk & Pony
  Ctr* TR9 . . . . .45 E6
Springhill PL2 . . . . .128 C8
Springhill Gn PL2 . . . . .128 C8

Springwell View PL31 . . . .109 F5
Springwood Cl PL7 . . . . . . .131 A3
Spruce Gdns PL7 . . . . .131 B5
Spurway Rd PL14 . . . . .113 D5
Square The
  ☑ Bere Alston PL20 . . . . . .41 B1
  Cawsand PL10 . . . . .133 A1
  Crowlas TR20 . . . . .89 A8
  Grampound Road TR2 . . . . .57 E1
  Gunnislake PL18 . . . . .41 A6
  Kilkhampton EX23 . . . . .5 A6
  Landrake PL12 . . . . .53 C3
  Leedstown TR27 . . . . .78 E1
  ☑ Lizard TR12 . . . . .102 F2
  Manaccan TR12 . . . . .101 A7
  Marazion TR17 . . . . .89 B5
  Pendeen TR19 . . . . .75 A1
  Penryn TR10 . . . . .144 D7
  Pentewan PL26 . . . . .73 C6
  Plymouth, Hooe PL9 . . . . .135 B6
  Plymouth, Stonehouse PL1 .128 A2
  Portreath TR16 . . . . .67 C6
  Portscatho TR2 . . . . .83 B2
  Praze-an-Beeble TR14 . . . . .79 B2
  Probus TR2 . . . . .71 C6
  Redruth TR16 . . . . .80 B5
  Saltash PL12 . . . . .122 C3
  St Columb Major TR9 . . . . .45 E6
  ☑ St Mawes TR2 . . . . .95 A6
  St Teath PL30 . . . . .23 E7
  Tregony TR2 . . . . .71 F3
  Veryan TR2 . . . . .83 F6
  Week St Mary EX22 . . . . . .11 E8
Squire La TR16 . . . . .80 F8
Squires La TR13 . . . . .91 C2
Stable Hobba Ind Est
  TR18 . . . . .142 C1
Stables The TR14 . . . . .67 B4
Staddiscombe Rd PL9 . . . .135 F4
Staddon Cres PL9 . . . . .135 E6
Staddon Gdns PL9 . . . . . . .135 D6
Staddon La PL9 . . . . .135 B4
Staddon Park Rd PL9 . . . . .135 E6
Staddon Terrace La
  PL1 . . . . .148 B4
Stafford Cl PL7 . . . . .131 D6
Stag La
  Plymouth, Elburton PL9 . . .136 B8
  Plymouth, Plympton PL7 . .136 A8
Staggy La PL21 . . . . .81 F7
Stamford Cl PL9 . . . . .135 A6
Stamford Fort Cotts
  PL9 . . . . .135 A6
Stamford La PL9 . . . . .135 A6
Stamps Hill
  Indian Queens TR9 . . . . . . .45 F1
  Summercourt PL26 . . . . . . .57 F8
Stamps The PL7 . . . . .40 D5
Stanborough Cross PL9 . .136 C7
Stanborough Rd PL9 . . . . .136 B7
Stanbury Ave PL6 . . . . .124 F1
Stanbury Cl PL15 . . . . .13 F1
Stanbury Cross EX23 . . . . . . .2 C1
Stanbury Ct PL9 . . . . .136 C7
Standarhay Villas PL9 . . . .136 C7
Stanford Cl ☑ TR18 . . . . . .143 D5
Stanford Terr TR18 . . . . . . .143 D5
Stangray Ave PL4 . . . . .128 F4
Stanharrer Cl TR7 . . . . .111 E6
Stanhope Rd PL5 . . . . .123 C1
Stanley Pl PL4 . . . . .129 B2
Stanley Terr ☑ TR15 . . . . .140 B5
Stanley Way TR15 . . . . . . .140 C6
Stannary Bridge Rd
  PL19 . . . . .147 D6
Stannary Rd PL26 . . . . .59 C8
Stantons Row PL14 . . . . . . .38 A3
Stanways Rd TR7 . . . . .111 D7
Staple Cl PL6 . . . . .121 C1
Stapleford Gdns PL5 . . . . .123 F5
Stapleton Rd EX23 . . . . . . .104 F4
Star Pk PL18 . . . . .41 A6
Statham Rd PL31 . . . . .109 D4
Station App
  Newquay TR7 . . . . .110 F6
  St Columb Road TR9 . . . . .45 E2
  St Erth TR27 . . . . .77 E2
Station Hill Hayle TR27 . . . .142 B5
  Lelant TR26 . . . . .77 E4
  Praze-an-Beeble TR14 . . . . .79 B2
  Redruth TR15 . . . . .140 B4
Station La PL18 . . . . .41 A3
Station Par TR7 . . . . .110 F6
Station Rd
  Bere Alston PL20 . . . . .41 B1
  Bere Ferrers PL20 . . . . . . .119 E3
  Bugle PL26 . . . . .47 C2
  Camborne TR15 . . . . .139 C5
  Carnhell Green TR14 . . . . . .78 F4
  Chacewater TR4 . . . . .68 F4
  Fowey PL23 . . . . .116 D5
  Grampound Road TR2 . . . . .57 E1
  Gunnislake PL18 . . . . .40 F6
  Helston TR13 . . . . .146 C7
  Horrabridge PL20 . . . . .42 C4
  Kelly Bray PL17 . . . . .39 F4
  Launceston PL15 . . . . .106 C6
  Liskeard PL14 . . . . .113 B4
  Looe PL13 . . . . .117 C4
  Mary Tavy PL19 . . . . .30 F5
  North Brentor PL19 . . . . . . .30 E8
  Padstow PL28 . . . . .107 D5
  Par PL24 . . . . .60 C5
  Penryn TR10 . . . . .144 B8
  Penzance TR18 . . . . .143 F6
  Perranporth TR6 . . . . .55 B5
  Perranwell Sta TR3 . . . . . . .81 E6

Station Rd *continued*
  Plymouth, Elburton PL9 . . .136 C8
  Plymouth, Keyham PL2 . . .127 E5
  Plymouth, Plympton PL7 . .130 E7
  Plymouth, Tamerton Foliot
  PL5 . . . . .124 C6
  Redruth TR15 . . . . .140 C5
  Saltash PL12 . . . . .123 A2
  St Columb Major TR9 . . . . .45 E6
  St Newlyn East TR8 . . . . . . .56 F2
  Truro TR1 . . . . .137 E2
  Wadebridge PL30 . . . . .34 C6
  Yelverton PL20 . . . . .42 E3
Station View PL19 . . . . .30 E8
Steamers Hill TR27 . . . . . . .78 C1
Steamers Mdw TR27 . . . . . .78 C1
Steeple Cl Plymouth PL9 . .135 E8
  St Ives TR26 . . . . .141 B5
Steeple La TR26 . . . . .141 B5
Steeple View Ct TR26 . . . .141 C1
Steer Park Rd PL7 . . . . .131 C3
Steer Point Cotts PL8 . . . .136 F4
Stefan Cl PL9 . . . . .135 E8
Stenalees Hill PL26 . . . . . . .59 C7
Stenlake Pl PL4 . . . . .129 B3
Stenlake Terr PL4 . . . . .129 B3
Stennack Gdns ☑ TR26 . . .141 A5
Stennack Parc TR19 . . . . . . .86 F7
Stennack Rd PL25 . . . . .115 B3
Stennack The TR26 . . . . . . .141 B5
Stentaway Cl PL9 . . . . .135 E5
Stentaway Dr PL9 . . . . .135 E5
Stentaway Rd PL9 . . . . .135 E5
Stephens Rd PL14 . . . . .113 D4
Stephney Cl TR11 . . . . .144 C1
Steppy Downs Rd TR27 . . . .78 A5
Stewarts Rd EX22 . . . . .11 E1
Stiles The TR8 . . . . .56 F2
Stillman Ct ☑ PL4 . . . . . . .149 A4
Stillman St PL4 . . . . .149 A4
Stirling Ct PL5 . . . . .123 C2
Stirling Rd PL5 . . . . .123 C2
Stithians Com Prim Sch
  TR3 . . . . .80 F3
Stithians Row TR16 . . . . . . .80 B8
Stoggy La PL7 . . . . .131 A4
Stoke Climsland Prim Sch
  PL17 . . . . .28 D1
Stoke Damerel Bsns Ctr ☑
  PL3 . . . . .128 A4
Stoke Damerel Com Coll
  PL1 . . . . .128 B4
Stoke Damerel Prim Sch
  PL3 . . . . .128 A4
Stoke Hill La PL20 . . . . .42 B8
Stoke Rd Bray Shop PL17 . . .28 A4
  Kelly Bray PL17 . . . . .39 E1
  Linkinhorne PL17 . . . . .39 A4
  Plymouth PL1 . . . . .148 A4
Stoke Terr PL17 . . . . .39 E1
Stokes La PL1 . . . . .149 A4
Stokingway Cl PL9 . . . . . . .135 E8
Stone Barton Cl PL7 . . . . . .130 C6
Stone Barton Rd PL7 . . . . .130 C6
Stone Chair La TR19 . . . . . .96 B8
Stone Cross PL16 . . . . .19 F7
Stone La EX23 . . . . .4 E1
Stonehall Flats PL1 . . . . . .128 A1
Stonehouse Bridge PL1 . . .128 A2
Stonehouse St PL1 . . . . . . .148 A3
Stonewood Ct TR9 . . . . .45 E6
Stoney Hill PL25 . . . . .59 A4
Stoney La Polgooth PL26 . . .59 A1
  St Austell PL25 . . . . .114 C6
Stoney Lands PL12 . . . . .53 D3
Stony La Bodmin PL31 . . . . .34 D2
  Gunnislake PL18 . . . . .40 F7
Stopford Pl PL1 . . . . .127 F3
Stott Cl PL3 . . . . .129 D5
Stour Cl PL3 . . . . .129 D6
Stourscombe PL15 . . . . . . .106 F3
Stourscombe Wood
  PL15 . . . . .106 F3
Stowe Gdns PL5 . . . . .124 B2
Stowford Cl PL20 . . . . .42 C3
Stowford Cross EX22 . . . . . . .7 E4
Stracey Rd TR11 . . . . .145 B2
Strafford Cl EX23 . . . . .104 C2
Strand TR18 . . . . .143 C2
Strand St Padstow PL28 . . .107 D5
  Plymouth PL1 . . . . .134 A8
Strand The Bude EX23 . . . .104 D5
  Padstow PL28 . . . . .107 D5
Strangways Terr TR1 . . . . .137 D3
Stratton Hospl EX23 . . . . . . .4 D1
Stratton Pl TR10 . . . . .144 A6
Stratton Prim Sch EX23 . . . .4 D1
Stratton Rd Bude EX23 . . . . .4 D1
Stratton Terr
  Falmouth TR11 . . . . .145 A6
  Truro TR1 . . . . .137 B4
Stratton Wlk PL2 . . . . .128 D8
Strawberry Cl TR15 . . . . . .140 B6
Strawberry Cres TR15 . . . .140 B6
Strawberry Fields TR16 . . .140 A2
Strawberry Gdns TR16 . . .140 A2
Strawberry La
  Hayle TR27 . . . . .142 C2
  Lelant TR26 . . . . .77 E4
  Redruth TR15 . . . . .140 B6
Stray Park Cres TR14 . . . . .138 F2
Stray Park Rd TR14 . . . . . .138 F2
Stray Park Way TR14 . . . . .138 E2
Street-An-Garrow ☑
  TR26 . . . . .141 B5

reet-An-Pol 3 TR26 ...141 B5
retyn 5 TR3 ...81 F7
rickland Cotts 6
　FR18 ...143 C2
ringers Hill TR20 ...88 A5
rode Rd PL7 ...130 F6
roma CI PL6 ...124 F7
roud Park Rd PL2 ...128 C7
uart Rd PL3 ...148 A4
uart Road Prim Sch
　PL1 ...148 A4
ucley Rd EX23 ...4 D1
urdee Rd PL2 ...128 A5
ursdon Cross EX23 ...5 A8
ugar Mill Bsns Pk PL9 ...129 C1
ummer La PL13 ...62 D6
ummer Lodge Holiday
　Village TR8 ...45 B2
ummercourt TR10 ...144 D7
ummercourt Com Prim Sch
　TR8 ...57 C7
ummerfield CI PL26 ...73 B3
ummerfield La PL22 ...122 D1
ummerheath PL10 ...81 C1
ummerhill Rd PL15 ...106 A4
ummerlands Ct PL7 ...131 C5
ummerlands Gdns PL7 ...131 C5
ummerlane PL13 ...62 D6
ummerleaze EX23 ...104 D7
ummerleaze Cres
　EX23 ...104 D7
ummers CI PL6 ...129 B7
ummers St PL22 ...122 C2
ummerville Cross EX39 ...3 C6
un Girt La PL14 ...113 C5
uncrest PL14 ...38 A4
uncrest Est TR9 ...45 E1
underland Gr PL9 ...135 A6
underland Rd PL27 ...31 F3
unland Holiday Est
　TR16 ...67 C5
unley Orford Ho 6
　TR1 ...137 D4
unningdale TR1 ...137 A4
unningdale Rd PL22 ...122 C2
unny Bank PL30 ...48 E8
unny Cnr TR20 ...89 F5
uns TR4 ...81 B7
unny Corner La TR19 ...96 C7
unny Dene PL5 ...123 D1
unny Terr PL13 ...143 B2
unnybank CI TR13 ...98 C8
unnybanks PL12 ...53 E4
unnycroft PL13 ...117 C3
unnyside Carnkie TR13 ...80 D1
　Menheniot PL14 ...51 F5
　Menheniot PL14 ...52 B5
　2 Perranporth TR6 ...55 A4
　Portscatho TR2 ...83 B2
unnyside Mdw PL32 ...106 D4
unnyside Parc TR15 ...139 C8
unnyside Rd PL4 ...129 B2
unnyvale Rd TR16 ...67 C6
unnyvale Rd TR16 ...67 D6
unrising Est PL13 ...117 D5
unset Dr 3 TR13 ...98 C8
unset Gdns 3 TR13 ...98 C8
unway CI PL19 ...147 A6
unwell La Antony PL11 ...65 E4
　St John PL11 ...132 A8
unset View TR7 ...110 A6
ussex PI PL1 ...148 B2
ussex Rd PL2 ...127 F5
ussex St PL1 ...148 C2
ussex Terr 5 PL2 ...127 F5
utherland Rd PL4 ...149 A4
utton Ct PL1 ...127 F1
utton Mews 22 PL4 ...149 A2
utton Rd PL4 ...149 A2
uvale Rd 8 PL3 ...128 E6
wale CI PL3 ...129 B6
wallow CI EX23 ...104 D5
wallowfield CI PL24 ...60 D5
wallows End PL9 ...133 A8
wan CI PL10 ...133 A6
wan Gdns PL7 ...130 F5
wanpool CI TR11 ...145 A1
wanpool Hill TR11 ...145 A2
wanpool Rd TR11 ...144 F3
wanpool St TR11 ...145 C3
wanvale Rd TR1 ...143 F3
weet Briar Cres TR7 ...111 A4
wift Gdns PL15 ...106 C3
winburne Gdns PL5 ...124 C2
wingate Cross EX22 ...13 E8
ycamore Ave
　Plymouth PL4 ...149 C2
　St Austell PL25 ...114 E5
　Tavistock PL19 ...147 C2
ycamore CI
　Bodmin PL31 ...109 B4
　Launceston PL26 ...59 A1
　Praze-an-Beeble TR14 ...79 B2
　Rock PL27 ...21 E3
ycamore Dr
　Illogan TR15 ...139 D7
　Plymouth PL7 ...131 A5
　Torpoint PL11 ...127 A3
ycamore Gdns TR8 ...57 B7
ycamore Rd PL12 ...122 B3
ycamore The PL25 ...114 C4
ycamore Way PL6 ...125 E6
ydenham Cross PL19 ...29 C2
ydney CI PL7 ...130 E4
ydney Rd Newquay TR7 ...110 D6

Sydney Rd continued
　Torpoint PL11 ...127 B3
Sydney St PL1 ...148 B4
Sylvan CI PL25 ...114 E6
Sylverton PI 2 TR18 ...143 C7
Symons CI Blackwater TR4 ...68 C5
　St Austell PL25 ...115 A5
Symons Hill TR11 ...145 A5
Symons Rd PL23 ...122 D2
Symons Row PL4 ...37 F3
Symons Terr TR15 ...140 B5
Syra CI PL30 ...23 B2

T
Tabernacle St TR1 ...137 D4
Tackbear Rd EX22,EX23 ...7 E4
Tailyour Rd PL6 ...124 F2
Talbot Gdns PL7 ...127 D7
Talexandra Terr PL15 ...106 D5
Talgos CI TR16 ...140 E8
Talland Hill PL13 ...62 E2
Talland Rd PL13 ...62 E2
Talmena Ave PL27 ...108 A5
Talveneth
　Camborne TR14 ...138 F3
　Pendeen TR19 ...75 A1
　Redruth TR15 ...140 C6
Tamar Ave Plymouth PL2 ...127 E5
Tamar CI
　17 Bere Alston PL20 ...41 B1
　20 Callington PL17 ...39 F4
Tamar Cotts PL19 ...29 C1
Tamar St Plymouth PL1 ...127 E3
　Saltash PL12 ...123 A2
　Torpoint PL11 ...127 C3
Tamar Terr Calstock PL17 ...41 A3
　Saltash PL12 ...123 A2
Tamar Units PL15 ...18 E2
Tamar Bridge PL5 ...123 A2
Tamar View
　Launceston PL15 ...106 D5
　Milton Abbot PL19 ...29 C6
　St Dominick PL12 ...40 D2
Tamar View Ind Est
　PL12 ...122 D5
Tamar Villas PL9 ...135 D7
Tamar Way PL18 ...41 A6
Tamar Wharf PL1 ...127 E3
Tamarisk La PL7 ...131 A4
Tamarside Com Coll
　PL5 ...123 E1
Tamblin Ave PL14 ...50 E7
Tamerton Ave PL5 ...123 D1
Tamerton CI PL5 ...124 A6
Tamerton Foliot Rd
　PL6 ...124 D5
Tamerton Rd PL6 ...121 B2
Tamerton Vale Prim Sch
　PL6 ...124 C6
Tangmere Ave PL5 ...123 E5
Tangye CI TR16 ...67 C5
Tangye Rd TR16 ...139 C6
Tanhouse Rd PL22 ...112 C2
Tanwood View PL1 ...109 C5
Tapson Dr PL9 ...135 A6
Taranto Rd TR13 ...146 D4
Taroveor Rd TR18 ...143 E6
Taroveor Terr 3 TR18 ...143 E5
Tarr PL22 ...49 E3
Tarrandean La PL9 ...81 E6
Tarten Cross PL12 ...53 B4
Tate Gallery* TR26 ...141 B6
Taunton Ave PL5 ...123 D1
Taunton PI PL5 ...124 B5
Tavern Barn PL23 ...116 C5
Tavistock Coll PL19 ...147 A3
Tavistock Cross PL20 ...41 C2
Tavistock General PL19 ...147 B6
Tavistock Mus* PL19 ...147 C6
Tavistock PI PL4 ...149 A3
Tavistock Prim Sch
　PL19 ...147 B4
Tavistock Rd
　Callington PL17 ...39 F4
　Launceston, Stourscombe
　PL15 ...106 E3
　Plymouth PL6 ...125 B5
　Plymouth, Manadon PL5 ...124 E1
　Yelverton PL20 ...42 C3
Tavy PI PL4 ...149 A4
Tavy Rd Saltash PL12 ...123 A3
　Tavistock PL19 ...147 D5
Taw CI PL3 ...129 D6
Tayberry Dr TR16 ...140 F1
Taylor CI PL7 ...131 A3
Taylor Ct PL22 ...122 C3
Taylor Sq PL19 ...147 B6
Taylor's Cross EX23 ...5 B7
Teats Hill Flats PL4 ...149 B1
Teats Hill Rd PL4 ...149 B1
Tedder Rd 4 PL26 ...59 D7
Tees CI PL3 ...129 C7
Teetotal St TR16 ...139 C4
Tehidy CI TR14 ...138 F7
Tehidy Copse TR14 ...67 B4
Tehidy Ctry Pk* TR14 ...67 B4
Tehidy Rd
　Camborne TR14 ...138 D4
　Par PL24 ...60 D5
Tehidy Terr TR11 ...145 A6

Teign PL3 ...129 B6
Telcarne CI TR27 ...78 D6
Telegraph Hill TR16 ...68 E1
Telegraph St TR16 ...68 C5
Telegraph Wharf PL1 ...134 A8
Telephone La PL26 ...59 C8
Telford Cres PL5 ...123 F2
Temeraire Rd PL5 ...124 D2
Tenacres La PL14 ...38 E4
Tenby Rd PL5 ...123 C1
Tencreek Ave TR18 ...143 E5
Tencreek Cvn & Camping Pk
　PL13 ...117 B2
Tenderah St PL13 ...146 C2
Tenderah Rd TR13 ...146 C6
Tennyson Gdns PL5 ...124 B1
Tern Gdns PL7 ...130 F5
Terr The Crafthole PL11 ...65 B5
　Portwrinkle PL11 ...65 A4
Terra Nova Gn PL2 ...128 B5
Terrace The
　Chacewater TR4 ...68 F3
　Dobwalls PL14 ...50 D7
　Downderry PL11 ...64 C5
　East Portholland PL26 ...84 E5
　Harrowbarrow PL17 ...40 D5
　Penryn TR10 ...144 C2
　Pentewan PL26 ...73 D6
　Port Isaac PL29 ...22 E7
　Rock PL27 ...21 D2
　St Ives TR26 ...141 B5
　Yeolmbridge PL15 ...18 E6
Terras Hill PL22 ...112 C3
Terras Rd PL26 ...58 A4
Tethadene PL30 ...23 E7
Tewington PI PL25 ...114 B4
Tewkesbury CI PL2 ...128 A8
Thackeray Gdns PL5 ...124 B1
Thames Gdns PL3 ...129 D5
Thanckes CI PL11 ...127 A3
Thanckes Dr PL11 ...127 A4
The Hillocks PL13 ...117 D4
Theatre Ope PL1 ...127 F1
Theatre Royal PL1 ...148 C2
Therlow Rd PL2 ...128 A5
Theydon Rd TR11 ...144 F3
Third Ave
　Plymouth, Billacombe PL9 ...130 A1
　Plymouth, Camels Head
　PL2 ...127 E7
　Plymouth, Stoke PL1 ...128 A2
Thirlmere Gdns PL6 ...124 F4
Thistle CI PL5 ...124 D3
Thomas Bullock CI PL30 ...48 C2
Thomas Johnson Ct 6
　TR1 ...137 C4
Thomas St 4 TR13 ...98 C8
Thomas Terr 5 TR13 ...98 C8
Thorn CI PL15 ...26 C7
Thorn La PL12 ...122 C3
Thorn Moor Cross PL15 ...19 F7
Thorn Pk PL3 ...128 F5
Thorn Terr PL14 ...113 B5
Thornberry Terr PL13 ...143 F6
Thornbury Park Ave
　PL3 ...128 D6
Thornbury Prim Sch
　PL6 ...125 D4
Thornbury Rd PL6 ...125 E4
Thorndon Cross EX22 ...8 F5
Thorne Cross EX23 ...4 F2
Thornhill Rd PL3 ...128 E6
Thornhill Way PL3 ...128 E6
Thornpark Rd PL25 ...114 E5
Thornton Ave PL4 ...149 B4
Thornton CI PL26 ...46 F3
Thornville Terr PL9 ...135 C8
Thornwell La PL27 ...53 E2
Thornyville CI PL9 ...135 D8
Thornyville Villas PL9 ...135 D8
Three Cross TR13 ...98 E3
Three Holes Cross PL27 ...34 A8
Threemilestone Ind Est
　TR4 ...69 C3
Threemilestone Prim Sch
　TR3 ...69 D3
Thurlestone Wlk PL6 ...129 D8
Tiddy St St Germans PL12 ...65 B8
　Tavistock PL19 ...147 B3
Tideford Cross La PL12 ...52 F3
Tideford Dr
　Landrake PL12 ...53 A2
　St Germans PL12 ...65 B8
Tideford Rd PL12 ...53 C2
Tides Reach TR7 ...111 B7
Tillard CI PL7 ...131 C5
Tillie St 5 PL17 ...39 E4
Tilly CI PL9 ...135 F4
Timber CI PL25 ...114 B4
Tin La PL4 ...149 A2
Tincombe PL12 ...122 C2
Tincroft Rd TR15 ...139 B4
Tinners Dr PL27 ...21 D6
Tinners Way
　Callington PL17 ...39 F5
　New Polzeath PL27 ...21 D6
Tinners Wlk TR15 ...145 D3
Tinney Dr TR1 ...137 F5
Tintagel Castle* PL34 ...14 B8
Tintagel Cres PL2 ...128 C8
Tintagel Hts PL34 ...14 C6
Tintagel Prim Sch PL34 ...14 C5
Tintagel Terr 5 PL2 ...128 C8
Tintagel Terr PL29 ...22 D7
Tintagel Visitor Ctr*
　PL34 ...14 C7

Tintern Ave PL4 ...149 C2
Tiny Mdws
　Launceston PL15 ...18 E1
　South Petherwin PL15 ...27 B8
Tipple Cross PL15 ...19 C6
Tithe Rd PL7 ...130 B7
Tiverton CI PL6 ...125 B8
Tobruk Rd PL12 ...122 E3
Toby Way TR7 ...110 D7
Tolcarne CI PL25 ...114 E5
Tolcarne Com Prim Sch
　TR18 ...143 C3
Tolcarne Mews TR7 ...110 F6
Tolcarne Rd
　Camborne TR14 ...79 D5
　Newquay TR7 ...110 F6
　St Day TR16 ...68 D1
Tolcarne Terr TR18 ...143 C3
Tolgarrick Rd TR14 ...138 F5
Tolgus Hill TR15 ...140 A5
Tolgus PI TR15 ...140 A6
Tolgus Vean TR15 ...140 A6
Tolgus Wartha TR15 ...140 A6
Tollgate CI PL14 ...113 B4
Tollox PI PL3 ...129 B4
Tollyfrank Hill TR12 ...103 B6
Tolpeon Flats TR26 ...141 E2
Tolponds Rd TR13 ...91 A1
Tolroy Holiday Village
　TR27 ...142 C2
Tolroy Rd TR27 ...142 D1
Tolskithy La TR15 ...139 E6
Tolticken Hill TR16 ...67 E6
Toltuff Cres TR18 ...143 C4
Toltuff Rd TR18 ...143 C4
Tolvaddon Energy Pk
　TR14 ...138 F7
Tolvaddon Rd TR15 ...139 A5
Tolvan Cross TR12 ...91 C2
Tolver PI PL18 ...143 E6
Tolver Rd TR18 ...143 E6
Tolview Terr TR27 ...142 B4
Tom Lyon Rd PL14 ...113 A4
Tom Nicolls St 7 PL14 ...38 A3
Top Hill TR2 ...57 F1
Top Of The Town Ctyd
　PL12 ...122 F2
Top Rd PL11 ...64 C5
Tor CI
　Plymouth, Hartley PL3 ...128 E7
　Plymouth, Marsh Mills PL3 ...129 F5
　Porthleven PL13 ...91 B1
Tor La PL12 ...122 E3
Tor Rd Newquay TR7 ...110 E6
　Plymouth PL3 ...128 E7
Tor View Bugle PL26 ...47 C2
　8 Horrabridge PL20 ...42 C4
　Tregadillett PL15 ...106 A3
Torbridge CI PL12 ...122 D2
Torbridge Rd
　7 Horrabridge PL20 ...42 C4
　Plymouth PL7 ...130 D6
Torland Rd PL3 ...128 E7
Torleven Rd TR13 ...91 B2
Torpoint Com Sch PL11 ...127 A4
Torpoint Inf Sch PL11 ...127 B3
Torr Cres PL3 ...128 D7
Torr La PL3 ...128 D7
Torr Rd PL3 ...128 E7
Torr View Ave PL3 ...128 D7
Torridge CI PL7 ...130 F6
Torridge Rd PL7 ...130 F6
Torridge Way PL3 ...129 C5
Tors View CI PL17 ...39 F4
Torver CI PL6 ...124 D2
Tory Brook Ave PL7 ...130 E6
Tory Brook Ct PL7 ...130 D6
Tory Way PL7 ...130 D6
Tosberry Cross EX39 ...3 B7
Tothill Ave PL4 ...149 B3
Tothill Rd PL4 ...149 B3
Totnes CI PL7 ...131 B4
Towan Blystra Rd PL7 ...111 A5
Towan CI PL28 ...31 D2
Towan Prom TR7 ...110 C6
Towan Rd Pentewan PL26 ...73 D8
　Porthtowan TR4 ...68 A7
Towednack Rd TR26 ...77 A6
Tower CI Pelynt PL13 ...62 B6
　Sennen TR19 ...96 B6
Tower Ct PL12 ...122 C2
Tower Hill Looe PL13 ...117 D3
　Wadebridge PL27 ...108 C5
Tower Ho PL1 ...127 E1
Tower Mews TR19 ...97 A6
Tower Park Est TR15 ...62 D6
Tower Park Rd PL13 ...62 C6
Tower Pk Fowey PL23 ...116 B3
　Pelynt PL13 ...62 B6
Tower Pk Cvn & Camping Pk
　TR15 ...87 C1
Town Farm CI PL28 ...31 E4
Town Farm Cl 6 PL20 ...42 C4
Town Hill TR5 ...54 C4
Town Mills PL15 ...106 C5
Town Mills Flats PL15 ...106 B7
Townfield TR15 ...139 C6

Townsend PL23 ...116 D2
Townshend Ave PL2 ...127 E5
Townswell CI PL12 ...53 E2
Townswell La PL12 ...53 E2
Traboe Cross PL12 ...100 C3
Tracarus Ind Est PL28 ...107 B4
Tracey Ct PL1 ...148 B3
Trafalgar CI PL15 ...127 D8
Trafalgar PI 3 PL1 ...127 F3
Trafalgar Place La PL1 ...127 F3
Trafalgar Sq PL1 ...137 D4
Trafalgar St PL4 ...149 A3
Traine Brake PL9 ...136 C1
Traine Rd PL9 ...136 B1
Traly CI EX23 ...104 C4
Tram La TR16 ...140 E1
Tramway Rd PL6 ...125 E7
Tranalt Terr TR1 ...137 C3
Trannack Com Prim Sch
　TR13 ...91 E5
Trannack Mill Ind Est
　TR13 ...91 E5
Trannack Terr TR18 ...143 E7
Tranquil La PL31 ...109 C5
Transit Way PL5 ...124 C3
Travellers Rest TR12 ...99 B8
Travers CI PL14 ...113 A6
Tre-El-Verne CI TR1 ...137 A4
Tre-Pol PL26 ...58 F1
Treago Gdns PL26 ...125 C8
Trease TR19 ...75 A1
Treassowe Rd TR18 ...143 E6
Treban Gdns* TR11 ...93 C2
Treban Rd TR18 ...117 B1
Trebartha CI PL17 ...39 E3
Trebartha Rd TR1 ...137 B1
Trebarthen Terr TR4 ...55 D5
Trebarva CI TR15 ...140 A6
Trebarvah La TR20 ...89 E4
Trebarwith Cres TR7 ...110 E6
Trebarwith Rd PL33 ...14 D4
Treberran Gdns TR1 ...136 F6
Treboul Cross PL12 ...64 F8
Treboul Way PL12 ...122 A1
Treburden Dr PL26 ...125 C8
Treburley CI PL15 ...28 C4
Treburley Ind Est PL15 ...28 C4
Treby Rd PL7 ...130 F4
Trebyhan Parc TR3 ...80 F3
Trecarn CI PL15 ...106 B5
Trecarne Falmouth TR11 ...144 F5
　Tremar PL ...38 A3
Trecarne CI Polgooth PL26 ...59 A1
　St Austell PL25 ...115 B5
Trecarne Gdns PL33 ...14 E3
Trecarne View PL14 ...37 F3
Trecarrack Rd TR14 ...138 F3
Trecarrel PL15 ...106 C4
Trecarrell CI PL15 ...106 D4
Tredanek CI PL31 ...109 B5
Tredarrup Cross PL15 ...11 A1
Tredarvah Dr TR18 ...143 C5
Tredarvah Rd TR18 ...143 B1
Tredavoe La PL18 ...143 B1
Tredenham CI 4 PL24 ...60 C4
Tredenham Rd PL2 ...95 B6
Tredethy Rd PL30 ...34 F6
Tredinnick Cotts TR20 ...76 A1
Tredinnick La PL12 ...53 E3
Tredinnick Lane-End
　PL13 ...64 A8
Tredinnick Way 12 TR6 ...55 A4
Tredinnick Wood CI
　PL13 ...146 D8
Tredour Rd PL7 ...110 E4
Tredova Cres TR11 ...145 B2
Tredragon CI TR8 ...31 C2
Tredragon Rd TR8 ...31 C2
Tredrea Gdns PL31 ...21 E5
Tredrea La PL27 ...77 E2
Tredrizzick CI PL27 ...21 F3
Tredour Rd TR7 ...110 E4
Tredustan Rd PL27 ...33 B8
Tredydan Rd PL15 ...106 B6
Tredynas Rd PL15 ...145 D3
Tredyson PI TR11 ...145 A3
Treen Flats TR14 ...138 F3
Treen Hill TR19 ...96 F4
Treetops Hill PL13 ...117 A3
Treeve Farm Ind Units
　TR27 ...78 C6
Treffile La TR27 ...78 C6
Treffry CI PL30 ...48 C6
Treffry Way 12 PL24 ...60 B4
Trefinnick Rd PL17 ...39 B8
Trefloyd CI PL17 ...39 E6
Trefloyd Ct PL17 ...39 E6
Treforda Rd TR14 ...110 F4
Treforest Rd PL28 ...107 A8
Treforthlan 7 TR16 ...67 E4
Treforthlan CI TR16 ...67 E4
Trefrew Rd PL32 ...105 C6
Trefusis CI TR1 ...137 F5
Trefusis Ct TR11 ...144 A3
Trefusis Gdns PL3 ...129 A4
Trefusis Rd
　Falmouth TR11 ...144 F2
　Flushing TR11 ...145 C6
　Redruth TR15 ...140 C4
Trefusis Terr
　Millbrook PL10 ...132 E6
　Redruth TR15 ...140 C5
Tregadillett Com Prim Sch
　PL15 ...18 C2

Trevena Dr PL34 ....14 C7
Trevena Gdns TR11 ....19 D3
Trevena Rd TR18 ....143 C4
Trevena Terr TR7 ....110 D6
Trevendon PL17 ....28 D1
Treveneague Gdns PL2 ...128 D8
Treveneth Rd TR13 ....146 C5
Treveneth Cres TR18 ......143 C1
Treveneth PL █ TR18 ......143 C1
Trevenna Cross TR8 ....45 A8
Trevenner La TR7 ....89 C5
Trevenner Mews █
TR15 ....140 B5
Trevenner Sq TR17 ....89 C5
Trevenson Ct TR15 ....139 B6
Trevenson La
Camborne TR14 ....138 D2
Camborne, Pool TR15 .....139 A6
Trevenson Rd
Camborne TR15 ....139 B5
Newquay TR7 ....111 B6
Trevenson St TR14 ....138 D2
Treventon Cl
Falmouth TR11 ....144 E4
Portscatho TR2 ....83 B2
Treventon Rd TR2 ....83 B2
Trevenwith TR1 █ TR9 ....45 E6
Treverbyn Com Prim Sch
PL26 ....59 C8
Treverbyn Cl
Liskeard PL14 ....113 C6
Plymouth PL7 ....130 D6
Treverbyn Gdns PL25 .....114 F4
Treverbyn Rd
Falmouth TR11 ....144 E1
Padstow PL28 ....107 E4
Plymouth PL7 ....130 D6
St Austell PL25 ....114 E7
St Ives TR26 ....141 A6
Stenalees PL26 ....59 C8
Truro TR1 ....137 C6
Treverbyn Rise TR10 .....144 A8
Trevere Cl TR27 ....78 C6
Treverno Rd TR14 ....138 E6
Treveryn Parc TR11 ....144 C2
Trevessa Cl PL2 ....128 D8
Treveth La TR13 ....146 D8
Treveth Vlyn TR14 ....45 A8
Trevethan Cl TR11 ....145 A4
Trevethan Ct █ TR11 .....145 A5
Trevethan Gdns █
TR11 ....145 A4
Trevethan Hill TR11 ......145 B5
Trevethan Rd TR11 ....145 A4
Trevethan Rise TR11 .....145 A4
Trevethenick Rd TR13 ...137 E3
Trevia La PL32 ....105 B4
Trevia Pk Terr PL32 .....105 C3
Trevian Cl TR8 ....55 A4
Treviglas Cl TR7 ....111 D7
Treviglas Com Coll TR7 .111 D7
Treviglas La TR2 ....71 C6
Treviglas Rise TR1 ....71 C6
Trevilley La PL30 ....23 E8
Trevillick La PL30 ....23 F6
Trevilling Rd PL27 ....108 B6
Trevillis Pk PL14 ....113 B4
Trevince Parc TR16 ....80 F8
Trevingey Cl TR15 ....140 A3
Trevingey Cres TR15 .....140 A3
Trevingey Parc TR15 .....140 A4
Trevingey Rd TR15 ....140 A3
Trevisker Com Prim Sch
PL27 ....[blank]
Treviskey Hill TR2 ....84 B3
Trevissome Ct TR11 ......144 F6
Trevithick PL28 ....31 F8
Trevithick Ave PL11 ......126 F4
Trevithick Cl
Newquay TR7 ....110 F4
St Merryn PL28 ....31 F8
Trevithick Cres TR27 ....142 D5
Trevithick Ct
Camborne TR14 ....138 C3
Truro TR1 ....137 C6
Trevithick Rd
Camborne TR14 ....138 D3
Camborne, Illogan Highway
TR15 ....139 C6
Chacewater TR4 ....69 A3
Falmouth TR11 ....144 E5
Plymouth PL5 ....123 E2
St Austell PL25 ....114 E3
Truro TR1 ....137 C5
Trevithick Sch TR14 .....138 D1
Trevoarn TR27 ....142 B5
Trevol Bsns Pk PL11 .....126 D3
Trevol Pl PL11 ....126 E3
Trevol Rd PL11 ....126 E3
Trevollard PL11 ....61 F7
Trevollard La PL12 ....53 D1
Trevone Cres PL14 ....114 A4
Trevone Gdns PL2 ....128 D8
Trevone Rd PL28 ....20 F2
Trevoney TR11 ....144 C2
Trevorder Cl PL11 ....126 E2
Trevorder Dr TR1 ....69 C2
Trevorder Rd PL11 ....126 F2
Trevorgans Cross TR19 ...87 B2

Trevozah Cross PL15 ....28 B8
Trevu Ho TR14 ....138 E1
Trevu Rd TR14 ....138 E2
Trevurvas La TR13 ....90 C3
Trewall Hill PL11 ....64 D5
Trewans Terr TR15 ....140 C4
Trewardreva Cross TR11 ...92 E4
Trewarlett Cross PL15 .....28 A7
Trewartha Cl TR26 ....141 B1
Trewartha Ct █ PL14 ....113 C6
Trewartha Est TR26 ......141 D1
Trewartha Flats TR26 ...141 D1
Trewartha Rd TR20 ....90 C3
Trewartha Terr █ TR18 .143 A4
Trewarton Rd TR10 ....81 D2
Trewarveneth Farm Cotts
TR18 ....88 C2
Trewarveneth St █ TR18 .143 C2
Trewassa Flats PL32 .....105 C1
Trewavas Cres TR13 .....146 C5
Trewavas Rd TR18 ....143 C1
Trewbeath Rd TR18 ......143 C1
Treweege Row TR3 ....80 E4
Treweeks Rd TR19 ....75 A1
Treweese Cross PL14 .....52 B7
Treweese Rd
Menheniot PL14 ....52 B7
Quethiock PL14 ....52 B8
Trewellard Hill TR19 ......87 A8
Trewellard End Est TR19 ...86 F8
Trewellard Rd TR19 ....86 F8
Trewelm La TR18 ....68 E1
Trewen Rd TR11 ....144 C2
Trewen Terr TR11 ....144 C2
Trewern La TR20 ....87 F4
Trewetha Farm Lodges
PL29 ....22 E7
Trewetha La TR29 ....22 E7
Trewey Hill TR26 ....76 B4
Trewhella La TR20 ....89 F7
Trewhella Terr TR20 ......90 A6
Trewidden Rd TR26 ......114 C2
Trewidden Cl TR1 ....137 E5
Trewidden Ct TR1 ....137 E5
Trewidden Rd TR1 ....141 B5
Trewidland Prim Sch
PL14 ....51 C3
Trewince TR1 ....93 B3
Trewince La
Grampound Road TR2 .....57 E1
Lostwithiel PL22 ....112 C3
Porth Navas TR11 ....92 E3
Trewince Manor TR2 ......95 C6
Trewince Terr █ TR18 ...143 C1
Trewince Villas TR7 ....32 E6
Trewinnard Ct TR1 ....137 B6
Trewinnard Rd TR1 ....137 B6
Trewinnard La TR7 ....77 E1
Trewinnard Rd TR16 ......77 E1
Trewinnick Council Hos
PL27 ....32 A5
Trewinnick Rd PL27 ....32 A5
Trewinnow Cross PL15 ....27 D6
Trewint Cres TR13 ....117 D4
Trewint Est PL14 ....52 A5
Trewint La Landrake PL12 ...53 B2
Rock PL27 ....21 D3
Trewint Rd PL14 ....52 A5
Trewirgie Hill TR15 ......140 B3
Trewirgie Inf Sch TR15 .140 B3
Trewirgie Jun Sch TR15 .140 A4
Trewirgie Rd TR15 ....140 B4
Trewirgie Vean TR15 ....140 B3
Trewiston La PL27 ....21 E3
Trewithan Parc PL12 ....112 D2
Trewithen Gdns* TR2 ....71 C6
Trewithen Parc TR8 ....56 B7
Trewithen Rd TR18 ....143 D5
Trewithen Terr TR13 ......90 D5
Trewithy Dr PL6 ....124 F1
Trewoollock Cl PL26 ......85 C5
Trewoollock La PL26 .....85 C5
Trewoolte Terr █ PL14 ...38 C4
Trewoon Rd TR12 ....99 B2
Treworder La TR27 ....108 F5
Treworder Rd TR1 ....137 B3
Treworgan Ct TR4 ....56 D1
Treworlis Ct TR13 ....146 D8
Treworthal Rd TR3 ....81 D5
Treworveneth Dr █
TR17 ....89 C5
Trewreck La PL11 ....65 A5
Trewyn Flats █ TR26 ....141 B6
Treyarnon Bay YH*
PL28 ....20 B1
Treyew Pl TR16 ....80 F8
Treyew Rd TR1 ....137 B3
Treyew Sch TR1 ....137 A4
Treza Rd TR13 ....90 C3
Trezaise Ave PL26 ....47 A2
Trezaise Cl PL26 ....47 A2
Trezaise Rd PL26 ....46 F2
Trezela Rd TR18 ....143 C4
Trinity Cl Bere Alston PL20 ...48 A1
Carnkie TR16 ....80 C2
Trinity House National
Lighthouse Ctr* TR4 ...... [blank]
Trinity St PL25 ....114 C3
Trinity Way PL19 ....147 A4
Tripp Hill PL14 ....36 F2
Trispen Hill TR4 ....56 D1
Trolver Hill TR3 ....82 B6
Trolvus Vean TR10 ....81 A1
Troon Com Prim Sch
TR14 ....79 E4
Troon Moor TR14 ....79 E4

Troon Row TR13 ....90 F3
Troubridge Rd TR13 .....146 C4
Trowbridge Cl PL5 ....124 C4
Troy Ct PL23 ....116 C4
Truck Hill TR2 ....71 B6
Trungle Parc TR19 ....88 C2
Trungle Terr TR19 ....88 C2
Trumpleasure Cotts TR19 ...88 C2
Truro Coll TR1 ....69 E3
Truro Dr PL5 ....124 A5
Truro High Sch for Girls
TR1 ....137 C3
Truro Hill TR10 ....144 C8
Truro La TR10 ....144 C8
Truro Rd Lanivet PL30 ....47 F7
St Austell PL25 ....114 A2
Truro Sch TR1 ....137 E3
Truro Sta TR1 ....137 B4
Truro Vean Terr TR1 .....137 D5
Truthwall La TR19 ....86 F7
Tryhall Com Prim Sch
TR20 ....89 C7
Trythogga Hill TR18 .....143 F8
Trythogga Rd TR18 ......143 F8
Tubbon Hill TR3 ....81 A4
Tubby's Terr TR19 ....88 C2
Tucker Cl PL5 ....127 F8
Tuckers St TR18 ....111 B4
Tuckingmill Terr TR13 ...91 E4
Tudor Cl PL1 ....135 E5
Tudor Ct PL12 ....122 E1
Tudor Lodge Holiday Pk
TR20 ....89 C7
Tuke Cl TR11 ....144 E5
Turbill Gdns █ PL7 ....131 B5
Turf St PL31 ....109 E5
Turdown Rd PL30 ....48 E8
Turnavean Rd PL25 ......114 A5
Turnaware La TR3 ....84 A1
Turnpike Hill TR11 ....92 A7
Turnpike Hill █ TR17 .....89 C5
Turnpike Rd
Connor Downs TR27 ......78 D6
Marazion TR17 ....89 C5
Turnpike The TR19 ....86 F6
Turnquay PL9 ....135 C7
Turret Gr PL4 ....128 F4
Turton Cl PL7 ....131 C3
Twelveroods Cl PL14 .....50 E8
Twelvewoods PL14 ....50 E8
Two Hills Pk PL12 ....122 C2
Two Trees PL27 ....108 B4
Two Trees Rd PL22 ....112 F1
Tyacke Rd TR13 ....146 B5
Tybesta TR2 ....72 A7
Tye Hill Cl PL25 ....59 A3
Tyland Rd PL32 ....105 F4
Tylney Ct PL6 ....125 B6
Tyndale Cl PL5 ....124 B1
Tyringham Pl TR7 ....77 E4
Tyringham Rd TR26 ....77 F4
Tyringham Row TR26 .....77 F4
Tyshute La PL26 ....59 A1
Tything Wlk █ PL3 ....128 E6
Tywardreath Highway
PL24 ....60 C6
Tywardreath Hill PL24 ...60 D4
Tywardreath Sch PL24 ...60 D5
Tywarnhale Way TR4 ......64 A8
Tywarnhayle Rd TR6 ......55 A5

U

Uglow Cl TR14 ....138 C3
Ulalia Rd TR7 ....110 F6
Ulswater Cres PL6 ....124 E4
Umfulla Pl █ TR26 ....141 B5
Under Chapel Yd TR18 ...143 F4
Under La PL15 ....18 C3
Under Rd Boscastle PL35 ...9 C1
Bridgerule EX23 ....8 A5
Gunnislake PL18 ....41 A6
Undercliff PL10 ....142 D7
Undercliff Rd PL9 ....135 D7
Underhayes La PL15 ......35 A6
Underhill Rd PL3 ....128 A4
Underhill Villas █ PL3 ...128 A3
Underlane Boyton PL15 ...13 A2
Marhamchurch EX23 ....7 B6
Plymouth, Plympton PL7 ..130 C5
Plymouth, Plymstock PL9 ..135 E6
Underways PL20 ....41 B1
Underwood Rd PL7 ....130 D4
Unicorn Cl PL7 ....130 B6
Union Cnr TR11 ....144 D5
Union Hall
St Columb Major TR9 .....45 E6
█ Stratton EX23 ....4 D1
Truro TR1 ....137 D4
Union Pl Fowey PL23 .....116 D4
Plymouth PL1 ....148 A2
Union Rd TR11 ....144 D6
Union Sq TR9 ....45 E6
Union St Camborne TR14 .138 D2
█ Penzance TR18 ....143 E5
Plymouth PL1 ....148 A2
Union St PL12 ....61 A5
Unit Hos PL27 ....33 D5
United Downs Ind Pk
TR16 ....81 A8
United Rd TR16 ....80 F8
Unity Cl PL6 ....125 D5
Unity Rd TR13 ....98 C8
Univ of Plymouth PL1,
PL4 ....148 C3

Univ of Plymouth
(Cookworthy Bldg)
PL4 ....149 A3
Univ of Plymouth Bsns Sch
PL4 ....148 C4
Univ of Plymouth The Hoe
Ctr PL1 ....148 C2
Upcott Cross EX39 ....2 F5
Upland Cl TR1 ....137 E6
Upland Cres TR1 ....137 E6
Upland Rd PL6 ....125 A5
Uplands Saltash PL12 ....122 E1
Tavistock PL19 ....147 A4
Uplands Vean TR1 ....137 F5
Upper Castle Rd TR2 ......95 A6
Upper Chapel PL15 ......106 A4
Upper Dobbin Cl PL28 ....20 F2
Upper Dobbin La PL28 ....20 F2
Upper Eastcliffe Rd PL24 ..60 D4
Upper Hillcrest █ TR6 ....55 A4
Upper Knollys Terrace La
PL3 ....128 C4
Upper Ridings PL6 ....131 B7
Upper School La TR1 .....137 C3
Upper Tredrea TR3 ....81 D5
Upper Vean PL6 ....121 F3
Upton Cl PL3 ....129 B7
Upton Cross EX23 ....104 C2
Upton Cross Prim Sch
PL14 ....38 C7
Upton Mdws EX23 ....104 C3
Upton Terr EX23 ....104 C2
Urban Terr PL17 ....39 F5
Uxbridge Dr PL5 ....123 E4
Uzella Pk PL22 ....112 C2

V

Vaagso Cl PL11 ....127 E2
Valency Row PL35 ....9 C2
Valentine Row █ PL17 ....39 E4
Valiant Ave PL5 ....124 A4
Vallard's La PL12 ....53 E4
Valletort Flats PL1 ....148 A2
Valletort Ho PL1 ....148 C3
Valletort La PL1 ....128 A3
Valletort Pl █ PL1 ....128 A2
Valletort Pl PL1 ....128 A3
Valletort Rd PL1 ....128 A3
Valley Cl Goonhavern TR4 ...55 C3
Truro TR1 ....69 F3
Valley Gdns █ TR16 ....67 E4
Valley La TR3 ....81 F7
Valley Park La PL26 ....73 C3
Valley Rd Bude EX23 ....104 E5
Carbis Bay PL26 ....141 C2
Mevagissey PL26 ....73 C4
Plymouth PL7 ....130 B5
Saltash PL12 ....122 E2
Valley View Bodmin PL31 .109 E3
█ Illogan TR16 ....67 E4
Liskeard PL14 ....113 D7
Redruth TR16 ....140 E1
St Teath PL30 ....23 E7
Wadebridge PL27 ....108 C4
Valley View Cl PL3 ....129 B6
Valley View Dr TR1 ....69 F3
Valley View Rd PL3 ....129 B7
Valley View Terr PL3 ......81 B5
Valley Wlk PL6 ....125 E6
Vanguard Cl PL5 ....124 D1
Vapron Rd PL3 ....128 F6
Vardun Terr PL14 ....113 B5
Varfell La TR20 ....89 A7
Varley La PL14 ....113 B5
Varley Terr █ PL14 ....113 B5
Vauban Pl PL2 ....127 F4
Vaughan Cl PL2 ....128 C7
Vauxhall Cl PL4 ....149 A2
Vauxhall St █ PL4 ....149 A2
Vauxhall Street Flats
PL4 ....149 A2
Vean Rd PL14 ....113 B5
Vean Terr TR14 ....138 E2
Vear Ho TR14 ....138 E2
Vear Rd TR14 ....138 E2
Vellan Cl TR14 ....79 B5
Vellan Parc Ave TR27 .....78 C5
Vellan Vrane TR27 ....78 C5
Vellandrucia TR3 ....80 F3
Vellanhoggan Mews
TR18 ....88 C6
Venland Cl █ PL6 ....38 A3
Venn Cl █ PL3 ....128 E6
Venn Cres PL3 ....128 E6
Venn Ct PL3 ....128 E6
Venn Gdns PL3 ....128 E6
Venn Gr PL3 ....128 E6
Venn Hill PL19 ....29 C6
Venn La PL2,PL3 ....128 C6
Venn Way PL3 ....128 E7
Venslooe Hill PL14 ....113 B7
Ventnor Terr TR26 ....141 A6
Venton Cl PL15 ....18 B8
Venton East Sq TR19 .....86 F6
Venton Lace Rd TR7 ......57 E1
Venton Rd
Falmouth TR11 ....144 E4
Truro TR1 ....137 C4
Ventongauge Hill PL27 ...142 E7
Ventonleague Row
TR27 ....142 E7
Ventonleague Row █
TR27 ....67 E4
Veor Rd TR7 ....111 C7
Vermont Gdns PL2 ......127 F7
Verna Pl PL5 ....123 D2

Verna Rd PL5 ....123 E2
Vernigo Cross PL12 ....40 B1
Vernon Pl TR11 ....145 B4
Verran Rd TR14 ....138 A2
Viaduct Hill TR27 ....142 E6
Viaduct La TR14 ....138 A1
Vicarage Cl
Budock Water TR11 ......144 C3
Menheniot PL14 ....51 F5
Vicarage Gdns
Milton Abbot PL19 ....29 C6
Plymouth PL5 ....123 B1
Vicarage Hill
Budock Water TR11 ......144 C3
Penzance TR18 ....73 C4
█ St Austell PL25 ....114 C3
St Day TR16 ....68 E1
Tintagel PL34 ....14 C7
Vicarage La Lelant TR26 ...77 E1
Manaccan TR12 ....101 A8
Poundstock EX23 ....6 F2
Vicarage Mdw PL23 ......116 C4
Vicarage Rd Bude EX23 .104 D5
Bude PL28 ....107 E4
Plymouth PL7 ....130 C6
Porthleven TR13 ....91 A1
St Agnes TR5 ....54 D1
Torpoint PL11 ....127 B2
Vicarage Row TR11 ....90 F3
Vicarage Terr TR11 ....92 F4
Victoria Ave PL1 ....148 A4
Victoria Bsns Pk PL26 ...47 A4
Victoria Cl PL14 ....113 C6
Victoria Cotts
Falmouth TR11 ....145 B3
Plymouth PL6 ....129 B8
Victoria Ct █ TR18 ......143 E6
Victoria Gdns
St Columb Road TR9 ......45 E2
Threemilestone TR3 ....69 D3
Victoria La PL12 ....122 F2
Victoria Mews █ TR18 ...143 E6
Victoria Pk PL27 ....108 D6
Victoria Pl
█ Penzance TR18 ....143 E5
Plymouth PL1 ....148 A2
Plymouth, Devonport PL2 .127 C4
█ St Austell PL25 ....114 C3
█ St Ives TR26 ....141 B6
Victoria Quay
Falmouth TR11 ....145 B5
Truro TR1 ....70 D1
Victoria Rd Bude EX23 ...104 D7
Camelford PL32 ....105 B4
Plymouth PL5 ....123 D2
Roche PL26 ....47 A4
Saltash PL12 ....122 F2
St Austell PL25 ....114 F3
█ St Ives TR26 ....141 B6
Threemilestone TR3 ....69 D3
Victoria Row TR19 ....86 F6
Victoria Sq Bodmin PL31 .109 F3
█ Penzance TR18 ....143 E6
Truro TR1 ....137 C4
Victoria St
Camborne TR14 ....138 D2
St Columb Major TR9 .....45 E6
Torpoint PL11 ....127 B3
Victoria Terr
█ Lelant PL14 ....113 B5
Nanpean PL26 ....58 D6
Plymouth PL4 ....148 C4
Portscatho TR2 ....83 B2
St Breward PL30 ....24 B3
Victory Rd EX22 ....13 A8
Victory St PL2 ....127 E6
Vigo Mews PL19 ....147 C6
Vigobridge Rd PL19 .....147 C6
Villa Marina TR17 ....89 B5
Village Dr PL6 ....121 C1
Village Farm Cl EX23 ......7 B6
Village The
Buckland Monachorum PL20 .41 F3
Dulce PL14 ....51 A1
Villiers Cl PL9 ....135 D7
Vincent Way PL12 ....122 F2
Vine Cres PL2 ....128 B6
Vine Gdns PL2 ....128 B6
Vine Pl █ PL25 ....60 D5
Vinefield Ct TR1 ....145 B7
Vinery La PL7,PL9 ....130 E1
Vineyard The TR3 ....82 D3
Vingoe's La TR20 ....88 B7
Vinstone Way PL5 ....123 D1
Violet Dr PL6 ....125 E8
Virgil Cl La PL19 ....147 C6
Virgin Hill TR17 ....89 C6
Virgin St █ TR26 ....141 B6
Virginia Gdns PL1 ....127 F2
Visicks Works TR3 ....81 E6
Vivian Cl TR1 ....137 C3
Vivian Ct TR1 ....137 D3
Vivian Pl PL20 ....42 C3
Vivian Rd PL31 ....109 B4
Vixen Tor Cl PL20 ....42 C3
Vogue Hill TR16 ....68 D1
Vogue Terr TR16 ....68 D1
Vorfield Cl TR15 ....140 B6
Vosporth Hill TR8 ....110 A3
Voss Rd PL12 ....53 E1
Vounder Glaze TR19 ......86 E6
Voundervour La █
TR18 ....143 E5

Vyvyan Dr TR8 ....44 E3
Vyvyan Pl TR13 ....146 C5
Vyvyan St TR14 ....138 D3
Vyvyan's Terr TR14 ....79 B2

W

Waddon Cl PL7 ....130 E2
Wadebridge Com Prim Sch
PL27 ....108 C6
Wadebridge Rd
St Tudy PL30 ....23 E3
Wadebridge PL30 ....34 C8
Wadebridge Sch PL27 ...108 D6
Wadeland Terr [3] PL14 ...51 A7
Wadham Cl [4] PL14 .....113 C5
Wadham Dr PL14 ....113 D5
Wadham Ho [5] PL14 .....113 D5
Wadham Rd PL14 ....113 D5
Wadham Terr [6] PL2 ....128 A5
Wagg La TR2 ....71 C6
Waggon Hill PL7 ....131 A4
Wain Pk PL7 ....130 F4
Wainsway TR6 ....55 A4
Wainways EX23 ....10 F6
Wake St PL4 ....148 B4
Wakefield Ave PL5 ....123 E1
Walcot Cl PL6 ....123 E3
Waldon Cl PL7 ....131 B6
Walk The PL15 ....106 C6
Walker Lines Ind Est
PL31 ....48 D8
Walker Terr [3] PL14 ...148 B3
Walkham Bsns Pk PL5 ...124 B1
Walkham Cl PL19 ....147 D5
Walkham Mdws PL20 ......42 C4
Walkham Terr [5] PL20 ...42 C5
Walkhampton Rd PL20 ...42 C4
Walkhampton Wlk PL6 ...125 E1
Wall Gdns TR27 ....78 E3
Wall Pk TR27 ....78 E3
Wall Vean TR27 ....78 E3
Wallace Mews [1] PL31 ..109 D5
Wallace Rd Bodmin PL31 109 D5
Plymouth PL7 ....131 A4
Wallpark Cl PL7 ....130 F7
Walnut Cl PL7 ....131 B5
Walnut Dr PL7 ....131 C5
Walnut Gdns PL7 ....131 C5
Walreddon Cl PL19 ......147 B4
Walsingham Ct PL7 ......131 B6
Walsingham Pl [1] TR1 ..137 D4
Walters La PL15 ....113 D5
Walters Rd PL5 ....123 C2
Waltham Pl PL2 ....128 A8
Walton Cres PL5 ....124 C1
Wandle Pl PL3 ....129 D5
Wansford Mdw PL26 ......85 C5
Wanstead Gr PL5 ....124 A2
Wantage Gdns PL1 ......148 A3
Warbstow Com Prim Sch
PL15 ....11 B1
Warburton Gdns PL5 .....123 C1
Ward Cl [4] EX23 ....4 D1
Ward Pl PL3 ....129 B5
Wardlow Cl PL6 ....128 F8
Wardlow Gdns PL6 ....128 F8
Warfelton Cres PL12 ....122 E2
Warfelton Gdns PL12 ....122 E2
Warfelton Terr PL12 ....122 E2
Waring Rd PL6 ....124 D7
Warleigh Ave PL2 ....127 E5
Warleigh Cres PL6 ......124 F5
Warleigh La PL2 ....127 E5
Warleigh Rd [4] PL4 ....128 E4
Warmwell Rd PL5 ....123 E4
Warne Cl TR2 ....71 F3
Warran La PL19 ....147 C3
Warraton Cl PL12 ....122 D3
Warraton Gn PL12 ....122 D3
Warraton La PL12 ....122 D3
Warraton Rd PL12 ......122 D3
Warren Cl PL31 ....141 B5
Warren Cl [10] TR13 .....98 C8
Warren La PL5 ....124 A8
Warren Pk PL6 ....125 C1
Warren Rd TR9 ....45 F2
Warren St PL2 ....127 E4
Warrens Field PL32 .....105 D5
Warspite Gdns PL5 ......124 D3
Warton Cl PL5 ....124 D3
Warwick Ave Illogan TR16 67 D4
Plymouth PL5 ....124 D3
Warwick Cres [5] PL27 ...31 F3
Warwick Orchard Cl
PL5 ....124 B3
Warwick Rd EX23 ....104 E4
Wasdale Cl PL6 ....125 D7
Wasdale Gdns PL6 ......125 D7
Washbourne Cl PL1 .....127 E3
Water La Crantock TR8 ..110 A3
Delabole PL33 ....14 E1
Golant PL23 ....61 B5
Hayle TR27 ....142 B3
St Agnes TR5 ....54 D1
Water's Edge PL28 ......107 E6
Water-Ma-Trout TR13 ..146 C8
Watergate Bay Holiday Pk
TR8 ....44 D8
Watergate La PL30 ....34 C8
Watergate Rd TR8 ....44 C6
Watering Hill Cl PL25 ..114 E3
Waterings Rd TR11 ....82 A2

Waterloo Ave PL3 ....128 E5
Waterloo Cl
Plymouth PL1 ....128 A2
St Mawes TR2 ....95 A6
Waterloo Ct PL1 ....128 A2
Waterloo Rd TR11 ......145 B4
Waterloo St
Plymouth PL1 ....149 A4
Plymouth, Stoke PL1 ....128 A3
Waterloo Yard Flats
PL1 ....128 A2
Waters Edge TR7 ....110 A6
Waterside Ct PL25 .....114 B4
Watersmead Parc TR11 144 C3
Watery La Bodmin PL31 109 D5
Milton Combe PL6 ....120 D6
Watson Gdns PL4 ....149 B3
Watson Pl PL4 ....149 B2
Watts Park Rd PL2 ......128 C7
Watts Rd PL19 ....147 B5
Watts' Rd PL4 ....149 C3
Waveney Gdns PL5 .....124 C3
Waverley Rd PL5 ....123 D2
Wavish Pk PL11 ....126 D4
Waycott Wlk PL6 ....124 D6
Wayfield Rd TR11 ....82 B2
Wayside Cl PL7 ....111 A4
Wayside Folk Mus*
TR 26 ....76 B5
Wearde Rd PL12 ....122 E1
Webb St PL23 ....116 D4
Webber Hill PL11 ....145 B4
Webber St TR11 ....145 B4
Weeke Cross PL25 ......115 A4
Weekstone Cross EX22 ...8 C8
Weet Cnr EX14 ....138 C3
Weeth Com Prim Sch
TR14 ....138 C4
Weeth La TR14 ....138 C4
Weeth Rd TR14 ....138 C3
Weethes Cotts [8] TR18 143 D5
Weir Cl PL6 ....125 D7
Weir Gdns PL6 ....125 F2
Weir Rd PL6 ....125 F2
Welay Terr PL14 ....37 F3
Welbeck Ave PL4 ....148 C4
Welcombe Cross EX39 ...3 B4
Welcome Cl TR4 ....56 D1
Well Cl PL14 ....148 B3
Well La Constantine TR11 .92 F4
Falmouth TR11 ....145 B4
Goldsithney TR20 ....89 F5
Liskeard PL14 ....113 C6
Looe PL13 ....117 C3
St Buryan TR19 ....97 E5
St Cleer PL14 ....37 F3
St Keverne TR12 ....101 D4
Tregony TR2 ....71 F3
Well Way TR7 ....111 C7
Welland Gdns PL3 ......129 C5
Weller Ct TR11 ....145 B3
Wellfield Cl
Coad's Green PL15 ....27 D3
Plymouth PL7 ....131 C5
Wellhay Cl PL9 ....136 C6
Wellington Cl TR14 ....138 C3
Wellington Gdns TR11 145 B4
Wellington Pl
Falmouth TR11 ....145 B4
Penzance TR18 ....143 D5
Wadebridge PL27 ....108 C4
Wellington Plantation
TR3 ....82 B7
Wellington Rd
Camborne TR14 ....138 D3
Porthleven TR13 ....91 B1
St Dennis PL26 ....58 C8
St Eval PL27 ....31 F3
Wellington St
Plymouth PL4 ....149 A4
Plymouth, Stoke PL1 ....128 A3
Torpoint PL11 ....127 B3
Wellington Terr
Falmouth TR11 ....145 B4
Porthleven TR13 ....91 B2
Portscatho TR2 ....83 B2
[2] Truro TR1 ....137 C4
Wellpark Rd PL18 ....40 F5
Wells Ct PL10 ....132 E4
Welsford Ave PL3 ....128 E6
Welway TR6 ....55 A4
Wembury Park Rd PL3 ..128 D6
Wembury Rd PL9 ....136 A4
Wendron CE Prim Sch
TR13 ....91 F5
Wendron St TR13 ......146 C6
Wenlock Gdns PL2 .....128 B8
Wensum Cl PL7 ....131 A4
Wentwood Gdns PL6 ....125 E3
Wentwood Pl PL6 ....125 E3
Wentworth Cl
Lynstone EX23 ....104 C3
Polzeath PL27 ....21 D5
Wentworth Pl PL14 ....129 B2
Wentworth Way PL12 ..122 C2
Werrington Dr PL17 ......39 E4
Werrington Prim Sch
PL15 ....18 F7

Waterloo Cl Kelly Bray PL17 ..39 F6
Stenalees PL26 ....59 C7
Wesley Cottage* PL15 ...26 B7
Wesley Ct Penryn TR10 144 C8
[1] Heamoor TR18 ....38 D4
Pensilva PL14 ....38 B2
Torpoint PL11 ....127 C3
Wesley La PL12 ....122 F2
Wesley Pl
[5] Newlyn TR18 ....143 C2
Plymouth, Mutley PL4 ..128 E5
[1] Plymouth, Stoke PL2 128 A4
St Austell PL25 ....114 F3
[7] St Ives TR26 ....141 B5
Wesley Rd Cubert TR8 ...55 D8
Pensilva PL14 ....38 D4
Saltash PL12 ....122 F2
Wesley St
Camborne TR14 ....138 E3
[1] Redruth TR15 ....140 C5
Wesley Terr Bugle PL26 ...47 C2
Looe PL13 ....117 D4
Wesley Way PL15 ....26 B7
[4] St Ives TR26 ....141 B5
West Ave [4] PL19 .....147 B5
West Beach TR4 ....68 A6
West Beckon Cl EX23 ...2 D1
West Bridge Rd PL15 ..106 C5
West Camps Bay PL11 ...64 C4
West Charles St TR14 ..138 D2
West Cliff TR4 ....68 A6
West Cnr [1] TR2 ....81 F7
West Cornwall Hospl
TR18 ....143 D6
West Devon Bsns Pk
PL19 ....147 B3
West Down Cl PL17 .....117 C4
West Down Rd PL20 ....128 B6
West End Goldsithney TR20 89 E5
Marazion TR17 ....89 C5
Pentewan PL26 ....73 C6
Redruth TR15 ....140 B4
St Day TR16 ....68 D1
West End Cotts PL11 ...64 B8
West End Ct [2] TR15 ..140 B4
West End Sq [7] PL17 ...39 E4
West Fairholme Rd
EX23 ....104 E7
West Hill St Austell PL25 114 C3
Wadebridge PL27 ....108 A6
West Hill Rd PL4 ....128 F4
West Hoe Rd PL1 ....148 B1
West Kitty TR5 ....54 C1
West La Crafthole PL11 ...65 B5
Delabole PL33 ....14 E2
Landrake PL12 ....53 B3
West Looe Hill PL13 ...117 B3
West Looe Sq PL13 .....117 C3
West Malling Ave PL5 ..123 E5
West Park Dr PL7 ......131 C5
West Park Est PL27 ....108 D5
West Park Hill PL7 .....131 B7
West Park Prim Sch
PL5 ....124 A2
West Rd EX23 ....104 D7
West Pentire Rd TR8 ...43 D3
West Pk Liskeard PL14 ...51 C3
Liskeard PL14 ....113 B6
Millbrook PL10 ....132 E5
Penryn TR10 ....144 C8
Polruan PL23 ....116 C2
St Columb Major TR9 ...45 E6
Tideford PL12 ....52 F2
West Porthmeor Cotts
PL25 ....115 B2
West Rise TR11 ....144 F3
West St Grimscott EX23 ...5 B1
Liskeard PL14 ....113 B6
Millbrook PL10 ....132 E5
Penryn TR10 ....144 C8
Polruan PL23 ....116 C2
St Columb Major TR9 ...45 E6
St Just TR19 ....86 E6
West Tehidy TR14 ....138 F7
West Terr Hayle TR27 ..142 B6
Newlyn TR18 ....143 C3
West Tolgus TR15 ....139 D8
West Trevingey TR15 ...140 A3
West Trewirgie Rd
TR15 ....140 B4
West View
Porthleven TR13 ....91 A1
Tavistock PL19 ....147 E2
Trevone PL28 ....20 F2
West View Rd [5] PL20 ..41 B1
West Villas TR5 ....57 B7
West Week Cl EX22 ......11 E8
West Wharf PL26 ....73 C3
Westbeare Hts PL15 ....140 B3
Westborne Rd TR14 ....138 B4
Westbourne Rd PL25 ...114 B3
Westbourne La PL14 ...113 B6
Westbourne Rd PL3 ....128 D5
Westbourne Terr
Fraddon TR9 ....57 D8
Saltash PL12 ....122 F3
Westbridge Cotts PL19 147 B4
Westbridge Rd PL25 ....59 A3
Westbridge Ind Est [3]
PL19 ....147 B4
Westbury Cl EX23 .....104 E5
Westbury Rd EX23 ....104 E5

Westcombe Cres PL9 ...135 D5
Westcott PL27 ....108 A6
Westcott Cl PL6 ....129 A8
Westcountry Cl PL2 ....127 F7
Westcroft Rd PL5 ....123 D1
Westdown Rd PL13 .....62 D2
Westella Rd PL20 ....42 D2
Westend Terr PL10 ....144 C8
Westeria Terr PL2 ......128 C7
Western App PL1 ......148 B2
Western Ave [9] PL4 ....51 A7
Western College Rd
PL4 ....128 F5
Western Dr PL3 ....129 B4
Western Pl TR10 ....144 B8
Western Promenade Rd
TR18 ....143 E4
Western Rd PL15 ......106 B5
Western Terr
Falmouth TR11 ....145 A3
Launceston PL15 ....106 B5
Western Wood Way
PL7 ....131 D5
Westfield PL7 ....131 A6
Westfield Ave PL9 .....135 C6
Westgate St PL15 .....106 C5
Westground Way PL34 ..14 D7
Westhampnett Pl PL25 ..115 C4
Westhaul Pk PL25 .....115 C4
Westhays Cl PL9 ....135 F4
Westhead Rd PL10 .....64 B2
Westheath Ave PL30,
PL31 ....109 B3
Westheath Rd PL31 ....109 B3
Westlake Cl PL11 ......126 F3
Westmoor Cl PL17 .....131 C6
Westmoor Cres TR3 ....81 B6
Westmoor Pk PL19 ....147 C4
Weston Mill Com Prim Sch
PL2 ....127 E7
Weston Mill Dr PL5 ....127 F8
Weston Mill Hill PL5 ..123 F1
Weston Mill La PL5 ....124 A1
Weston Mill Rd PL5 ...123 E1
Weston Park Rd PL3 ..128 D6
Westpark Rd PL27 ......108 A4
Westward PL27 ....21 D5
Westward Rd TR26 ....141 A6
Westways PL9 ....135 B5
Westwinds PL23 ....16 A8
Westwood PL14 ....113 B6
Westwood Ave PL6 ....125 D6
Wetherham La PL30 ....23 C3
Wharf Rd Penzance TR18 143 F5
St Ives TR26 ....141 B6
Wharf The
[21] Mousehole TR19 ....88 C1
St Ives TR26 ....141 B6
Wharfdale Rd PL3 ......129 C6
Wharfside Village [9]
TR18 ....143 E5
Wheal TR6 ....55 B5
Wheal Agar TR15 ......139 D6
Wheal Alfred Rd TR27 142 F5
Wheal Bull PL26 ....58 D5
Wheal Busy La TR4 .....68 F3
Wheal Catherine Cl TR6 ..55 B5
Wheal Dream TR26 ....141 C6
Wheal Eliza Cl PL25 ...115 B5
Wheal Fortune La TR5 ..54 C2
Wheal Friendly La TR5 ..54 C2
Wheal Gerry TR14 .....138 E4
Wheal Golden Dr TR8 ...43 D3
Wheal Gorland Rd TR16 ..68 D1
Wheal Harmony Terr
TR15 ....140 B7
Wheal Jane (Gipsy Site)
TR3 ....68 E1
Wheal Kitty TR5 ....54 D1
Wheal Kitty La TR5 .....54 D1
Wheal Leisure TR6 ......55 B6
Wheal Leisure Cl [1] TR6 55 A5
Wheal Margery TR26 ..141 C3
Wheal Maria Cophs PL19 29 D1
Wheal Martyn Mus*
PL26 ....59 B6
Wheal Northey PL25 ...115 B5
Wheal Quoit Ave TR5 ...54 C1
Wheal Regent Pk PL25 115 D3
Wheal Rodney Holiday Bglws
TR17 ....89 B5
Wheal Rose [1] TR13 ...98 C8
Wheal Silver TR15 ....140 B5
Wheal Speed Rd TR26 .141 C2
Wheal Tehidy La TR15 ..139 D6
Wheal Trefusis TR15 ..140 D2
Wheal Venture Rd TR26 141 C3
Wheal View PL26 ....58 B4
Wheal Vor TR15 ....140 D8
Wheal Vyyyan TR11 ....92 F4
Wheal Whidden TR26 ...92 F4
Wheal-An-Wens TR17 ...89 C5
Wheatfield Cres PL7 ...111 A4
Wheatridge PL7 ....130 B7
Wheal Ayr Terr TR26 ..141 A6
Wheeler Higman Cl PL26 59 C7
Wheelwright Ct PL20 ...42 E4
Wherry Pl PL23 ....116 D2
Wherry Way PL14 ......50 E7
Wheildon Rd PL25 ....115 A4
Whimple St PL1 ....148 C2
Whin Bank Rd PL5 ....124 C2
Whipsiderry Cl TR7 ....44 C6
Whistley Down PL20 ....42 B3
Whitby Cres PL6 ....125 A1

Whitby Rd PL6 ....125 A1
Whitchurch Prim Sch
PL19 ....147 D2
Whitchurch Rd
Horrabridge PL20 ....42 C5
Tavistock PL19 ....147 C3
Whitcross Hill TR15 ...139 C3
White Cross Cury TR12 ...99 B4
Redruth TR16 ....68 D3
White Cross Ct PL4 ....149 A3
White Hart Arc The
PL15 ....106 C5
White Horse TR13 ......91 A6
White House Cl TR26 ..141 C2
White La PL1 ....149 A2
White Lodge EX23 ......10 C7
White Smock Mdw [7]
PL35 ....9 C1
White Walls Ct [10] TR26 ..55 A4
White's Cl [5] TR5 .....54 C1
Whiteacres Holiday Pk
TR8 ....45 B3
Whitebarrow Cotts PL14 .37 A4
Whitecroft Way EX23 ...5 A6
Whitecross Blisland TR30 35 C7
Fowey PL23 ....116 D5
Whitecross End TR8 ....45 B2
Whitefield Terr PL4 ....149 B4
Whiteford Rd PL3 .....128 E6
Whitefriars La PL4 ....149 B3
Whitegate PL26 ....58 B8
Whitegate Mdws PL26 ..58 B8
Whitegate Rd TR7 ....111 A7
Whitegate Sh Ctr TR7 ..111 A7
Whitehall Bgws PL30 ...23 B2
Whitehall Dr
[8] Bere Alston PL20 ....41 B1
Plymouth PL9 ....136 B7
Whitehall Est PL30 .....23 A2
Whitehill Cross PL15 ...19 C6
Whitehill Terr TR13 ...146 C4
Whitemoor Prim Sch
PL26 ....58 E8
Whiterock Cl PL27 ....108 B5
Whiterock Rd PL27 ....108 B5
Whiterock Terr PL27 ..108 A5
Whiterocks Pk PL18 ....40 D6
Whitestone Cres PL31 109 C3
Whitestone Rd PL31 ..109 C3
Whitham Pk PL19 .....147 C4
Whitleigh Ave PL5 ....124 B2
Whitleigh Cotts PL5 ..124 A3
Whitleigh Ct PL5 ......124 D4
Whitleigh Gn PL5 .....124 B3
Whitleigh Prim Sch
PL5 ....124 D4
Whitleigh Villas PL5 ..124 C2
Whitleigh Way PL5 ...124 C3
Whitley Cl TR1 ....137 A6
Whitley Grange PL14 ..113 A6
Whitpot Hill PL12 ......64 F8
Whitsam Cross PL20 ....42 A4
Whitsand Bay View PL11 .65 A4
Whitson Cross PL15 ...45 D5
Whitsoncross La PL5 ..124 C7
Whitstone Com Prim Sch
EX22 ....7 F1
Whitstone Head Sch EX22 .7 F1
Whittington St PL1 ....148 B4
Whitworth Cl TR5 ......54 C1
Whity Cross PL12 .....122 A4
Widegate Nursery PL9 136 D8
Widemouth Bay Cvn Pk
EX23 ....6 E3
Widemouth Bay Holiday
Village EX23 ....6 F4
Widewell La PL6 ....125 B7
Widewell Prim Sch PL6 125 B7
Widewell Rd PL6 ....125 B7
Widey Court Prim Sch
PL6 ....124 F1
Widey Cross PL6 ......124 F1
Widey Ct PL6 ....124 F1
Widey La PL6 ....124 F1
Widey View PL3 ....128 F6
Wilcove La PL11 ......126 E5
Wildebeest Rd [7] PL27 ..31 F3
Wilderness Rd PL3 ....128 E5
Wildflower La
Newquay TR7 ....111 A6
Newquay TR7 ....111 B5
Wilkes Wlk TR1 ....137 D4
Wilkinson Rd PL5 ......127 D8
Will's Row TR15 ....139 D8
Willas Rd PL16 ....19 F4
William Edwards Cl
EX23 ....104 E6
William Evans Cl PL6 ..125 A1
William Laundry Cl PL14 52 A5
William St
Camborne TR14 ....138 D2
Truro TR1 ....137 D4
William Young Mews
PL14 ....113 E5
Williams Ave PL4 .....149 C4
Willis Vean TR12 ....99 A1
Willoughby Pl PL17 .....39 E4
Willow Cl
[22] Callington PL17 .....39 F4
Mylor Bridge TR11 ....82 A3
Plymouth PL3 ....129 E5
Quintrell Downs TR8 ....44 E2
Willow Cotts PL7 ......130 D6
Willow Cres PL7 ....130 E8
Willow Ct PL14 ....138 B4
Willow Gn PL12 ....122 D3
Willow Rd PL19 ....147 C5
Willow Way PL14 ......113 B6

Willow Wlk PL6 ....125 D5
Willowby Pk PL20 ......42 D2
Willowfield Flats TR18 ..143 C5
Willows The Bugle PL26 ...47 C1
Whipsiderry TR7 ....44 C6
Wills Cl PL6 ....124 E7
Wills Moor PL26 ....85 C5
Wilminstone Ind Est
  PL19 ....147 E7
Wilmot Gdns PL5 ....124 D3
Wilsey View PL15 ....17 B7
Wilson Cres PL2 ....128 B5
Wilson Way
  Camborne TR15 ....139 D5
  4 Par PL24 ....60 B4
Wilsworthy Cross EX22 ..12 C7
Wilton Rd PL1 ....123 A3
Wilton St PL1 ....148 A4
Wilton Terr PL13 ......62 D6
Wiltshire Cl PL4 ......128 F4
Winchester Gdns PL5 ..124 A5
Windermere Cres PL6 ..124 F4
Winding Terr TR10 .....81 A1
Windmill PL23 ....116 C4
Windmill Hill
  Launceston PL15 .....106 C5
  Saltash PL12 ....122 E2
  St Just In Roseland TR2 ..82 F2
Windmill Hill Terr PL15 ..106 C5
Windmill Ind Est PL23 ..116 C4
Windmill La PL15 ......106 C5
Windsor Ct
  Falmouth TR11 ....145 B4
  Newquay TR7 ....110 D5
Windsor Dr PL25 ......115 C3
Windsor Gr PL31 ......109 F5
Windsor Hill 8 TR26 ..141 B5
Windsor La
  Kelly Bray PL17 ......39 F6
  Saltash PL12 ....122 E2
Windsor Mews PL31 ...109 E5
Windsor Pl
  Liskeard PL14 ....113 C5
  22 Penzance TR18 ...143 E6
  Plymouth PL1 ....148 C2
Windsor Rd PL3 ....129 B7
Windsor Terr
  Falmouth TR11 ......145 B4
  Penzance TR18 ......143 D6
  4 St Ives TR26 ......141 A5
Windsor Villas PL1 ...148 C2
Wingfield PL31 ....35 B2
Wingfield Rd PL3 .....148 A4

Wingfield Way PL3 ....148 A4
Winifred Baker Ct 5
  PL4 ....149 A4
Winnard's Perch TR9 ...32 D1
Winnicott Cl PL6 ......124 E7
Winnow Cl PL9 ....135 F4
Winns Row TR13 ....146 C6
Winsbury Ct PL6 ......125 A1
Winsor Cotts PL15 ....106 B7
Winsor Est PL13 ....62 D5
Winstanley Wlk PL3 ...129 D6
Winston Ave PL4 .....148 C4
Winstowe Terr TR8 ....110 A3
Winwell Field PL27 ....108 D6
Witham Gdns PL3 .....129 C5
Withnoe La PL10 ......132 B6
Woburn Rd PL15 ......106 B4
Woburn Terr PL9 .....135 C7
Wodehouse Terr TR11 ..145 B4
Wolcocke Cl TR17 ......89 D5
Wollaton Gr PL5 ......123 F3
Wolrige Ave PL7 ......131 B5
Wolrige Way PL7 .....131 A5
Wolsdon Pl PL1 ....148 A3
Wolsdon St PL1 ....148 B3
Wolseley Bsns Pk 2
  PL2 ....128 A5
Wolseley Cl PL2 ......128 A5
Wolseley Rd
  Plymouth, Camels Head
  PL5 ....127 F6
  Plymouth, St Budeaux PL5 ..123 C1
Wolseley Road Flats
  PL2 ....127 F6
Wolverton Cl PL7 .....131 C3
Wolverwood La PL7 ...131 B3
Wombwell Cres PL2 ...127 E7
Wood Acre PL12 ......122 B4
Wood Cl PL12 ....122 B3
Wood Dr PL12 ....53 C8
Wood La Landrake PL12 ..53 D2
  Par PL24 ....60 D5
  Truro TR1 ....137 D3
Wood View TR10 ......144 B7
Wooda La PL15 ....106 B6
Wooda Rd PL15 ......106 C6
Woodbine Cotts PL7 ..130 E4
Woodbine La TR16 .....67 D4
Woodbury Gdns PL5 ..124 A3
Woodchurch PL20 .....42 B3
Woodcock Cl PL10 ....133 A6
Woodend Rd PL6 .....125 D7
Woodfield Prim Sch
  PL5 ....124 C5

Woodford Rd EX23 ....104 E7
Woodford Ave PL7 ....130 A7
Woodford Cl PL7 .....130 A7
Woodford Cres PL7 ...130 A6
Woodford Cross EX23 ...2 C1
Woodford Gn PL7 ....130 B6
Woodford Inf Sch PL7 ..130 B6
Woodford Jun Sch PL7 ..130 B7
Woodgate Rd PL6 ....125 D6
Woodgate Rd PL14 ...113 A5
Woodgrove Pk PL26 ...59 A1
Woodhey Rd PL2 .....128 A7
Woodland Ave
  12 Par PL24 ....60 D5
  Penryn TR10 ....144 B6
Woodland Cl Lanivet PL30 ..47 E7
  St Austell PL25 ......114 E3
Woodland Ct TR1 ....137 E5
Woodland Dr PL7 ....130 B4
Woodland Glade PL30 ..47 F7
Woodland Hts TR1 ...137 E5
Woodland Rd
  Plymouth PL7 ....130 C6
  St Austell PL25 ......114 E3
Woodland Rise
  Penryn TR10 ....144 B7
  Rilla Mill PL17 ....38 E8
Woodland Terr
  Plymouth PL4 ....149 B4
  St Columb Road TR9 ..45 E2
Woodland View
  Coombe PL26 ....58 C2
  Lanivet PL30 ....47 E6
Woodland Way
  Gunnislake PL18 ......41 A7
  Torpoint PL11 ....126 F3
Woodland Way Cl PL18 ..40 F6
Woodlands Dousland PL20 ..42 E3
  Plymouth PL9 ....99 A2
  4 Mullion TR12 ......99 A2
Woodlands Ct PL5 ...124 A3
Woodlands End PL6 ..125 D5
Woodlands La PL6 ...125 F1
Woodlands Sch PL5 ..124 B4
Woodlands Terr 3
  TR16 ....140 F1
Woodlands The TR16 ...67 B4
Woodlands View PL13 ..117 B4
Woodlane TR11 ....145 B3
Woodlane Cl TR11 ....145 B3
Woodlane Cres TR11 ..145 B3
Woodlane Dr TR11 ...145 B3
Woodley Cl 8 EX23 .....4 D1

Woodman's Cnr PL20 ...42 D3
Woodovis Holiday Pk
  PL19 ....29 F1
Woodridge Cl TR27 ....78 E1
Woods-Browning Ind Est
  PL31 ....109 F2
Woodside Crapstone PL20 ..42 B2
  Penryn TR10 ....144 B7
  Plymouth PL4 ....149 B4
Woodside Ave PL9 ...135 C6
Woodside Cl PL7 .....130 E4
Woodside La PL4 ....149 B4
Woodstock Gdns PL5 ..123 D1
Woodvale Terr PL15 ..106 C5
Woodview Pk PL9 ....136 A6
Woodville Cl PL2 .....127 F7
Woodville Rd
  Morwenstow EX23 .....2 C1
  Plymouth PL2 ....127 F6
  Woodford EX23 ....4 D8
Woodway Penryn TR10 ..144 B7
  Plymouth PL9 ....136 A7
Woolacombe Cross PL20 ..41 C1
Woolacombe Rd PL20 ..41 C1
Woollcombe Ave PL7 ..130 F4
Woolster Ct 9 PL4 ...149 A2
Woolwell Cres PL6 ...125 C8
Woolwell Dr PL6 .....125 C7
Woolwell Rd PL6 .....125 D7
Woon La 3 TR3 ....81 F7
Worcester Rd PL25 ...115 A4
Wordsworth Cres PL2 ..127 F7
Wordsworth Rd PL2 ..127 F7
Wotton Cross PL12 ....53 B4
Wreford Cl 11 TR9 ....45 D6
Wren Gdns PL7 ......130 C6
Wren Ind Est TR1 .....69 E4
Wrens Gate PL9 .....135 E8
Wrey Ave PL14 ....113 C7
Wright Cl PL1 ....127 E3
Wyatts La PL19 ....147 B6
Wych Hazel Way TR10 ..144 F4
Wycliffe Rd PL3 ......129 B4
Wye Gdns PL3 ....129 D7
Wykeham Dr PL2 ....128 A7
Wyleaf Holiday Pk EX23 ..4 F3
Wyndham La PL1 ....148 A3
Wyndham Sq PL1 ....148 A3
Wyndham St E PL1 ...148 B3
Wyndham St W PL1 ..148 B3
Wyndhurst Orch PL27 ..108 B6
Wyoming Cl PL3 .....129 C6
Wythburn Gdns PL6 ..125 D3

Y
Yardley Gdns PL6 ....125 E3
Yarg Cheese Farm*
  PL14 ....38 D8
Yarrow Mead PL9 .....136 D7
Yealmpstone Cl PL7 ...131 B4
Yealmpstone Dr PL7 ...131 B3
Yealmpstone Farm Prim Sch
  PL7 ....131 B3
Yeats Cl PL5 ....124 C2
Yellow Tor Ct PL12 ...122 C2
Yellow Tor La PL12 ...122 C2
Yellow-wort TR16 ......80 C3
Yellowtor Rd PL12 ...122 B2
Yelverton Bsns Pk PL20 ..42 B2
Yelverton Cl PL5 .....123 E4
Yelverton Paperweight Mus*
  PL20 ....42 C2
Yelverton Terr
  Tavistock PL19 ......147 D6
  Yelverton PL20 ....42 D2
Yeo Cl PL3 ....129 B5
Yeoland La PL20 ......42 C1
Yeomadon Cross EX22 ...8 E4
Yeomans Cl PL14 ....113 D5
Yeomans Way PL7 ...131 A4
Yew Tree Ct TR1 ....137 F6
Yewdale Gdns PL6 ...125 D2
Yonder St PL9 ....135 B6
York Pl PL2 ....127 F4
York Rd Plymouth PL5 ..127 E8
  Torpoint PL11 ......127 B3
York St Penzance TR18 ..143 D6
York Terr 7 PL2 .....127 F5
Youldon Way PL20 .....42 C4

Z
Zaggy La PL17 ....39 E4
Zion St PL1 ....148 C2
Zodiac Ho TR19 ....96 E3

Any feature in this atlas can be given a unique reference to help you find the same feature on other Ordnance Survey maps of the area, or to help someone else locate you if they do not have a Street Atlas.

The grid squares in this atlas match the Ordnance Survey National Grid and are at 500 metre intervals. The small figures at the bottom and sides of every other grid line are the National Grid kilometre values (**00** to **99** km) and are repeated across the country every 100 km (see left).

To give a unique National Grid reference you need to locate where in the country you are. The country is divided into 100 km squares with each square given a unique two-letter reference. Use the administrative map to determine in which 100 km square a particular page of this atlas falls.

The bold letters and numbers between each grid line (**A** to **F**, **1** to **8**) are for use within a specific Street Atlas only, and when used with the page number, are a convenient way of referencing these grid squares.

Example   *The railway bridge over DARLEY GREEN RD in grid square B1*

Step 1: Identify the two-letter reference, in this example the page is in **SP**

Step 2: Identify the 1 km square in which the railway bridge falls. Use the figures in the southwest corner of this square: Eastings **17**, Northings **74**. This gives a unique reference: **SP 17 74**, accurate to 1 km.

Step 3: To give a more precise reference accurate to 100 m you need to estimate how many tenths along and how many tenths up this 1 km square the feature is (to help with this the 1 km square is divided into four 500 m squares). This makes the bridge about **8** tenths along and about **1** tenth up from the southwest corner.

This gives a unique reference: **SP 178 741**, accurate to 100 m.

Eastings (read from left to right along the bottom) come before Northings (read from bottom to top). If you have trouble remembering say to yourself "Along the hall, THEN up the stairs"!

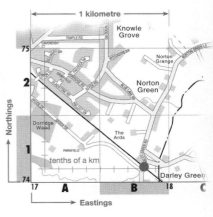

Addresses

Name and Address	Telephone	Page	Grid reference

Addresses

Name and Address	Telephone	Page	Grid reference